Distributed Cognition in Enlightenment and Romantic Culture

The Edinburgh History of Distributed Cognition
Series Editors: Miranda Anderson and Douglas Cairns

Scholars from across the disciplinary spectrum track the notions of distributed cognition in a wide range of historical, cultural and literary contexts from antiquity through to the twentieth century.

Distributed Cognition in Classical Antiquity
Edited by Miranda Anderson, Douglas Cairns and Mark Sprevak

Distributed Cognition in Medieval and Renaissance Culture
Edited by Miranda Anderson and Michael Wheeler

Distributed Cognition in Enlightenment and Romantic Culture
Edited by Miranda Anderson, George Rousseau and Michael Wheeler

Distributed Cognition in Victorian Culture and Modernism
Edited by Miranda Anderson, Peter Garratt and Mark Sprevak

Visit the series website at edinburghuniversitypress.com/series/ehdc

Distributed Cognition in Enlightenment and Romantic Culture

Edited by Miranda Anderson, George Rousseau
and Michael Wheeler

EDINBURGH
University Press

Edinburgh University Press is one of the leading university presses in the UK. We publish academic books and journals in our selected subject areas across the humanities and social sciences, combining cutting-edge scholarship with high editorial and production values to produce academic works of lasting importance. For more information visit our website: edinburghuniversitypress.com

Edinburgh University Press Ltd
The Tun – Holyrood Road
12(2f) Jackson's Entry
Edinburgh EH8 8PJ

Typeset in 10/12 Monotype Baskerville by
Servis Filmsetting Ltd, Stockport, Cheshire
and printed and bound in Great Britain.

A CIP record for this book is available from the British Library

ISBN 978 1 4744 4228 2 (hardback)
ISBN 978 1 4744 4230 5 (webready PDF)
ISBN 978 1 4744 4231 2 (epub)

Contents

List of Illustrations

Series Preface

This book, like the series of which it is part, explores the notion that the mind is spread out across brain, body and world, for which we have adopted 'distributed cognition' as the most comprehensive term. Distributed cognition primarily draws evidence from philosophy, cognitive science, psychology, linguistics and neuroscience. Distributed cognition covers an intertwined group of theories, which include enactivism and embodied, embedded and extended cognition, and which are also together known as '4E cognition'. An overview and explanation of the various strands of distributed cognition are provided in the general introduction.

Distributed cognition can be used as a methodology through which to pursue study of the humanities and is also evident in past practices and thought. Our series considers a wide range of works from classical antiquity to modernism in order to explore ways in which the humanities benefits from thinking of cognition as distributed via objects, language and social, technological and natural resources and environments, and to examine earlier notions that cognition is distributed. Theories of distributed cognition are transformative in terms of how we understand human nature and the humanities: they enable a different way of perceiving our interactions in the world, highlighting the significant role of texts and other cultural artefacts as part of a biologically based and environmentally grounded account of the mind. Theories of distributed cognition offer an opportunity to integrate the humanities and the sciences through an account that combines biologically and culturally situated aspects of the mind. The series illuminates the ways in which past ideas and practices of distributed cognition are historically and culturally inflected and highlights the cognitive significance of material, linguistic and other sociocultural developments. This evidence has the potential to feed back into cognitive science and philosophy of mind, casting new light on current definitions and debates.

Each volume provides a general and a period-specific introduction. The general introduction, which is replicated across all four volumes, aims to orientate readers unfamiliar with this area of research. It provides an overview of the different approaches within distributed cognition and discussion of the value of a distributed cognitive approach to the humanities. The period-specific introductions provide a more detailed analysis of work in the cognitive humanities in the period covered by the volume, before going on to reflect on how the essays in the volume advance understanding in the humanities via distributed cognition.

The project from which this series emerged provided participants with an online seminar series by philosophers working on various aspects of distributed cognition. These seminars are publicly available on the project's website (http://www. hdc.ed.ac.uk/seminars). The seminars aim to help researchers in the humanities think about how ideas in distributed cognition could inform, and be informed by, their work. Four workshops were held in the summer of 2015 at the University of Edinburgh and were attended by nearly all the volume contributors. The workshops brought participants together to collaborate in ways that contributed not just to the making of this series but to the development of this approach to the humanities. From the springboard of the seminar series, through the gathering together of scholars from across a range of disciplines and by ongoing interaction with the editorial team during the production of the final essays, the aim has been to provide a set of rigorous analyses of historical notions of distributed cognition.

The series is deliberately exploratory: the areas covered by the essays are indicative of the benefits of the general approach of using distributed cognition to inform cultural interpretations. The first four volumes of the series concentrate primarily on Western Europe; however, we envisage further future volumes that will expand the scope of the series. If distributed cognition is understood as we contend, then this understanding has the potential to be valuable across the humanities as part of a new type of intellectual history. The four volumes are arranged chronologically and each of the volumes is edited by a period specialist (Cairns, Anderson, Rousseau, Garratt), a philosopher (Wheeler or Sprevak), and Anderson, whose central involvement in all four volumes ensured overall consistency in approach and style. At the very moment when modern-day technological innovations reveal the extent to which cognition is not just all in the head, this series demonstrates that, just as humans have always relied on bodily and external resources, we have always developed theories, models and metaphors to make sense of the ways in which thought is dependent on being in the world.

Acknowledgements

This series emerged from the project 'A History of Distributed Cognition' (2014–18), funded by the Arts and Humanities Research Council (AHRC), whom we should like to thank most warmly for their support. The idea for the project first came about in 2010. Miranda Anderson realised that the resonances she was exploring between recent ideas on distributed cognition and Renaissance notions of the mind were not just a matter of a correlation between two points in time, but reflected an important aspect of the mind in history that has been neglected, one that, fittingly, might be best explored through a collaborative project. Our interdisciplinary team has worked closely together developing the project, the monograph series and this general approach to the humanities: ours has been an intellectual endeavour akin to Hutchins's description of a ship's crew successfully navigating by means of collective computation (1995). With Douglas Cairns as Principal Investigator and the core project team of Miranda Anderson, Mark Sprevak and Michael Wheeler, we have collaborated closely both between ourselves and with other scholars. For volumes 3 and 4 respectively, the editorial team were joined by period specialists George Rousseau and Peter Garratt, who helped shape these volumes. Boleslaw Czarnecki, research assistant on the project during 2016–17, helped liaise with contributors and with the organisation of public engagement activities during this time. We were fortunate to have had two excellent auditors, in the shape of Terence Cave and Tim Crane, who used their years of accumulated experience and wisdom to help monitor our progress. Our advisory board offered expertise from across a wide spectrum of academic disciplines: Andy Clark, Giovanna Colombetti, Christopher Gill, David Konstan, Karin Kukkonen, Duncan Pritchard, Andrew Michael Roberts and Patricia Waugh. We are very grateful to the philosophers who came on board to provide us with the online seminars and joined us in online discussion: Andy Clark, Giovanna Colombetti, Shaun Gallagher, John Sutton, Deb Tollefsen, Dave Ward, Dan Zahavi, as well as our own Michael Wheeler. The editors would also like to thank those scholars (Marius Kwint and Blakey Vermeule) who made valuable contributions to the third project workshop but whose papers could not for various reasons be included in the final volume.

The editorial team is especially grateful to Duncan Pritchard and Eidyn, the University of Edinburgh's Philosophy Research Centre, for their support of a pilot of this project in 2012–13. The Balzan Project, 'Literature as an Object of Knowledge', led by Terence Cave, also kindly supported the project, providing funds for the images on our website. The project has benefited from the involvement of many of the participants from the Balzan Project in our workshops and volumes including Guillemette Bolens, Terence Cave, Mary Crane, Jennifer Gosetti-Ferencei, Karin Kukkonen, Raphael Lyne, Emily Troscianko, and our own Miranda Anderson. Meanwhile, the AHRC-funded Cognitive Futures in the Humanities Network (2012–14), co-led by Peter Garratt, with Michael Wheeler as a founding steering-committee member, has also fostered further productive interactions and cross-fertilisation.

We warmly thank the National Gallery of Scotland for helping us to source and secure our website images. The National Museum of Scotland (NMS) was our supportive project partner, and NMS staff met with the team to discuss and assist with the development of public engagement activities. These activities included a series of recorded public lectures, during which museum curators and academics provided their perspective on the cognitive implications of museum artefacts. Malcolm Knight, the multitalented man behind the Scottish Mask and Puppet Centre, illustrated the cognitive dimensions of masks and puppets and provided much entertainment during one of the NMS lectures. NMS also provided us with their classrooms for our school workshops. Lisa Hannah Thompson was an invaluable contributor to the development of our ideas on how best to shape the material and the programme for children in order to connect in fun and effective ways. Finally, we are grateful to our copy-editor, Cathy Falconer, for her consistently sharp-eyed attention to detail and to Edinburgh University Press for their support throughout the process.

Editorial Notes

Contributors have been allowed to follow their own preferences with regard to the use of original spelling and capitalisation in primary texts. The editors have sought to impose consistency within rather than between chapters.

Distributed Cognition and the Humanities

Miranda Anderson, Michael Wheeler and Mark Sprevak[1]

Consider counting on your fingers; or solving a challenging mathematical problem using pen and paper (or Napier's bones, or a slide-rule); or the way in which we routinely offload the psychological task of remembering phone numbers on to our ubiquitous mobile phones; or a brainstorming scenario in which new creative ideas emerge from a process of collective group interaction; or the manner in which the intelligent feat of ship navigation is realised through a pattern of embodied, information-communicating social exchanges between crew members who, individually, perform purely local information-processing tasks (such as bearing taking) using specialised technology. All of these examples of brain-body-world collaboration are, potentially at least, instances of the phenomenon that, illuminated from a historical perspective, is the topic of this volume. That phenomenon is *distributed cognition*.

So what, precisely, is distributed cognition? The term itself is standardly traced to the pioneering work of the cognitive anthropologist Edwin Hutchins (see, canonically, Hutchins 1995, from where the example of ship navigation is taken). However, in using this introduction to sketch the conceptual background for the chapters that follow, we shall adopt an understanding of distributed cognition that arguably diverges somewhat from Hutchins's own (for one thing, we make no demand that the target elements, whether located inside or outside the brain, should be understood as representational media; see e.g. Hutchins 1995: 373). Here we are aiming for a general and inclusive notion of cognition alongside a general and inclusive notion of what it means for cognition to be distributed. Thus the term 'cognition' should be understood liberally, as it routinely is in the day-to-day business of cognitive science, as picking out the domain of the psychological, where that domain encompasses phenomena that we often identify using

[1] We warmly thank Douglas Cairns for his assistance with this chapter. The authors would also like to thank the participants in a workshop at the University of Edinburgh in June 2017 who provided feedback on an earlier draft of this chapter: Felix Budelmann, Peter Garratt, Christopher Gill, Elspeth Jajdelska, Karin Kukkonen, Adam Lively, Andrew Michael Roberts, George Rousseau, William Short, Jan Söffner, Eleanore Widger and Clare Wright.

terms such as mind, thought, reasoning, perception, imagination, intelligence, emotion and experience (this list is not exhaustive), and includes various conscious, unconscious-but-potentially-conscious, and strictly non-conscious states and processes. Given this broad conception of what cognition is, cognition may be said to be distributed when it is, in some way, *spread out* over the brain, the non-neural body and (in many paradigm cases) an environment consisting of objects, tools, other artefacts, texts, individuals, groups and/or social/institutional structures. Advocates of distributed cognition argue that a great many examples of the kinds of cognitive phenomena identified above (reasoning, perception, emotion, etc.) are spread out in this way.

To see why the notion of distributed cognition has attracted so much attention, here's a way of thinking about how the contemporary discourses stationed in and around cognitive science arrived at what might justifiably, in the present context, be called the received (non-distributed) view of mind. Although the very brief history lesson that follows involves the odd caricature, it is surely broadly accurate. According to the much-maligned substance dualists (the most famous of whom is arguably Descartes), mind is a non-physical entity that is metaphysically distinct from the material world. Here the material world includes not only the external tools and artefacts that human beings design, build and use, but also the thinker's own organic body. On this model, the minds of other people become peculiarly inaccessible, and indeed one's indirect knowledge of those minds, such as it is, seems to result from a precarious analogy with the correlations between thought and action in one's own case. For this reason, plus a whole battery of others – some scientific, some philosophical – substance dualism is now officially unpopular in most of the relevant academic circles. Indeed, in the twentieth and twenty-first centuries, mind has been placed firmly back in the material and social world. Or rather, it has been placed firmly in a particular segment of that world, namely the brain.

As apparently demonstrated by all those 'pictures of the brain thinking' that we regularly receive from functional magnetic resonance imaging (fMRI) scans and the like, the received view is now that the brain is where the cognitive action is. This neuro-centric orthodoxy is not an irrational position. Indeed, there is no doubt that many a good thing has come out of research programmes in psychology, neuroscience and elsewhere which embrace it. Nevertheless, the contemporary distributed cognition perspective is usefully depicted as a reaction against neuro-centrism's (allegedly) distorting influence. To be clear, no advocate of distributed cognition believes that the brain is somehow unimportant. Rather, (part of) the proposal is that to understand properly what the brain does, we need to take proper account of the subtle, complex and often surprising ways in which that venerable organ is enmeshed with, and often depends on, non-neural bodily and environmental factors, in what is the co-generation of thought and experience.

One consequence of adopting a general and inclusive notion of distributed cognition is that there turns out to be more than one version of the idea from which to choose when developing the view. How, then, may we articulate the notion further? One taxonomic move that is increasingly popular in the literature is to unpack distributed cognition in terms of *4E cognition*, where the four Es in question are *embodied, embedded, extended* and *enactive*. In other words, it is possible to provide a more detailed picture of distributed cognition by thinking in terms of the four Es and the pattern of symbiotic and sometimes not-so-symbiotic relationships between them. That's what we shall now do, starting with the notion of *embodied* cognition.

According to the hypothesis of embodied cognition, psychological states and processes are routinely shaped, in fundamental ways, by non-neural bodily factors. In a full treatment of this idea, *much* more would need to be said about what the terms 'shaped' and 'fundamental' mean, but for present purposes the motivating thought will do: in order to understand cognition, the structures and forms of the non-neural body need to be foregrounded in ways that are absent from the neuro-centric orthodoxy. From this shared point of departure, the embodied cognition community has become home to a diverse kaleidoscope of projects. Thus embodiment is said to determine or condition the nature of concepts (e.g. Lakoff and Johnson 1980), the character of perceptual experience (e.g. Noë 2004), various factors such as orientation and posture that do not themselves enter into the content of experience, but which preconceptually structure that experience (e.g. Gallagher 2005), and the architectures, assemblages and processing mechanisms that enable intelligent action (in the philosophical literature, see e.g. Clark 1997, 2008; Haugeland 1998; Wheeler 2005).

As just one example of embodied cognition research, consider groundbreaking work in cognitive semantics on the role of embodiment in human sense-making (how we experience the world to be meaningful). Johnson (1987) argues that we experience our bodies fundamentally as three-dimensional containers into which we put things (e.g. food) and out of which things come (e.g. blood). The result is that the metaphor of containment becomes a preconceptual cognitive schema that heavily constrains other contexts of meaning. Thus, building on Johnson's idea, Lakoff (1987) argues that the containment schema, as determined by our human experience of embodiment, even underlies abstract logical structures such as 'P or not P' (inside the container or outside of it). One apparent implication of this approach is that creatures with different experiences of embodiment will possess different preconceptual schemata and thus will inhabit different semantic landscapes.

To the extent that embodiment is grounded in bodily acts, such as, say, the physical manipulations of instruments or tools, embodiment naturally encompasses a rich mode of environmental interaction, which is just to say that there is a natural route from embodied cognition to the second of the four Es, namely *embedded* cognition. According to the embedded view, the distinctive adaptive richness and/ or flexibility of intelligent thought and action is regularly, and perhaps sometimes necessarily, causally dependent on the bodily exploitation of certain environmental props or scaffolds. As an illustration, consider the phenomenon that Andy Clark has dubbed *cognitive niche construction* (e.g. Clark 2008; see also Wheeler and Clark 2008). This occurs when human beings build external structures that, often in combination with culturally transmitted practices, transform problem spaces in ways that promote, or sometimes obstruct, thinking and reasoning. A compelling example, which Clark sources from Beach (1988), is the way in which a skilled bartender may achieve the successful delivery of a large and complex order of cocktails (a relatively daunting memory task) by exploiting the fact that different kinds of cocktail often come in differently shaped glasses. Bartenders learn to retrieve the correct glass for each drink as it is requested, and to arrange the differently shaped glasses in a spatial sequence that tracks the temporal sequence of the drinks order, thus transforming a highly challenging memory task into a simpler (roughly) perception and association task. This reduces the burden on inner processing by exploiting a self-created environmental structure according to a culturally inherited social practice.

Of course, as indicated in the definition given of cognitive niche construction, not all cases of the environmental scaffolding of cognition will result in enhanced performance. The background picture here is of 'our distinctive universal human nature, insofar as it exists at all, [as] a nature of biologically determined openness to deep, learning- and development-mediated, change' (Wheeler and Clark 2008: 3572) and thus, given a technologically saturated environment, of human organisms as what Clark (2003) calls *natural born cyborgs*, creatures who are naturally evolved to seek out intimate unions with non-biological resources. Overall, the ongoing operation of this evolved tendency has yielded myriad adaptive benefits, but sometimes the couplings that result will be adaptively neutral, inappropriate or dysfunctional. This observation points to an important vein of research on how ideas that are central to distributed cognition can contribute to areas such as psychopathology (e.g. Gallagher 2004; Fuchs 2005; Drayson 2009; Sprevak 2011).

Despite the fact that the embedded theorist seeks to register the routinely performance-boosting, often transformative, sometimes necessary, but occasionally obstructive, causal contributions made by environmental elements (paradigmatically, external technology) to many cognitive outcomes, she continues to hold that the actual thinking going on in such cases remains a resolutely skin-side phenomenon, being either brain-bound or (on a less common, more radical iteration of the view) distributed through the brain and the non-neural body. By contrast, according to the advocate of *extended* cognition, it is literally true that the physical machinery of mind itself sometimes extends beyond the skull and skin (see, canonically, Clark and Chalmers 1998; for a collection that places the original Clark and Chalmers paper alongside a series of criticisms, defences and developments, see Menary 2010). More precisely, according to the hypothesis of extended cognition, there are actual (in this world) cases of intelligent thought and action, in which the material vehicles that realise the thinking and thoughts concerned are spatially distributed over brain, body and world, in such a way that certain external factors are rightly accorded fundamentally the same cognitive status as would ordinarily be accorded to a subset of your neurons. Thus, under the right circumstances, your mobile phone *literally* counts as part of your mnemonic machinery, alongside some of your neurons.

To bring home the distinction between embedded and extended cognition, as we have just introduced it, consider the example of a mathematical calculation achieved, in part, through the bodily manipulation of pen and paper. For both the embedded and the extended view, what we have here is a brain-body-pen-and-paper system involving a beyond-the-skin element that, perhaps among other things, helps to transform a difficult cognitive problem into a set of simpler ones (e.g. by acting as storage for intermediate calculations). For the embedded theorist, however, even if it is true that the overall mathematical problem could not have been solved, at least by some particular mathematician, without the use of pen and paper, nevertheless the external resource in play retains the status of a non-cognitive aid to some internally located thinking system. By contrast, for the advocate of the extended view, the coupled system of pen-and-paper resource, appropriate bodily manipulations, and in-the-head processing may itself count as a cognitive architecture, even though it is a dynamically assembled (rather than hard-wired) and essentially temporary (rather than persisting) coalition of elements. In other words, each of the differently located components of this distributed (over brain, body and world) multi-factor system enjoys cognitive status, where the term 'cognitive status' should be understood as indicating whatever status it is that we ordinarily grant the brain.

Here it is worth pausing to note that, in the distributed cognition literature, one can certainly find the term 'extended cognition' being given a less specific reading than we have just suggested, a reading which is tantamount to the interpretation we have adopted here of the term 'distributed cognition', and which thus encompasses embedded cognition and (at least many forms of) embodied cognition. This liberal usage is not negligent. For one thing, the boundary between internal and external is, in some contexts, fixed by the skin – in which case gross bodily forms count as internal – while in others it is fixed by the limits of the brain or central nervous system – in which case gross bodily forms count as external. On the latter view, at least some forms of embodied cognition would count as cases of extended cognition. For another thing, given certain projects and purposes, the distinction between being a non-cognitive but performance-boosting scaffold and being a genuine part of one's mental machinery may be a distraction, even if it is metaphysically legitimate. Nevertheless, it does seem clear that if one uses the term 'extended cognition' in the more inclusive way, one will need to find a different term for the case of what we might identify as metaphysical or constitutive extension ('strictly extended' maybe). Otherwise one will risk succumbing to what extended cognition theorists call cognitive bloat, an undesirable outcome in which one is forced to concede all sorts of mundane and unexciting cases of causal coupling between inner and external elements to be cases of extended cognition, thus generating a wildly counter-intuitive position. It looks, then, as if there is a genuine argument to be had over whether it is possible to make the transition from embodied-embedded cognition to extended cognition. And, indeed, this is a complicated and contested area (to sample just a small subset of views and the sometimes ill-tempered debate, see e.g. Rowlands 1999, 2010; Menary 2007, 2010; Adams and Aizawa 2008; Clark

2008; Rupert 2009; Sprevak 2009; Sutton 2010; Wheeler 2010a). And it is possible that there won't be a universal resolution. That is, it may be that while some cognitive phenomena reward an extended treatment (leading candidates might include memory, reasoning and problem-solving), others will not. There is, for example, an ongoing debate over the credentials of extended consciousness (Hurley and Noë 2003; Noë 2004; Clark 2009; Hurley 2010; Ward 2012; Wheeler 2015).

Our final 'E' is *enactive*. In the most general terms, a position is enactivist if it pursues some version of the claim that cognition unfolds (is enacted) in looping sensorimotor interactions between an active embodied organism and its environment. For the enactivist, then, cognition depends on a tight and dynamic relationship between perception and action. Enactivism also tends to foreground the disciplined examination of lived experience as a methodological tool in cognitive theory. This leads many enactivists to draw on the phenomenological philosophical tradition, as represented centrally by thinkers such as Husserl, Heidegger and Merleau-Ponty, a tradition which concentrates on the structures of, and the conditions for, lived experience. This productive engagement with phenomenology is especially prominent in relation to the enactivist understanding of the body not simply as a physical mechanism, but as a lived structure through which the world is experienced. (Although enactivism foregrounds phenomenology more so than the other branches of distributed cognition, that is not to say that it has a monopoly on phenomenology's insights and conceptual machinery; see e.g. Gallagher 2005; Wheeler 2005; Zahavi 2014 for essentially non-enactivist yet systematic appeals to phenomenology, in and around the distributed cognition literature.)

The two most common forms of enactivism are sensorimotor enactivism (e.g. O'Regan and Noë 2001; Noë 2004) and autopoietic enactivism (e.g. Varela et al. 1991; Di Paolo 2005; Thompson 2007), although another recent, and increasingly important, variant that we shall not discuss here is the so-called radical enactivism of Hutto and Myin (2012). Sensorimotor enactivism is rooted in the thought that perceptual experience is constituted by implicit knowledge of so-called sensorimotor contingencies – the law-like effects that either my movement or the movements of objects in my sensory field have on the sensory input that I receive – where the implicit knowledge in question is to be understood in terms of the possession and exercise of certain bodily skills. Thus consider my visual perception of a tomato. Although my visual access to that entity is aspectual (there is an obvious sense in which, given my embodied spatial perspective, I have visual access only to certain portions of it), my ordinary experience is nevertheless of the tomato as an intact, solid, three-dimensional object. As one might put it, the tomato's hidden-from-perspectival-view aspects are nevertheless experientially present to me. According to the sensorimotor enactivist, this is explained by my implicit mastery of the relevant sensorimotor contingencies – very roughly, the visual inputs my eyes would receive if I moved around the tomato, or if I turned it, or if it span round. This implicit sensorimotor knowledge is constitutive of my perceptual experience.

Autopoietic enactivism is based on the idea that cognition is a process of sense-making by adaptively autonomous systems, where an autonomous system is a network of interdependent processes whose recurrent activity (a) produces and maintains the very boundary that determines the identity of that network as a unitary system, and concurrently (b) defines the ways in which that system may encounter perturbations from what is outside it while maintaining its organisation. A system is adaptively autonomous when it is able to alter its behaviour in response to changes in its environment in order to improve its situation, for example by sensorimotor activity. To illustrate this with an example that the autopoietic enactivists themselves often use, bacteria sense and swim towards the environmental area containing the greatest concentration of glucose molecules. Thus, as a consequence of the specific metabolically realised autonomy of the bacteria, glucose emerges as – is brought forth as – significant for those organisms as food. As this example nicely illustrates, autopoietic enactivism is distinctive in forging a close connection between life and mind (cognition). As Thompson (2007: 128) puts it: 'life and mind share a set of basic organizational principles, and the organizational properties distinctive of mind are an enriched version of those fundamental to life. Mind is life-like and life is mind-like.'

One effect of enactive life-mind continuity is to place affective phenomena such as emotions and moods at the very centre of the cognitive stage. As the glucose example highlights, enacted significance is fundamentally a matter of valence, that is, of being appropriately attracted and repelled by environmental factors that might improve or diminish organisational integrity. In this way, these factors are things that the organism *cares* about. This is the enactive root of affectivity. (For a developed enactive account of emotional episodes as self-organising patterns of the whole embodied organism, see Colombetti 2014.) More generally, a 4E-friendly treatment of affective phenomena will tend to reject a commonly held view in the psychology of emotions according to which there is a neat distinction between the cognitive components of emotions (e.g. the appraisal of a situation in relation to one's well-being) and their bodily components (e.g. arousal and facial expressions). For the advocate of embodied emotions, appraisal is itself a phenomenon that is spread out over both neural and non-neural bodily factors (see, again, Colombetti 2014). In the background here is Damasio's (e.g. 1999) influential notion of somatic markers, i.e. specific feelings in the body that accompany specific emotions (e.g. nausea with disgust) and which strongly shape subsequent decision-making. A more controversial application of 4E thinking in the vicinity of affective phenomena is the claim that such phenomena may be extended beyond the skin of an individual, either over artefacts such as musical instruments (see e.g. Colombetti and Roberts 2015) or over other people (see e.g. Slaby 2014; Krueger and Szanto 2016).

This final point brings us neatly to the issue of the social dimension of the 4E mind. Consider three possible ways in which cognition might be socially distributed:

1. I think some of the thoughts I think because, or perhaps only because, I am part of a particular social group.
2. My cognitive states or processes are socially as well as technologically extended,

such that some of my cognitive machinery is located partly in the brains of other people.

3. Groups may have minds in much the same way that individuals have minds.

Option 1 is perhaps most naturally understood as an embedded view according to which some psychological capacities realised wholly by neural states and processes are nevertheless manifested only in certain kinds of social circumstances, because they are socially scaffolded by those circumstances. Option 2 is the social version of the hypothesis of extended cognition. Consider Tom and Mary, a couple with a long and interdependent relationship. Perhaps Tom might come to trust, rely on and routinely access information stored in Mary's brain, in such a way that, in certain contexts, her brain comes to play essentially the same role as his own neural resources, and thus constitute a repository of his memories (cf. Clark and Chalmers 1998). Both option 1 and option 2 may count as versions of what Wilson (2005) calls the social manifestation hypothesis, which maintains that cognition remains a 'property of individuals, but only insofar as those individuals are situated or embedded in certain physical environments and social milieus'. By contrast, option 3 shifts the ownership of the relevant psychological states and processes from the individual to the group. According to 3, the group mind hypothesis, we should take at face value statements such as 'the team desires a victory' and 'the crowd thinks the game is over'. Whole groups, and not merely the individuals out of which those groups are constructed, may non-metaphorically be attributed with beliefs, desires, other psychological states and processes of reasoning (for versions of this view, see e.g. Huebner 2014; Tollefsen 2006). As one might imagine, much of the philosophical debate in this area concerns the conditions and circumstances under which it would be correct to adopt either option 2 or option 3, both of which might, to our modern thinking at least, seem counter-intuitive or, from a theoretical perspective, metaphysically profligate (for an argument for the latter conclusion, see e.g. Rupert 2014). But even the seemingly less radical option 1 constitutes a prompt for a careful examination of the distributed causal mechanisms and social contexts that drive the processes concerned.

Two further modulations of social cognition, when developed in a 4E register, bring out a final way in which the distributed perspective changes the shape of the received theoretical terrain. It has become a commonplace view in the psychology of social cognition that we navigate our social spaces either by predicting and explaining one another's observable behaviour using what is tantamount to a commonsense theory of the hidden inner causes of that behaviour – the beliefs, desires and other mental states inside other people's heads – or by predicting and explaining that behaviour by internally simulating what we ourselves would think and experience in the same circumstances, in order to produce the same behaviour. On either of these models, and partially echoing the Cartesian dualism of days gone by (see above), our access to the mental states of the other person is fundamentally *indirect*, involving inference or simulation. However, some distributed cognition theorists (e.g. Gallagher 2008), drawing centrally on phenomenology, argue that our grasp of the mental states of another person with whom we are in perceptual contact is ordinarily *direct*, in that, rather than, for example, inferring another person's joy from some of her facial movements, we see that joy directly, in her laughter. Relatedly, but moving away even further from the conventional assumption that a theory of social cognition should begin with a conception of people as isolated spectators, a distinctively enactive account of social cognition has emerged in the form of the *participatory sense-making* approach (De Jaegher and Di Paolo 2007). This approach begins with a conception of people not as spectators, but as engaged participants, and focuses on the ways in which individuals interactively coordinate their movements and utterances in social situations. For participatory sense-making theorists, the interaction process itself can come to exhibit an enactive form of autonomy (see above), one that is generated by, but also constrains and scaffolds, the activity of the interacting individuals. The alleged directness of social cognition is grounded in the fact that we are so proficient at social interaction that the interactive process becomes transparent to us (De Jaegher 2009).

This section has surveyed views that fall under the general heading of 'distributed cognition'. What these views have in common is that they accord some kind of special role to the environment (perhaps including the bodily environment or social environment) that is missing in the traditional Cartesian or in more recent neuro-centric cognitive theories. More to the fore in this introduction, however, is the *diversity* of views within the distributed cognition camp. We have seen that distributed cognition can roughly be split into 4 Es (embodied, embedded, extended and enactive) with each 'E' admitting of further, sometimes competing, articulations in the hands of different philosophers and cognitive scientists (we have already met two kinds of enactivism). Philosophers and cognitive scientists who work in this area often adopt what might appear to be a mix-and-match approach: they accept some 'distributed' claims but reject others. Moreover, they may accept a different combination of distributed (or non-distributed) claims about different parts of human mental life: some aspects of our mental life (perhaps our feelings of joy and pain) may be treated as purely internal while others (perhaps some of our memories and decision-making) are distributed. A further complication is that, even if attention is restricted to a single aspect of human mental life, a distributed theorist may give a different distributed/non-distributed answer for different human subjects in different environmental contexts at different times (some humans are more inclined than others to distribute their memory on to external devices).

How should researchers in the humanities make sense of all this disagreement and diversity within the distributed cognition camp? We suggest that they cut through philosophical disagreements and explore the specific combination of distributed views that suits their interests. An application of distributed cognition in the humanities should be assessed on its own merits. A specific combination of 'distributed' views may prove more or less fruitful to understanding a particular historical phenomenon. And different combinations of 'distributed' views may prove suited to different historical phenomena.

There is no reason why a single, one-size-fits-all approach should be adopted.

The merits of a particular combination of distributed views, in a particular historical setting, should be based on its pay-off for our understanding in the humanities. We hope that the essays in the volume demonstrate both the value and the diversity of conceptual tools offered by a distributed cognition approach.

Distributed Cognition and the Cognitive Turn

The question of how new insights into the nature of the mind illuminate our understanding of being human and our engagement with the world is one of the greatest issues facing the current generation of humanities scholars. Knowledge that is emerging from cognitive science and neuroscience, along with related research in disciplines such as philosophy, psychology and linguistics, casts a new light on issues that are central to the humanities, and enables us to better explain the nature of forms of human culture and how and why they emerge and evolve. Knowledge from the sciences can help to make a case for culture's significance to being human. In turn, the humanities provide an archive of examples concerning how humans develop in a range of environments and evidence diverse ways in which we use and create resources as means to extend our capacities. This section provides a general overview of the emergence of the cognitive humanities and considers how distributed cognition interrogates and supplements existing humanities methodologies.

In spite of the humanities' increasing interdisciplinarity since the late 1950s, the long-standing disciplinary antagonism between the arts and sciences continues (Snow 1993; Leavis 1962; Ortolano 2005). This tension is now further exacerbated by wider movements towards education's commodification, quantification and rebranding as merely employment-based training, with accompanying questions about the relevance and value of the arts and humanities (Collini 2009; M. C. Nussbaum 2010). The defensive response by many in the humanities has been to fall back on claims about the qualitative and irreducible nature of aesthetic values in the humanities and to view humanities scholars who draw on scientific knowledge as reductionists.[2] The presumption is that scientific knowledge entails a constraint on, and a diminution of the value of, their own complex material and methodologies, rather than adding a further perspective. Yet, even for the hard problem of consciousness – that is, the way it feels to be me or you – philosophers draw on insights from neuroscience. There is no reason why questions about the qualitative nature of our experience of cultural artefacts cannot be addressed, even if not solved outright, by neuroscientific insights. Moreover, a broad-based approach that draws not just on the mind's neural basis, but on the whole range of the human mind as evidenced in cultural texts and practices, seems likely to provide us with the fullest insights into these enduring questions.

Phenomenology has influenced both philosophers focusing on culture or lan-

---

[2] As Helen Small describes, 'the humanities value qualitative above quantitative reasoning' (2013: 57). Raymond Tallis (2011) provides an example of the anti-scientific bent with his dismissal of a focus on the physical aspects of being human as 'neuromania' or 'Darwinitis'.

guage (so-called 'continental' philosophers, such as Foucault, Derrida and Lacan) and models (in particular enactivism) that attempt to conceptualise scientific evidence of distributed cognition. However, in cultural studies phenomenological ideas became entangled with a tendency towards relativism, as part of a backlash against earlier humanist or structuralist notions of culture as revealing universal human attributes and values. Throughout history, oscillating drives towards universalism and relativism often culminate in polarised models, or one extreme sets the pendulum swinging back to the other extreme. In recent decades literary, historical and cultural criticism have focused on various kinds of postmodern relativism and social constructivism which resist anything interpretable as 'facts', 'truth' or 'reality' and in which human bodies are presented as merely cultural constructs (the tendency is notable in new historicism, cultural materialism and feminist, queer and globalisation studies). From classical antiquity onwards, there have been those who have questioned the extent of our access to a mind-independent world: from Plato's shadow-watchers in the cave, to Descartes's sceptical *cogito ergo sum*, to more recent thought experiments suggesting that our experience might be the same were we brains in a vat, to Bayesian predictive coding models, which some internalist-minded philosophers argue are a basis for assuming that cognition is skull-bound, so that 'conscious experience is like a fantasy or virtual reality' (Hohwy 2013: 137).

Early artificial intelligence and cybernetics influenced both cognitive scientists and the continental philosophers who in turn have informed cultural theory. Lacan, for instance, discussed the influence that cybernetics had on him, though in his dark version, humans become the processed rather than the processor: 'It is the world of words which creates the world of things . . . Man speaks therefore, but it is because the symbol has made him man' (Lacan 1981: 39). Higher-level shifts in norms of understanding and focus cascade down, and so shape and are reshaped by disciplines into idiosyncratic manifestations of the higher-level propensities into which (along with many other factors) they feed back. The linguistic turn in the humanities in the 1970s and 1980s argued that language consisted of a system of codes, with words caught up primarily in their relation to other words, with a consequent endless deferral of meaning and a disconnectedness to referents in the world. At the same time, classical cognitive science described cognition as occurring through computational manipulation of internal symbols. Such theories emphasised the role of arbitrary, abstract syntactic structures at the expense of attention to the emergence of meaning through our engagement in the world.

More recently, Daniel Dennett suggested that 'A scholar is just a library's way of making another library' (1991: 202). This may seem to relate straightforwardly to Lacanian-type claims. Dennett himself has commented on the correspondences between these ideas and postmodern deconstructionism (410). However, Dennett reaches his suppositions through biologically grounded or organically inspired notions, such as memes, an idea developed by Richard Dawkins (who coined the term) to describe units of cultural transmission akin to genes as units of biological transmission (202–3). In contrast to such biologically grounded accounts, prevailing postmodern methodologies have argued that sociocultural forces are entirely responsible for human concepts and behaviour. For example, the elision of the physical body is evident in Judith Butler's claim that 'gender is a performance that produces the illusion of an inner sex' (1998: 728). Whilst such accounts make visible sociocultural influences on biological categories, their rebuttal of the hegemony of the natural world and of the fixed nature of biological categories is problematic to the extent that it simply inverts the relationship and asserts the dominance of sociocultural forces over the realm of the natural and physical. The significant difference between a postmodern stance and Dennett's viewpoint is highlighted by his concluding comment that 'I wouldn't say there is nothing outside the text. There are for instance all the bookcases, buildings, bodies, bacteria . . .' (1991: 411).

Embodied cognition – that is, the notion that our physical bodies enable and constitute cognitive processes – presents a greater challenge to postmodern accounts than do claims about its extended nature. Furthermore, distributed cognitive models make evident that the mind's embedded or extended nature is not simply a matter of unconstrained cultural determinism. The elision of the physical body and world in postmodern accounts helps to perpetuate an apparent conflict between the arts and sciences that risks miring notions of being human (and the humanities) in isolated idealism. The recent rise of digital humanities, despite its use of distant reading and quantitative analyses,[3] might be explained in part by technological advancements. These advancements massively increase the ways in which we can creatively use programs and technologies to inform and study our interaction with texts and artefacts. However, its rise may also be due to a theoretical tendency towards the virtual and virtualisation, with an over-emphasis on the distinctiveness of human nature as arising from meta- or trans-physical capacities, a tendency which has been evident throughout history in idealist accounts of human nature (Hayles 1999; Nusselder 2009). As part of a countermovement in the humanities today, there is a shift towards the study of material culture, with a renewed focus on specific physical objects, physical environments and ecological contexts.

We also find elision, if not of the physical body as a whole, then at least of the significance of the specifics of it, in some more functionalist accounts of the extended mind. Andy Clark accuses thinkers such as Damasio of biochauvinism because of the essential role they ascribe to the body in cognition. Instead, Clark argues, 'the perceptual experience of differently embodied animals could in principle be identical, not merely similar to our own' (Clark 2008: 193). Clark's functionalist approach allows for the possibility that a non-biological resource can play the same role as a biological one. Yet, elsewhere, Clark emphasises that external resources

---

[3] Franco Moretti coined the term 'distant reading' to describe the need for a world-scale study of literature, which would draw on other researchers' scholarship, in contrast to the conventional close reading of a small number of canonical texts (Moretti 2000). In his later work, and more generally, the term is now often used to describe the study of literature through data analysis or text-mining of large-scale corpora (Moretti 2013).

need not be functionally identical to internal ones to qualify as extended (1997: 220): a laptop does not store or compute information in the same way as a brain, and it can, for that reason, be useful in supplementing our neural capacities. On Clark's view, there is a question about how much the material nature of a resource matters to how it fulfils its function, and this is important for how we evaluate the significance of different resources – neural, bodily and non-biological ones – in different historical contexts. Our view is that in certain contexts, or while performing certain functions, a difference between human bodies or physical resources may matter; in other cases, it may not be significant. The richer idea that emerges from this perspective is that through differences, as well as similarities, various forms of representational, computational and mnemonic resources can supplement our biological limitations.

We have seen that distributed cognition presents an array of competing and sometimes conflicting theories. This may appear a sign of fragility, but this diversity can be seen as reflecting the ways in which different cognitive models come to the fore in relation to different mental capacities or contexts. Shifting trends and debates about cognitive hierarchies, such as an emphasis on the role of embodiment or on particular methods or resources as extending representational or phenomenological possibilities, can be seen to emerge in relation to the development of, or reaction against, new genres, cultural modes and technological, scientific and sociocultural changes. Therefore, the multifaceted nature of distributed cognition as a theory is, in our view, a strength that reflects the operation of different cognitive norms and modes in the world.

From the late 1980s and 1990s onwards a few 'first-wave' thinkers in the cognitive humanities, primarily based in the US, adopted notions from evolutionary psychology or from cognitive linguistics that emphasised the universal aspects of humans' cognitive and physical characteristics.[4] A particularly influential idea was that humans tend to conceptualise non-physical domains in terms of physical ones, and in contrast to postmodern deconstructionism, this suggested a specific way in which language is embodied. Engagement with these ideas in the humanities challenged existing disciplinary divisions and opened up new ways to think about what human beings have in common and how humans from diverse cultures can have some understanding of one another. Yet both evolutionary-psychological and cognitive-linguistic humanities approaches tend to operate without due attention to the many historical (and geographical) variables involved in cultural, linguistic and literary constructions. Such early cognitive humanities scholars therefore tended to set postmodern and cognitive approaches in irreconcilable opposition to one another. This risked simply repeating within the humanities the persisting methodological tensions between the arts and sciences through the siding of critics with oppositional explanatory paradigms. However, these first-wave thinkers have remained largely on the peripheries of mainstream literary and cultural methodologies, against which some of them tend to situate themselves.

---

[4] See, for example, Lakoff and Johnson 1980; Carroll 1994; Gottschall and Wilson 2005.

Yet even from the early stages, cognitive humanities scholars drew attention to the benefits of engaging with scientific work on the mind, and not all their efforts were so oppositional. One of the first scholars to adopt a cognitive approach, which he argued was compatible with the more conventional approaches he was already using, was the psychoanalytical literary critic Norman Holland (1988). Most other early adopters of scientific work, models and metaphors as a means to inform our reading of texts in the emerging field of 'cognitive poetics' (such as Tsur 1992; Gibbs 1994; Turner 1991, 1996) were influenced by and developed cognitive linguistics' notion of conceptual schema and argued for the everyday nature of figurative thought and language. There were, however, already outliers such as Ellen Spolsky, who was instead focused on reapplying the then fashionable theory of the modular mind to her analysis of literary texts as a means of engaging with poststructuralism (1993).

Distributed cognition suggests another perspective to universalising models, one that takes account of the way in which embodiment is a crucial aspect of our extendedness, since it is our biological nature that enables us to incorporate sociocultural and technological resources into our cognitive systems. The significance of the human body arises also from its capacity for engagement and interaction. The dynamic cognitive roles of linguistic, sociocultural and technological resources are made possible by neurological plasticity.[5] This raises the possibility that social constructivist models may have a neurological basis, as our ability to be (at times transparently) constructed by sociocultural forces relates to the adaptability of the human brain. At the same time, human adaptability and extendedness temper any notion of universal communal features shared across all humans that could be based on embodiment. While humans exhibit certain enduring biological characteristics, these characteristics dynamically interact with our sociocultural and environmental contexts. Together these lead to the manifestation of different kinds of minds and to the expression or suppression of particular forms of cognitive paradigms. This perception enables a reassessment of polar representations of the mind as either fixed and universal or as socially constructed and culturally relative – two models which have constrained understandings of historical, as well as modern, concepts of the mind. Humans are particularly talented not just at evolutionarily adapting to niches, but also at adapting our niches to supplement our cognitive and other needs (Wheeler and Clark 2008). While humans' capacity to exist within cognitive niches, with ongoing reciprocal interactions between niches and organisms, is shared across generations, these niches also reflect technological and sociocultural developments; ultimately, rather than either universalism or relativism, this implies that we shall find a rich combination of shared features and particular divergences across history and cultures.

The paradigm of distributed cognition provides a middle way between relativ-

---

[5] For just a few works that discuss neurological plasticity and adaptivity, see Ramachandran and Ramachandran 1996; Berti and Frassinetti 2000; Maravati and Iriki 2004; Gallagher 2005; Rizzolatti and Sinigaglia 2008; Clark 2008.

ism and universalism by highlighting the vital roles played by both physical and cultural resources in cognition. As a methodology, this provides a potential strategy for making headway in the science wars. In the conflict between radical postmodern relativism and science-based realism, the question is whether facts about the world are merely culturally determined or whether those facts are grounded in some mind-independent reality. Analysis of cognition needs to take into account not only the findings of current cognitive science, but also the imagery and narratives used in scientific, cultural and literary discourses. Cultural factors play an essential role in shaping the world, and acknowledging this should not require rejecting or devaluing the role of science. The influence of culture and its role in cognitive niche construction shapes even our disciplinary taxonomies – constantly evolving scaffolds that accrete knowledge about specific domains. A combination of scientific and cultural knowledge is necessary to understand the nature of cognition and of being human in the world. Distributed cognition is a theoretical framework that enables one to grasp the mutual entanglement of science and culture. The importance of distributed cognition as a methodological approach grows out of its rootedness in bodies of knowledge from across the disciplinary spectrum, which together are reflective of the full scope of human nature.

During the period in which our project has taken place, second-wave thinkers in the cognitive humanities have begun to consider a more diverse range of approaches to the mind; the expansion of recent work in the field is discussed in each of the period-specific introductions to the volumes. Our project sought to strengthen and stimulate increased interest in distributed cognition. The current book series provides a rigorous engagement with these ideas by humanities scholars and demonstrates that distributed cognition can helpfully illuminate cultural studies. Our aim is to inspire a broader re-evaluation in the humanities of what is understood to count as cognition and to suggest a new way of doing intellectual history. The four current volumes on distributed cognition examine the practices and the explicit and implicit conceptual models that were in use from antiquity to the early twentieth century. Together the essays trace across Western European history developments and divergences among various concepts of distributed cognition that were circulating. The essays engage with recent debates about the various models of distributed cognition and bring these into discourse with research in the humanities through examination of the parallels to (and divergences from) these models and these debates in earlier cultural, philosophical and scientific works. The essays make evident some of the explicit and implicit grounds on which our present suppositions about cognition stand and also some of the knowledge and insights, as well as superstitions and ungrounded beliefs, that have been lost and obscured along the way. The reiterations and the diversity in expressions and practices of distributed cognition enrich and enlighten our understanding of wider forces and rhythms in the history of cognition. One important point that emerges is that notions of cognition can be shown to be fundamental to how we conceptualise debates in every discipline – the study of cognitive phenomena cannot be considered a specialist niche, but is rather a necessary underpinning of any study of humans in the world. This series bears out the premise that 'current philosophical notions [of distributed cognition] are simply the most recent manifestation of an enduring paradigm that reflects the non-trivial participation of the body and world in cognition' (Anderson 2015b: xi).

In return for providing a scientific basis to our understanding of the mind in the humanities, historical studies have the potential to feed back and interrogate our current philosophical and scientific understanding of how cognition may be distributed across the body and the world. The historical lineage of non-brain-bound concepts of cognition demonstrates that such ideas are not merely a product of our own age. Cultural beliefs and philosophical interpretations map on to underlying physical features and processes in ways that function practically within a society.

The volume introductions provide detailed overviews of the development of the cognitive humanities in relation to the periods they cover, but to briefly outline how distributed cognition can illuminate cultural interpretation by challenging models that view the body or the environment as peripheral to understanding the nature of cognition, we shall present a few instances that arise from our collaboration with the National Museum of Scotland.

Distributed cognition raises questions about the nature and role of galleries and museums, demonstrating ways in which many of the artefacts extend either human cognitive or other physical capacities. There are some (perhaps obvious) examples of distributed cognition, such as the tally stick, which was a piece of bone or wood scored across with notches that was used, from around 30,000 years ago, to record numbers or messages. This was an ancient memory aid. Like the oft-cited modern example of an iPhone, it remembers, so you need not. Basic tools controlled by bodily action gave way to mechanised tools that outsourced mechanical processes, through devices such as steam engines, and to automated and programmable agents, such as the Jacquard Loom. The Jacquard Loom not only moved faster and more reliably than a human weaver, it took over the weaver's cognitive load and allowed greater design complexity than would ordinarily be available from the average human weaver's brain alone. In a trajectory familiar to those who work on the history of the book, a museum also makes evident the shift from oral traditions to literacy through the preservation of early memorial stones carved first with only images, then manuscripts which enabled more detailed storage, manipulation and communication of information, then printed books and presses that enabled the sharing of information on a larger scale, and finally we emerge into the modern world of computers and the internet.

Encounters with museum artefacts involve both a conceptual encounter with an object's caption and an experiential encounter with the object itself – a metal helmet may automatically trigger a sense of weightiness (Bolens 2017). Yet, in some instances the contingent nature of one's tacit knowledge may affect the extent to which artefacts prompt a kinesic or kinaesthetic response, with the cognitive capacity to simulate holding, wearing or interacting with an object relating partly to prior embodied and cultural experience, with more conceptual scaffolding (for example, via illustrations of past uses) needed for more obscure artefacts. Similarly, devices that may seem intuitive in one period often require significant amounts of culturally embedded knowledge that belie their apparent simplicity (Phillipson 2017). Distributed cognition invites a broad spectrum of multidisciplinary approaches, enabling a richly diverse appreciation of the reciprocal ways in which artefacts and humans have shaped each other.

Distributed cognition creates a scientific basis for understanding the fundamental significance of culture to humans and the humanities. Describing perception, Alva Noë says, 'We continuously move about and squint and adjust ourselves to . . . bring and maintain the world in focus' (2015: 9). When we read literature, view art or engage with historical artefacts in a museum, we remain linked to our own particular ever-shifting perspective and yet these cultural resources allow us to experience the world beyond our usual cognitive range. Each genre, each author or artist, and each work provides distinct forms of cognitive mediation. It does this in a way that reflects back on ourselves and the world around us, at the same time as it recalibrates and adds to the numerous virtual coordinates through which we more generally orient ourselves and enact our worlds. Texts, artworks and other cultural artefacts are imbued with mind, the mind of their creator and their context, and that of the spectator, reader or interactor. Objects, images and language, particularly those in consciously crafted literary and art works, provide catalytic scaffolding for perceptual flights into and beyond the usual constraints of our own imaginations, and can trigger a rich array of responses that are grounded in and recalibrate our emotional, physical and cultural natures, extending and revitalising our mental panoramas.

Our series questions assumptions that have been made about historical notions of the mind, begins to trace the lineages of ideas about the mind across periods and cultures, and highlights the ways in which certain aspects of the mind come to the fore in certain contexts and traditions. The realisation of the distributed nature of cognition, which can induce both mind-forged manacles and mind-extending marvels, upholds the role of the humanities in wider society and more broadly challenges humans' ways of being in the world. The extent of our capacity to extend our minds, across our current sociocultural panorama and physical world, and via the cognitive scaffolding provided by earlier generations, places in question the relatively short-term individualistic ends that are currently being prioritised and endorsed in most modern societies. The value of the humanities in concert with the sciences is their capacity to extend our cognitive range beyond everyday constraints, by scaffolding critical thinking and enabling our minds to soar to the heights needed to tackle world-sized and epic-scale issues, as well as to supplement our ability to grasp more fully the diversity of other minds. Distributed cognition invites a more inclusive approach, which acknowledges that experience and understanding of the world and of the humanities is multifaceted and involves biological and sociocultural dimensions. Distributed cognition offers a reconsideration of the nature of the human mind, and so of being human, and, in turn, of the humanities.

2

Introduction

I. Distributed Cognition in Enlightenment and Romantic Studies – An Overview

George Rousseau

This chapter deals with the long eighteenth century and offers guideposts for further exploration. It distinguishes between cognitive approaches at large and specific versions of distributed cognition, and, where appropriate, comments on the four Es within this range. It specifically aims to engage readers already interested in both the long eighteenth century and cognitive approaches to literature who may be wondering how distributed cognition can benefit their own work.

Recent cognitive approaches to the period focus on didactic thinkers, especially philosophers of the period who challenged prevailing views of mind, rather than the literary figures – poets, dramatists, novelists, essayists, memoirists – who absorbed, and often applied, the former's theories. A sentence in a recent collection of essays makes the point: 'Well before Romanticism criticized the murdering dissection of the intellect by appealing to a plastic imagination that was not detached from the life of the world, the ideal of living praxis has frequently acted as a challenge to *theoria*' (Danta and Groth 2014: 37). The author is referring to pre-1800 theories and practices embedding mind and body, and tracing antecedents of plastic imagination in the history of ideas. The mind's plasticity was not a major theme in the large body of pre-1800 thought but traces of its appearance then began to surface in medical and philosophical thought (Ione 2016). After 1800, Coleridge and his circle adumbrated notions of plasticity more fully and forged ahead with new approaches, especially the well-known theory of esemplastic imagination capable of shaping things into a seamless and unified whole. Nevertheless, Coleridge and other Romantics represented the end, rather than the beginning, of a wave of interest in imagination starting with Descartes (Rousseau 1968, 1972). By the middle of the eighteenth century a counter-tradition arose that was grounded in vitalist notions of spirit and soul which were resistant to the quantifying laws of mechanics. Embedded between these positions – post-Cartesian mechanics and vitalistic spirit – were a wide range of inchoate notions of distributed cognition, sprouting and waiting to be gathered.

The most noteworthy aspect of Cartesian ideas for eighteenth-century cognitive science was not its dualism but the tyranny of its mechanics in establishing body as the basis of mind. As philosopher D. M. Armstrong (1993) has claimed, mind emerged almost exclusively from the materialism of Cartesian mechanics. Set the time dials to circa 1700 and few theories of mind look beyond those formulated in the Renaissance. For example, when John Locke published his *Essay Concerning Human Understanding* in 1689 he altered the whole course of the philosophy of mind by devaluing Cartesian mechanics (Crane and Patterson 2000). A robust case can indeed be made that the rest of the century amounted to sets of foot-notes on Locke's *Essay*, even the radical ideas of David Hume and Adam Smith which further punctured Descartes's main premises. Literary writers – poets Pope to Chatterton, novelists Defoe to Mary Wollstonecraft, playwrights Congreve to Sheridan – contributed little to this developing theory of mind except by occasion-ally embellishing the ramifications and fine-tuning the differences. A small anthol-ogy dating between 1700 and 1820 of literary pronouncements about mind could be gathered.[1] But only when the heirs of associationist philosopher David Hartley – literary authors from Blake to Coleridge and Wordsworth – grappled with dilem-mas about matter yielding itself to mechanical analysis versus fluid spirits flowing through all bodies did a new post-Lockean – and many would also claim post-Humean – cognitive pathway follow. When recent scholars detect literary input to the post-Cartesian philosophical juggernaut of body and mind, consciousness and cognition, it is often in the domain of embodied experience and the materialisation of thought. Literary and artistic contributions, however, have fuelled some major research by the last generation of humanities scholars (Fox 1987; Fox et al. 1995; Reeves 2010). As recently as 2016 a group of North Americans documented the eighteenth century's two predominant approaches to cognitive science in terms of its embodied experience and materialisation of thought (Conway and McMurran 2016).

Concurrent with this research, the present vitalistic strand of mind-body science has recently focused on the souls of animals in comparison to humans. Descartes wrote two treatises on this topic, Bayle another, their commentators many more.[2] Enlightenment vitalist thinkers proceeded on the premise that spirit consisted of some type of 'fluid', but they indicated little more about its material or immaterial substance than this. What they believed was that this 'spirit', and its attendant 'fluid', distinguished human from beast, and they sometimes demonstrated the political consequences by analogical reasoning (Israel 2010). The idea was that the body's constitutional arrangement corresponded to the divided sovereignty of material and spiritual substance, and that similar division ruled eighteenth-century British political thought, riven by struggles among parliament, monarch and pop-ulace. The recent history of science covering the first half of the eighteenth century has sought to situate the precise anatomical sites of the mechanical operations of this vitalistic fluid. And when electricity was discovered in the middle of the eight-eenth century, the discussion changed, presupposing that if spirit is an 'electrical fluid' then electricity must distinguish human from beast.

[1] No such anthology exists but many candidates for inclusion are found in Rousseau 1990.
[2] For a panopticon survey of post-Cartesian responses see Berchtold and Guichet 2010.

Ideas about cognition lurked everywhere in these pursuits. For instance, the method to differentiate mind from body in both mechanistic and vitalistic approaches was itself embodied. But numerous Enlightenment natural philosophers approached the matter with an embodied empiricism noticeably different from that of Descartes's contemporaries (Wolfe 2014). Concurrently, eighteenth-century mind, both mechanical and vitalistic, showed itself to be increasingly extended. Yet if body remained the primary site through which mind and imagination were being forged, by the mid-eighteenth century it was no longer a model of body composed of four humours, three different types of spirits and various faculties of the soul, as it had been earlier (Anderson 2015b: chapter 3; Rousseau 1968: 111–14). The Renaissance had constructed an elaborate edifice of the body's material components consisting of these humours, multiple spirits and several faculties of the soul situated in essential anatomical organs (Anderson 2015b: 77–80). Complicating this imposing scheme in the period before 1700 were the differences of these 'body parts' among plants, animals and man. Within the eighteenth-century theory of body, mind assumed an increasingly important role as the century wore on, and by mid-century – when electricity was discovered – the number of different anatomical 'spirits' had dwindled (some would claim amalgamated) into a single 'spirit' (Baynes 1738; Sutton 1998). This contraction had the unintended effect of expanding a formerly embodied mind toward a more extended mind, as well as reconceptualising mind as extending into non-bodily components of the environment. By the second half of the eighteenth century it seemed as if the whole terraqueous globe was being configured as a single, continuous, animated body with both matter and spirit flowing through it (Glacken 1967). Eighteenth-century poet and physician Erasmus Darwin should not be enlisted as having anticipated the modern Gaia hypothesis (the belief that organisms interact with their inorganic surroundings on earth to form a synergistic and self-regulating, complex system), but he would have approved of its fundamental tenet about a universe composed of continuous bodies in the animal, vegetable and mineral world (Fara 2012).

Brain was rarely omitted from these discussions, especially its radical degree of sovereignty over the body. Only in philosophical discourse postulating innate ideas as the organism's first principle of consciousness was brain downplayed (Mayne 1728). Yet if continental post-Cartesian mechanists pronounced about the brain's material and mechanistic role in consciousness, it was an English physician – Thomas Willis (1621–75) – who, like his Oxford student John Locke, altered the course of Stuart and Georgian cognitive science by fixing the brain as its indisputable centrepiece. For Willis the anatomic human brain is organised into tripartite divisions. Intellectual historians Wolfe and Gal (2010a) have demonstrated the sociopolitical significance of this ternary model. Others have shown how Willis's primacy of nerves and brain eclipsed other body parts to create a revolution in the understanding of human interaction. George Rousseau traced this development of 'brain science' in eighteenth-century culture (Rousseau 1989, 1991, 2004, 2007a) and mounted a strong case for the part it played in the rise of

Enlightenment sensibility (Rousseau 1975).[3] Peter Logan (1997) demonstrated how nerves, popularly understood, became a stock feature of Enlightenment narrative, while Alan Richardson has written books purporting that the 'neural paradigm' is of prime importance to the development of Romanticism (Richardson 2001, 2010; Richardson and Spolsky 2004). To the present moment most treatments of eighteenth-century sensibility include brain and nerves as implicated in sensibility's formation – from Samuel Richardson to Blake and Coleridge – complemented by the role played by human sociability (Mullan 1990; Quinlan 2013). Gazing at sensibility's cognitive threshold, it is fair to claim that if this book is the first to apply distributed cognition to a selective swathe of literature and the arts, it has done so by building on the shoulders of pioneers of cognitive approaches.[4] It is too ambitious to claim this volume maps out a new model of the double periods: Enlightenment and Romantic. More accurately, its case studies suggest how such a model could be constructed, noting how many more figures and genres, poets, novelists and thinkers, would need to be consulted to make the leap.

These proliferating references to historical periodisation – Renaissance, Enlightenment, Romanticism, long eighteenth century – are of course given to slippage. However widely invoked today, these labels have contested meanings, chronological as well as ideological. Their boundaries are fraught, their overlaps myriad.[5] We the editors took the decision to conceptualise the two periods – Enlightenment and Romantic – as if amalgamated into one. And if we have insufficiently dwelled on their similarities and differences, it is only in deference to the larger task of demonstrating beyond doubt what the four Es could yield.

The two periods are strikingly controversial in literary history and cultural criticism because 'the Enlightenment' has been construed principally as a scientific-philosophical historical development and 'the long eighteenth century' principally as a literary one – and one whose segments are often split into pre-Romantic and proto-Romantic (Elam and Ferguson 2005). The consequences of these conventions within literary history for distributed cognition can be made explicit: given our attention to genres (for example, women novelists' representations of the theatre) and philosophical currents (Sterne's cognitive underpinnings in *Tristram Shandy*), small advantage would have accrued from dividing the period chronologically in half by carving up the book into two volumes. If we had done so, further case studies could have been added, especially based on canonical texts (for example, eighteenth-century poetry from Pope to Blake is absent in the present contents). But the case that four E manifestations of distributed cognition are robustly embedded in the primary literature would not have been strengthened. What one

---

[3] Before Rousseau's work in the 1970s the rise of sensibility was attributed to social manners and domestic morals, with science, medicine and philosophy playing little, if any, role. Rousseau documented the importance of the latter three. Recently Rousseau has also demonstrated the social ramification of brain science (Rousseau 2007b).

[4] Turner 1991; Vermeule 2010; Zunshine 2010; Anderson 2015b; Cave 2016.

[5] Outram 1995; Reeves 2010; Siskin and Warner 2010; Pagden 2013.

wants in an eclectic collection of case studies such as this one is the demonstration, wherever possible, that distributed cognition emanates naturally from the texts and cultural practices themselves rather than exhaustive chronological coverage of authors and genres.

Even so, the distributed cognition we discuss appears across different genres and a broad range of authors. The analysis of its appearances in two discrete segments (Enlightenment and Romantic) would have had to presuppose a more variegated, historical map of cognition in the long eighteenth century. Our inclusion of authors and texts – topics ranging from reading practices to theories of mind, as well as French Jesuit poets to Kant's theory of knowledge – can appear to be random. But its scatter-shot content will also strike readers immersed in the canon as innovative. This is because most treatments of the 'cognitive turn', to cite Steve Fuller (1989) who initiated the much-quoted phrase, have so far focused on canonical texts (Cave 2016; Phillips 2016a). Furthermore, a combined field of Enlightenment and Romantic studies offers comparative benefits. Amalgamating them provides contrast, and in some cases (such as Keats's notion that the poet and reader jointly create affect) offers the exploration of a specific type of distributed cognition sprung from a particular moment, for example its appearance four decades earlier or later. The growth of the eighteenth-century novel offers another instance of an extended entente between author and reader. Or, perhaps less tangibly but no less consequentially, the conceptual intersections between scientific and literary frameworks still possible before the solidification of modern academic disciplines occurred in the nineteenth century. Further case studies will be needed before the coalescence of these developments (especially the rise of the novel as one of the period's great enablers of distributed cognition) can be asserted as emblematic of the era. Not that the era itself was homogeneous: entire libraries have been compiled demonstrating just the opposite, nor do we suggest homogeneity. But literary history has so long been carved up into such narrow units that most readers – especially those wondering about the *longue durée* – will appreciate the yoking of Enlightenment and Romanticism.[6]

Consider the further example of eighteenth-century materialism in the decades from Leibniz and Locke to those of Kant and the post-Kantians in the early nineteenth century. Advantages accrue from demonstrating their models of machines and matter during that whole, long, chronological sweep, especially Leibniz's natural and artificial machines. By identifying these frameworks of materialism in the long stretch, and consulting some of the imaginative literature probing its concerns, it becomes palpable that representations of the material body had been embedded in philosophical discussion all along (Fox 1988).[7] Then, by mid-century,

---

[6] Parallel literary-historical fields exist in 'the early Middle Ages' and 'later Middle Ages', or 'the early seventeenth century' and 'later seventeenth century'. Advantages and disadvantages exist in all these parallels.

[7] Fox's (1988) is an important book for demonstrating how au fait with contemporary cognitive theories the Scriblerians – Pope, Swift, Arbuthnot, Parnell, Bolingbroke et al. – were.

cadres of eighteenth-century materialists envisioned the body as a self-regulating homeostatic machine – with internal communications systems – and non-human machines as bodies (La Mettrie and Vartanian 1960; Moravia 1978; Riskin 2015). Yet, concurrently, it was a perilous task in Catholic France to inquire if the body regulated itself, as La Mettrie soon found after clandestinely publishing his *Man a Machine* in 1749 (La Mettrie and Thomson 1996). He renounced the dualistic Cartesian notion of a corporeal soul within a material body, and demolished post-Cartesian versions of soul composed of substances different from the rest of the body's matter (Thomson 1981). La Mettrie trod delicately over Willisian corporeal versions of the soul because Willis's model was less dualistic than that of his forebear Descartes, as historian Alison Muri (2006) has shown. Muri historicised myriad eighteenth-century man-machine systems in *The Enlightenment Cyborg*. She showed how the 'cybernetic organism' had existed since the Enlightenment as both anatomical model and literary figure. Its composite essence was the body imagined as a self-regulating homeostatic machine replete with internal communication systems. The implications for embodied cognition are significant: if brain is equivalent to mind as an assemblage of mechanistic parts, what differentiates man-machine from lifeless automaton? Put otherwise, if spirit is an electrical fluid, a chemical or mechanical by-product, what distinguishes human from beast, both of which are also animated by electrical fluids (Bell 1802)? The vigour of Muri's 'Enlightenment cyborg' is not merely that she collapses artificial distinctions between modern and postmodern borders but also that she elevates cyber theory for pre-1800 notions of extended cognition. And she does so by reinvigorating materialist philosophy from Descartes to La Mettrie and, above all, by placing Willis in the limelight to a degree only seen in George Rousseau's *Nervous Acts*.

Issues about philosophical monism and dualism were less vexatious thorns than the embodied self. That is, the sense that human beings are not merely present in their bodies but intrinsically commingled with them. It may be one reason why eighteenth-century poetry from Pope to Johnson did not dwell on the differences of monism and dualism to the degree of Romantic poetry: the sublime was not among this poetry's chief concerns as it later became.[8] Here, then, resides one new pathway to extended and distributed cognition even if the world of Spinoza and Malebranche to Hume and Hartley did not see it that way. These philosophers assumed brain was more or less equivalent to mind to a degree underplayed in recent treatments of philosophical monism (Crane and Patterson 2000; Gaukroger 2010; Weir 2012). Muri, more than these other recent authors, confronts the complications of early modern distributed cognition in her Enlightenment cyborgs.

Then, as now, the thorny issue was cognition, specifically the physiological source of the arising cognisance, the riddle of how consciousness and cognition arose from animated matter. The answers depended on the balance of mechanism and vitalism more than extrinsic categories grounded in philosophical dualism and

---

[8] A transitional literary work demonstrating a shift in concerns about monism and dualism is Zimmermann's *Solitude Considered with Respect to its Influence upon the Mind and Heart* (1794).

monism; or, further afield, the disciplinary origins of the thinker (i.e. whether toiling in the sciences, medicine, theoretical experimentation and so forth). An example in Germany were the cognition debates about the life force commencing in the 1740s, during the same decade when La Mettrie sketched his man-machine (McCarthy et al. 2016). From the start the German controversies privileged vitalism. Debates about vitalism, or *Lebenskraft*, endured well into the Romantic era and constituted one reason why the English Romantics discussed in this book were so eager to travel to Germany. Further ahead in the nineteenth century, vitalistic dilemmas in relation to embodied cognition continued to trouble no less an influential critic than Mikhail Bakhtin.[9] Historians Jonathan Sheehan and Dror Wahrman (2015), on the other hand, trace Enlightenment vitalism and self-organisation in relation to individual cognition. These discussions continued to raise questions about a stable concept of mind emerging from contested models (Danta and Groth 2014). Recent studies tracing the Enlightenment contributions to extended cognition have also begun to explore how such radically shifting models of mind can have produced a blueprint of cognition capable of satisfying anyone (Bruhn and Wehrs 2013).[10]

Scholarship devoted to the history of the book has often homed in on Enlightenment and Romantic attention, especially the attentive spans of readers and writers, including a study of the didactic eighteenth-century poetry devoted to attention itself (Koehler 2012). Two decades ago John Sutton's (1998) important retrieval of 'memory traces' suggested that attention might become a subdiscipline of extended cognition studies. The eighteenth-century preoccupation with madness – a rival to memory – further suggests the rich resonances of 'distracting' components embedded in configurations of attention (Pashler 1998; Crary 2001; Daston 2004; Phillips 2016a). Considering the amount of empirical data recently generated about attention in cognitive psychology as a basis for the medical study of dementia, this development is not surprising, and no more unpredictable than the turn to emotion and emotional history in eighteenth-century studies (Lemmings et al. 2016). However, less agreement exists about adequate theoretical models for cognitive attention, especially when the cogitating subject is viewed as a self-operating autopoietic system.[11]

---

[9] During his most Kantian phase Russian theorist Bakhtin spent several years in the 1920s emphasising the role of Enlightenment vitalism for the material mind, and in 1926 he published a long article entitled 'Contemporary Vitalism' in the Russian journal *Chelovek I Priroda* (*Man and Nature*); for the Enlightenment background and text of the essay see Rousseau 1993. Charles T. Wolfe has recently demonstrated the powerful force of vitalism in all Enlightenment debates about embodied cognition (see Wolfe 2012, 2014; Wolfe and Gal 2010a).

[10] In his special edited issue of *Poetics Today* M. J. Bruhn (2011) suggests that our type of book offering a historicised distributed cognition is what he has sought.

[11] N. M. Phillips (2016b) has highlighted some of the disputes and called attention to the role of cognitive overload during the eighteenth century as information exploded and to the new forms of metropolitan distraction in Britain's growing cities. But these well-founded historical observations do not yet shed much light on attention's enacted versions. It shed abundant light on its embodied forms as the subject became increasingly enmeshed in the agents of distractions, whether animate or inanimate.

The crucial vitalistic component of these debates continues to be reflected in scholarship about reproduction (Stephanson and Wagner 2015), predictably as Enlightenment biology, with its inherent materialism, captured the stakes of vitalistic riddles. Scholars have even considered to what degree vitalism's unseen forces played roles in shaping concepts of eighteenth-century sympathy (Scheler 1973; Terrall 1996). It has now become clear to what extent Enlightenment philosophical pronouncements about sympathy emanated from the reproduction debates, especially those pertaining to preformationism and epigenesis, even if little evidence has been found that anatomical body parts – heart, stomach, liver, nerves, spirits and fibres – were functioning autonomously (Csengei 2011; Lemmings et al. 2016). One thread has been that Romantic interaction with a natural environment beckoning urbanites to view its pleasures was a source of extended cognition more potent than the five senses.[12]

Few topics in Enlightenment and Romantic scholarship have been more discussed recently than the rise of sensibility. Numbers of books have been written about its genesis (Riskin 2002; Lloyd 2013) and sensibility itself has been configured as the main shift from an early Enlightenment mindset predicated on an aesthetic of balance, proportion and reason to a more passionate one grounded in ecstasy and excess. A second thread in the sensibility paradigm has demonstrated it emanating from the ongoing mind-body debates (Rousseau 1989, 1991); while a third, more recent strand has focused on biological topics pertaining to animal economy and living organic form (Jackson 2008). None of these recent trends discounts vitalism even when called by other names (i.e. animal economy, organic form, self-regulating system). The Enlightenment construction of the perplexing automaton – the self-operating machine designed automatically to follow a predetermined sequence of operations – was configured in terms both mechanistic and vitalistic despite the automaton's lack of an anatomical brain (Riskin 2015).

American historian of neuroscience Harry Whitaker and his colleagues (2007) recently produced a substantial volume of essays mapping the space, as it were, between the brain and the mind in eighteenth-century writing. Their results demonstrate the progress mind had made from 1700 to 1820. Nerves and neural pathways remained constant during that century but the degree to which mind overtook brain was replete with implications for the later development of cognitive science along the lines of our four Es. When historian Rita Carter and neuroscientist Christopher Frith collaborated in the late 1990s 'mind' was still inchoate, in their words 'waiting to be mapped' (Carter and Frith 1998: 3–4). In the aftermath of Kant, brain partially dropped out: first in favour of abstract transcendental minds and, second, because of a more extended cognition. Brains would soon return, of course; in early-nineteenth-century research the neurologists had never dropped out (Bell 1802; Wade 2000). But mind's increments and inroads trumpeted later forms of distributed and extended cognition, as John Sutton (1998)

---

[12] As long ago as 1998 Clark and Chalmers suggested that the environment plays an active role in driving cognitive processes; for more recent work see Malafouris and Renfrew 2013.

suggested in his work on post-Cartesian connectionism. And the pathway continues to the present moment in Daniel Dennett's latest book (2017), revisiting and extending a half-century of work on the anthropological evolution of minds.

Dennett has provisionally configured extended cognition as proximate to an 'organ of unification' within a control system produced by an evolutionary process (see Dennett's chapter in Ross 2007: 157–89). But among scholars of the humanities and social sciences his view begs to be historicised, particularly the role vitalism played in relation to materialist paradigms of the man-machine (Mitchell 2013). Hartley's associationism may have changed the course of Enlightenment psychology and philosophy when postulating a neurological model of mind grounded in vibrations in the nerves curbing free will. Yet not until Coleridge and other Romantics refuted Hartley was it clear what a leap was taken from Hartleyan associationism to the transcendental mind Coleridge postulated. The latter mind stood apart from its surroundings: in this sense it was not yet extended or distributed in the ways contemporary philosophers construe it. But the Romantic mind was gradually moving in this distributed direction as an evolving mind aggregating ever-greater powers to itself. It may be the reason why recent books have been preponderantly drawn to Romantic theories of cognition, especially in the work of Alan Richardson (Richardson 2001, 2010; Richardson and Spolsky 2004). That scholarship has not yet proffered its fine lenses to distributed and extended cognition suggests the novelty of our book for historicising mind science.

Nevertheless, it would be misleading to think the long eighteenth century has become distributed and extended along the lines of 4E cognition. It has been moving in directions privileging consciousness but not yet the 4E distributed models forming the focus of our approach. Over a decade ago John Beer (2003) surveyed the whole period in terms of 'Romantic consciousness' and, more recently, Marcus Iseli (2015) has focused on Thomas De Quincey's 'cognitive unconscious', but these approaches are not those of the four Es. So too David Herman's (2011) team of scholars who recently traced the *longue durée* of 'consciousness in narrative discourse' from Chaucer to the present, and those now enlisting cutting-edge neuroimaging technology to scrutinise the localised brains of students reading Jane Austen (Carroll 2012; Phillips 2016b). Such cognitive turns were probably predictable ever since Michel Foucault imported science and medicine into the cultural analysis of the long eighteenth century almost a half-century ago, and assessed their extended role in shaping 'knowledge, power, and discourse' in *Folie et déraison: histoire de la folie à l'âge classique* (Foucault 1961: ii–iii). More consequential have been the historical configurations of cyborgs, whether in Donna Haraway's (1991) version in her manifesto for feminism, or in Andy Clark's (2003) construction of human beings as 'natural-born cyborgs'. Their embodiments have not been subtly historicised, or enriched, with long-eighteenth-century sources to the extent of Alison Muri's version (2006).

Foucault became invested in the power and politics of the body at a time when psychoanalysis still held high cachet. It eroded in the decades after his death in 1984, and – in partial response to its demise – significant numbers of scholars concluded he had done more harm than good for historical comprehension of the Enlightenment. While Foucault tapped into a long eighteenth century obsessed with the body and its forms of power, others began to launch an era based on capital and commodity, print culture and consumerism, literary selfhood and sociability. Yet both versions partook of social networking capable of arising only through shared forms of cognition. The new networks generated new ethical systems stimulated, in part, by Scottish Common Sense philosophy, which, in turn, was altering modes of human interaction as well as a sense of human interaction with the natural environment. Even new attitudes toward animals augured what was coming. And an unprecedented explosion of books and other printed matter certainly rivalled any transformations that had occurred in relation to the anatomical body.

Foucault's versions of embodiment – in hindsight whether damaging to understanding of the epoch or not – minimised cognition but never silenced it. Indeed, could he return from the dead he would be enthralled by the bouillon the new cognition has given his *Folie et déraison: histoire de la folie à l'âge classique*. For even the madness Foucault found riddled in classical eighteenth-century civilisation depended on distributed cognition. And the time cannot now be far away when our post-post-Foucaldian Enlightenment and Romantic studies will begin to invoke the four Es. When they do, a new dimension of the inner, yet still isolated, minds of its Pamelas and Clarissas, Robinson Crusoes and Tom Joneses, will unfold. The progression to a 4E conception of the era will pose an alternative to the more anthropocentric, imperialist and patriarchal eighteenth century still prevalent today, and to the charge, broadly made, that theoretical cognitive studies are inherently antihistoricist in their preference for nature over nurture. Placing these just-mentioned canonical and other long-eighteenth-century texts under the lens of the four Es will also yield another kind of 'cognitive turn': one emphasising the cultural and historical dimensions of the period rather than its transhistorical niche. If and when that occurs, the historicist threshold of eighteenth-century literary studies will in turn also rise, which must be beneficial to the understanding of the era.

II. Distributed Cognition in Enlightenment and Romantic Studies – Our Volume

Miranda Anderson

This volume brings together eleven chapters by international specialists working in the period between the late seventeenth and early nineteenth centuries in the fields of literature, philosophy, art, material culture and history of science and medicine. The chapters revitalise our understanding of the long eighteenth century by bringing to bear recent insights in cognitive science and philosophy of mind on the distributed nature of cognition. Distributed cognition claims that cognition does not occur just through sociocultural forces or disembodied information flow, nor merely in our brains as some distilled miniature of our situation in the world. Instead, cognition occurs through brain-body-world interactions. The first section of this introductory chapter has provided a background to current research in Enlightenment and Romantic studies on topics related to distributed cognition, while this second section considers how the various chapters in this volume represent, reflect and advance work in this area.[13]

The aims with which we presented participants in the research project from which this volume derives were either to consider the ways in which Enlightenment and Romantic sources might be regarded as representing approaches that in some way prefigure modern theories of distributed cognition, or to explore the ways in which these modern theories cast new light on Enlightenment and Romantic phenomena, or the traditions through which they have been interpreted. A further aim is to demonstrate, and to stimulate wider critical investigations on, how approaches to distributed cognition in philosophy and cognitive science can inform, and be informed by, Enlightenment and Romantic culture, through making evident the constraints and capacities of past and current definitions and debates. The contributors represent an array of disciplines, with literary scholars having contributed the most chapters overall, due to the breadth of literary studies as a discipline and its pioneering interest in cognitive approaches to the humanities. The chapters directly engage with the various models in modern philosophy of mind and cognitive science which challenge standard models that view the body and the environment as peripheral to an understanding of the nature of cognition. Distributed cognition covers an intertwined group of theories, which include enactivism and embodied, embedded and extended cognition, which are also together known as '4E cognition'.[14] Together the chapters make evident the ways in which particular notions and practices of distributed cognition emerged from the particular range of sociocultural and technological contexts that existed during this period. The eleven chapters that follow illuminate notions and practices of distributed cognition in Enlightenment and Romantic thought and culture.

The long eighteenth century saw the development of a wide range of theories that attempted to revise existing explanations of the basis for human cognition which, in the face of scientific, empirical and epistemological developments, were perceived to be incomplete or unsatisfactory. Especially prominent during this period are a range of theories whose opposition to the rise of mechanistic and dualistic notions produced forms of proto-enactivism. Enactivism claims continuity between mind and life, describing cognition as enacted (unfolding) via

---

[13] I would like to thank Elspeth Jajdelska, Karin Kukkonen, George Rousseau and Michael Wheeler for proofreading a draft of this section.

[14] Brief outlines of these theories are provided here where needed and the series introduction to this volume (Chapter 1) provides a detailed overview.

looping interactions between the organism and its environment. There are two main branches – the first emphasises the sensorimotor aspects and the second autopoiesis (self-creation).[15] One of the roots from which the blossoming of pro-to-enactivist notions emerged in this period is traced in our opening chapter by Charlotte Lee on the poetry of Barthold Heinrich Brockes (1680–1747) set against the background context of physico-theology (Chapter 3). Physico-theology claimed continuity between worldly and divine phenomena such that study of the natural world could provide evidence for God's existence. The radical Protestantism and Pietism of late-seventeenth- to mid-eighteenth-century Germany encouraged ideas that the emotions inform reason, as well as a unified view of body and soul. As Lee observes, there is clearly a difference between recent embodied and enactive theories and the religious belief system of Brockes and his contemporaries – and yet the general supposition that earlier periods mostly viewed the mind as dis-embodied is shown to need rethinking.[16] Brockes's poem *Irdisches Vergnügen in Gott* (*Earthly Pleasure in God*) anticipates enactivism and influenced later Romantic works in terms of its emphasis on the profound significance of the natural world and on feeling as an aspect of thinking. Not only the natural but the created environment is of consequence to cognition. Distributed cognition's focus on the ways in which human beings' shaping of environments recursively shapes our own potential also extends into conceptual realms: theoretical, cultural and literary forms and tra-ditions provide diverse means to structure and widen the scope of our thought-worlds. This further fundamental contribution of distributed cognitive approaches to the humanities is explored by Lee in the second section of her chapter through an analysis of the alignment between Brockes's *Irdisches Vergnügen* and cognitive scientific notions of 'epistemic engineering'[17] – since human design, inheritance and cumulative modifications to habitats encompasses the epistemic environment, including that conjured by literary works. The poem is held up as both a product of and an instrument for passionate engagement with the world and as unearthing the entwined nature of subjective and objective domains.

Ideas of the emotions' cognitive role and of mind-world flow that the open-ing chapter reveals at work in the seventeenth to mid-eighteenth century, Renee Harris shows appearing in new guises from the mid-eighteenth to early nineteenth century (Chapter 4). Harris discusses the development of notions of affectivity in psychology, medicine and moral philosophy as a background to an investigation into their expression in the works of Wordsworth (1770–1850) and John Keats (1795–1821). Earlier notions of the flow of the passions around and between bodies by means of the spirits[18] became associated with the newly renamed 'sympathetic

---

[15] For a more detailed account see the series introduction to this volume (Chapter 1) and the 'Enactivism' seminar by Dave Ward (2014), available online at <www.hdc.ed.ac.uk/seminars/enactivism> (last accessed 1 February 2019).

[16] Lakoff (2003) is also critiqued by other volumes in this series in this respect.

[17] Clark 2008: 66 following Sterelny.

[18] On Renaissance notions of the spirits and the emotions see, in volume 2 of this series, Wojciehowski 2019 and Lochman 2019; also see Anderson 2015b, 2016 and Paster et al. 2004.

nervous system' and discussion of the roles of sympathy and the emotions pervaded Enlightenment and Romantic medical, philosophical and cultural discourses. Adam Smith and David Hume's notions of fellow-feeling and affective transmission anticipate and attempt to explain phenomena we now know to be underpinned by neurophysiological mechanisms, such as the mirror neuron system, which causes us to mentally simulate others' actions and emotions, and which can also be activated by language.[19] Wordsworth's early description of the power of poetry as the spontaneous outpouring of 'emotion recollected in tranquillity'[20] and his insertion of his own experiences of (what we now call) cognitive processing are critiqued by the later Romantics, including Keats, as insulating aesthetic experience from sensation. The roots of Keat's notions of cognition and emotion as interdependent and intersubjective are uncovered in notes from his medical training and, less directly, in the works of Hume and Smith. The resonances of late Romantic notions with enactive concepts of transubjective affectivity and enacted spaces of empathy (Colombetti 2014) help articulate and ground their idealistic impulses. These notions of transubjective affectivity and aesthetics, Harris concludes, show that the 'radical openness of the distributed cognition model and the physiological sympathy imagined by the eighteenth century . . . offers a hope for societal change through the bond of shared feeling and the creative activity it inspires' (p. 62).

Embodiment and our situatedness in the world also contributed to eighteenth-century epistemological notions of mental representations. Jennifer Mensch deploys notions of distributed cognition as a means to re-examine the relation between the critiques of materialism by Bishop George Berkeley (1685–1783) and Immanuel Kant (1724–1804), and provides an unexpected twist to conventional views of their works' intellectual foundations (Chapter 5). Kant's concern to distance his idealism from Berkeley's theories is shown to be fuelled in part by their mutual reliance on embodied cognition. Consequently, the theoretical move made by current embodied cognition scholars, which is to claim that certain challenges faced by perception and cognition can be solved by examining the nature of our embodiment, is revealed to have a long history. Berkeley argued that tangible ideas of spatial distance and position acquired through the course of bodily experience – for example, motion and touch – lead to and provide the meaning of our ideas of geometry and space. While Berkeley presented God as the active source of all our sensible ideas, he does not claim a necessary connection between these ideas and the things they represent. For Kant it is an otherwise unknowable material realm of things-in-themselves that is behind, or beyond, the sensory impressions out of which the mind constructs experience. Kant claims that our innate sense of the difference between the left and right sides of our body gives us our sense of situatedness in the

---

[19] See also, for example, theories on motor simulation of language content and theories of language processing in which production (action) and comprehension (perception) are interwoven, with motor simulation a route to comprehension (e.g. Rizzolatti and Sinigaglia 2008; Pickering and Garrod 2013).

[20] Wordsworth 2001: 273, quoted in Harris, p. 56.

world: it enables us to orient ourselves in space, and 'this cognition is functionally extended beyond the body with the use of compasses, star charts and other tools for understanding spatial position'.[21] Thus embodied and enacted cognition is shown as poised to be extended by external tools, as in extended mind accounts. Furthermore, our intuitive capacity to distinguish between left and right ultimately relates to and proves the independent existence of space: 'embodied cognition of directions in space, a cognition of unquestioned worth and necessity, could only be made sense of, in other words, if space were outside us and real' (Mensch, p. 92). In Kant's account the ideal nature of space entailed that geometry was not arbitrary, and geometry's mathematical certainty demonstrated intuition's contribution to knowledge. Despite their differences, Mensch shows that both Berkeley and Kant sought to describe a system in which our experience of the world was of appearance only *and* was empirically real. Moreover, both use proprioception, our embodied cognition of space, to demonstrate that our representations constitute our reality, sharing a fundamentally phenomenological and enactive account of the body as enabling orientation in space.

The following couple of chapters focus again on the ways in which current notions about enactivism are anticipated and come particularly to the fore during this period. Quite what the protagonist of *Tristram Shandy* makes of mind and life and what insights can be revealed by re-examining his confused sense of time and identity via distributed cognitive approaches form the core of Chapter 6. Enactivism foregrounds the examination of lived experience as a methodological instrument. Here through the narrator's comical dissection of Tristram's views and behaviour the kinds of issues that might emerge through naive and overly simplistic notions of distributed accounts of mind and life surface in a deliberately dysfunctional form. Tristram's fumbling forays are contrasted by George Rousseau with Laurence Sterne's (1713–68) own wide knowledge of eighteenth-century theories of cognition, which included those by Locke, against whose blank slate of the mind as populated by ideas formed from sensory impressions as part of a proto-input-output system Sterne created his polemic. Rousseau explores the fault lines between various of the distributed cognitive approaches – particularly extendedness and enactivism – against the backdrop of Michael Wheeler's (2010b: 34) claim that 'cognition enacted cannot be cognition extended', since autopoietic enactivism can be argued to entail continuity between the cognitive system and the living system. Yet Tristram appears unable either cognitively to extend or to maintain his own integrity as an autopoietic system, instead appearing as a cog of an allopoietic system beyond his ken or control. Rousseau ultimately concludes that both Sterne's protagonist and his book *Tristram Shandy*, and more generally genre development, make evident that arbitrariness rather than dependability of boundaries can be a feature of autopoiesis. Characters, people, books and genres, like living organisms, can incorporate disparate matter into integrated evolving dynamic forms, though do not necessarily do so without problematic perturbations, and are subject to an

---

[21] Mensch, p. 91; cf. Hutchins (1995) and Roby (2018) on Ptolemy in volume 1 of this series.

intimacy and dependency – that is not necessarily desirable – with wider allopoietic systems, as expressed here through the characters, form and content of Sterne's prose satire.

Enactive theories' grasp of the interwoven nature of mind and life and of the subject and world similarly enable a new reading of Samuel Taylor Coleridge's (1772–1834) theory of knowledge in *Biographia Literaria*, and insight into its complementary relation to his 'Theory of life' (Chapter 7). While modern accounts of distributed cognition respond to Cartesian dualism and isolation of mind from environment by neuro-centric, cognitivist and computational approaches, Romantic thinkers were caught between striving to reject dualism and avoiding the pitfalls of other materialist, vitalist or idealist theories. In the process, as Lisa Ann Robertson shows, Coleridge develops complementary theories of knowledge and life which anticipate a range of enactive concepts, such as structural coupling, co-emergence and co-dependence. Drawing on German transcendentalism combined with British empiricism, Coleridge develops an ontological theory whereby the absolute and transient are mutually constitutive. His epistemological theory describes a similarly dynamic co-constitution and recursiveness between subjective mind and objective nature. Rather than flattening the subject into matter alone, making the world entirely a product of mind, or dualistically positing an ontological distinction between mind and matter, Coleridge describes the body and spirit as merely different 'degrees in perfection, of a common substratum'.[22] The enactive distinction between autopoiesis and allopoiesis is expressed by Coleridge in terms of life's 'organisation ab intra' versus death's 'organisation ab extra', with life, the world and the laws of nature emerging from, and as driven by, the dynamic pull of two poles, unity versus individuality.[23] As in Berkeley's and Kant's theories (discussed in Chapter 5), the world cannot be known other than through the mind that perceives it. For Coleridge knowledge emerges, as in enactive theories, through 'a reciprocal concurrence' of subject and object.[24] Understanding of cognition as 'an emergent process between percipients and their surroundings', Robertson argues, might lead us to more 'continuously engage in the difficult task of considering whether we are in the right relationship with ourselves, our surroundings, our community, and with the ground of being' (p. 138).

The transformation of our understanding of Coleridge's works is also the aim of John Savarese's chapter, this time primarily from the angle of extended cognition, in terms of humans' textual and social extendibility (Chapter 8). Coleridge asserts that we should make use of textual resources, such as his own *Aids to Reflection*

---

[22] Coleridge 1983: 114, quoted in Robertson (p. 133). Looking in the other direction, the influence of Aristotelian notions on Coleridge's notions is strongly evident.

[23] Robertson comments on the influence of *Naturphilosophie* here, and we can also see the influence of classical models discussed in volume 1 of this series, which had re-emerged in Boethius (Anderson 2007) and later in Francis Bacon's notions of a fundamental tension between a striving towards unity and individuality (Anderson 2016), again more recently expressed by Freud's 'Beyond the Pleasure Principle' (also discussed in Anderson 2007).

[24] Coleridge 1983: 255, quoted in Robertson (p. 133).

(1825), in order to extend our cognitive capacities. This is less self-serving of Coleridge than it may at first appear. The word 'reflection' in Coleridge's work does not entail mere introspection – which after Robertson's chapter on his theory of knowledge as emerging from subject-object interaction is not as surprising as it might otherwise seem. *Aids to Reflection* itself acts as a manual for reflection and sets out the case that external aids can scaffold internal processes by performing part of the cognitive labour: this is 'private thought scaffolded not by divine action but by an integrated network of texts and information management systems' (p. 155). It is against the backdrop of Clark and Chalmers' seminal 'Extended Mind' hypothesis regarding the potential for parity between biological and non-biological resources, and its hypothetical case of the memory-impaired Otto using a notebook in place of his biological memory, that Coleridge's work is initially set by Savarese. Both Coleridge's views on textual aids and his related beliefs that language is a cognitive tool, a culturally specific resource and a living expression of Logos evidence the influence of earlier thinkers,[25] but he resets these within the context of transcendentalism. For Savarese the work 'is positioned as a vehicle of enlightenment that would promote intellectual autonomy' (p. 142). The apparent paradox, that intellectual autonomy emerges via our capacity to use and internalise external scaffolding, is one that has more recently been tackled by distributed cognition theorists, including Varela, Thompson and Rosch (1991). Comparison with Wheeler and Clark's notion of 'cognitive niche construction' (2008) – which describes our engineering of societies for cognitive optimisation across time with inherited learning transmitted via practices and artefacts – further helps us to view the meaning of this work as part of Coleridge's broader framework of ideas. Coleridge's claim that we require such aids is grounded in a socially extended cognition claim: all humans across space and time are 'one Individual Mind', hence we have access to a shared storehouse of memory.[26] When we set Robertson's and Savarese's chapters side by side we can see particularly well why Coleridge had a 'divided legacy later in the nineteenth century', 'at once a sage in the transcendentalist tradition and a more empirical, eclectic figure of materially and textually mediated thinking' (Savarese, p. 142). In many respects this vision captures a more general insight into the way the period has been perceived in the past. When approached via a distributed cognition framework, the coalescence between both aspects – the transcendental and empirical – and the ways in which human and world emerge together become visible.

The following cluster of chapters expand this exploration of the cognitive effects of textual resources in further fruitful directions, reconsidering through a cognitive lens the effects of widening literacy, increasing availability of texts and the emergence of new genres. Elspeth Jajdelska shows how changes in the material and conceptual environment combine to support the development of writing as a means to cognitively process experience rather than just chart events (Chapter 9).

---

[25] See Anderson 2015b and volume 2 of this series.
[26] Coleridge 1956–71: II, 701, quoted in Savarese, p. 144.

Tracking diary-writing practices between the seventeenth and eighteenth centuries, Jajdelska observes that amidst the more general utilitarian religious 'credit and debit' accounts there emerged those in which 'entries became micro-narratives, and diaries macro-narratives, of continuous personal experience' (p. 160). One influence here is the rise in the eighteenth century of the novel, which also selects information in order to convey experiential trajectories. Narrative's potential for flexibility along with its durability made it a means of dynamic self-formation. Rather than the more stable semantic memory of facts, as in the seminal Clark and Chalmers account, it is the more malleable, episodic memory of autobiographical information that is supplemented, the episodic memory's adaptive nature making its relatively stable pen and ink imprinting potentially even more transformative. Jajdelska draws on recent research on eye activity during writing that shows various scales of oscillating movements back and forth across the text, which 'blurs processing with production', as has been previously shown to be the case in regard to the entangled nature of gesture and speech processing and production (p. 162). The eighteenth-century diarist's generation of 'a coherent self is shared with the environment through the gesture of writing and the act of reading' (p. 168). Changes in reading practices not only affected the ways in which diaries were being written; the increasing equality of expression possible in written texts and the reading of elite texts by wider audiences began to place in question the gender and class hierarchies that persisted in face-to-face interchanges. Jajdelska concludes that it was such subtle shifts in the conceptual framework accompanying the spread of books and literacy which helped to create fertile ground for dissemination of more radical ideas and ways of co-existing. The argument has broadened out again then, in this case opening out from the ways in which writing systems can scaffold individual minds to the ways in which consequently sociocultural norms can be transformed.

A more epistemological form of ongoing hierarchical struggle is the focus of Ros Ballaster's chapter on the evolving eighteenth-century literary tradition: text versus body, manifested as prose versus performance (Chapter 10). Prose forms, particularly newly emerging genres, such as the novel and theatre criticism, seek to establish their superiority over the established genre of theatrical performance by ranking textually enabled aspects of social cognition over bodily ones, echoing in the secular sphere religious tensions over the superiority of text-based versus sensorially rich forms of worship, which came to the fore in the preceding centuries. Women writers tended to be motivated by their marginalisation from mainstream playwriting, and defensively responded by emphasising the greater capacity of a narratorial voice to evoke presence, versus that of the embodied voices, expressions and gestures of theatrical performers. The emphasis on sociability in eighteenth-century Britain, Ballaster argues, is expressed by the new prose genres in terms resonant with the current concept of a 'group mind', to the extent that they promoted an epistemology of collectively thinking together, in a way that elite prose had not. Furthermore, the reframing of the genre system as a 'mental institution' – which is created via '(shared) mental processes' that combine the 'products constituted in mental processes already accomplished by others' and our reshaping of them' (Gallagher 2013: 7) – helps bring to light not only the cognitive functions of evolving, emerging and hybrid genres, but also the constantly recalibrated nature of inherited values as part of a dynamic cognitive ecology. In this instance the dominant norms and attributes of theatrical production and performance in the eighteenth century inform the ways in which the other genres define and measure themselves. Drawing on a wide range of prose works by women writers, including Eliza Haywood, Sarah Fielding, Charlotte Lennox and Frances Brooke, Ballaster demonstrates the new prose media's evoking of theatrical performance and embodied co-presence. As if to underline this, Fielding and Collier conjure ghostly presence associatively through their reference to the need that 'the mind's eye' be assisted by their fable, as the body's eye is corrected by glasses,[27] evoking *Hamlet*, as well as echoing George Puttenham's (1589: 256) description of rhetoric as spectacles for the mind, a prosthetic for the understanding. Indeed, prose texts were argued to be more productive of socially distributed cognition, via the wider and more reflective operation, than that of being in the audience of a theatre performance. Though Ballaster also mentions an assertion of 'the superior power of the framing narrator to ensure the moral affect of this shared experience' (p. 186), we know from Harris (Chapter 4) such views shall meet a challenge in the later Romantics' attitudes to such filtering and directiveness.

Another countermovement arises in the following chapter, which conversely charts a defence of the superior capacity of theatrical performance to prose. The apologists' stance again emerges, though, from a combination of their own particular cultural situatedness and the particular cognitive capacities enabled, enhanced or extended by the different media. Karin Kukkonen examines the ways in which the Jesuits theorised media differences, focusing on Porée and Brumoy's treatises as a means towards analysis of Brumoy's didactic poem *De motibus animi* (1741) and Bougeant's novel parody *Voyage merveilleux du Prince Fan-Férédin dans la Romancie* ([1735] 1992) (Chapter 11). Drawing on Sterelny (2003, 2014) and Wheeler and Clark (2008), Kukkonen analyses eighteenth-century Jesuit poetics as a form of 'designer environment' – 'spatial and procedural arrangements that scaffold and amplify cognition' – extending this notion 'beyond the usual focus on problem-solving and the immediate task at hand' (p. 187). The apologists' defence may seem familiar from the last chapter: the Jesuits' practice of theatrical performance is argued to have a superior capacity for moral improvement through emotionally moving an audience in a more controlled fashion than is possible via a textual medium. Despite the contrast with the previous chapter in terms of the particular form of medium lauded, the Jesuits' defence is still grounded in more general concerns and anxiety about the role of the uncontrolled body and emotions in cognition, which appear reflexively to accompany notions of their intimacy or integration with mind. Reflecting on the work of Ed Hutchins, and the application of his theories in Evelyn Tribble's work on distributed cognition in the Globe theatre

---

[27] In 'Prologue to Part the Third', Fielding and Collier 2018: 133, quoted by Ballaster, p. 175.

and in English Protestant worship, Kukkonen raises as an issue that attention has tended to focus too much on distributed cognition in terms of problem-solving. Examining the Jesuits' theory and practice of a 'literary designer environment', she argues that such a fictional extension allows for a state between immersion and reflection by drawing on embodiment and linguistic elements, as well as detachment from immediate problem-solving: through these methods literature enables manipulations of readers' expectations and enhancement of readers' cognitive processes.

The last two chapters expand the scope of their reflections to encompass various forms of visual arts. In the first of these, Richard Sha examines the resonances between distributed cognition and eighteenth-century philosophical, scientific and literary ideas, before narrowing the focus to a detailed analysis of the poem and print of William Blake's 'London', as a means to consider 'where we mark the boundaries and why and when we feel the need to mark them' (p. 205) (Chapter 12). Sha touches on a wide range of Enlightenment and Romantic ideas in evidence across the volume – the brain as extending into the body via a nervous system which processes experience; mental capacities as emerging from thinking about the motions of objects in the world; and sensibility as extended across nature – all spurred on in part by reactions against Cartesian notions of two different kinds of matter, *res extensa* and *res cogitans*. Kant reappears here with his emphasis on the structuring role of the imagination and his inversion of Descartes's 'I think therefore I am' to 'I am therefore I think'.[28] This makes self *a priori*, since for Kant a unified self is necessary for thought, rather than the Cartesian model of thought being proof of self. However, as Sha points out, this still relies on a homology between self and cognition. It is the issue of this homology, which is also at the heart of enactive ideas, that Sha sceptically probes in this chapter, tackling similar questions to George Rousseau (Chapter 6) regarding whether or not autonomy and autopoiesis require a border, whether that border is flexible, and whether the border of the self and of cognition are identical, along with the issue of whether some forms of distributed cognition should be evaded rather than embraced. Sha argues that Blake's 'London' illustrates the collapsing together of mind and self, as a critique of the reductive nature of a conflation of mind and self. Cognition appears cramped by the threat of such a confinement. The urban landscape itself is shown to instantiate institutions that are formed from and formative of social and cognitive norms, with such 'mind-forg'd manacles' corralling biological forces.[29] The content and structure of the work, from the marks making up the print to the metre and rhythm, are shown to transmit the speaker's sense of constriction, and simultaneously to invite reflection on the moveable nature of the boundary between mind and world. The 'blurring of where inputs and outputs begin and end', Sha argues, makes evident the potentially 'stiff price to be paid for all this cognitive efficiency: the inability to distinguish between affordances and ideology' (p. 205).

[28] Kant 1996a: B135, quoted in Sha, p. 218.
[29] Blake, 'London', quoted in Sha, p. 215.

Competing forms of classical reception in the late eighteenth century are set side by side in the final chapter, revealing at work three forms of distributed cognition: extended, embodied and enacted (Chapter 13). Helen Slaney explores how 'cognising' – which she also terms '*connaissance*' or 'coming-to-know' – antique artefacts was understood to be a means to access antiquity: this is cognition as extended across time via artefacts. The emergence of competing ideas about the best means of cognising antiquity are rooted, Slaney argues, in the en masse uncovering of antique artefacts around Naples during this period, at the same time as antiquarianism began to be approached more scientifically and systematically. The catalogues of William Hamilton's Greek vase collection represent a form of cognition as extended via the two-way dynamic between the collection and perceivers of it, with the vases' agency evident through their 'informing, instructing and . . . initiating [the antiquarians] into sacred mysteries' (p. 223). By contrast, Emma Hamilton's approach to her husband's collection involved a form of embodied cognition, yet another eighteenth-century notion of coming-to-know through the body and its relation to motion, here termed 'kinaesthetic cognisance'. This took on a more performative aspect than it did for thinkers such as Berkeley or Kant: Emma's 'Attitudes' involved dressing in costumes inspired by the vases and posing as characters from Greek mythology. At the time her *tableaux vivants* were celebrated and yet seen merely as an amusement. Philosopher Johann Gottfried Herder was one of those who were dismissive of Emma's performance art, preferring an aesthetic approach to antiquity that more closely anticipates enactivism. Herder believed that ancient Greek sculptures were visual stimuli that caused kinaesthetic responses most richly virtually in the imagination – he argued that a simulation of movement in the beholder's imagination is triggered through merely being in the presence of a sculptural artefact. These three forms of cognisance relate to the artefacts' attributes and to the ways they were presented and organised, such that different cognitive stances emerge. In preference to Herder's fantasies, Slaney upholds Emma's embodied sculpting of a knowledge of antiquity through her flesh by means of which she 'made herself a vessel' (p. 236). The catalogue, dance and the simulation are reflective of the prioritisation of different strands of distributed cognition by differently situated individuals or groups. The variety of methods applied to grasp phenomenologically the bygone experience of the classical past is suggestive of broader trends and debates in the long eighteenth century (and beyond) about artistic and cognitive hierarchies, which form a persistent theme throughout this volume.

As is evident from the essays in this volume, the two-way conversation in the long eighteenth century between literary writers and scholars working on the philosophical or scientific nature of the mind means that literary works often reflected, debated and interrogated philosophical and scientific concepts. One such concept, vitalism, is often defined as concerned with belief in a metaphysical self-determining force or forces, yet in the long eighteenth century it was not always the case that the vital power of the spirits or spirit was conceived of as immaterial, as George Rousseau demonstrates in the first section of this chapter. For as in the

Renaissance, whose influence still lingered, the spirits or spirit flowing around and between bodies were one means by which the concept and the common phenomenological experience of cognition as distributed across brain, body and world were then expressed – and can take us beyond mainstream modern distributed cognition in terms of suggesting the sharing of aspects of consciousness. In fact, stemming from such experiences, as we have seen, there abounded a wide range of holistic notions of embodiment and environment as dynamically entangled, with human minds emerging in concert with biological and sociocultural environments. As Sha observes: 'In the study of Romanticism, poststructuralist approaches have emphasised the gap between mind and world, with an aporia where there is relationality' (p. 206).[30] Yet neither humans being poised in this way, nor the cognitive niches with which they could become enmeshed, were necessarily viewed positively, as they tend to be in more recent cognitive scientific approaches, and this in itself can helpfully prompt reconsideration as to the extent of optimism generally inherent in recent models. Contributions across the series have brought to the fore not only epistemological and ontological questions, but the ethical issues that are raised by notions of the intimacy or integration of mind with its spatial and sociocultural surround. Another issue that emerges is that while distributed cognition takes a liberal approach to defining what is included under the term 'cognition', even enactivism can default to framing it primarily in terms of 'problem-solving', betraying the influence of decades of dialogue involving philosophers grounded in analytical philosophy and computational theories.[31] In the long-eighteenth-century belief system, notions such as the sympathetic nervous system, vitalism and transcendental idealism provided a biological basis for humans' capacity to fluidly and reciprocally interact with their environment, and a natural grounding for models that extended this dynamic interactivity to the social and cultural realms.

A topic that increasingly became a matter of debate in the long eighteenth century was the ways in which different media present diverse stances and trajectories through which cognitive processes and states could be articulated, adapted or advanced. A dominant theme in the essays is the effect of more widespread print and increasing literacy as a wider range of literary media develop and are supplemented by the emergence of new genres. The diversification of literary species was accompanied by increasing competition to establish dominance of one's own preferred kind. The competition between forms of cognitive scaffolding is also evident more generally in the culture of the long eighteenth century. For instance, another manifestation of this rivalry is between historiographical, sculptural and performative forms of experiencing and expressing antique culture (as described in the final

---

[30] Anderson has observed this of postmodern approaches more generally (2015b); also see the series introduction (Chapter 1).

[31] Thompson and Stapleton's critique of the extended mind thesis argues that it has 'treated cognition as if it were largely affectless problem-solving or information processing' (2008: 26), yet we can also see the tendency to slip into a focus on problem-solving in recent seminal enactivist works (e.g. Gallagher 2017).

chapter). This competition signals the period's heightened concern with interrogating the cognitive role of the body versus other cognitive resources that are available, as well as the struggle to clarify the relation between life and mind, both of which remain central topics of debate today. In turn, these competing models reflect attempts to establish hierarchies among different distributed cognitive models, which vary between prioritising (their own particular eighteenth-century variants or hybrid forms of) embodied, embedded, enacted or extended claims, and which were, and are, associated with claims about the superiority of particular scientific and cultural beliefs, forms and practices.

This volume on the thought-world of the long eighteenth century has uncovered notions of flux between brain, body and world, of mind-life and subject-object structural couplings, of affective cognition and sympathetic circulations, of mind metamorphoses and manacles, and of texts, performances and artefacts as cognitive aids and as modes of access to other minds and past phenomenologies. Encountering the historically inflected and culturally situated beliefs and practices of eighteenth-century distributed cognition provides a new perspectival depth and broadening of our own limited purview – current debates and definitions have themselves been created and constrained by their own developmental trajectories. Through addressing the ways in which the distribution of cognition across brain, body and world encompasses all human domains, the cognitive significance of humanities' research matter emerges, as does, in turn, the humanities' significance to attempts to grasp the multifaceted nature of human cognition.

3

Barthold Heinrich Brockes
and Distributed Cognition:
The Delicate Flux of World and Spirit

Charlotte Lee

human minds . . . are the surprisingly plastic minds of *profoundly* embodied agents: agents whose boundaries and components are forever negotiable and for whom body, sensing, thinking, and reasoning are all woven flexibly and repeatedly from the accommodating weave of situated, intentional action.

Andy Clark, *Supersizing the Mind*

Barthold Heinrich Brockes (1680–1747) was one of the most prolific poets of the German Enlightenment. His magnum opus was *Irdisches Vergnügen in Gott (Earthly Pleasure in God)*,[1] a nine-volume collection of lyric pieces, each one geared to the praise of God. Many of the poems offer fascinating early explorations of what the editors of this volume call 'brain-body-world collaboration'. Brockes was predisposed by certain trends in his own time to think in a manner resonant with modern approaches. While his work is not concerned with the specifics of neutrally located thinking, the bodily nature of knowledge-formation, understood in more general terms, is an important theme. He was working in the context of a general relaxation of taboos around the senses, and of a rise of empiricism in natural philosophy. A consequence of this new attention to the senses was the frequent extension of 'bodily consideration to all aspects of cognition and mental life' (Wolfe and Gal 2010b: 4). Of perhaps even greater relevance to this volume is the intensive flux between body and mind on the one hand, and 'world' or environment on the other, which – owing to both religious and scientific influences on his thought – features with high frequency in his poetry. It is above all this glide from mind to world, presented with such ease and assurance in his work, which makes it possible to argue for Brockes as a precursor of modern notions of distributed cognition.

Brockes's intellectual development was shaped by an eclectic mix of theories. The University of Halle, where he studied law and philosophy between 1700 and 1702, provided some vital formative influences. An important inspiration for Brockes was the jurist and philosopher Christian Thomasius, whose lectures

---

[1] The publication gives this as *Irdisches Vergnügen in GOtt*; the capitalisation has been adjusted throughout.

he attended, and whose 1699 treatise *Versuch vom Wesen des Geistes* in particular left discernible traces in *Irdisches Vergnügen*.[2] Thomasius argued, against Descartes, that 'the active principle which extends matter . . . is spirit' (Ahnert 2003: 263). Spirit, or 'Geist' in German, he describes as 'etwas edlers als das leibliche Wesen, das ausser und in allen leiblichen Wesen ist' ('something more noble than physical being, which is outside and within all physical beings', Thomasius 2004: 35). For him, matter is essentially passive, inert and requires animation by spirit: in a delightful image, he compares this process to a child using its breath to blow a bubble from soapy water (36). Thomasius's thought, then, was closer to the ancient tradition of hermeticism – which conceived of the world as 'ensouled organism, an organic body'[3] – than to the mechanistic interpretations of nature which were gaining ground in the wake of Descartes.

The general atmosphere at Halle has been described as a 'bastion of anti-Cartesianism',[4] a reputation which it owes not least to the influence of Georg Ernst Stahl, who was Professor of Medicine there. Stahl mounted a direct and sustained challenge both to post-Cartesian philosophy and to the increasing tendency in medicine to view the body in mechanistic terms. Some of Stahl's ideas were wide of the mark in their details: take, for example, his opposition to the notion of the heart as a more or less mechanical regulator of pulse and blood flow.[5] Yet his general approach to the unity of body and soul is remarkable in its foreshadowing of modern embodied and enactive theories, and of psychosomatic medicine and psychotherapy.[6] It was also highly influential at the time: Stahl's association with radical Protestantism ensured that his ideas reached beyond scientific circles – though, of course, disciplinary boundaries of this kind were in any case less clearly delineated in the eighteenth century than they are today. In his time at Halle, therefore, Brockes would have been steeped in an environment which encouraged more holistic approaches to the relation of the material and the immaterial.

Brockes himself was never fully invested in a particular school of thought, but the poetry of his maturity, above all *Irdisches Vergnügen*, is most commonly associated with physico-theology, an approach to religious apologetics underpinned by the rigorous observation of natural phenomena. This movement was actively represented in Hamburg, the place of Brockes's birth, to which he returned in 1704 after his studies at Halle and a brief spell travelling. Physico-theology derived in part from a perceived need to ensure that theology retained its validity in the face of the

---

[2] See e.g. Fry 1990: 167–72.

[3] 'Aus hermetischer Sicht ist das Weltsystem ein beseelter Organismus, ein organischer «Leib», der «in sich selbst bewegt» ist, der also wirklich – nicht bloß im metaphorischen Sinn – *lebt*.' See Liedtke 1996: 62. Despite the general tendency to associate the influence of Hermes Trismegistus and the *Corpus Hermeticum* with esoteric traditions, above all alchemy, hermeticism was, until the nineteenth century, a widely recognised current of natural philosophy.

[4] '[E]ine Hochburg des Anticartesianismus': Hans-Georg Kemper's phrase in his notes to *Irdisches Vergnügen in Gott. Naturlyrik und Lehrdichtung* (Stuttgart: Reclam, 1999), p. 149.

[5] See Geyer-Kordesch 1990: 76.

[6] On Stahl's role in the prehistory of psychotherapy, see e.g. Dewhurst and Reeves 1978: 96.

rapidly developing natural sciences – and, equally, to give scientists themselves a means of reconciling their faith with the rest of their intellectual activity. Brockes was not himself an experimental scientist, but he was widely read: as Harold P. Fry (1990: 280) has argued, '[p]hysics, or natural history, provided Brockes with a wealth of material . . . [and] shaped his diction and descriptive techniques'. The development of physico-theology signified both 'the breakdown of traditional disciplinary boundaries' and 'the disintegration of the traditional vocational demarcations of the middle ages' (Harrison 2005: 179). The first recorded use of the term in English is attributed to the philosopher-physician Walter Charleton, in *The Darkness of Atheism Dispelled by the Light of Nature. A Physico-Theologicall Treatise* (1652); but it was Robert Boyle who, towards the end of the seventeenth century, developed its ramifications more fully, arguing that the Christian philosopher had a *duty* to progress beyond physics to the realms of the sublime and the spiritual (Harrison 2005: 178). Adherents of the 'mixed science' of physico-theology sought to demonstrate the existence of God on the basis of the miracle that is the everyday physical world. This impulse underlies each and every one of the poems in *Irdisches Vergnügen in Gott*, as the title makes plain. For Brockes, God reveals himself in that which is earthly, and minute observation of the latter renders us open to communion with Him.

Brockes's religious belief was the unifying factor in his varied intellectual explorations. Physico-theology was, of course, intrinsically concerned with the dialogue between science and faith, but even some of the apparently secular influences on him were bound up in religious debate – and politics. As Johanna Geyer-Kordesch (1990) has shown, Stahl's medical theories aligned conveniently with the ideological aims of radical Protestantism, in particular early Pietism. Stahl's opposition to mechanistic and dualistic approaches, together with his insistence on the unity of body and soul, and on the deep connections between reason and emotion, resonated strongly with the beliefs and practices of Enthusiast Protestants; the unorthodox nature of his positions also appealed to religious groups campaigning to preserve their confessional and political freedom. Brockes's writing does not, arguably, have the same polemical, anti-Cartesian thrust as that of Stahl, nor was he necessarily a 'radical' Protestant, even though he was concerned to move beyond religious orthodoxy. Nonetheless, his dissatisfaction with dualistic models of being and cognition lends his work an aspect of subtle challenge to the intellectual 'mainstream', and this he shares with many proponents of modern cognitive approaches. George Lakoff (2003: 49), one of the leading theorists of embodied mind, pits the philosophical and scientific revolutions of the end of the twentieth and the beginning of the twenty-first centuries against more than two thousand years of 'philosophical baggage', which, for the most part, characterised the mind as disembodied. While Lakoff exaggerates here, dualistic philosophy has indeed been a formidable opponent. Thus, although there is a gap between Brockes's religious thought-world on the one hand and, on the other, the thoroughly secularised context from which modern embodied and enactive approaches have arisen, the gulf is perhaps not quite as great as it appears at first sight.

In fact, once we start to look properly, the preoccupations shared between cognitive theorists in our own time and those late-seventeenth- and early-eighteenth-century Protestant thinkers who influenced Brockes are surprising in number. Just as Georg Ernst Stahl sought to challenge exclusively mechanistic conceptions of how human beings work, so (for example) Andy Clark's (2008: xxvii–xxviii) theory of extended mind derives partly from a concern to counter the idea that cognition is 'brainbound' – that is, situated solely within the brain and nervous system – and, moreover, to counter the conception of the brain as a computer, commonplace in the discourse of artificial intelligence. Moreover, the centrality of affect to religious experience, promoted by Brockes and eighteenth-century Pietists, has a modern-day secular echo in (again, to take one example) Giovanna Colombetti's (2014: xiii) use of enactivism to demonstrate that affectivity is 'an essential dimension of the mind'. Clearly, there are limits to the comparison: the theories deployed and developed by Colombetti operate at a level of scientific specificity – particularly in terms of the differentiation between affectivity on the one hand, and emotions and moods on the other – which is not present in the work of Brockes and his contemporaries. Yet the notion of 'the *deep continuity* of life and mind' (Colombetti 2014: xvi) which underpins the enactive approach also resonates with the work of many thinkers of the Enlightenment period. If some flexibility is brought to those terms – if 'mind', for example, can also be expanded to include earlier notions of the 'spirit' and 'soul' – then the relevance of the notion of deep continuity to Brockes comes into full relief. His poem 'Ein klares Tröpfgen'[7] ('A Clear Droplet'), for example, includes the line: 'Die schöne Kleinheit drang durchs Auge selbst in den Sitz der Seelen ein' ('This small thing of beauty penetrated through the eye to the seat of the soul'). Here, an impression is formed somatically, through the eye, and proceeds directly to the level of spirit. An aesthetic judgement (die schöne Kleinheit) is also emotional, and the passage from the physical to the abstract (eye to soul) is unproblematic. Indeed, a high degree of permeability between self and world is implied here. The droplet, the window of the eye, and the soul are juxtaposed within a single line, and that sense of proximity is enhanced by the verb 'drang' ('penetrated'), which in the German has a particularly energetic, urgent quality.

The parallel between Stahl and his contemporaries, on the one hand, and Clark and his peers on the other is perhaps not surprising. There were many thinkers in the eighteenth century who questioned the notion of the human being as entirely mechanistic. Of greater interest, arguably, is the fact that these resonances extend to a work like Brockes's *Irdisches Vergnügen*: a collection of didactic poems which seek to inculcate an understanding and appreciation of God's grandeur. The

---

[7] Barthold Heinrich Brockes, 2012–16 edition, vol. 4: 229. I use this edition because it is the most recent and in terms of typeset the most accessible, but it is not yet complete, with the final three parts of *Irdisches Vergnügen* still to come. For that reason, when I come to treat 'Untersuchungen eines vom Körper getrennten Geistes', which is from Part Eight of *Irdisches Vergnügen*, I shall use the abridged Reclam edition of 1999, which is also an excellent resource.

possibility of including Brockes in this survey of the history of distributed cognition attests partly to the influence of Stahl, Thomasius et al., which evidently went far beyond scientific discourse. Yet the relevance of Brockes's poetry to this volume also derives from the fact that, for him, feeling is an aspect of thought: emotion and sensation are essential to the process of understanding. The didactic aim of *Irdisches Vergnügen* is achieved partly through description and argument, and partly through moving the reader, by lifting his or her spirits and communicating a sense of awe. This combination of offices derives from the influence of rhetoric, still the 'chief ally' (Fry 1990: 8) of poetics in Brockes's day: Cicero, of course, had argued that persuasion was to be achieved by instructing (*docere*), delighting (*delectare*), and by engaging the emotions of the audience (*movere*). Feeling is as central, arguably, to the enterprise as rationality. This is not confined to the desired effect on the reader; it is also a central thematic concern in *Irdisches Vergnügen*. The word 'fühlen' (to feel), used in both a physical and an emotional sense, recurs throughout, as do cognate words such as 'spüren' (to sense) or 'rühren' (to stir). This general attitude, in combination with his acute attentiveness to nature and the environment, accounts for the numerous alignments which can be discerned between his work and modern theories of distributed cognition. The key terms in the excerpt from Andy Clark quoted at the start of this chapter – profound embodiment, situated action, flexibility and plasticity – provide a contemporary vocabulary for many of the figures of thought in *Irdisches Vergnügen*.

There are two areas of the comparison between Brockes's work and the notion of distributed cognition which merit particular attention: first, the inherent flux between mind, body and world; and second, the opportunities that humankind creates to further that exchange, the productive use of which, through 'intentional action', it can make of its environment.

Flux and Permeability

'Der gestirnte Himmel'[8] ('The Starry Sky/Heaven') encapsulates many of the themes that concern us here, and it will serve as a useful introduction to Brockes's work. The poem is set at night, after a heavy rain shower has refreshed the parched earth. In a long first strophe, the speaker contemplates the stars flashing in the firmament, and muses on the vastness of their height and number. In its second and final strophe, the poem rises into sonnet form as the speaker dwells rhapsodically on the magnificence of God which has been revealed to him in this scene. The poem is striking for its depiction of 'profound embodiment' (one of the key terms in the opening quotation from Andy Clark). In accordance, perhaps, with the hermetic notion of the world-system as a body, the description of the natural environment is replete with bodily metaphors: before the shower, the air is 'pregnant with heaven's seed' ('vom Himmels-Samen schwanger'), whilst the meadows are 'thirsty' ('den durst'gen Anger') and the bushes 'panting' ('das lechzende Gesträuch'), which

---

[8] Brockes 2012–16: 160–1 (vol. 2.1, Part One/Erster Teil).

conveys a desperate desire for hydration. Although it is a profoundly spiritual experience which the speaker describes, he does not shy away from using explicit physical images as he conjures up the setting. His own physicality is echoed in that of his surroundings; his spirit is, as it were, profoundly embodied. Nor is this necessarily a state to be abandoned in the pursuit of transcendence. In the sonnet section, the speaker desires for God to become visible, tangible, fully present to all the senses. This would require, on the part of the human subject, not just the passive reception of revelation, and certainly not a relegation of the body, but a maximal opening out of all one's faculties, spiritual and physical. Take the lines:

> die Seele wird gerühret;
> Es lässt, als wenn mein Hertz des Schöpfers Gegenwart
> In unaussprechlicher Pracht, Gröss' und Klarheit spüret.

> my soul is stirred;
> It seems as if my heart can sense the presence of the creator
> In indescribable radiance, grandeur and clarity.

The impression that the entire spectrum of feeling is co-opted in this spiritual experience is reinforced by the rhyming of 'gerühret' ('stirred, moved') and 'spüret' ('senses, perceives').[9] The heart, the soul itself, is sensate. Indeed, it has taken over the function of feeling from a body momentarily stunned by the magnificence of the divine: just before the lines quoted above, the speaker puns subtly with the word 'starrt', describing both the action of his eye ('starren' means 'to stare') and its temporary, awestruck impotence ('starr' means 'rigid' or 'numb'). The poem ends, finally, on a (somewhat surreal) image of an ideal cooperation between body and soul in the perception and admiration of God: 'Ach mögte Leib und Geist, zu GOttes [*sic*] Ehr, zu Augen, / Und dann, zu Seinem Ruhm, zu lauter Zungen werden!' ('Ah, would that body and spirit could become eyes to honour God / And then simply tongues to praise Him!') Thus body, sensing, thinking (and, we might add, believing) are – or should be – as 'flexibly interwoven' as they are for Clark.

The notion of radical separation between the spiritual and the corporeal is problematised at every turn in another piece, namely 'Untersuchungen eines vom

---

[9] This notion is given more detailed, explicit treatment in the long poem 'Zur Neuen-Jahrs-Betrachtung des 1735sten Jahres'. In a section calqued on the opening passage of the second book of John Locke's *An Essay Concerning Human Understanding*, Brockes includes the lines: 'Erstlich kann man in der Seelen durch Erfahrung gleichsam fühlen, / Daß von äusserlichen Dingen, welche Cörperlich sind, Zeichen, / (So mit Lettern einer Schrift nicht unfüglich zu vergleichen) / Und aus diesen, wenn dieselben wohl gefüget sind, Ideen, / Die von aussen an sie kommen, sinnlich in der Seel entstehen.' 'Firstly, one can feel through experience that, from those external things which are physical, signs arise (which can justly be compared to the letters of a written text) in the soul; and from these signs, if they are well formed, ideas from without develop sensibly and palpably within the soul.' (My own translation; due to complex syntax this does not follow the original line breaks.)

Körper getrenneten [*sic*] Geistes'[10] ('Deliberations of a Spirit Separated from the Body'). Of all the poems in *Irdisches Vergnügen in Gott*, it is arguably this one which has the most obvious bearing on the theme of distributed cognition. The disembodied spirit reflects on what its connection with the world can be, what action it might still be capable of taking, after its existence in matter has ceased. The spirit-voice considers the possibility that the end of normal sensory activity ('das Sinnliche') through death means the sundering of all connections between spirit and world: 'So scheint die Welt und Geist getrennet'. Immediately, however, it registers its dissatisfaction with this explanation, and proposes an important nuance: the notion that the body's sensory faculties ('das sinnliche Vermögen') themselves contain a spiritual element ('Was Geistigs'), which itself is not eradicated by the simple fact of physical death. This part of the poem is a little convoluted, but the point is that 'Kraft' (which I understand as that energetic connection with the world which characterises sensate bodies) is always already mingled with spirit, and that this energy can outlast the apparent disappearance of the physical body. The fact of death, the poem seems to be saying, need not lead us to assume that the world of matter and the world of spirit are separate kingdoms. Further on, the spirit-voice proposes that the cruder physique of our ordinary earthly existence may be succeeded by a bodily vessel more 'subtle and fine' ('subtil und fein'): one which eludes ordinary powers of perception ('nicht sicht- nicht fühlbar'), but which is nonetheless capable of carrying and perpetuating that aforementioned 'Kraft'. By this understanding, death does involve an element of separation from physical parts ('trennt und scheidet'), but only in the context of a process of metamorphosis. In an image reminiscent of Clark's description of 'negotiable boundaries' or of 'flexible and repeated weaving', a comparison is drawn with the moulting of the silkworm from larva ('die groben Hülsen') to pupa ('einer schönern Haut'). The spirit-voice then concedes that there can be no proof for this theory, but the attraction of an alternative, immortal shape for the soul persists. At the end of the piece, the notion of the astral body – described as a 'marriage' of the soul with a 'delicate substance' ('zarter Stoff'), a 'thin being' ('dünnes Wesen')[11] in which souls cloak themselves – is posited as the most satisfactory resolution.

It is the preoccupation with the place of the individual in the world which makes this poem a particularly interesting forerunner of theories of distributed cognition. The commitment to presence and materiality that it demonstrates is not just a commitment to form, though it is that too: towards the end of the poem, for example, the spirit-voice emphasises the need for contours of some kind in order for individual souls not to lose their identity and 'run into one another like water'. However, the desire for corporeal existence not to end with death derives primarily

---

[10] Brockes 1999: 178–82 (Reclam edition – see note 7).

[11] Brockes's choice of 'Wesen' is highly suggestive, and difficult to translate. It can mean a creature (a 'being' in that sense), or it can indicate the nature, essence, the core of a thing. It is at once open-ended and peculiarly specific as an indicator of concepts of being; in this context, it is an apposite choice to reflect the ontological debates in which the spirit-voice has been engaged.

from a concern for – to use Clark's words again – situated, intentional action in the world. In the opening lines, the disembodied spirit expresses anxiety that it can no longer have any impact on the world:

Die ganze Welt bleibt vor sich still
Und fühlet nichts von meinem Denken:
Nichts kann sich ändern, regen, lenken.

The whole world remains silent, closed
And feels none of my thinking:
Nothing can change, stir, shift its course.

The sense of isolation and impotence is agonising for the disembodied spirit, as conveyed by the doubling of 'nichts', nothing, in these lines. The formulation in the second line in particular is intriguing. The suggestion is that thinking and feeling or sensation are intimately linked; cognition, once again, is portrayed as physical as well as 'intellectual'. Moreover, the world itself is depicted as sentient ('fühlet'), and it is implied that thinking is only effective if it is received by a sensing being or collection of beings. If they are to count, to matter, processes of cognition must be fully embedded in the world. They must also be enactive: movement is a key part of the connection which the spirit so craves, as the verbs 'ändern, regen, lenken' make plain. What the spirit misses is inclusion in that life-giving flux which makes the world, and for which the body is the vehicle, or 'tool' ('Werkzeug'), as it is called later in the poem. The poem is not necessarily advocating total permeability between 'mind' and world, self and other, as is clear from the resistance to the notion of souls merging into one another; but the thought that the reciprocal flow of energy might cease is a desolate one and, the poet decides, is not to be borne.

Innovation and Epistemic Engineering

The word 'tool' brings us conveniently to the second aspect of the distributed cognition hypothesis which is relevant for this enquiry: namely, the ways in which humankind shapes its environment – and, in a doubling-back of the process, shapes its own potential. There is no need to debate the absolute centrality of God to Brockes's system; to an extent, all recognition of human potential in his work is tantamount to the praise of God. Yet human achievements are also explored for their own sake: Florian Welle, for example, suggests an important nuance to standard interpretations of Brockes's approach, namely the decoupling (up to a point) of religious apologetics from human self-discovery.[12] The two aspects are intimately linked, but each can also be examined on its own terms. Intellectual innovation is

[12] Welle (2009: 71, esp. fn. 120) observes that, whilst God is the enduring and unquestioned heart of Brockes's physico-theological programme, the poems themselves focus their attention on the human subject and on the *relationship* to God, rather than on God Himself.

central to his whole enterprise, and his consistent aim is to facilitate more precise modes of seeing and understanding. In 'Kirsch-Blühte bey der Nacht'[13] ('Cherry Blossom by Night'), which is arguably Brockes's best-known poem, the speaker continually revises his perception of light and colour as he contemplates the cherry tree. As he becomes more immersed in the scene, his awareness gradually opens to a light more purely radiant than even the whiteness of the blossoms which he had been admiring first:

> Es fiel mir ins Gesicht
> Von einem hellen Stern ein weisses Licht,
> Das mir recht in die Seele strahlte.

> Upon my face there fell
> From a bright star a white light,
> Which shone through to my very soul.

To a certain extent, this is an act of grace: the 'bright star' is laden with biblical connotations, clearly, and the word 'fell' suggests that the event is partly out of the hands of the observer. The poem draws to a close with a reflection on the modesty of earthly riches by comparison with those of the heavens, which must always remain largely beyond the reach of human understanding. Yet there is still a clear and powerful role for human agency here. The poem opens with the line 'Ich sahe mit betrachtendem Gemüthe'. This translates roughly as 'I saw (or watched) with my mind in active contemplation' – although, once again, cognition is more than 'simply' intellectual, for 'Gemüt' also connotes (in addition to mind) spirit, mood and disposition. Insight, then, derives from a combination of divine grace and human self-teaching; the purpose of *Irdisches Vergnügen* is to promote the latter, whilst remaining all the while in awe of the former.

This duality is developed more fully in 'Die himmlische Schrift'[14] ('The Heavenly Script'). Awe is the constant melody, but the harmony oscillates between, on the one hand, perplexity, which sinks occasionally into despair at the inadequacy of the human mind, and, on the other, a determination to improve. In its early stages, the poem expresses an almost giddy delight at the immensity of God's universe, and appears to renounce any ambition to understand it:

> O Wunder, das kein Mensch begreifen
> Und keine Klugheit fassen kann!

> O wonder, which no person can understand,
> No intelligence grasp!

---

[13] Brockes 2012–16: 469 (vol. 2.2, Part Two/Zweiter Teil).
[14] Brockes 2012–16: 603 (vol. 2.2, Part Two/Zweiter Teil).

This then modulates into a sense of terror at the insignificance not only of his own being, but of the combined efforts of the most penetrating intellects: despite the work of mathematicians and philosophers – listed in a group which includes Huygens, La Hire and Newton – to describe 'unserer Sonnen Grösse' ('the greatness of our suns'), there remains something terrifying ('entsetzlich') about that greatness. Yet the poem is thoroughly informed by recent scientific discoveries: one of the greatest thrills for the poet, mingled though it is with 'Seelen-Schwindel' ('dizziness in the soul'), comes from contemplating the speed of Venus. Galileo's observation that Venus showed phases and must therefore be in orbit of the sun had, of course, been a key step in disproving Ptolemy's geocentric model; Brockes's use of the example here attests to an unsqueamish and productive attitude to scientific progress. This sustains the poem even through the existential terror that it explores, and the closing few stanzas are given over to the wish for greater powers of understanding. The poet appeals to God:

Laß unsere Seelen doch dein unbegreiflichs Wesen
Im Buch der Creatur erstaunt mit Ehrfurcht lesen!

But still, let our souls read your incomprehensible being
In the book of creation, with wonder and reverence!

The self-limitation of the earlier phases of the piece persists in the words 'unbegreiflich', 'erstaunt', 'mit Ehrfurcht', yet the emphatic 'doch' ('but still', 'and yet') communicates a certain defiance – not of God Himself, but of the paralysing fear of human weakness – and the postponement of 'lesen' ('read') until the moment of rhyme creates a powerful sense of purpose. This is continued to the end of the poem in the imagery of learning to decipher the script of an unfamiliar language, and in the ultimate confidence that that very human effort can yield a greater appreciation of divinity.

The ability of humankind to influence or 'engineer' its own knowledge-making is, then, an important theme in the collection. Tools and instruments can themselves be manifestations of new forms of thought, and they serve in turn to further human understanding, and to drive on intellectual innovation. An awareness of this cumulative aspect of what Clark (2008: 66), following Sterelny, has called 'epistemic engineering' can be detected in *Irdisches Vergnügen*. Brockes takes a particular interest in the optical instruments, the telescope and the microscope, invented in the Netherlands in the previous century. Here, too, in his view, human ingenuity has required the prompting of the divine: in 'Die Wunder-reiche Erfindung'[15] ('The Wondrous Invention'), for example, the poet comments that God has 'allowed the spyglass and the magnifying glass to be invented' ('[Hat] [e]in Fern- und Grösserungs-Glas erfinden lassen'). That formulation 'erfinden lassen' implies a similar combination of grace and agency to that which we saw previously:

[15] Brockes 2012–16: 585–9 (vol. 3, Part Four/Vierter Teil).

he has allowed it and humanity has invented it. Yet Brockes also demonstrates a keen awareness of the transformative effect of instruments such as these on human perception and thought. Critics have remarked on the open-mindedness, the lack of suspicion which he displays (in contrast to various seventeenth-century predecessors in Germany) in his treatment of the telescope and the microscope.[16] The change in perspective which they afford is welcomed as an opportunity, rather than a threat; the 'problem space' (to use Clark's terms) which is transformed is the relatively limited visual field of the naked human eye, and the 'target domain' is the miraculous world of God's creation. In 'Gedanken über ein Perspektiv'[17] ('Thoughts on a Spyglass'), the poet describes the accumulated benefits of the use of this instrument:

> Je mehr ich durch diesen Grund des Perspektivs betrachte;
> Je mehr kann ich, was mir und andern nützt,
> Aus der verkleinten Grösse lernen
>
> The more I observe in the mode of this spyglass;
> The more I can learn, of use both to me and to others
> From the vastness made miniature.

Insight breeds insight, and human self-teaching also assumes a social aspect ('mir und andern', 'me and others'). 'Vastness made miniature' might seem counterintuitive as a description of the view through the telescope: what tends to capture the imagination is the *magnified* detail in which, with the aid of the glass, we are able to see distant, or even hidden, objects. Yet that formulation reflects the mindset which governs these poems: a desire for human understanding to become commensurate with the magnificence of God's world, and vice versa. The telescope *does* make the universe smaller, in the sense that it brings it nearer; at the same time, it brings about an expansion of the mind, conveyed in this poem in the repetition of 'je mehr' ('the more . . .').

Karl Richter writes of the affinity between the possibilities offered by instruments and by descriptive poetry;[18] indeed, the poems of *Irdisches Vergnügen* are them-

---

[16] See e.g. Richter 2002: 3–4.

[17] Brockes 2012–16: 560–1 (vol. 3, Part Four/Vierter Teil). Given in this edition as 'Gedanken über eine Perspectivische Aussicht', but 'Gedanken über ein Perspektiv' is the more commonly used title.

[18] 'Die optischen Instrumente erweitern den Bereich des «Wirklichen» über das mit Augen Anschaubare hinaus; sie machten ein neues Sehen, Beobachten und Beschreiben möglich und vermittelten neue Vorstellungen von der Größe der Schöpfung und des Schöpfers; sie forderten die staunende Haltung des Menschen vor der Schöpfung heraus. Das alles aber waren Einstellungen, die auch sonst für die Poesie des *Irdischen Vergnügens* konstitutiv sind. Anders gesagt: Die Thematik der Instrumente und die Poetik des Werks konnten sich wechselseitig begünstigen und verstärken' (Richter 2002: 5). The gist of Richter's argument here is the sense of wonder at the sights revealed by optical instruments which was precisely the attitude that Brockes wanted to promote with his poetry. The scientific theme and the poetic conception were thus intimately linked.

selves designed to promote precisely that attentiveness which looking through the
telescope or microscope can also engender. They have a crucial part to play in the
process of (self-) teaching, and therefore they, too, can be seen as 'instruments'. In
his recent exploration of cognitive modes of literary criticism, Terence Cave (2016:
52) argues that '[l]anguage itself is for humans the key empowering affordance,
allowing the development of secondary language-based affordances, artefacts or
instruments made out of language, such as metaphors, literary genres, poetic and
narrative forms, and individual literary works'. The notion of the affordance was
coined by James J. Gibson (1986 edition: 127) to describe what the environment
offers animals and humans, 'what it provides or furnishes, either for good or ill'.
Crucially for our purposes, Gibson posits that:

> An affordance cuts across the dichotomy of subjective-objective and helps us to
> understand its inadequacy. It is equally a fact of the environment and a fact of
> behaviour. It is both physical and psychical, yet neither. An affordance points
> both ways, to the environment and to the observer. (129)

The affordance thus defined is a magnificent demonstration of the principle of distributed cognition, of the flux between mind, body and world, and Brockes's whole
approach to the poetic undertaking indicates his instinctive grasp of this principle in relation to language. Take the poem 'Anmuthige Frühlings-Vorwürfe'[19]
('Graceful Spring-Sketches'), for example, which opens thus:

> Ich höre die Vögel; ich sehe die Wälder;
> Ich fühle das Spielen der kühlenden Luft;
> Ich rieche der Blühte bebiesamten Duft;
> Ich schmecke die Früchte. . . .

> I hear the birds; I see the woods;
> I feel the play of the cooling air;
> I smell the perfumed scent of the blossom;
> I taste the fruit. . . .

In these lines and throughout the piece, the enumeration of sensory impressions
from the spring scene prompts the reader to look around, mentally if nothing
else, and the heaping of details, one upon the other, combines with the lilting
metre to evoke the lush, energetic feel of the season. The rhythms do not run on
mindlessly: enforced pauses mid-line (as we see introduced in line four above) and
variations in sentence length require the reader to stop and reflect. Nonetheless,
the cumulative effect of the rhythms over the course of the poem is powerfully
evocative. Sensorimotor experience is both recorded and reinvoked here through
the affordance, or affordances, of language. Not all the pieces in *Irdisches Vergnügen*

---

[19] Brockes 2012–16: 494 (vol. 2.2, Part Two/Zweiter Teil).

deploy mimetic linguistic effects as this one does, but common to all of them is the endeavour to bring the reader closer to his or her environment – and, by extension, to God – by enhancing their powers of observation. Brockes's poetry 'points both ways', and that is essential to their didactic purpose. Each piece has been called into being by a combination of intellectual and emotional engagement on the part of the poet, and it becomes, in turn, an instrument by which to educate and move the reader. Each one is a product of the deep continuity between life and world, which for Brockes are both encompassed by the divine.

Our examination of alignments between Brockes's poetry and theories of distributed cognition has brought a number of insights. First, it has reintroduced a religious dimension into a secular area of modern intellectual investigation. *Irdisches Vergnügen in Gott* is an energetic demonstration of how worldviews associated with religion and science, often pitted against one another, might be brought together. The piece had already served this purpose in its own time, rooted as it was in the field of physico-theology; in the context of our present-day cognitive enquiries, Brockes's admiration of the workings of the divine on earth adds a further touch of passion to our own appreciation of the world in which we collaborate, whether or not we ourselves believe in God. That passion is reinforced by the pleasure in words which is the business of verse, and which brings us to the second gain of this brief study. Poetry is language working at full pressure, and the best pieces in *Irdisches Vergnügen* offer delicate, prism-like structures through which to view modern scientific theories. The direct line which can be traced between anti-mechanistic thought in the eighteenth century and current cognitive approaches prevent this activity from being anachronistic. Reading his work in the context of distributed cognition also benefits the reception of Brockes himself. He has sometimes been underestimated, not least because the scale of *Irdisches Vergnügen in Gott* is as likely to induce a sense of exhaustion as it is a sense of wonder in the reader. Yet the numerous parallels which it has been possible to uncover here attest to the enduring relevance of his work. One of the central aims of this volume is 'to reinvigorate our understanding of Western European culture'; the lens of distributed cognition has certainly opened up new perspectives on Brockes.

Brockes was and remains a pivotal figure in the development of German poetry. What Cave calls the 'empowering' aspect of the 'secondary language-based affordance' – in this case, poetry – works on a variety of levels. On a local, individual scale, a piece of writing can shape the thinking of the individual reader and, perhaps, send him or her out into the world with a modified mode of being and acting. Moreover, each new literary work may also contain within it the seeds of future innovations, if it is of sufficient quality and is planted into a fertile mind. Building on his legacy, later poets such as Klopstock and Goethe produced still more radical work, supreme examples of cognition in action, which would transform the German language itself.

4

Wordsworth, Keats and Cognitive Spaces of Empathy in *Endymion*

Renee Harris

Historians of science and literary critics alike trace the overlap in mental science and literature of the Romantic period. Scientists like J. G. von Herder and Erasmus Darwin theorised about the mind as it was depicted in poems, and poets read, critiqued and revised theories on associationism, memory, dualism and materialism. Indeed, Coleridge and Wordsworth read and revised the work of mental scientists like Hartley, Darwin and Franz Gall, while John Keats was himself a trained physician with a working knowledge of the latest theories on bodily sensation and brain function. Alan Richardson writes of the blended disciplinary interests of the period:

> It was a time when poets (like Coleridge) consorted with laboratory scientists and when philosophical doctors (like Darwin) gave point to their scientific theories in verse, when phrenology and mesmerism gained adherents across the medical community, when Bell could work out his physiological psychology in a series of lectures to London artists, scientists could perform as showmen, and Galvani's experiments with 'animal electricity' could be replicated by an eager public 'wherever frogs were to be found'. (Richardson 2001: 7)

Late-eighteenth- and early-nineteenth-century mental science favoured an anti-dualistic psychological model, which anticipates what we now call embodied cognition. The understanding of the mechanics of cognitive processing as distributed through the body and even beyond the body coincided with a trend in moral philosophy that saw potential revolutionary power in the passions. Travelling from external stimuli through the senses and to the brain, passions appeared contagious. However, philosophers, scientists and poets, too, found evidence that affect was not unidirectional: feelings seem not only to circulate but to exist transsubjectively, across and between bodies, objects and experiences.

While the notion of the human body's porousness to the outside world can be traced to Renaissance medical thinking,[1] advances in seventeenth- and

---

[1] Take for example Francastoro's *De sympathia* (1555), which established the modern notion of contagion, the passing of animal spirits between bodies (Ackerknecht 1974: 2).

eighteenth-century medical science provided an anatomical basis for the belief that our skin is not a barrier against but a channel to the feelings of others. Experiments and dissections led to a more intricate knowledge of the nervous system and its function in sensation. The system was believed responsible for processing external stimuli as sensations. Though calling it by a different name, Thomas Willis was the first to locate the sympathetic nerve (or *intercostalis*), descending from the brain via the spinal column. The cerebrospinal connection here led to the conclusion that the sympathetic nerve is receptive to external stimuli via the larger network of nerves throughout the body (Robinson 1907: 14). Moreover, his *De cerebri anatome* distinguishes voluntary motion from involuntary motion, locating involuntary motion in the intercostal nerve (Ackerknecht 1974: 2). Because of its role in involuntary motion, Willis held that the intercostal nerve system coordinates the reactions of various organs in the body, as they respond autonomically to stimuli. Revising Willis's terminology, Jacques Benigne Winslow (1732) renamed the *intercostalis* 'the sympathetic nervous system' (Ackerknecht 1974: 3). As Erwin Ackerknecht explains, 'through Winslow, the notion of sympathy remained forever associated with the nervous system' (1974: 3). This newly untangled anatomy gave physiological credence to beliefs that the function of an individual body takes cues from objects and bodies external to itself and that a body's reactions to said stimuli happen beyond the immediate control of the subject.

The adoption of 'sympathy' as the preferred term for the intercostal nervous system coincided with the rise in discussion of 'sympathy' in eighteenth-century moral philosophy. Given the physiological mechanics of sympathy accepted by aesthetics, the overlap in disciplinary use of the term exceeds metaphor to speak to the way Enlightenment and Romantic-era culture understood the relation of the body to its environment. Medical thought about the body's openness to external influence inspired contrasting sentiments, from those who celebrate the possibility for radical interconnectedness and those who fear the threat of a penetrable self. Analysing the cultural effects, Karin Littau (2006) traces a shift that occurred in reading practices and, consequently, in literary criticism between the early nineteenth century and now. She explains how historically reading was a bodily experience, and, as late as 1799, it was thought of as a cardiovascular exercise that sets the blood in motion.[2] Citing Immanuel Kant's disinterested reader as a key influence for this shift, she writes: 'The dispassionate, disinterested pleasure we now take in art is far removed from those passionate encounters which for centuries justified aesthetic theory and practices' (Littau 2006: 2). As I will argue below, Romantic writers conceived of reading as an embodied social practice, understanding literary affect as a physiological connection between writer and reader. These writers turned the phenomenon of 'feeling' into one of 'feeling with'. Nevertheless, anxiety surrounding embodied aesthetic experiences and the distributed cognition they engage in through physiological sympathy led to debate among Romantic poets. In moments of intense aesthetic experience, were readers' bodies,

---

[2] Littau cites as a source for this claim Bergk [1799] 1966: 69.

emotions and minds at the mercy of the text? In this chapter, I explore how two Romantic-era writers experimented with poetic form to find how best to manage a reader's engagement with the text and thereby shape their sympathetic faculties. Examining acts of reading and dreaming in Keats's *Endymion*, I apply Giovanna Colombetti's work on enacted spaces of empathy to show how Keats's theory of feeling contrasts with Wordsworth's conservative aesthetic model. Ultimately, Keats's theory of feeling goes beyond the Enlightenment models available to him and envisions a more revolutionary model of social cognition.

Wordsworth's Mental Science and Disinterested Reading

Wordsworth's model for engagement with a text takes cues from contemporaneous mental science and moral philosophy, yet he also seeks to delineate the body's role in the formation of poetic meaning from the mind's role in the process. Wordsworth's knowledge of scientific study has received a significant amount of scholarly interest, with many scholars investigating his and Coleridge's use of Hartleyan associationism in the 1790s (Jackson 2008; Richardson 2001; Miall 1993). As the father of associationism, David Hartley's proto-physiological psychology revolutionised mental science, and Coleridge was a devoted follower for many years before ultimately dismissing Hartley as too mechanistic in his *Biographia Literaria* (1817). Hartley explained that a process of vibrations along the brain formed the foundation of associated ideas (Richardson 2001: 9–10). Jackson explains that Wordsworth himself demonstrates a 'partially materialist orientation towards questions of human thought and feeling' and that many of his works 'sought to systematize a model of individual poetic consciousness closely if ambivalently tied to bodily feeling' (Jackson 2008: 8). Hints of Wordsworth's play with Hartleyan associationism and Galvanic animal magnetism[3] can be seen in often-quoted lines from 'Tintern Abbey' (1798: ll. 22, 27–30):

> These beauteous forms . . .
> In hours of weariness, sensations sweet,
> Felt in the blood, and felt along the heart;
> And passing even into my purer mind,
> With tranquil restoration.

The sensations received from external stimuli (the 'beauteous forms' of the River

---

[3] In 1830 John F. W. Herschel wrote of Galvani's theory: the 'principle once established, that there exists in the animal economy a power of determining the development of electric excitement, capable of being transmitted *along the nerves* . . . it became an easy step after that to refer the origin of muscular motion in the living brain to a similar cause; and look to the brain, a wonderfully constituted organ, for which no mode of action possessing the least plausibility had ever been devised, as the source of the required electrical power' (quoted in Richardson 2001: 7, emphasis added). While Wordsworth obviously did not read Herschel, we can see based on the common language evidence for a shared cultural knowledge of the contemporaneous scientific hypotheses.

Wye and the abbey) travel through his blood, along his heart, and into his mind.
The felt movement or vibrations produce memories that recall to the city-bound
Wordsworth pleasanter moments of immersion in nature. As we see from the
insistence on memory, Wordsworth imagines a writer (and reader) removed from
the immediacy of sensual absorption inherent in the aesthetic experience of nature.

Wordsworth's poetry utilises a physiologically informed rendering of affect;
however, the poet responds to the possibility for radical openness of the body by
mediating aesthetic experience for his reader. I argue that rather than engaging
in a distributed cognition where distinctions between his own body, the outside
world and the body of his readers become blurred, Wordsworth offers a model
that seeks to contain and control feeling. For Wordsworth, preventing his reader
from being overwhelmed by direct and immediate sensation serves to protect the
integrity of a reader's independent, thinking self. Richardson (2001: 71) posits that
Wordsworth's poetic sensibility is 'organic' as the poet's sensations are gathered
from external stimuli but are also produced by emotional awareness. Quoting the
1799 *Prelude*, Richardson (2001: 71) writes,

> A genuine poetic sensibility, for Wordsworth, is one that continues to register the
> permeation of thought with feeling and remains in touch with the sensational,
> bodily, and emotive origins of mind, the 'lovely forms / And sweet sensations'
> and the 'passions' that 'build up our human soul' (*Prelude*, 1.134, 461–62).

This dynamic model of the poetic mind acquires a temporal element as Wordsworth
proceeds to define poetry later in the 1802 *Preface*: 'the spontaneous overflow of
powerful feelings: [poetry] takes its origin from emotion recollected in tranquillity'
(Wordsworth 2001: 273). Importantly for Wordsworth, this synthetic process is
first at work for the artist who must distance himself or herself from the immediacy of sensory events in order to 'read' his or her own experience properly. This
auto-read model establishes a self-reflective stance for a poet's engagement with an
art object, and Wordsworth believes the time of reflection is necessary to improve
on the initial sensory experience. Then, the reflective poetry (often lyric in form)
guides the reader's own intellectualisation of the sensual experience of reading the
poem. After this multi-phase act of writing and reading, Wordsworth's ideal poetry
reconciles bodily sensation and intellectual processing through memory and reflective distance. In the first book of the 1805 *Prelude*, Wordsworth explains the process:

> Thus often in those fits of vulgar joy
> Which through all seasons on a child's pursuits
> Are prompt attendants, 'mid that giddy bliss
> Which like a tempest works along the blood
> And is forgotten, even then I felt
> Gleams like the flashing of a shield. The earth
> And common face of Nature spake to me
> Remembrable things; sometimes, 'tis true,

By chance collisions and quaint accidents

. . .

Not profitless, if haply they impressed
Collateral objects and appearances,
Albeit lifeless then, and doomed to sleep
Until mature seasons called them forth
To impregnate and to elevate the mind.

(Wordsworth [1805] 1979: *Prelude* I, 610–25)

The first phase of Wordsworth's scheme is the event itself. Often taking place in nature during his childhood, this 'spontaneous overflow of powerful feeling' is pre-reflective and seemingly a pure-bodily experience of sensation travelling along the veins on its way to the brain. He calls these experiences of affect 'fits of vulgar joy', dismissing them as ephemeral and low. He describes the moments via a seemingly Hartleyan materialism as 'that giddy bliss / Which like a tempest works along the blood' (Wordsworth [1805] 1979: *Prelude* I, 612–13). This overflow of powerful emotion takes over the body, working its way in a rush of sensation through the blood. Yet, as mere sensation, the feeling evoked by these moments is fleeting. However, the event is stored as unconscious memory for later use. In a later time of tranquillity, when the poet's mind takes precedence over the original bodily experience, the moment in nature can be recalled. Once the environment and condition of the mind is right (the poet is not immersed in nature and/or the poet has had long enough to be able to rationally and productively reflect upon the event), the poet employs his fancy in imagining the scene and its associated affect. Therefore poetry, the product of this third phase of recollection and imagination, improves upon the original sensory experience. In the end, the reader's aesthetic experience is thoroughly insulated from the original sensation. Ultimately, Wordsworth's model of reading shows distrust in the distributed cognition of eighteenth-century medical and philosophical discourse on the sympathetic capacities of the body. Much like Kant's disinterested reader in the 1790 *Critique of Judgment*, Wordsworth's ideal reader (and writer) is never without the power of reasoning, never consumed or absorbed in the sensual effects of aesthetic experience with their consequent emotional upheaval.

Emerging Romantic writers of the 1810s believed that Wordsworth's mode of intellectualising his sense experience in lyric poems prohibits sympathetic identification. By 'explaining in too much detail, by patronizing and lecturing his reader' over the significance of the sublime moment, Wordsworth prevents his reader from actually feeling the sublimity (Bennett 1994: 29). According to John Keats and the wider Hunt Circle, Wordsworth does not seek to feel with the reader so much as he wishes to pass down his feelings or knowledge to the reader. In a letter to John Hamilton Reynolds, Keats famously complained that Wordsworth's poetry had 'a palpable design upon us' (Keats 1958: I, 271). Keats believed the insertion of the poet's mental processing of embodied experience disrupts the reader's sensory experience of and pleasure in the poem. The later Romantics understood that a too visible authorial hand seems to generate resistance from the reader, but a more egalitarian and sociable approach to feelings, where author and reader occupy the same position as beholder of a scene or object, allows for ready sympathetic identification between the parties.

Eighteenth- and Nineteenth-Century Medicine and Moral Philosophy

Keats's medical training from 1814 to 1816 gave him confidence in the most recent anatomical findings and these informed his own attempt to trace the mechanics of cognitive distribution through narrative. Contained in his *Anatomical and Physiological Notebook*, Keats's lecture notes from his years at Guy's Hospital are full of scientific thought on the brain and nervous system from the period's foremost surgeons and anatomists such as Astley Cooper, John Abernethy and Henry Cline, under whom the poet studied. Most of his anatomy notes are on the brain and nervous system, and discussions of muscles and bones appear secondary to related points on sensation and movement. In notes from the tenth lecture, Keats uses the term 'grand sympathetic', in reference to the sympathetic nerve. Following Willis's distinction between involuntary and voluntary motion, Keats writes that the sympathetic nervous system has two main functions: sensation and volition. Keats learned that sensation begins at the extremities and tracks to the brain through the network of nerves. His notes describe:

> Volition is the contrary of Sensation it proceeds from the internal to external parts. It does not reside entirely in the Brain but partly in spinal Marrow which is seen in the Behaviour of a Frog after having been guilloteened. (Keats 1934: lecture 10, page 9)

Volition, then, as Keats understood it, is distributed beyond the brain through the spine. More strikingly, he continues:

> Volition is sometimes present while sensation is destroyed. In a Gentleman who had lost sensation and yet had powers of Volition it was observed that he could grasp and hold a substance which his whole attention was directed thereto, but on his turning to a fresh occupation the substance dropped. (Keats 1934: lecture 10, page 9)

Not only did early-nineteenth-century medical science understand volition to be distributed along the sympathetic nervous system, these notes also indicate a belief that volition can replace sensation. In the absence of sensation, concentrated attention can perform motor tasks thought to require input from external stimuli.

From his *Anatomical and Physiological Notebook*, we see the way Keats's medical training informed his development of a cognitive model of reading that anticipated current models of distributed cognition; however, his notebooks also point to an anatomical understanding of sympathy that aligns with the moral philosophy of his period. Exploration of how sympathy was understood and theorised further elucidates the way Keats imagines affect to circulate among and join bodies to create a shared aesthetic experience. In both medical science and moral philosophy, the concept of sympathy traverses the internal and external, the voluntary and involuntary. Sympathy takes what is individual and makes it communal. Though no physician, David Hume traces the cognitive pathways of ideas and impressions (corresponding, I argue, to volition and sensation with their respective internal origins and external origins) and shows how sympathy can replicate the sensations felt by another. Impressions become ideas as they lose the original force with which they entered the mind. The act of smelling a rose conveys the impression of the smell through the cognitive pathways of the body processing it into the abstract idea of sweetness. This process is unidirectional except where sympathy is at play. Sympathy reverses the trajectory, acting as the vehicle by which sensation can be replicated, making ideas into impressions. Sympathy conveys an idea that increases in intensity until it approximates the original impression held by the object of sympathy. We read about the sweet smell of a rose growing along the road, and, by imagining ourselves in the space described, we activate the cognitive pathways that translate the idea of the sweetness into the smell of rose. We experience in our own bodies the sensations we read and witness through sympathy (Hume [1748] 2001: paras 3–9).

Continuing to study sympathy's mechanics two decades after Hume, Adam Smith theorised 'fellow-feeling' as an act upon the body through the senses and involving the imagination. He writes in *Theory of Moral Sentiments*:

> This is the source of our fellow-feeling for the misery of others, that it is by changing places in fancy with the sufferer, that we come either to conceive or to be affected by what he feels, may be demonstrated by many obvious observations, if it should not be thought sufficiently evident of itself. When we see a stroke aimed and just ready to fall upon the leg or arm of another person, we naturally shrink and draw back our own leg or our own arm; and when it does fall, we feel it in some measure, and are hurt by it as well as the sufferer. The mob, when they are gazing at a dancer on the slack rope, naturally writhe and twist and balance their own bodies, as they see him do, and as they feel that they themselves must do if in his situation. (Smith [1759] 1976: I, i, 3)

Here the senses take cues from what they perceive and imagine, joining what is external to what is internal. The spectator sees an action or sees the promise of an action (the stroke ready to fall), and his or her body registers the sensation. According to Smith, the fancy makes the necessary connection between visual object and sympathetic subject by enabling him or her to enter the 'place' of the sufferer.

We have seen how the advances of eighteenth-century medicine provide an anatomical basis for cultural beliefs regarding the body's relationship to the outside

world, and twenty-first-century medical knowledge further expands our understanding of how we take in and process sensation. In her book *Feeling Beauty*,
Gabrielle Starr explains how magnetic resonance imaging of intense aesthetic
experiences in subjects shows the joint activity of sensual perception and the default
mode network. Since the default mode network is responsible for the cognitive
functions of memory and imagination, its activity during moments of perception,
specifically during intense aesthetic experience, is surprising. An intense aesthetic
experience would seem to overwhelm the internal with the external, but Starr
explains how the brain architecture is at work in these moments:

> In general anatomical terms, neural activation moves from sensory cortex for-
> ward toward the basal ganglia (reward process) and toward the hippocampus and
> amygdalae (memory and emotion – though these functions are not exclusively
> carried out in these structures). Activation in the orbitofrontal cortex follows, but
> there are interactive loops that reach between these frontal areas and the basal
> ganglia so that higher-order, complex processes of cognition, and emotional and
> reward processes, may continually feed one another. (Starr 2013: 24)

As Smith posited in the eighteenth century, the imagination is active in moments
of visual intake. Moreover, modern cognitive science suggests that the imagination and associated emotions supplement the sensory registry to create the image
seen, and that, therefore, in the act of seeing, the imagination is always already at
work. Ultimately, here where the imagination and perception interweave, volition
and sensation (the internal and the external) join together to create a space of
collaboration.

Giovanna Colombetti's *The Feeling Body* presents a phenomenological approach
to empathy that expands on the medical findings, as well as on the eighteenth-
century medical science and moral philosophy discussed thus far. Her work on
direct accessibility of feeling proposes an enacted space of empathy where the
translation of feeling between bodies is virtually uninhibited (Colombetti 2014:
131). She challenges Theory Theory[4] and Simulation Theory,[5] which both see a
stage of mediation between perceiving and feeling the emotions of another. She

[4] Theory of Mind maintains that we attribute mental states to behaviours or other outward cues.
Theory Theory derives from Piaget's developmental psychology and represents the earliest stages
of mind-reading; it is a 'naive' theory of mind that we use when first forming the cognitive architecture and knowledge of how to interact with the world. The term 'Theory Theory' derives from
the notion that this process is represented in the mind and is structured like a scientific inquiry.

[5] Shanton and Goldman (2010: 1) explain the differences between Simulation Theory (ST) and
Theory Theory (TT): 'Rejecting the TT emphasis on theoretical inference, ST (in its original
form) says that people employ imagination, mental pretense, or perspective taking ("putting
oneself in the other person's shoes") to determine others' mental states. A mentalizer simulates
another person by first creating pretend states (e.g. pretend desires and beliefs) in her own mind
that correspond to those of the target. She then inputs these pretend states into a suitable cognitive
mechanism, which operates on the inputs and generates a new output (e.g. a decision). This new
state is taken "off line" and attributed or assigned to the target.'

says while these approaches 'make . . . the minds of others never directly experientially accessible', phenomenological understandings of empathy believe in a direct accessibility between the mental states of the observer and observed; seeing a balled-up fist, for example, I 'live' the tenseness of the fist (Colombetti 2014: 130). Therefore, a work of art such as literature that engages the imagination to replicate smell, sound, taste or movement writes feelings in the brain and on the body of its reader. Starr explains that similar pathways are activated in mental imagery (the creation of an image in the mind) as in the experience of perception (when the object is present). Someone's suffering when read about in a text (or heard about from a witness) must be imagined by the reader; however, this mediation of a real-life sensory experience into an imagined sensory experience does not hamper the translation of feeling. Brain activity during imagined sensory experience correlates most closely to that of active perception when a text evokes multisensory or motor imagery (Starr 2013: 75). Eighteenth-century philosophers believed this to be true as well. Adela Pinch (1996: 45) writes of Hume's theory, 'whether one is responding to a person or to a representation of a person suffering seems, in many cases, ultimately not to make any difference to the emotional experience itself.' This direct translation of phenomenological experience, the similitude between the observed feeling and that which registers on the body of the observer, further disintegrates the self/other boundaries that could inhibit the free circulation of affect and sympathy, thus allowing for the ideal interconnectedness of writer and audience during acts of reading.

Keats's understanding of sympathy as a model for the writer-reader relationship exceeds the Smith model of 'fellow-feeling' and its modern counterparts. Much like Hume, who sees feeling as existing between bodies, Keats imagines feeling to be jointly created rather than transferred. Pinch (1996: 45) explains that, for Hume, 'feelings are transsubjective entities that pass between persons; that our feelings are always really someone else's; that it is passion that allows us to be persons, rather than the other way around'. Sympathy is the vehicle through which feelings circulate between bodies in a distributed cognition of embodied emotion. Passion allows us to be persons because, for Hume ([1738] 2012: II, i), the self only comes into being through association with others' feelings. Therefore the self is fundamentally social by nature. As the next section makes evident, Keats's writing style embraces this bodily, affective and transsubjective model of feeling in *Endymion*. Whereas Wordsworth presents the writer-reader dynamic as that of a teacher to his student, Keats's contract with readers assumes a social and emotional bond between friends. Rather than transferring feeling from writer to reader (a model that does not seem to require the sympathy or the imagination of the reader),[6] Keats's poem

---

[6] Adam Smith ([1759] 1976: IV) runs up against the tension of self-interest and a communal outlook when he addresses Dr Mandeville's claim that private vices can be public benefits. Whereas Mandeville reads self-interest in all acts that serve a public good insofar as they gain the beneficent citizen social esteem, Smith argues such self-interest can be seen as virtuous when the outcomes benefit the larger community. This complicates my reading of Wordsworth's self-reflective poetics. Wordsworth's self-interest lies in his efforts to protect and fortify the integrity of his identity or

seeks to demonstrate and allow the free circulation of feelings between the writer, reader and text. In scenes of reading, Keats's audience witnesses moments of sympathetic engagement, marking how these experiences manifest physiologically in the characters. The interconnectedness of the characters in these moments mirrors the type of enacted empathic environments that Colombetti theorises. The interconnectedness of his characters allows for their joint creation of a new narrative or even a new reality, as we shall see, for example, in the case of Endymion's dreams. Thus the radical openness of the distributed cognition model and the physiological sympathy imagined by eighteenth-century moral philosophers, mental scientists and Romantic poets, like Keats, offers a hope for societal change through the bond of shared feeling and the creative activity it inspires.

Sympathetic Reading in *Endymion*

Keats famously opens his attempt at epic poetry, *Endymion* ([1817] 2009),[7] with the declaration 'A Thing of beauty is a joy for ever' (I, 1). By the end of his inaugural stanza, Keats narrows his scope from 'a thing of beauty' to the art of storytelling in particular. He writes, 'All lovely tales that we have heard or read: / An endless fountain of immortal drink, / Pouring unto us from the heaven's brink' (I, 22–4). Literature itself is immortal, and in hearing and reading it, we taste immortality. Importantly, Keats employs the plural pronoun to create a sense of community between the bodies involved in aesthetic experience. 'We' read and are poured unto. 'We' receive the quiet bower, health and sweet dreams from the immortal fount of literature. Moreover, the source of beauty is all one, a single 'endless fountain' pouring from '*the* heaven' (emphasis mine). Fluidity and movement circulate feelings as they ebb and flow. By the way it engages the mind and the senses, literature taps a deep interconnectedness of being and from this creates community across mortality and immortality, earth and heaven.

Endymion's second stanza imagines a symbiotic relationship between beautiful 'essences' and our souls (I, 25). We are intrinsically intertwined with cosmic entities, essences such as 'the moon, / The passion poesy, glories infinite' (I, 28–9), and the relationship is such that if one party were to pass into nothingness, the other too would perish. This cosmic vision, this pretty piece of paganism, as Wordsworth famously commented on Keats's recitation of 'The Hymn to Pan', declares communion necessary to mortal and immortal existence. Pan is the source of 'universal knowledge' (I, 289), and, as Cox notes, etymologically his name means 'all',[8] so that the pagan festival in Latmos that opens the poem joins all bodies in worship

cogito through his auto-read practices. However, as Adam Smith would argue, Wordsworth also seeks to protect the integrity of his readers' thinking selves by insulating their aesthetic experience. His motivation is not self-seeking, after all, though other Romantic writers, as I show, believe his methods to limit the public benefits literature can perform.
[7] All citations of *Endymion* in this chapter are to this edition.
[8] Editorial note in Keats 2009: 155.

of shared truth. But Keats takes this radical interconnectedness a step further by claiming that beautiful things cannot exist without human community and love:

> What I know not: but who, of men, can tell
> That flowers would bloom, or that green fruit would swell
> To melting pulp, that fish would have bright mail,
> The earth its dower of river, wood, and vale,
> The meadows runnels, runnels pebble-stones,
> The seed its harvest, or the lute its tones,
> Tones ravishment, or ravishment its sweet,
> If human souls did never kiss and greet? (I, 835–42)

Interconnectedness is enacted in the very form of this passage. Keats repeats grammatical objects as subjects in their subsequent clauses, 'the meadows runnels, runnels pebble-stones'. The poem famously uses uncontrolled 'Cockney' couplets that overrun their prescribed bounds. The enjambment in the first three quoted lines demonstrates the unconventional openness of the Cockney couplets, how they expand into the line that follows, pushing into the space of the next thought and fusing together the items in Keats's catalogue of imagery. Indeed, the Cockney couplets themselves effectively mirror the model of distributed minds as they reach outward, beyond the bounds of individual bodies to participate in a transsubjective system of shared feeling. While in this quoted passage we have some control exerted with the primarily end-stopped lines, ultimately the passage is a teeming list of natural beauty. The rhyming pairs and the repetition create an echoing effect that seems to carry beyond the concluding question mark. While Keats's message is clear (we are all interconnected), he makes a bold claim for the lynchpin of this interconnected existence. Human community is the necessary prerequisite for universal harmony. The beautiful essences that connect with our souls require human fellowship in order to manifest as beautiful objects in nature and even in art. In the 'Pleasure Thermometer' section, Keats says richer entanglements than even 'Eolian magic' (a Romantic symbol for poetry), the enthrallments forged by love and friendship are the crown of humanity (I, 786). Keats concludes, 'melting into its radiance, we blend, / Mingle, and so become a part of it' and from this the world 'benefits unknowingly' (I, 810–11, 827).

The Keatsian model of radical cognitive and emotional interconnectedness that forms the philosophical foundation of *Endymion* anticipates the exchange of feelings that distributed cognition theorists imagine happens between sympathetically engaged bodies. In a phenomenon she calls 'feeling close', Giovanna Colombetti cites and revises Edith Stein ([1917] 1989). Stein describes a system of shared feeling that unites two subjects in an experience of a common object or event. Elaborating on Stein, Colombetti summarises the empathy experienced in these situations:

> awareness of sharing a feeling leads to 'a subject of a higher level' (17), a 'higher unity' (122) between self and other. I do not just experience the other via basic

empathy; I am also aware that the other and I feel the same, and this awareness induces a stronger experience of connectedness. It is as if the others' feelings, which I usually experience as nonprimordial (i.e., as belonging to them and not to me), have lost their nonprimordial character and become 'live to me' like my own feelings. (Colombetti 2014: 135)

The shared feeling and the awareness of the shared feeling create a compounded intimacy that represents a new level of connectivity between sympathetic bodies. Feeling close is, then, a new space of shared cognition. However, both Stein and Colombetti believe that the self/other boundary remains within this new space: 'I neither "lose myself" in the others nor incorporate the others' experience into mine in a sort of extended awareness of myself' (Colombetti 2014: 134–5). Keats, on the other hand, describes love and friendship as 'self-destroying', dissolving the ego to allow the interpenetration of our essence with others in the grand cosmos of love and fellow-feeling (I, 799–801). He sees human fellowship as individually and societally transformative and points to reading literature as critical in promoting this change. The world benefits from this loss of 'self', this radical interconnectedness that goes beyond 'feeling close' and even the 'fellow-feeling' of sympathy or basic empathy to imagine the self as entirely within and made up of a larger cosmic, cognitive community.

Throughout *Endymion*, Keats shows his radical sense of sympathy at work when a character hears (or reads) the tale of another. Let us take for instance our reintroduction to the poor wanderer Endymion in Book II. The 'brain-sick shepherd prince' has stopped at a spring, weary with his quest and 'old grief' (II, 42; II, 46). A rose bud 'snares his fancy' (II, 56). He plucks it, dips its stem into the water, and watches it bloom. From the now blossomed bud, a golden butterfly is released. Endymion's 'wide eye' is captivated by the butterfly, whose wings 'must be surely character'd strange things' (II, 62; II, 61). His imagination activated by 'reading' nature, he becomes physiologically sympathetic to the butterfly, who flies lightly away. Endymion himself feels emotionally lighter and his own seemingly weightless movements mirror that of the butterfly. Endymion rises and follows it. 'From languor's sullen bands / His limbs are loos'd, and eager, on he hies / Dazzled to trace it in the sunny skies. / It seem'd he flew, the way so easy was' (II, 65–8). Similarly, in Book III, Keats introduces Glaucus as a text telling a story:

A cloak of blue wrapp'd up his aged bones,
O'erwrought with symbols by the deepest groans
Of ambitious magic: every ocean-form
Was woven in with black distinctness; storm
And calm, and whispering, and hideous roar,
Quicksand and whirlpool, and deserted shore
Were emblem'd in the woof. (III, 197–203)

Glaucus's cloak is full of characters and marks, depicting the ocean and its mythologies. He pores over a book open on his lap. His forehead is margined by wrinkles.

Though initially repulsed by Glaucus (Endymion believes Glaucus a wretched sorcerer who will burn him, freeze him, tear him to pieces to feed his army of fish, etc.), when he sees the old man weeping, he recognises his humanity. Keats writes,

> Lo! his heart 'gan warm
> With pity for the grey hair'd creature wept.
> Had he then wrong'd a heart where sorrow kept?
> Had he, though blindly contumelious, brought
> Rheum to kind eyes, a sting to human thought,
> Convulsion to a mouth of many years?
> He had in truth; and he was ripe for tears.
> The penitent shower fell, as down he knelt
> Before that care-worn sage. (III, 282–90)

Tracing the circulation of affect, we first note that Endymion has a physiological change as his heart warms with emotion, with pity. Endymion then appraises the old man's embodied emotions. The tears indicate pain, a sting to a human being who must feel as he does, not to a cruel, otherworldly sorcerer. The 'human thought' here further suggests that self-consciousness and perhaps sympathy is the marker of humanity. I say sympathy because, as Cox notes, the fair copy of this line read 'humane thought'.[9] Endymion then weeps, too, catching the feelings of another being through sympathy and the recognition of common humanity. Glaucus's reaction to Endymion's shared emotion recapitulates the circulating affect. He declares: 'I know thine inmost bosom, and I feel / A very brother's yearning for thee steal / Into mine own' (III, 292–4). Endymion feels Glaucus's pain, and Glaucus's own body conveys the sympathetic reaction, and reciprocates with a familial bond. They are brothers in shared feeling and reading.

The cognitive process represented in the Glaucus scene requires further scrutiny, however. Keats portrays the mechanics of circulating affect in a level of detail that begs the question of whether his cognitive model engages in the same reflective practices for which Wordsworth is so infamous. As he reads the emotions on Glaucus's face, Endymion recognises their common humanity. This is cognitive appraisal, and, ultimately, Endymion reflects upon his hasty judgement. Or rather, we infer through the third-person narrator (the speaker of the poem, who enters the space of the hero's mind) that Endymion processes the reading experience in this way. However, this reading experience is arguably one of distributed cognition, distinctly different from the auto-read practices of Wordsworth. Even though, as readers, we see into the mind of the hero and the ways he processes an experience, the narrator poses questions that encourage the reader's own cognitive processing alongside Endymion's. The narrator asks, 'Had he then wrong'd a heart where sorrow kept?' (III, 284). The third-person grammatical construction asks the question simultaneously from the perspectives of the narrator and the reader.

---

[9] Editorial note in Keats 2009: 200.

Indeed, Endymion himself might be asking the question in a moment of existential self-reflection. In this way, Keats foregoes the use of a Wordsworthian guiding hand that would philosophise the experience for his readers. We witness the scene as a tableau of sympathetic engagement, a story of human compassion unfolding before us in the present, in which we are invited to participate and learn.

Dreams as Enacted Spaces of Empathy

Even as he wanders from scene to scene, from person to person on his journey, Endymion falls prey to feelings of loneliness and melancholy. Solitude by definition cannot be a shared feeling, but even in moments of isolation Endymion escapes solitude through sleep. Sleep is where Cynthia (also referred to as Phoebe or the moon) joins our hero. He feels lonely on his journey, finds himself in a bower, and falls asleep. Then, his goddess lover appears, or she sends him to visit another suffering lover. Thus dreams are particularly interesting sites to study cognition and fellow-feeling in this poem. In the article 'Romantic poetry and the idea of the dream', Grevel Lindop introduces two primary ways of understanding dreams in early-nineteenth-century Britain. The first way Romantic writers would have understood dreams emerges from the biblical tradition that sees dreams as 'caused by spiritual agency: God, angels, good or evil spirits intervening in the sleeper's consciousness to give messages which might be either helpful or misleading' (Lindop 2004: 20). The second lens through which many understood dreams was medical. Many believed 'dreams were caused by bodily factors – in particular the food you had eaten before sleeping, but also the position of the body, temperature, breathing, one's general state of health, and so on' (20). Keats draws upon both of these traditions in *Endymion*. The protagonist's dreams are often visions or challenges imposed by Phoebe, as she trains him in the ways of compassion and prepares him for ascension to immortality. However, Keats also shows how external experiences and imagined experience pass through the body and blur the border between waking and sleeping. Both of these historical understandings of dream space constitute enactive approaches to distributed cognition, where the narrative of the dream is co-created through the interactions of the dreamer, his body and his environment.

The dreams act as narrative texts for Endymion as he participates in the dreams in ways that mirror immersive reading. Keats believes texts join people across time and space through shared feeling, and dreams do the same type of work. Both experiences necessitate the lapse of the conscious actor. A dreamer must be open to the activity of the dream (including the feelings that coincide) in much the same way as readers suspend disbelief in order to immerse themselves in narrative action or a character's perspective. Even as the reader is at the mercy of the text, the dreamer's experience is often organised by sensual perception. A dreamer's body will take cues from her surroundings, a conversation from the next room, her quilt's texture, the smell of breakfast on the stove. Each of these can translate into the dream. At the same time the dream is a product of the dreamer's other cogni-

tive processes. She fills in the action to create a scene from the sensual details perceived. These dreams are pieced together from bits of memory, anxieties, desires
and so on. All of this coincides nicely with Keats's medical knowledge. As we have
seen from Keats's *Anatomical and Physiological Notebook*, he was taught that volition
and sensation are opposite forces, respectively internal production and externally
received information. These can supplement each other and combine to perform
tasks or create experience. Therefore, in its confusion of the internal and external,
the dream spaces in *Endymion* enact empathic spaces of lapsed selfhood where,
through affective communion with other characters and environmental entities,
the hero can usher into existence an ideal reality.

Dreaming may not be easily understood as a social phenomenon: the dream
experience will differ between sleepers based on their unique embodied exist-
ences, store of memories, individual desires and so on. However, the dream acts
in the same way a text does to necessitate the abdication of a reasoning self, laying
one open to the intervention of sensations. In fact, dreams may do so on a more
literalised level, being unmediated by a text. There is no translation from the
sign to the imagination, except in the cases of external sensations seeping into
the dream. Even in such cases, the sensation can be considered more original
because it occurs in the body and in real time. It is not 'just imagined'. In this way,
the sensual perception and volition in dreaming works backward, transitioning
from actual to imagined. Instead of the imagined becoming an actual feeling, as
in Humean sympathetic identification with another person, the actual becomes
part of the narrative, and the mind does not distinguish between the two until the
dreamer awakes and the *cogito* resumes control. I argue this is social insofar as the
same mechanisms for self-erasure and sympathetic embodied feeling are at work
in dreaming as in reading. Aside from this physiological realism, Keats's hero
Endymion dreams social existence into reality to cure his solitude.

For Keats, lived experience emerges from the dream experience. Here I must
attend to the famous 'Adam's dream' passage from his letter to Benjamin Bailey
on 22 November 1817:

> The imagination may be compared to Adam's dream, – he awoke and found it
> truth. I am more zealous in this affair because I have never yet been able to per-
> ceive how anything can be known for truth by consecutive reasoning – and yet
> it must be. Can it be that even the greatest philosopher ever arrived at his goal
> without putting aside numerous objections? However it may be, O for a life of
> sensation rather than of thoughts! It is a 'Vision in the form of Youth,' a shadow
> of reality to come. And this consideration has further convinced me, – for it has
> come as auxiliary to another favorite speculation of mine, – that we shall enjoy
> ourselves hereafter by having what we called happiness on earth repeated in a
> finer tone and so repeated. And yet such a fate can only befall those who delight
> in sensation, rather than hunger as you do after truth. Adam's dream will do
> here, and seems to be a conviction that imagination and its empyreal reflection
> is the same as human life and its spiritual repetition. (Keats 1958: I, 184–5)

The visionary becomes the empirical truth. Yet Keats calls the visionary 'sensation'. Strangely, he is not speaking of the phenomenological sensual perception here. Instead, he is using sensation to describe 'happiness on earth'. Delighting in sensation is set in opposition to hungering after truth, consecutive reasoning. Happiness and its eternal, immortal replication comes only to those who revel in the moment. Keats believes that striving for 'truth' rather than letting it come through immersive sensual experience is isolating. Importantly, Adam's dream is of a companion, and he awakes to find Eve. He dreams of communion, and he awakes to the reality of social existence. It is not good that the man should be alone. Endymion is drowning in grief over his lost immortal lover, his dream. He did not awake to find his lover true. Not in the first book of the poem, at least.

Throughout the poem, Endymion enters spaces of communion by dreaming. Peona finds Endymion in a restless trance as he sits with old men and an aged priest. They talk of crossing the bar into eternity and reuniting with their friends, family and fellow huntsmen in immortality. Peona takes him away to her favourite bower on a little island. He falls into a sleep, which heals and 'renovates' his mind:

> O magic sleep! O comfortable bird
> That broodest o'er the troubled sea of the mind
> Till it is hush'd and smooth! O unconfin'd
> Restraint! imprisoned liberty! great key
> To golden palaces, strange minstrelsy,
> Fountains grotesque, new trees, bespangled caves,
> Echoing grottos, full of tumbling waves
> And moonlight; aye, to all the mazy world
> Of silvery enchantment! – who, upfurl'd
> Beneath thy drowsy wing a triple hour,
> But renovates and lives? – Thus, in the bower,
> Endymion was calm'd to life again.
> Opening his eyelids with a healthier brain. (I, 453–65)

He celebrates sleep as the paradoxes of 'unconfin'd / Restraint! imprisoned liberty!'. The structure of these exclamations further interlocks and frees the very words as the adjectives and nouns reverse sentiment: a freeing confinement becomes a confining freedom. Yet the play between the structures grants its own kind of liberty. Sleep is a bounded space like a book, a poem, or even an enacted empathetic space of communion. Moreover, sleep and Endymion are very intimate, as lovers or family. He lies curled within Sleep's wing. Sleep as a bird brooding over a troubled sea of the mind echoes the Genesis creation story that envisions the Holy Spirit brooding over the earth's waters before the creation of light and darkness, day and night.[10] Sleep here is the dominant force between waking and sleeping,

---

[10] Genesis 1: 2.

the arbiter of each state, perhaps. What we can say more definitively, however, is sleep settles the mind through creation. The golden palaces, strange minstrelsy and host of other fantastic visions of fountains and grottoes resemble the dreamscape of Samuel Taylor Coleridge's 'Kubla Khan' (1816), which concludes with the image of an entranced poet with 'flashing eyes and floating hair',[11] who must have three circles woven round him (a triple hour is needed to calm Endymion's troubled mind). Sleep provides a site for fantastic creations and coincident renovation of the brain.

When Endymion awakes to talk with Peona, she plays a 'mournful strange' lay, which induces another sort of trancelike intoxication in her brother (I, 497). She stops playing and asks about his deeper knowledge of things immortal that 'weigh down' his nature. He explains that he has had a dream. A vision of mounting to the stars upon wings, seeing them disappear and the moon rise from the horizon. His 'dazzled soul / Commingl[es] with her argent spheres', and when she disappears, he seeks 'to commune' again with the stars (I, 594–5, 600). He has a vision of the deities. Then he describes Phoebe's beauty (he does not use her name; she is only 'the moon' here), and she takes his hand and they fly. He is so overcome that he nearly faints a couple of times and he goes into a madness, kissing her arms and face until she lays him down in another bower (I, 604–71). From here he loses the dream as he falls into a deeper 'stupid sleep' (I, 678).

The parallel between the dream experience and what Endymion undergoes while in his trance and asleep is too apparent to ignore. Endymion's dreamed journey mirrors the actual goings on of the scene. His vision of the deities from Mount Olympus is reminiscent of the circle of old men talking of eternity. Being escorted to a bower by Peona and falling out of the trance into deeper sleep further mirror his physical movements while unconscious. Though he does not awake to find his dream lover true, his dream takes cues from the external goings on his body perceives while asleep, enacting a cognitive space that is co-created by the dreamer and his environment.

In the exchange that follows this first sleep episode, Keats explores the distinction he draws in his letter to Bailey between a life of sensations and hungering after truth. Peona listens to her brother's lament over his lost opportunity for transcendence with Phoebe. Having heard enough, she chastises him and pokes fun at his sentimentalism. Instead of sighing, he should 'be rather in the trumpet's mouth, – anon / Among the winds at large – that all may hearken!' (I, 737–8). Rather than floundering in his emotions, he should be taking action. He should be more ambitious, a leader to whom all listen. She says of dreaming:

'– would I so tease
My pleasant days, because I could not mount
Into those regions? The Morphean fount
Of that fine element that visions, dreams

---

[11] See Damrosch and Dettmar 2006.

And fitful whims of sleep are made of, streams
Into its airy channels with so subtle,
So thin a breathing, not the spider's shuttle,
Circled a million times within the space
Of a swallow's nest-door, could delay a trace,
A tinting of its quality: how light
Must dreams themselves be; seeing they're more slight
Than the mere nothing that engenders them!
Then wherefore sully the entrusted gem
Of high and noble life with thoughts so sick?
Why pierce high-fronted honour to the quick
For nothing but a dream?' (I, 745–60)

Rather than seeing sleep as curative, she believes Endymion's sickness to derive from the dream, more specifically from the dream's failure to materialise into reality. She knows she cannot ascend to the realms she dreams of, and so she will not waste time trying. For Peona, dreams emerge from nothing and are even 'more slight / Than the mere nothing that engenders them!'. They bear no relation to reality and, therefore, should have no significance to the dreamer. To his sister's upbraiding, Endymion responds:

No, no, I'm sure,
My restless spirit never could endure
To brood so long upon one luxury,
Unless it did, though fearfully, espy
A hope beyond the shadow of a dream.
My sayings will the less obscured seem,
When I have told thee how my waking sight
Has made me scruple whether that same night
Was pass'd in dreaming. (I, 853–61)

Though Peona recognises that he 'know[s] of things mysterious, / Immortal, starry', she has missed the point here. Endymion understands that dreams extend beyond the moments of sleep, but not in the way Peona thinks, as a lingering sense of loss, a pointless pining after phantoms. Instead, the dreams extend toward a future reality, a 'hope beyond the shadow of a dream'. The shadow of a dream is a melancholic trace of the dream, and Endymion admits to a fearful attention to the shadow. However, the dream obscures the imagined and the lived, and this offers him a glimpse of hope beyond his fear. Lindop claims that Keats is most interested in 'a congruence between imagination and reality', notions of 'dreaming what is' (2004: 32). He writes, 'In *Endymion*, the protagonist's dream of the moon-goddess Phoebe is the inspiration that sends him on a quest through the elements for real union with the goddess. When he eventually finds her, in her earthly incarnation as the Indian maid, he falls asleep with her, dreams that he is in heaven with her and on waking, we are told "beheld his very dream" [IV, 436].' From this Lindop concludes that Endymion's quest is 'to make dream and reality coincide' (2004: 32). And yet Endymion cannot be sure that his experience is waking or dreamt. Endymion wonders, do I wake or sleep? And does the answer matter when he wakes to find the dream true? Indeed, dreaming of his lover's voice, Endymion awakes to find both his sister and his goddess-lover calling to him. Dreams are strange spaces where abandoning the reasoning self allows a sympathetic co-creation of narrative. Volition and sensation blend and confuse self and other, imagination and perception. The experience of the dream is written on the body and becomes truth in a process of direct accessibility of sensual experience that mirrors the way a text circulates affectively through the bodies engaged in acts of reading. For Keats, these moments of sympathetic engagement, these sites of physiological and cognitive interconnection, create cooperative compositions truer than what can be gathered in trumpet calls and consecutive reasoning.

Conclusion

To conclude, let me turn to Wordsworth's epic *The Excursion* (1814), in which the poet answers feelings of dejection and disillusionment following the violent turn in the French Revolution with solitude, the individual's communion with nature rather than love of man in society as the route to love of God. In response to *The Excursion*, Percy Bysshe Shelley presents what he feels is the true result of solitude in nature: self-centred seclusion, the inability to connect with the actual, and, most importantly, a fruitless life of idealisations rather than productive contention with realities. In his 1816 'Preface' to *Alastor*, Shelley recapitulates these dangers:

> Among those who attempt to exist without human sympathy, the pure and tender-hearted perish through the intensity and passion of their search after its communities, when the vacancy of their spirit suddenly makes itself felt . . . those who love not their fellow-beings live unfruitful lives, and prepare for their old age a miserable grave. (Shelley 2010: 5)

A life, or rather a life's work, produced within isolation proves sterile. Shelley even goes so far as to call these unsympathetic solitaries 'morally dead' (5).

Shelley's wanderer, like Wordsworth himself, starts in alienation and continues farther into 'a wide waste and tangled wilderness' (Shelley 2010: 8, l. 78). Though bearing company with 'savage men', boarding and eating among them, partaking of their hospitality, he does not connect with them (8, l. 80). In fact, the Arab maiden, an image of self-sacrifice and generosity, gives him her portions of food and bedding, yet he apparently fails to engage with her, substituting in her stead his own idealised vision of a beautiful maiden. Indeed, this ideal maiden proves little more than a reflection of the wanderer's own philosophical vision. Shelley writes, 'her voice was like the voice of his own soul' (10, l. 153). When she vanishes from his dreams, we hear echoes of the *ubi sunt* plaints of 'Intimations Ode'

$(1807)^{12}$ – the speaker cries, 'Whither have fled / the hues of heaven that canopied his bower / Of yesternight?' (11, ll. 196–8). Most significantly, the poet recognises his failure when looking on a swan pair, and mourns how he 'wast[es] these surpassing powers / In the deaf air, to the blind earth, and heaven / That echoes not my thoughts?' while the swan shares his voice with a beloved (13–14, ll. 288–90). In fact, Shelley turns 'Intimations Ode' on its head in the last lines of *Alastor*, proclaiming:

> It is a woe too 'deep for tears,' when all
> Is reft at once, when some surpassing Spirit,
> Whose light adorned the world around it, leaves
> Those who remain behind, not sobs or groans,
> The passionate tumult of clinging hope;
> But pale despair and cold tranquillity. (25, ll. 713–18)

The affective response, the pleasure, that once proved effective in cultivating sympathy and hope disintegrates. Moreover, Shelley seems to suggest that the cause of the pale despair and cold tranquillity is Wordsworth's own solipsism. Like Shelley's wanderer and Wordsworth's before him, Endymion and Keats simultaneously seek communion with immortality. Shelley's character Alastor and his real-life model Wordsworth fail to learn that immortality can only be achieved through tests of human compassion.

In spite of having passed his medical exams with ease the previous summer, Keats abandoned his medical career in December 1816. Hosting a Saturnalia dinner for his brothers and close friends, the young poet announced his intentions to devote himself fully to a literary career. *Endymion* was Keats's personal test of ability, his self-appointed and self-designed apprenticeship in his new career of poetry. Setting for himself the task of composing the poem in a year's time, Keats declared it 'a test, a trial of my Powers of Imagination and chiefly my invention which is a rare thing indeed – by which I must make 4000 Lines of one bare circumstance and fill them with Poetry . . . a test of Invention . . . [is] the Polar Star of Poetry, as Fancy is the Sails, and Imagination the Rudder . . .' (Keats 1958: I, 169–70). Even as his hero must prove himself, Keats views the epic attempt of *Endymion* as his own entrance exam to the everlasting community of poets he read and adored. Keats's *Endymion* would grant him immortality, like his hero who ascends to the heavens in the poem's end. Unlike the religiously conservative, older Wordsworth of *The Excursion*, Keats had no attachment to orthodox religion. His poem substitutes Christian faith for 'paganism' and classical mythology. Nevertheless, Keats did believe in a form of immortality, one that connects those who seek it through the act of reading and feeling. *Endymion* engages the reader's body and mind in an affective economy of sympathy, teaching the reader compassion even as the hero and the author learn it themselves. In a direct accessibility of phenomenological experience, the act of

---

[12] See Damrosch and Dettmar 2006.

reading Keats's epic attempt becomes a simultaneous journey of hero, author and reader from which a new reality of radical unity promises hope beyond the shadow of a dream, beyond the narrative text. Keats famously opens *Endymion* with a declaration of art's hedonic value: 'A Thing of beauty is a joy for ever: / Its loveliness increases; it will never / Pass into nothingness' (I, 1–3). Beautiful tales unite readers in shared feeling, 'for ever' across time and across space. Indeed, the work of art *itself* – its hedonic value – is for Keats, the poet-physician, the source of the distributed cognition. As he writes, despite despondence, the reality of the inhuman darkness and 'gloomy days' at hand, a beautiful thing 'bind[s] us to the earth', even to the tombs of 'the mighty dead', all while replenishing us with 'sweet dreams' of immortality (I, 9; I, 5; I, 21; I, 5).

5

Embodied Cognition in Berkeley and Kant: The Body's Own Space

Jennifer Mensch

Berkeley and Kant are known for having developed philosophical critiques of materialism, critiques leading them to propose instead an epistemology based on the coherence of our mental representations. For all that the two had in common, however, Kant was adamant in distinguishing his own 'empirical realism' from the immaterialist consequences entailed by Berkeley's attack on abstract ideas. Kant focused his most explicit criticisms on Berkeley's account of space, and commentators have for the most part decided that Kant either misunderstood or was simply unfamiliar with the Bishop's actual position. Rather than demonstrate that Kant understood Berkeley perfectly well – an argument that has already been forcefully made by Colin Turbayne – I want to take a different tack altogether. For it is by paying attention to Berkeley's actual account of space, an account oriented by his rejection of spatial 'geometers' like Descartes, and spatial 'absolutists' like Newton, that we discover an account of embodied cognition, of spatial distance and size that can only be known by way of the body's motion and touch. Perhaps even more striking, I suggest, is the manner in which Kant's approach to the problem of incongruent counterparts will equally need to rely on a proprioceptive cognition, one requiring a different geometry of position altogether. By focusing on these texts – Berkeley's *New Theory of Vision*, and Kant's repeated efforts to understand the problem of a mirrored difference between objects in space – I demonstrate that the solution to the issues under consideration require an account of embodiment. Thus while cognitive theorists today have recognised that certain challenges faced by perception and cognition can only be resolved by way of an appeal to the facts of embodiment, my aim in what follows is to show that such recourse is not new. My discussion proceeds in three stages, with stage one focused on Kant's efforts to distinguish his philosophical project from Berkeley's own idealist system, and stages two and three describing the manner in which their approach to spatial orientation both challenges and extends the traditional narrative of their differences as laid out in stage one.

Kant and his Critics: Dogmatic versus Critical Idealism

Some of the earliest and most persistent complaints against Immanuel Kant's theoretical programme included the charge of idealism, with critics immediately identifying Kant's transcendental idealism with the immaterialist philosophy put forward by George Berkeley, Bishop of Cloyne.[1] This charge was serious, and Kant was duly incensed by the comparison given Berkeley's reputation for having produced a system that, as Hume had famously put it, 'admits of no answer and produces no conviction'.[2] When the review appeared in 1782 Kant was in the midst of finishing a short précis of the *Critique*, a teacher's handbook that he felt could be used in high schools, which he titled a *Prolegomena to any future metaphysics that will be able to come forward as science* (1783). Kant's reaction to the review was swift, however, as he hastily added sections to the *Prolegomena*, ones now devoted to a careful distinction between his own 'critical' idealism and the 'mystical' and 'dogmatic' idealism put forward by 'the good Berkeley'. What is more, he included a separate section at the end of the *Prolegomena* demanding that the anonymous reviewer make themselves known, insisting that in the review itself 'a more miserable and historically incorrect judgment could hardly be made'.[3] Kant's worry over the comparison to Berkeley would continue throughout the 1780s, enough so that

[1] As one of the first reviews of Kant's *Critique of Pure Reason* put it, why should Kant insist on a difference between the two systems if, according to Kant's view, 'everything which we can know and talk about is only a representation and law of thought, if the representations which are modified in us and ordered according to certain laws are just what we call object and world'; if this was true, the anonymous reviewer asked, why fight the obvious: 'why fight against this commonly accepted language, *why* then and *from where* this idealist distinction?' ('Wenn, wie der Verfasser selbst behauptet, der Verstand nur die Empfindungen bearbeitet, nicht neue Kenntnisse und liefert: so handelt er seinen ersten Gesetzen gemäß, wenn er in allem, was Wirklichkeit betrifft, sich mehr von den Empfindungen leiten lässet, als sie leitet. . . . wenn die Vorstellungen in uns modificirt und geordnet nach gewissen Gesetzen just das since, was wir Objekte und Welt nennen: wozu den der Streit gegen diese gemein angenommena Sprache? Wozu den und woher die idealistische Unterscheidung?') This comment appeared in an anonymously published review of the *Critique* by Christian Garve – with significant emendations by the journal's editor, J. G. H. Feder (Anon. 1782: 48). An English translation is available in Sassen 2000: 53–8, and in Schultz 1995: Appendix C, 171–7. In Mensch 2006 I discuss the importance of this review for understanding the nature of Kant's changes to the *Critique* for its second edition in 1787.

[2] 'But that all his arguments, though otherwise intended, are, in reality, merely skeptical, appears from this, *that they admit of no answer and produce no conviction*. Their only effect is to cause that momentary amazement and irresolution and confusion, which is the result of skepticism' (Hume [1777] 1975: section 12, 155, n. 1). Harry Bracken (1965: 1) memorably described the general response to Berkeley as 'a source of low-class intellectual comedy'. For a more recent appraisal of responses to Berkeley's theory of vision see Atherton 2005.

[3] Kant 1985b: 115, corresponding to the Academy edition 4: 376. I will henceforth cite Kant's works in-text with volume and page number separated by a full colon. These citations will all correspond to the complete works of Immanuel Kant as published in German: *Kants gesammelte Schriften* (1900–). However, the *Critique of Pure Reason* uses an A/B system to indicate the 1781/1787 editions, e.g. A835/B863; where only A or B is given, this indicates passages either excised or added between the two editions.

when the chance came for a second printing of the *Critique of Pure Reason* in 1787, Kant added sections dealing with Berkeley, including one exclusively dedicated to a 'Refutation of Idealism' (B274–9).[4]

Although Kant only began to treat Berkeley by name during the 1780s, the spectre of idealism qua ontological immaterialism had already concerned him for years. When Kant had first assumed his professorship in 1770 it was required that he produce a work highlighting the philosophical direction to be inaugurated by him upon his assumption of the position. The result was Kant's dissertation 'On the form and principles of the sensible and intelligible world', a text whose significance becomes clearer with the benefit of hindsight so far as the main outlines of Kant's eventual epistemic strategy is already visible there. It was in this text that Kant first introduced what would come to be seen as one of the main innovations in his theory of cognition, namely the 'subjective' (the term 'transcendental' not yet being in use) ideality of space and time. What Kant meant by this in 1770 was that space and time were features of the mind, of the mind's subjective set of conditions imposed by it on the sense data apprehended, sorted and ultimately made into meaningful representations of a world by it. Insofar as space was a feature of the mind, Kant insisted that it could not have been abstracted from experience or otherwise derived from the senses but was instead generated by the mind itself in its work to make sense of the world.[5] As Kant summarised it,

> Although the *concept of space*, viewed as an objective and real being or affection, is imaginary, *relative to all sensible things (sensibilia)* it is not only *altogether true*, but the foundation of all truth in outer sensibility (*sensualitate*). For things cannot appear to the senses in any manner except by the mediating power of the mind, co-ordinating all sensations according to a constant law implanted in its nature. Nothing whatsoever, then, can be given to the senses save in conformity with the primary axioms of space and their consequences as taught in geometry. (2: 404)

Admitting that this distinguished his account of space from both the 'English view' and that held by the Leibnizians (2: 403), Kant argued that only his position was capable of explaining, and indeed securing, the necessary certainty of geometry,

---

[4] An excellent trio of articles have revisited the question of Kant's relationship to Berkeley. In the first of these we find Colin Turbayne (1955) itemising the striking resemblances between the two so far as each offers a concentrated attack on materialism (or 'transcendental realism', as Kant has it). Henry Allison (1973) offers a lucid response to Turbayne on Kant's behalf. Finally, we hear a rejoinder from the Berkeley scholar Kenneth Winkler (2008).

[5] 'Both concepts [space and time] are without doubt acquired, being abstracted not from the sensing of objects (for sensation gives the matter, not the form, of human cognition) but from the action of the mind in coordinating its sensa according to unchanging laws – each being, as it were, an immutable type to be known intuitively. Though sensations excite this act of the mind, they do not become part of the intuition. Nothing is here connate save the law of the mind, according to which it combines in a fixed manner the sense produced in it by the presence of the object' (2: 406). All citations taken from Kant's inaugural dissertation are translated by Lewis White Beck (Kant 1992b); the complete original Latin text is included in the Academy text as cited here.

For since geometry contemplates the relations of space, the concept of which contains in itself the very form of all sensual intuition, there can be nothing clear and evident in things perceived by outer sense except through the mediation of the intuition which that science is occupied in contemplating. (2: 403)

It was grounds such as these that led to Kant's pronouncing – in a statement anticipating what would come to be a core tenet of transcendental idealism – that 'The laws of sensibility will be laws of nature, in so far as nature falls within the scope of the senses' (2: 404). The only problem, and it was one Kant could immediately foresee, was the spectre of idealism.

To put the matter plainly, the issue for Kant turned on the connection between knowledge claims and the objects of everyday experience providing the content for them. Some sorts of knowledge claims – those regarding logic, for example – seemed to be both certain and true, but they were also not really about the objects of experience. Other sorts of claims, such as those based on sensible qualities – the pink, sticky sweetness of candyfloss, for example – seemed incurably subjective and open to just the sort of attacks led by Descartes and Locke regarding a sensible 'veil of illusion' between knower and thing. The trick, as Kant already understood in 1770, was to discover a means for making claims about the world of things such that those claims could be shielded from such illusion. The route taken by Berkeley, for whom ideas could only be produced by an active Intelligence, and never by some sort of indifferent piece of matter, was epistemically tight so far as no gap could exist between mental representation and material thing. But it also produced a system that, as Kant saw it, was convincing to no one.

In Kant's first attempt at a solution he simply asserted a materialist source for our sensations, declaring that as sensations are 'caused they bear witness to the presence of an object – which is opposed to idealism', before trialling his method for achieving certainty nonetheless. 'Consider judgments about things sensitively known,' he began,

> the truth of a judgment consists in the agreement of its predicate with the given subject. But the concept of the subject, so far as it is a phenomenon, can be given only by its relation to the sensitive faculty of knowledge, and it is also by the same faculty that the sensitively observable predicates are given. Hence it is clear that the representations of subject and predicate arise according to common laws, and so allow of a perfectly true knowledge. (2: 397)

The key to understanding Kant's preliminary solution here is found by focusing on his notion of 'common laws', for it is by means of these mental rules that sensible data received from a material source can be mediated in such a manner that a representation is formed. Since the laws producing predicates like 'hard' or 'grey' are identical to those regarding a subject like 'stone', it is this uniformity that is meant to undergird the certainty of a proposition like 'The grey stone is hard'. Kant is, however, walking a tightrope here. If the 'grey stone' representation is meant to be a mental copy of a material stone in the world then he will end up with a position much like Descartes or Locke and therefore generate the kind of scepticism leading to Berkeley's rejection of materialism altogether. Kant obviously does not want this and so he immediately insists on a disconnect between representation and thing, explaining that 'phenomena are, properly, semblances [*species*], not ideas, of things, and express no internal or absolute quality of the objects', even as he will also declare that 'knowledge of them is nonetheless perfectly genuine knowledge' given the common laws at work in providing for the propositional content of cognition (2: 397). The problem with Kant's position at this point, however, is just this disconnect between representation and thing, since it is hard to see how he can overcome his concerns regarding idealism as a result.

In the *Critique of Pure Reason*, Kant is in fact bolder in asserting the distinction between unknown material thing – the 'thing in itself' apart from any of the cognitive conditions required by us for knowledge of it – and its appearance; and bolder yet in asserting a strict ontological isomorphism between appearances and their mental representations. As Kant put it in what is perhaps his clearest formulation: 'By *transcendental idealism* I mean the doctrine that appearances are to be regarded as being, one and all, representations only, not things in themselves, and that time and space are therefore only sensible forms of our intuition, not determinations given as existing by themselves, nor conditions of objects viewed as things in themselves.'[6] Kant insisted that this position was sounder than any alternative, especially that of materialism, for 'After wrongly supposing that objects of the senses, if they are to be external, must have an existence by themselves, and independently of the senses, he [the materialist] finds that, judged from this point of view, all our sensuous representations are inadequate to establish their reality'.[7] But now, having closed the epistemic (and ontological) gap between our mental ideas of things and our experience of the appearances of things, Kant seemed closer than ever in his conclusions to Berkeley's position – a point that was not missed by his critics.

Anticipating criticisms along these lines, Kant developed a response to what he henceforth considered to be two distinctive strains of idealism: the 'dreaming' idealism of Descartes and the dogmatic idealism of Berkeley, where the former was constrained to doubting the existence of material objects, and the latter to outright denying them (A377). Given our focus on Berkeley in this discussion we can leave Descartes aside, noting only that Kant, like Descartes, faced ongoing difficulties in trying to convince readers that coherence could be a reliable criterion for

---

[6] 'Ich verstehe aber unter dem transscendentalen Idealism aller Erscheinungen den Lehrbegriff, nach welchem wir sie insgesammt als bloße Vorstellungen und nicht als Dinge an sich selbst ansehen, und dem gemäß Zeit und Raum nur sinnliche Formen unserer Anschauung, nicht aber für sich gegebene Bestimmungen oder Bedingungen der Objecte als Dinge an sich selbst sind' (A369).

[7] 'Dieser transcendentale Realist ist es eigentlich, welcher nachher den empirischen Idealisten spielt und, nachdem er fälschlich von Gegenständen der Sinne vorausgesetzt hat, daß, wenn sie äußere sein sollen, sie an sich selbst, auch ohne Sinne, ihre Existenz haben müßten, in diesem Gesichtspunkte alle unsere Vorstellungen der Sinne unzureichend findet, die Wirklichkeit derselben gewiß zu machen' (A369).

distinguishing between dreams and experience (especially given Kant's rejection of Descartes's eventual recourse to a proof for the existence of a non-scheming God for finally securing the criterion). As for Kant's treatment of Berkeley, this turned almost entirely on a critique of Berkeley's account of space, and here we must beware of the fact that Kant's discussion of other philosophers almost always began from what he took to be the *results* of a given position. Kant took Berkeley's immaterialism to be a logical reaction to the scepticism yielded up by materialists, and especially to their commonly held distinction between primary and secondary qualities. Indeed, Kant took materialism or 'transcendental realism' to be a Pyrrhonian system in its results, given that it led inexorably to an immaterialist ontology which no right-minded thinker could support. As Kant put it, 'we cannot blame the good Berkeley for degrading bodies to mere illusion [*Schein*]' if the only alternative was the kind of materialism espoused by Descartes and Locke (B71).

In the *Critique of Pure Reason* Kant developed a specific response to the epistemic problems posed by materialism. First, and in general continuity with his earlier presentation of it in his *Inaugural Dissertation* of 1770, there was the redefinition of space as a form of intuition. This entailed that we think of space as neither relational nor independent of objects but as instead a part of the subjective make-up of human knowers. Second, and as a consequence of this definition, all experience – from appearing objects outside us to mental representations within – was *a priori* subject to spatial conditioning. This entailed some linguistic difficulties when explaining what was meant by statements referring to objects 'outside us'. For as Kant described the transcendental idealist's position on this point, 'Matter is with him, therefore, only a species of representations (intuition), which are called external, not as standing in relation to objects *in themselves external*, but because they relate perceptions to the space in which all things are external to one another, while yet the space itself is in us.'[8] Kant admitted that 'The expression *outside us* is unavoidably ambiguous in meaning, sometimes signifying what *as thing in itself* exists apart from us, and sometimes what belongs solely to outer *appearance*',[9] but he was still confident that his system was not thereby tantamount to Berkeley's immaterialism. Why? Because, as he continued to insist, and this is the third point to make, the real, material content of our representations lay in sensation. And this fact was by no means eliminated by the demand that we were incapable of 'knowing' this content, in any meaningful sense, prior to its having been mentally taken up and synthesised according to space, time and the other required categories for

---

[8] 'Denn weil er diese Materie und sogar deren innere Möglichkeit blos für Erscheinung gelten läßt, die, von unserer Sinnlichkeit abgetrennt, nichts ist: so ist sie bei ihm nur eine Art Vorstellungen (Anschauung), welche äußerlich heißen, nicht als ob sie sich auf an sich selbst äußere Gegenstände bezögen, sondern weil sie Wahrnehmungen auf den Raum beziehen, in welchem alles außer einander, er selbst, der Raum, aber in uns ist' (A370).

[9] 'Weil indessen der Ausdruck: außer uns, eine nicht zu vermeidende Zweideutigkeit bei sich führt, indem er bald etwas bedeutet, was als Ding an sich selbst von uns unterschieden existirt, bald was blos zur äußeren Erscheinung gehört' (A373).

understanding the objects of experience. As Kant put it, 'Space itself, with all its appearances, as representations, is, indeed, only in me, but nevertheless the real, that is, the material of all objects of outer intuition, is actually given in this space, independently of all imaginative invention.'[10] On this basis Kant took it to be clear that our experience of the world – an experience uniformly taken by us to be real, that is, taken by us to form the 'empirically real' ground of a correspondence between thing and idea – this world of experience, and not immaterialism, was the happy yield of transcendental idealism. Kant explained in the *Prolegomena* that,

> As little as the man who admits colours not to be properties of the object itself but only to be modifications of the sense of sight should on that account be called an idealist, so little can my doctrine be named idealistic merely because I find that more, nay, *all the properties which constitute the intuition of a body belong merely to its appearance.* The existence of the thing that appears is thereby not destroyed, as in genuine idealism, but it is only shown that we cannot possibly know it by the senses as it is in itself.[11]

It was this last bit, however, that seems to have fallen on deaf ears. As one anonymous critic summarised the results of Kant's system as he saw it:

> It is a system of the higher or, as the author calls it, transcendental idealism. An idealism which encompasses spirit as well as matter, transforming the world and ourselves into representations.[12]

> All our cognitions arise from certain modifications of ourselves, which we call sensations. What these exist in, where they come from, is ultimately completely unknown to us. If there is an actual thing in which the representations inhere, or if they are created by actual things that exist independently of us, we still do not know the least predicate of either the one or the other.[13]

[10] 'Freilich ist der Raum selbst mit allen seinen Erscheinungen als Vorstellungen nur in mir, aber in diesem Raume ist doch gleichwohl das Reale oder der Stoff aller Gegenstände äußerer Anschauung wirklich und unabhängig von aller Erdichtung gegeben' (A375).

[11] '[U]nd so wenig wie der, so die Farben nicht als Eigenschaften, die dem Object an sich selbst, sondern nur den Sinn des Sehens als Modificationen anhängen, will gelten lassen, darum ein Idealist heißen kann: so wenig kann mein Lehrbegriff idealistisch heißen, blos deshalb weil ich finde, daß noch mehr, ja alle Eigenschaften, die die Anschauung eines Körpers ausmachen, blos zu seiner Erscheinung gehören; denn die Existenz des Dinges, was erscheint, wird dadurch nicht wie beim wirklichen Idealism aufgehoben, sondern nur gezeigt, daß wir es, wie es an sich selbst sei, durch Sinne gar nicht erkennen können' (4: 289).

[12] '[I]st ein System des höheren, oder, wie es der Verf. Nennt, des transcendentellen Idealismus; eines Idealismus, der Geist und Materie auf gleiche Weise umfaßt, die Welt und uns selbst in Vorstellungen verwandelt' (Anon. [Christian Garve] 1782: 40).

[13] 'Alle unsere Erkenntnisse entspringen aus gewissen Modificationen unserer selbst, die wir Empfindungen nennen. Worin diese befindlich sind, woher sie rühren, das ist uns im Grunde völlig unbekannt. Wenn es ein wirkliches Ding giebt, dem die Vorstellungen inhäriren; wirkliche

Space and time themselves are not something real outside of us. Neither are they relations or abstract concepts, but subjective laws of our faculty of representation, forms of sensation, [and] subjective conditions of sensible intuition. On this basis, sensation as mere modification of oneself (on which Berkeley too chiefly builds his idealism) is based on space and time, a basic pillar of the Kantian system.[14]

By claiming that Berkeley's idealism was built on an understanding of sensation in terms of its effect on us (as opposed to being a report on the material existence of things in the world), and that sensation was based on space and time as conditions set by us, the reviewer collapsed an epistemic claim regarding a set of mental conditions for knowing an object into an ontological claim regarding the source of our sensations – here inaccurately said to be 'based on space and time'.

Whether the reviewer was just careless in his wording or intentionally misleading – Kant took the latter to be the case given the journal's well-known lean toward the Scottish School of Common Sense philosophy – in Kant's subsequent treatments of Berkeley, his main effort was to respond to this claim. Thus to the *Prolegomena*, which he was writing when he read the review, Kant immediately added a section taking up the review in particular, calling the section 'A Specimen of a Judgment about the *Critique* Prior to its Examination'. Kant began with the reference to his system of 'higher idealism', suggesting that the term 'idealism' might need to be better explored.

The dictum of all genuine idealists, from the Eleatic school to Bishop Berkeley, is contained in this formula: 'All cognition through the senses and experience is nothing but sheer illusion, and only in the ideas of pure understanding and reason is there truth.'

The principle that throughout dominates and determines my idealism is, on the contrary: 'All cognition of things merely from pure understanding or pure reason is nothing but sheer illusion, and only in experience is there truth.'[15]

Dinge unabhängig von uns, die dieselben hervorbringen: so wissen wir doch von dem einen so wenig, als von dem andern, das mindeste Prädicat' (ibid.).

[14] 'Raum und Zeit selbst sind nichts wirkliches ausser uns, sind auch keine Verhältnisse, auch keine abstrahirte Begriffe; sondern subjective Gesetze unsers Vorstellungsvermögens, Formen der Empfindungen, subjective Bedingungen der sinnlichen Anschauung. Auf diesen Begriffen, von den Empfindungen als blossen Modificationen unserer selbst, (worauf auch Berkeley seinen Idealismus hauptsächlich baut) vom Raum und von der Zeit beruht der eine Grundpfeiler des Kantschen systems' (ibid. 41). My translation above differs from both Sassen and Morrison.

[15] 'Der Satz aller ächten Idealisten von der Eleatischen Schule an bis zum Bischof Berkeley ist in dieser Formel enthalten: "Alle Erkenntniß durch Sinne und Erfahrung ist nichts als lauter Schein, und nur in den Ideen des reinen Verstandes und Vernunft ist Wahrheit." Der Grundsatz, der meinen Idealism durchgängig regiert und bestimmt, ist dagegen: "Alles Erkenntniß von Dingen aus bloßem reinen Verstande oder reiner Vernunft ist nichts als lauter Schein, und nur in der Erfahrung ist Wahrheit"' (4: 374).

Kant's remarks here need careful unpacking. The 'dictum' starts from the position of the sceptic, the one who has discovered that materialism leads always to a veil of illusion between thing and idea. For this sceptic, truth can only be found in the ideas. While this sounds like a reference to the kind of Platonism latent within the doctrine of innate ideas, it is a logical conclusion – and the one that had indeed been reached by the materialist Hylas in Berkeley's *Three Dialogues between Hylas and Philonous* – once one has relinquished the demand that ideas refer to things. If ideas, as Berkeley argued, could only be meaningfully understood as referring to other ideas, then only in the ideas is there truth. Declaring, somewhat disingenuously, that 'my place is the fruitful bathos of experience' (4: 374), Kant distances himself from Berkeley's position by way of transcendental idealism's account of experience. In the *Critique* Kant had insisted that experience was impossible unless the mind was able to combine sensible intuition with intellectual concepts, telling his readers that 'thoughts without content are empty, intuitions without concepts are blind' (A51/B75). Truth or 'determinate knowledge' could only be had, according to Kant, within an experience of the world that was already conditioned by the mind's construction of it; this was experience of the 'empirically real' or of the world as it appeared to human cognisers, where objects were only ever objects-of-knowledge, never things in themselves.[16]

The role played by space and time, as parts of the *a priori* conditions for the possibility of experience, grounded Kant's response to the reviewer's specific reference to Berkeley. Thus a few lines later we read that

> Berkeley regarded space as a mere empirical representation that, like the appearances it contains, is, together with its determinations, known to us only by means of experience or perception. I, on the contrary, prove in the first place that space (and also time, which Berkeley did not consider) and all its determinations can be cognised *a priori* by us, because, no less than time, it inheres in us as a pure form of our sensibility before all perception of experience.[17]

Kant's point was just this: whereas Berkeley treated space like only one idea among many, for Kant, space was itself one of the formal conditions or 'common laws' set by the mind in its construction of experience. Since Berkeley had no such similar conception of a mental apparatus responsible for the construction of a uniform and coherent world of experience, Kant concluded that 'truth' itself was impossible in Berkeley's system. In Kant's words, 'as truth rests on universal and necessary

---

[16] I discuss Kant's position more fully in 'Kant on Truth' (Mensch 2004).

[17] 'Allein diese und unter ihnen vornehmlich Berkeley sahen den Raum für eine bloße empirische Vorstellung an, die eben so wie die Erscheinungen in ihm uns nur vermittelst der Erfahrung oder Wahrnehmung zusammt allen seinen Bestimmungen bekannt würde; ich dagegen zeige zuerst: daß der Raum (und eben so die Zeit, auf welche Berkeley nicht Acht hatte) sammt allen seinen Bestimmungen *a priori* von uns erkannt werden könne, weil er sowohl als die Zeit uns vor aller Wahrnehmung oder Erfahrung als reine Form unserer Sinnlichkeit beiwohnt und alle Anschauung derselben, mithin auch alle Erscheinungen möglich macht' (4: 475).

laws as its criteria, experience, according to Berkeley, can have no criteria of truth because its appearances (according to him) have nothing *a priori* at their foundation, whence it follows that experience is nothing but sheer illusion'. Whereas 'with us', Kant continued, 'space and time (in conjunction with the pure concepts of the understanding) prescribe their law *a priori* to all possible experience and, at the same time, afford the certain criterion for distinguishing truth from illusion therein'.[18] This epistemic security – a coherence theory of truth or, as Kant called it, 'transcendental truth', within which correspondence could easily operate within the empirically real field of experience – allowed Kant to dismiss the 'mystical and visionary idealism of Berkeley', an idealism 'against which and other similar phantasms, our *Critique* contains the proper antidote' (4: 293). This was not, however, Kant's final word on the matter.

When Kant published a second edition of the *Critique* in 1787 he focused his 'Refutation of Idealism' against Cartesian scepticism, telling readers that he had dealt with Berkeley already in the 'Transcendental Aesthetic'. This section opened the *Critique* and Kant's comments on Berkeley there had been specially drafted for the 1787 edition. As in the *Prolegomena*, Kant made it clear that he was responding to the 1782 review by repeating the charge connecting idealism and 'illusion' and emphasising once more the difference between a requirement that objects meet conditions set by a subject's cognitive possibilities, and the sense that any resultant appearances must be illusory. In this place, however, Kant advanced a new response, arguing that a truly illusory, even impossible world would be the result of insisting that space and time were somehow independent of human cognition. For

> if we reflect on the absurdities in which we are then involved, in that two infinite things, which are not substances, nor anything actually inhering in substances, must yet have existence, nay, must be the necessary condition of all existing things, and moreover must continue to exist, even although all existing things be removed – we cannot blame the good Berkeley for degrading bodies to mere illusion.[19]

[18] '[D]a Wahrheit auf allgemeinen und nothwendigen Gesetzen als ihren Kriterien beruht, die Erfahrung bei Berkeley keine Kriterien der Wahrheit haben könne, weil den Erscheinungen derselben (von ihm) nichts *a priori* zum Grunde gelegt ward, woraus denn folgte, daß sie nichts als lauter Schein sei, dagegen bei uns Raum und Zeit (in Verbindung mit den reinen Verstandesbegriffen) *a priori* aller möglichen Erfahrung ihr Gesetz vorschreiben, welches zugleich das sichere Kriterium abgiebt, in ihr Wahrheit von Schein zu unterscheiden' (4: 375).

[19] 'Denn wenn man den Raum und die Zeit als Beschaffenheiten ansieht, die ihrer Möglichkeit nach in Sachen an sich angetroffen werden müßten, und überdenkt die Ungereimtheiten, in die man sich alsdann verwickelt, indem zwei unendliche Dinge, die nicht Substanzen, auch nicht etwas wirklich den Substanzen Inhärirendes, dennoch aber Existirendes, ja die nothwendige Bedingung der Existenz aller Dinge sein müssen, auch übrig bleiben, wenn gleich alle existirende Dinge aufgehoben werden: so kann man es dem guten Berkeley wohl nicht verdenken, wenn er die Körper zu bloßem Schein herabsetzte' (B70).

Putting aside the patronising tone of 'the good Berkeley' for the moment, we can see that Kant is in fact exonerating him along earlier lines. Without focusing directly on Berkeley's account of space – that is, space as a mental representation but not, as for Kant, a *form* of mental representation – Kant reminded his readers that by ascribing transcendental reality to space we are asserting that some 'eternal and infinite, self-subsistent non-entity' exists (A39/B56), and that as such it functions as a parallel to God himself as the supposed ground and possibility of all reality.[20] It was in reaction to this conclusion, Kant now suggested, that Berkeley rejected all claims to independent reality, and for that we could hardly blame him.

Berkeley's New Theory of Vision

Nothing of what has been said so far would seem to suggest that either of these two idealist thinkers might have much to say about embodiment, and about embodied cognition as a bridge to distributed cognition in particular. But in this, I want to suggest, we would be wrong. Most of the story I have just rehearsed above regarding Kant's struggles against the charge of idealism, and especially his response to Berkeley's position, flows directly from Kant's first insights regarding the ideality of space. But in 1768, that is, two years earlier than his *Inaugural Dissertation* of 1770, Kant seems to have thought about space differently, turning to the body as a ground for proving the independent reality of space. What is more, Berkeley too had offered an account of embodied cognition for understanding our experience of space. The question of how or whether these respective accounts can be fitted into the idealist programmes advanced by each philosopher, and whether, in Kant's case, this changes his relationship to Berkeley, is something to address only after we have a sense of their respective positions.

Although Berkeley is today best known for the main works devoted to outlining his case against materialism, the *Treatise Concerning Principles of Human Knowledge* (1710) and its more popular counterpart, *Three Dialogues between Hylas and Philonous* (1713), Berkeley was a lively participant in discussions taking place in the natural sciences, and particularly so with respect to one of the more engrossing topics of the time: optics. On this subject Berkeley published first *An Essay Towards a New Theory of Vision* in 1709 and then, much later, *The Theory of Vision Vindicated and Explained* (1733).[21]

In these works Berkeley interrogated the manner in which vision had so far been treated by 'optical geometers' like Descartes and Newton, but his conceptual starting point lay in Locke's account of the relationship between sensible ideas. Locke had been interested in examining the manner in which regular experience led judgement to combine ideas in such a way as to form associations, habituating

---

[20] As we will see shortly, Kant advocated something close to this position in 1768.
[21] References to these works will be cited in-text as, respectively, NTV and TVV, with numbers corresponding with Berkeley's enumerated paragraphs. All citations from Berkeley 2000.

the mind to overlook its own contribution to our experience of the world. This was more so in the case of vision than in any of the other senses, for in that case 'by a settled habit', as Locke explained in his *Essay Concerning Human Understanding*, associations between 'things whereof we have frequent experience, is performed so constantly, and so quick, that we take that for the Perception of our Sensation which is an *Idea* formed by our Judgment; so that one, *viz.* that of Sensation, serves only to excite the other, and is scarce taken notice of itself'.[22] Locke interrupted the argument at this stage to quote from a letter sent to him by his friend William Molyneux. Molyneux's wife had lost her sight early in their marriage and his question for Locke turned on his claims regarding the associations made between vision and touch. Locke's rehearsal of the question in the second edition of the *Essay* would make what would come to be called 'Molyneux's problem' famous. The question, however, was relatively straightforward: if someone blind from birth had over the course of their life learned to distinguish a cube from a globe, would they, on being made to suddenly see, be able to correctly identify each by sight alone? Molyneux suggested that the answer was 'no' and Locke concurred (146).[23] In 1728 the English surgeon and anatomist William Cheselden successfully performed surgery to remove cataracts from a patient, restoring sight but also providing the world with an opportunity to test Molyneux's question. Although Cheselden's results on this matter were ultimately deemed inconclusive, they added important content to what would become a long history of discussion devoted to the topic.[24]

Locke had already died when Cheselden's historic feat occurred, but Berkeley included reference to it in his second work devoted to the issue, *The Theory of Vision Vindicated and Explained*. This made sense since the issue was in fact central to Berkeley's entire approach to the matter. I say 'central' because the starting insight was just this point already made by Locke in 1790, namely, that information received by the different senses was initially distinct and only later connected by means of mental processes. This point was of course not unique to Locke since many philosophers had by then understood the need to posit some kind of 'common sense' or other means for connecting discrete sensations, Descartes not least among them. But while many had made the point before, Berkeley's own approach offered an entirely different set of conclusions altogether.

Since the purpose here is for us to focus on the sense in which Berkeley seems to embrace embodied cognition in his discussion, I will simply state Berkeley's results for the sake of expediency. When Berkeley asked readers of the *New Theory of Vision* to consider the precise manner in which they came to visually estimate the distance, size and situation of things, he hoped to demonstrate that in each of these

---

[22] Locke 1975: 146–7.

[23] Molyneux's problem has been discussed by philosophers as much as by neuroscientists over the years. A recent interdisciplinary approach is taken by the philosopher Shaun Gallagher (2005: chapter 7) who uses neonate imitation studies to argue that Locke's response to Molyneux on this point is correct, though for the wrong reasons.

[24] The best place to start for this history, including its philosophical history, is Oliver Sacks's (1995: 108–52) absorbing account of the experiences had by a patient undergoing a similar procedure.

cases the estimation relied on a prior tactile experience. Locke had more or less believed this to be the case as well, but as a materialist Locke had also supposed an underlying reality to be grounding some kind of connection between tangible and visible ideas. For Locke, the smooth, round, red ideas of an apple referred the mind to the same one material object; a question might need to be raised regarding the accuracy of our sensible impressions perhaps, but not regarding their connection to a material world as their point of origin. For Berkeley, by contrast, there was no such material necessity holding between visible and tangible ideas. The manner in which the visible world referred, like a set of signs, to the tangible one was arbitrary, as arbitrary as any language was in reference to the meaning of its words. The constant association of tangible and visible ideas in experience had obscured this fact, leading us to falsely suppose that we could see distance or measure angles in space. This meant, for example, that tangible extension, not visible space, was the proper object of geometry (NTV, 151).[25] The purpose of visible images, as Berkeley understood it, was to function like a system of signs, a language composed of images instead of words, with the meaning of these image-words provided by the tactile world. In this vein the image or visible idea of an apple could be indexed over the course of experience to the tangible ideas of smooth and juicy. Learning to see, in other words, meant learning to associate a system of visual cues with their tangible meanings so that eventually visual ideas could work always to forewarn us of a tangible experience to come. Of course neither idea was to be counted as a more or less real idea than the other, but in the genetic order of experience, the means by which the signifiers could indeed function as such forewarnings depended on a prior history that began in the world of tactile experiences. As for the origin of these tangible ideas, the Bishop was clear: only an active intelligence could be the source. In Berkeley's words, 'God speaks to me by the intervention and use of arbitrary, outward, sensible signs, having no resemblance or necessary connexion [sic] with the things they stand for and suggest' (1950: 149). As for what this meant for the natural sciences, 'The scientist's task is to discover the laws of nature. These laws, however, do not pick out causes and their effects; they are, instead, the grammatical rules of the language in which God speaks to us for the sake of our well-being' (Winkler 2005: 140).

With the results of Berkeley's theory of vision before us, I want to take a closer look now at the precise means by which he explains our notions of distance, size and situation. For while it is easy for anyone who has spent time with an infant to believe in the primacy of touch for learning about the world, Berkeley's tack is in fact different. The first few paragraphs of the *New Theory of Vision* are meant to undermine support for the geometrical approach to optics as established by Descartes. This is done by showing the 'unsatisfactory' nature of a mathematical approach in general, given that it not only seems to belie everyday experience but

---

[25] A helpful account of Berkeley's approach to geometry is in Douglas Jesseph's *Berkeley's Philosophy of Mathematics* (1997: chapter 2).

indeed suggests that actual experience is dispensable.[26] According to the mathematical approach, 'men judge of distance by the angle of the optic axes, just as a
blind-man by the angle comprehended by two sticks, one whereof he held in each
hand. But if this were true, it would follow that one blind from his birth being made
to see, should stand in need of no new experience in order to perceive distance by
sight' (NTV, 42; TVV, 45).[27] Since this seems nonsensical, the question is how such
a counter-intuitive result might have been reached. This enquiry allows Berkeley
to postulate the heterogeneity of sight and touch, describing by one example after
another the manner in which meaning is supplied to every image by a prior history
of embodied experience.[28] We do not see distance, we remember the motion of our
body. This motion of the body, the movement of our head, the contraction of our
eye muscles, the sense of a changing terrain beneath our feet, these tangible ideas
literally form the landscape of meaning that will be later attached to the language
of visible signs (NTV, 45; TVV, 47). Of course, Berkeley does not suppose that distance can only be experienced when one has physically traversed it. Not only is the
mind capable of generalising from its tangible experience, the body itself provides
further modes of evidence (TVV, 51). 'First,' Berkeley explains,

> it is certain by experience that when we look at a near object with both eyes,
> according as it approaches or recedes from us, we alter the disposition of our
> eyes by lessening or widening the interval between the pupils. This disposition or
> turn of the eyes is attended with a sensation, which seems to me to be that which
> in this case brings the idea of greater or lesser distance into the mind. (NTV, 16)

Even as the pupil dilates we experience squinting as a different kind of felt response
to the 'confused appearance' of an object (NTV, 21). 'No man, I believe, will
pretend to see or feel those imaginary angles that the rays are supposed to form
according to the various inclinations of his eye,' Berkeley argues, but we can feel
ourselves struggling to see, and the tangible idea of squinting at something proves
'that instead of the greater or lesser divergency of the rays, the mind makes use
of the greater or lesser confusedness of the appearance, thereby to determine
the apparent place of an object' (NTV, 22). The question of magnitude or size is

---

[26] This would be central also to Diderot's 1749 'Letter on the blind for the use of those who see',
wherein the much celebrated optical mathematician Saunderson is both blind and rejecting of the
innate value of sight. As Diderot describes the attitude, 'I would just as soon have longer arms: it
seems to me my hands would tell me more of what goes on in the moon than your eyes or your
telescope' (1916: 77). Diderot discusses Berkeley's system in this work as well, complaining that 'to
the disgrace of the human mind and philosophy, it is the most difficult to combat, though also the
most absurd' (104–5).

[27] Here Berkeley is referring directly to Descartes's account in 1637 of the 'natural geometry' by
which a blind man holding two sticks discovers distance in the same manner that the eye observes
distance and position (1993).

[28] A contemporary discussion which is still helpful for understanding Berkeley on just this point is
found in Gallagher 2005.

treated in a similar manner, with Berkeley emphasising at all points the habitual overlooking of the body's tangible ideas as the basis for any visual estimation of extension.

For his discussion of situation, Berkeley returns to the case of the blind man. This allows him to consider the embodied meaning of situation without any of the usual distractions offered up by the language of vision. 'It is certain that a man actually blind, and who had continued so from his birth, would by the sense of feeling attain to have ideas of upper and lower,' Berkeley began.

> By the motion of his hand he might discern the situation of any tangible object placed within his reach. That part on which he felt himself supported, or towards which he perceived his body to gravitate, he would term lower, and the contrary to this upper. (NTV, 93)

> For a man born blind, and remaining in the same state, could mean nothing else by the words *higher* and *lower* than a greater or lesser distance from the earth; which distance he would measure by the motion or application of his hand or some other part of his body. (NTV, 94)

> Whence it plainly follows that such a one, if we suppose him made to see, would not at first sight think anything he saw was high or low, erect or inverted. (NTV, 95)

Exploiting the difference between touch and sight once more, Berkeley's argument for the proper understanding of directions in space appeals in every instance to the embodied cognition of subjects made to feel their way around the world. Notions of up and down, standing or flat, these ideas become meaningful only by touch: 'By the application of his hand to the several parts of a human body he had perceived different tangible ideas . . . thus one combination of a certain tangible figure, bulk, and consistency of parts is called the head, another the hand, a third the foot, and so of the rest' (NTV, 96). For the sighted, changes in perspective had to be indexed back to initial physical investigations of things, to the body's continuous experience of three-dimensionality, of its learned certainty that front sides will always have back sides (NTV, 97). Language aids us in this, Berkeley explains, by collecting ideas under a single name, and then experience teaches us to associate the named ideas of vision with the named ideas of touch (NTV, 49). At the end of this process, and without any special notice taken by us, Berkeley concludes, we are able to see an object and correctly identify it by name.[29]

Before turning finally to Kant's own use of embodied cognition for understand-

---

[29] In a scene described by Oliver Sacks, a newly sighted person is faced with a banana on a plate that has been placed next to a cut-out photograph of the banana on a plate. With the patient unable to decide which is the 'real' banana by sight alone, Sacks is reminded of William Cheselden's patient, who had reportedly asked, 'which was the lying sense, feeling or seeing?' (1995: 130).

ing location in space, it is worth noting the manner in which Berkeley's theory of vision seems to support an interpretation of his philosophy that is close to the empirical realism described by Kant. It is true that experience, for Kant, is constructed by the mind out of the raw material data taken up by the senses, and this is not the case for Berkeley. It is also true that whereas Kant posits an unknowable material basis for our sensations, Berkeley posits God as a benevolent and active Intelligence as the source for all of our ideas. But for all that, their results, their account of our experience of the world as appearance only, as real but only empirically so, and of experience as something that is there only 'for us', for humans with a set of cognitive conditions that must be met for us to find meaning in it: these results are as true for Berkeley as they are for Kant. And it is hard not to think that Kant grew to appreciate this, given that he felt forced to explain again and again why his results were so different from those of the Bishop of Cloyne.

Kant and the Embodied Geometry of Space

In this last piece of our discussion I want to focus on Kant's approach to the problem posed by 'incongruent counterparts'. Like mirror images of each other, these are objects which are identical in all ways apart from their spatial orientation and which thus require embodied experience in order for their difference in orientation to be grasped. Indeed, according to Kant, neither verbal nor mathematical descriptions could make sense of a mirrored reversal without it. Kant discussed incongruent counterparts in four places in his works: twice during the so-called Precritical years, first in an essay from 1768, 'Concerning the ultimate ground of the differentiation of directions in space', and then in the *Inaugural Dissertation* of 1770; then twice in the 1780s, in a passage just ahead of Kant's discussion of Berkeley in 1783's *Prolegomena* and then, for the last time, in Kant's delayed response to the fight over Lessing's alleged pantheism in the 1786 essay 'What does it mean to orient oneself in thinking?'. Kant's approach to the problem of incongruent counterparts has been long discussed in the scholarly literature, with some consensus that a break must be made between the 1768 essay and Kant's subsequent treatments in light of his later position on the transcendental ideality of space as a subjective form of intuition.[30] With Berkeley's arguments fresh in our mind, however, it can be seen that the issue cannot be resolved without embodied cognition, and that Kant came to understand this perfectly well. It can be seen as significant, in other words, that across the four discussions, the emphasis on embodiment remains constant, even as the account of space itself will change.

In the 1768 essay the task Kant set himself concerns the attempt to prove the

---

[30] A representative set of discussions can be found in *The Philosophy of Right and Left* (Van Cleve and Frederick 1991). Commentators focusing on the continuities across Kant's accounts include Jill Vance Buroker (1981), with attention to the Leibnizian strain in Kant's argument, and Angelica Nuzzo (2008). I discuss the issue in light of Kant's reading of Buffon's work to provide a physiological topology of left- and right-handedness in *Kant's Organicism* (Mensch 2013: 66–8).

reality of space apart from matter. Why? Because, he tells us, the geometers require this in order to make their science something more than a set of intuitive judgements about extension. This is interesting since it shows that Kant was already concerned that geometry might have a problematic status so long as the nature of space itself remained unsettled. As we saw in the first part of this discussion, Kant would eventually take geometric certainty and the ideality of space to be standing in a mutually supportive relation (A24–5). The ideality of space secured geometry as a non-arbitrary science even as the mathematical certainty of geometry demonstrated the positive epistemic contributions being made by intuition (B40–1; A87/B120). In Berkeley's account, by contrast, our ideas of space flowed directly from our tangible notions of distance and position, and geometry was accordingly a science whose meaning derived from tangible ideas as its proper objects of investigation. One of Kant's criticisms of Berkeley's account turned, as a result, on its inability to provide a certain framework for geometry, given what Kant took to be the lack of control over one's mental contents in Berkeley's system. The case of incongruent counterparts emerged as a different kind of problem altogether, one whose resolution required the embodied cognition of one's orientation in space. In 1768 Kant did not foresee this, however, since he had only introduced these objects into the discussion as part of his argument for the independent reality of absolute space. When Kant returned to the topic of incongruent counterparts in the 1780s, he continued to rely on embodied cognition for understanding them, a position that was if not at odds with his doctrine on the ideality of space then at least distinct from it, and indeed one that was close to Berkeley's own approach to geometry as a science based on our felt location in the world.

For our purposes we can reduce Kant's discussion in 1768 to two key steps. The first step entails a discussion of our sense of direction in space. Kant starts by asking his readers to visualise a person intersected by spatial planes. The planes transect the body into four distinct regions or quadrants such that the concept of sidedness – of left side and right side, of front and back side – can be meaningfully understood. Kant claims that it is only if space is conceived of as an independent reality that we can understand how a basic conceptual tool like sidedness ever arose for us. Without this concept, he argues, we would lose our native sense of the difference between right and left and orientation would be impossible. Kant lists examples of this, showing that the use of a compass can only be 'determined in relation to the sides of our body' (2: 379).

> Similarly, the most precise map of the heavens, if it did not, in addition to specifying the position of the stars relative to each other, also specify the direction by reference to the position of the chart relative to my hands, would not enable me, no matter how precisely I had it in mind, to infer from a known direction, for example, the north, on which side of the horizon I ought to expect the sun to rise.[31]

---

[31] 'Wenn ich auch noch so gut die Ordnung der Abtheilungen des Horizonts weiß, so kann ich doch

Insisting that all geographical and even ordinary knowledge of the position of places 'would be of no use to us unless we could also orientate the things thus ordered, along with the entire system of their reciprocal positions, by referring them to the sides of our body',[32] Kant moves from the embodied cognition of direction in space to the practical manner in which this cognition is functionally extended beyond the body with the use of compasses, star charts and other tools for understanding spatial position.[33] Kant's transition to the discussion of incongruent counterparts is made by way of an appeal to our native sense of the difference between left and right, a proprioceptive feeling so advantageous to us that Kant says it has been instilled in us by nature's establishment of 'an immediate connection between this feeling and the mechanical organization of the human body'.[34]

At this stage of the essay Kant was aware, perhaps, that he had not so far convincingly made a case for the independent reality of space. What he had done was demonstrate that our cognition of space relied on our being embodied, and that our use of tools for orienting our body in relation to others extended this cognition beyond the body and into the world. Kant thus effectively starts again at this point, reminding readers once more of the main task, and moving quickly to a discussion of incongruent counterparts. For this Kant describes screws that are identical in all respects apart from the direction of their threads, and winding helices that were equal apart from the direction of their turn. 'But the most common and clearest example', Kant tells us, 'is furnished by the limbs of the human body' (2: 381). Focusing on the fact that one's right hand could not be coincident with one's left hand, Kant takes this to be the pre-eminent example of our dependence on space for understanding the difference in orientation between them. We can, in other words, provide a lengthy linguistic or metrical account of any of these objects, but to comprehend the difference between one and its counterpart is to rely on a difference between their direction in space. This sense of situatedness, as Kant had just shown, is native to our body's experience in the world. But now Kant brings the two pieces of the argument together, arguing that all of this is ultimately made possible by the independent existence of space: 'differences, and true differences at

die Gegenden darnach nur bestimmen, indem ich mir bewußt bin, nach welcher Hand diese Ordnung fortlaufe, und die allergenaueste Himmelskarte, wenn außer der Lage der Sterne unter einander nicht noch durch die Stellung des Abrisses gegen meine Hände die Gegend determiniert würde, so genau wie ich sie auch in Gedanken hätte, würde mich doch nicht in den Stand setzen, aus einer bekannten Gegend, z. E. Norden, zu wissen, auf welcher Seite des Horizonts ich den Sonnenaufgang zu suchen hätte' (2: 379).

[32] 'Eben so ist es mit der geographischen, ja mit unserer gemeinsten Kenntniß der Lage der Örter bewandt, die uns zu nichts hilft, wenn wir die so geordnete Dinge und das ganze System der wechselseitigen Lagen nicht durch die Beziehung auf die Seiten unseres Körpers nach den Gegenden stellen können' (2: 379–80).

[33] Kant's discussion here can be meaningfully translated into current ones being had by philosophers like Andy Clark. See, for example, Clark's *Supersizing the Mind* (2008).

[34] 'Da das verschiedene Gefühl der rechten und linken Seite zum Urtheil der Gegenden von so großer Nothwendigkeit ist, so hat die Natur es zugleich an die mechanische Einrichtung des menschlichen Körpers geknüpft' (2: 380).

that can be found in the constitution of bodies,' he explains, but 'these differences relate exclusively to *absolute* and *original space*, for it is only in virtue of absolute and original space that the relation of physical things to each other is possible'.[35] Our embodied cognition of directions in space, a cognition of unquestioned worth and necessity, could only be made sense of, in other words, if space were outside us and real. Since no reasonable person could question the need to distinguish right from left, Kant reasons, the case for the reality of space has, by *reductio*, been made.[36]

Kant's reference to incongruent counterparts in the *Inaugural Dissertation* is brief, but what must be noted is that he has not changed the account in any significant sense. His examples of 'spherical triangles from two opposite hemispheres', and of right hands and left hands, are the same, as is the argument for the impossibility of describing the difference between them by any 'characteristic intellectual marks' (2: 403). What has changed is the account of space. Whereas before it was imperative for Kant to demonstrate that geometry was based on more than intuition, in 1770 (and from that point on, moreover) the proof was given on the basis of space as a form of human intuition. So too now for right- and left-handedness, with Kant declaring that such 'incongruity cannot be apprehended except by a certain pure intuition' (2: 403).

Kant would spend more time on the issue in the *Prolegomena*, opening his remarks with a rehearsal of the points raised in 1768 regarding the mirror-like quality of incongruent counterparts. The argument itself was a compressed account of the initial *reductio* with the important difference regarding the changed nature of space. As Kant put the matter, 'the difference between similar and equal things which are not congruent (for instance, helices winding in opposite ways) cannot be made intelligible by any concept, but only by the relation to the right and left hands, which immediately refers to intuition' (4: 286).[37] In this Kant gestures to the prior argument regarding our embodied cognition of direction in space as the basis for comprehending incongruence, but now the ultimate ground is asserted to be space as a form of intuition and as informing, therefore, all our experience of objects. When Kant took up the issue for the last time, in his 1786 essay on orientation in thinking, he warmed to the proper object of his discussion – a response to the so-called 'pantheism controversy' started by Jacobi's attack on Lessing – by way of describing the means by which we orient ourselves geographically. In these final

---

[35] '. . . in der Beschaffenheit der Körper Unterschiede angetroffen werden können und zwar wahre Unterschiede, die sich lediglich auf den absoluten und ursprünglichen Raum beziehen, weil nur durch ihn das Verhältniß körperlicher Dinge möglich ist' (2: 383).

[36] Note that Kant uses much the same strategy in his 'Refutation of Idealism' when arguing for the thesis that 'The mere, but empirically determined, consciousness of my own existence proves the existence of objects in space outside me' (B275).

[37] 'Wir können daher auch den Unterschied ähnlicher und gleicher, aber doch incongruenter Dinge (z.B. widersinnig gewundener Schnecken) durch keinen einzigen Begriff verständlich machen, sondern nur durch das Verhältniß zur rechten und linken Hand, welches unmittelbar auf Anschauung geht.'

remarks Kant focused once more on the body, observing again the specific feeling or proprioception by which nature had instilled in us a constant sense of the body's relative position and, as Kant emphasised, of the difference between right and left. Here Kant's discussion moved quickly past the test case posed by incongruence, to the critical role played by the body as the sole basis for orientation in space. Kant described this by way of a series of examples. We recognise the relative position of the sun to the horizon, for example, because we have a felt sense of our own body's movement in relation to objects. 'Even with all the objective data of the sky,' as he put it, 'I orient myself *geographically* only through a *subjective* ground of differentiation,' and thus even if the stars were to miraculously change their positions, we could still manage to reorient ourselves by falling back on our own body's sense of its position in space (8: 135). It is because of the body's native self-awareness that we are similarly able to find our way around a familiar but darkened room. For 'it is plain that nothing helps me here except the faculty for determining position according to a *subjective* ground of differentiation: for I do not see at all the objects whose place I am to find' (8: 135). And if, as in other cases, the positions of those objects had been somehow rearranged, it still would not matter since 'I can soon orient myself through the mere feeling of a difference between my two sides, the right and left'.[38]

What this long history reveals is the complicated nature of Kant's relationship to Berkeley. It is easy to focus on the differences between the two systems, to follow the narrative of Kant's angry rejection of any positive comparisons between them, but this would be to overlook too much of what they have in common. Each of them was centrally motivated by the rejection of materialism and each sought creative means by which to fashion an epistemic programme that could respond to the rich texture of sensible experience without thereby falling into the veil of illusion. Though they differed on the origin of our sensible ideas, each system focused on a description of the means by which our experience of the world was indubitably real.

Kant struggled to explain the difference between our experience of an empirically real space 'outside us' and the fact that all space was nonetheless 'inside us' given its status as an *a priori* form of intuition. But when it came to our embodied cognition of space, Kant was not only clear but in perfect agreement with Berkeley – just as, for Berkeley, we only know ourselves as we sensibly appear. Our representations of ourselves, of our body as much as of the mental contents of our mind, are neither more nor less than collections of ideas. But these representations, as each of these idealists would argue, constitute the entirety of what counts as

---

[38] 'Also orientire ich mich *geographisch* bei allen objectiven Datis am Himmel doch nur durch einen *subjectiven* Unterscheidungsgrund ... Im Finstern orientire ich mich in einem mir bekannten Zimmer, wenn ich nur einen einzigen Gegenstand, dessen Stelle ich im Gedächtniß habe, anfassen kann. Aber hier hilft mir offenbar nichts als das Bestimmungsvermögen der Lagen nach einem *subjectiven* Unterscheidungsgrunde: denn die Objecte, deren Stelle ich finden soll, sehe ich gar nicht ... So aber orientire ich mich bald durch das bloße Gefühl eines Unterschiedes meiner zwei Seiten, der rechten und der linken (8: 135).

reality for us. And so it is not a misnomer to insist on the central role played by embodiment, or a misunderstanding of idealism to provide a phenomenological account of the modes by which the body grounds the very possibility of orientation in space. On this point, I think, Kant and Berkeley would agree.

6

Is Laurence Sterne's Protagonist Tristram Shandy Embodied, Enacted or Extended?

George Rousseau

Cognitive scientist John Sutton has designated Laurence Sterne's *The Life and Opinions of Tristram Shandy* (1759–67) the eighteenth-century literary text *par excellence* for serving up an extended analysis of human cognition.[1] His rationale is that Sterne is meticulous in locating 'memory traces' in fleeting animal spirits and nervous fluids rummaging through the pores of brain and body. Only Diderot in those decades approximates such clarity, Sutton opines, in *Le Rêve d'Alembert*. Sterne's analysis may not be as fine-tuned as a twenty-first-century cognitive philosopher's analysis, but it matches any other text of the long eighteenth century, he believes, as a blueprint delineating the perils and pitfalls of cognition. Sutton particularly calls attention to Sterne's celebrated opening passage about the animal spirits and their parodic manner of challenging Locke's belief that the source of associated ideas is located in the physiological motion of these mysterious fluids (1998: 207). Sutton further extols Sterne for coming down hard on Locke: 'Sterne is even less sanguine than Locke about our chances of voluntarily putting the fleeting spirits anywhere' (207–8). *Tristram Shandy* indeed starts as a virtuosic attempt to deracinate Locke's claim that ideas in the brain are 'but Trains of Motions in the animal Spirits, which once set a going continue on in the same steps they have been used to, which by often treading are worn into a smooth path, and the Motion in it becomes easy and as if it were Natural' (Locke 1975: II, 33). This chapter builds on a century of literary criticism about *Tristram Shandy* and aims to extend exploration of the book's contexts beyond literary criticism. The chapter's main lesson is to explore the ways *Tristram Shandy* anticipated the four Es within a firmly historical approach and, furthermore, to demonstrate that Sterne's biographical fascination with Enlightenment science and medicine, especially its anatomy, biology, neurology and psychology, prefigured his ideas of the embodied mind. Most of all, the chapter's lesson attempts to pursue Sterne's intuitive cognitive impulses and address the question whether, and specifically how, his book is embodied, enacted

---

[1] See Sutton 1998: 207–13, the chapter entitled 'the scholar's fragile virility'; for the secondary sources Sutton has used for Sterne and cognition, see 208, n. 21. To Sutton's list should be added Sinding 2012 for the sensitive way genre figures in the discussion.

or extended. The main components of enactivism are not defined here because they have been developed earlier in this book, especially in the introductions. But the argument about autopoiesis is fully described, even if it unfolds at various stages of the chapter.[2]

Neurology and Consciousness

The book's opening paragraphs invoke biological language we would classify as neural or neuroscientific – nerves, spirits, fibres, animal spirits, neural pathways – and it soon becomes evident that neuroanatomy and neurophysiology occupy the main part of the protagonist's thoughts about his autobiographical origins. Tristram refers to his gestation as an 'homunculus' or 'little gentleman' – the human being in sperm – and tries to comprehend how an apparently normal homunculus was transformed into the aberrant Tristram.[3] He comments on his biological dysfunction as the key to his mental operations – errant animal spirits, damaged fibres and wanton nerves – and especially the sense that his consciousness developed by establishing awkward connections of contiguity, similarity, and cause and effect, a view enshrined in Enlightenment materialist theories of associationist philosophy (Israel 2010; Bourdin 1996; Yolton 1983). Yet his mother Elizabeth cannot have conjugal sex with her husband Walter without thinking of him 'winding up the clock', which Mr Shandy does on the first Sunday night of every month. As a result Mrs Shandy is habituated to link intercourse with time, and the *idée fixe* mars her foetus with an aborted sense of time according to eighteenth-century biological theory.[4]

As the opening two volumes evolve, Tristram foregrounds his subjective plight in terms (ranked in order of perceived importance in relation to himself) of: neurophysiological dysfunction; distorted sense of time; wayward cognition (especially the relation of body and mind); inability to concentrate and keep his attention focused on one topic; his idiosyncratic selfhood and troubled subjectivity. I have already commented on the first but let us consider the second: how can Tristram have become so confused about time? Repeatedly he asks himself why his parents were so egregiously negligent at the moment of his conception to permit this defect. But he cannot concentrate on the dilemma and wanders off to the connections between his mind and body. He keeps asking himself who he is. More excruciating for him, he questions how he knows what he knows, another tangent sprung from the quandary about time. Sterne's reading was vast (Sterne 1930; Hawley 1990), but not even its reconstruction has addressed the questions most vexatious

---

[2] The author wishes to thank the Centre for the History of Childhood at Oxford University for presenting versions of this chapter in its programmes during 2008–9 devoted to child psychology and adolescent cognition.

[3] We will see later on how Sterne anticipates the philosophical zombies so controversial in our era.

[4] See Stephanson and Wagner 2015 for the prevalence of this view throughout Europe during Sterne's adulthood. Numerous contemporary literary critics opine this opening to be the clue to Sterne's whole book, as does cognitive critic Lisa Zunshine (2010: 281–2).

to Tristram, who also speculates whether he is *au fond* some type of mutant neuro-biological configuration. If only he can answer these questions he opines that his failures might become intelligible to him and – more pressingly – to his developing sense of his identity. At forty-one (his age when the narrative opens) he has no idea where he is heading, nor how he arrived here. His perception of time is muddled. His psychological unease stems from his sense that because his perception of linear time is so unpredictable he has not evolved into a 'normal' human being, despite never using this word. He embraces little, if any, sense of (what we would call) entropic time: the notion that as entropy increases and potentially decays, disorder arises. Indeed, he cannot connect his development to his mutant sense of time. Tristram's maker Sterne tells the reader that all nine volumes have evolved in just one day, that is one day inside Tristram's head, but disoriented Tristram thinks it has taken him one year to write out the forty-one years of his lifetime extending over nine volumes, so mentally distorted is his temporal awareness and so charged the role of time in this narrative.[5]

Who then is Tristram Shandy, however genial and confused he may be, and what did Sterne think he was doing by inventing him? If we aim to answer the question by applying historical categories of Enlightenment explanation, Tristram is a mutant neurological monster (Landa 1963; Rousseau 2004: 255–9, 284–90). Sterne himself explains how Tristram's 'convulsive birth' (he is literally 'black in the face' when first born), with the baby's head emerging first, led to possible brain damage and a clipped nose.[6] However, biological beliefs linking the mother's imagination and its imprint on her foetus were not jettisoned until the nineteenth century, long after Sterne's death. Yet a different figure emerges if Tristram is explained in today's terms: someone who suffered brain damage during birth that has altered the plasticity and size of his human cortex, whose transformations take a toll on his cognitive and metacognitive system. The latter system can account for Tristram's penchant for incessant storytelling, especially as this form of self-reflection impinges on his sense of memory, time and his inability to extract meaning from his past. Other possibilities also exist: for example, the notion that Tristram is some type of zombie; not in our loose parlance as a freak or weirdo, but a living creature who duplicates another creature whose consciousness strays from the ordinary (Kirk 2005). Specifically, this is the so-called philosophical zombie who demonstrates outward behaviour similar to that of a normal human being but does not have his own subjective phenomenology. Here lies the caveat of recent philosophers who hold that a necessary condition for the possibility of philosophical zombies is that there should be no specific part, or parts, of the

[5] Dozens of articles have been written about the time scheme of this book and it would be pedantic to attempt to list even a few; the salient point is Tristram's disordered cognition in relation to time and his certainty that its origins are neurophysiological.

[6] The point of the hapless Tristram's birth is that the errant Dr Slop has got his instrument backwards and pulls out the head first using forceps, which, in turn, renders possible a damaged brain and crushed nose.

brain that directly gives rise to what it feels like to be inside the consciousness of the original creature. Hence the zombie can only exist if subjective consciousness is causally separate from physical brains. While arguing against the possibility of philosophical duplicates (i.e. physical duplicates of people), philosopher Robert Kirk has described this 'zombie difference' in terms so proximate to Sterne's concerns that one wonders whether he had *Tristram Shandy* in mind when historicising the zombie:

> Locke asserted that 'Consciousness is the perception of what passes in a Man's own Mind' (*Essay concerning Human Understanding* II. i. 19). Without further explanation, this suggestion conjures up the deceptive picture of a homunculus facing a procession of mental phenomena: the Cartesian Theatre. . . . It puts the original problem one step back. The problem is that we are faced with the world, and we want to explain how we can have perceptual experience of it. We are told that instead of perceiving the world perfectly, we (or if not we, then some component of ourselves) perceive a representation of the world. (2005: 30–2)

The zombie type, for Kirk, is one whose 'representations of the world' are inherently imperfect. He remains dubious that zombies exist (for reasons we cannot explore here) and presents the most extended exploration of what that type could be if it were to exist. Even so, Kirk taps into many of the same dilemmas the biographical Sterne struggled with in the eighteenth century to construct the philosophical content of his book, especially Locke's *Essay on Human Understanding* vis-à-vis consciousness, the inadequacy of Locke's reply to Cartesian mechanism, the biology of the homunculus in its progression toward becoming human, and, finally, representations of the world in the minds of ordinary human beings. Kirk concedes the complexity of all four matters and notices how much less fraught the 'purely materialist view of consciousness' is rather than the 'zombie view' (2005: 31), and he endorses philosopher David Armstrong's historical approach to these matters (1993: 326). But a primarily historical approach will not resolve them (Rousseau 1990; Wright and Potter 2000), as Tristram's eternal dilemma pertains to representations of the world, not the world itself. This is a thorny point requiring significant unpacking if we are to comprehend how Sterne was anticipating concerns of embodiment and extendedness.[7] Tristram cannot understand why his experience of the representations is so stressed: their prolific number, sequential flow, and the inexplicable way the representations give rise to his images of an external reality beyond himself. Armstrong's materialist explanation of mind, one of many recent accounts, can appear applicable to the historical world Sterne inhabited. Nevertheless, however historically useful Armstrong's approach is, it proves of limited utility if pursued at length, nor can Sterne have known, of course, about Armstrong's account of mind. Any number of other modern historical-

---

[7] It is worth noting that some thinkers do not consider embodiment, enactivism and extendedness to be mutually exclusive; see, for example, the discussion in Wheeler and Di Paolo 2011.

philosophical approaches to mind could be pursued in addition to Armstrong's. The point is that all return us to Tristram's original dilemma: namely, how he has arrived at such a pathetic (or comic, if the spectator wishes to ridicule it) point after forty-one years of deciphering representations of the world.

Tristram's Cognitive Universe

Literary criticism of *Tristram Shandy* has shown interest in these matters but not along the cognitive lines of autopoiesis, embodiment, enactivism or – more generally – Tristram's cognitive universe. Not even Tristram's biological terror – his enduring fear that his 'animal spirits' were brutally compromised at birth – has been glossed beyond the milieu of mid-eighteenth-century theories of generation and related philosophical debates about epigenesis and preformationism (Roger and Benson 1997; Finucci and Brownlee 2001; Stephanson and Wagner 2015). Only one commentator, James E. Swearingen, seized upon Tristram's 'phenomenological dilemma' in a full-length book: *Reflexivity in Tristram Shandy: An Essay in Phenomenological Criticism.*[8] Swearingen was struck during the 1970s by the light hermeneutics and phenomenology shed on literary criticism, yet the world of Maturana and Varela, who were then generating biological theories culminating in their influential 1980–1 statement about autopoiesis, was closed to him. Now, a generation later, some of the philosophical riddles of autopoiesis have been clarified, if not resolved, and its outgrowths in enactivism, embodiment and distributed cognition are topics of primary concern in the history of cognition. Put otherwise, if the troubled Tristram could have known about these categories of cognition during the 1760s he, like his maker Sterne, would have attentively listened. Or would he? Tristram often cannot listen attentively to any ratiocination without distorting what he hears.

The fact of literary history is that Sterne's canonical masterpiece has no fictional rival in the long eighteenth century for engaging with contemporary concerns of autopoiesis, enactivism and embodied mind. And if the biographical Sterne were alive today, by all accounts he would be intrigued by the disagreements these concepts have instaurated since Maturana and Varela and, more recently, Milan Zeleny, Evan Thompson, Andy Clark and Michael Wheeler.[9]

---

[8] Swearingen was influenced by Heidegger, Bachelard, Merleau-Ponty and Poulet. Jean H. Hagstrum's (1987) study of the word 'conscious' in eighteenth-century English literature includes Sterne and asserts he was immensely invested in cognitive matters. Tristram, for his part, routinely refers to his mental insides as part of his 'conscience': 'I think in my conscience' (I, lii) or, as he addresses his readers, 'as your good consciences think' (II, xiii).

[9] See Maturana and Varela 1980 and especially the first four chapters within Zeleny 1981: 1 [Zeleny], 2 [Maturana], 3 [Varela] and 4 [Uribe]. Uribe shrewdly comments on randomness of experience as the basis for Tristram's type of confusion. Furthermore, it is not at all ancillary to cite polymath Kenneth Boulding's comments about the historical status of autopoiesis in Sterne's intellectual milieu featured in his splendid introduction (Zeleny 1981: xii): 'I would certainly argue as an economist that Adam Smith in *The Wealth of Nations* [1776] discovered the concept of

For years before composing *Tristram Shandy* Sterne immersed himself in the eighteenth-century equivalents of modern neuroscience. He gathered more information about these matters into his head than his library catalogue reveals, as the text of *Tristram Shandy* demonstrates. He read voraciously about consciousness and cognition in the works of contemporary philosophers, theologians, doctors and scientists, while remaining vigilant in the literary construction of his magnum opus to distance himself from his idiosyncratic protagonist (Sterne 1978–84: I, 167–8). Moreover, he worked hard to legitimate his book as transcending the genre of autobiographical memoir camouflaged as fiction. And he launched his 'cock-n-bull story' as a massive polemic against *Locke's Essay Concerning Human Understanding*, because he viewed as flawed its mono-dimensional notion of cognition based on mechanistic neuroanatomical processes. Locke believed mind at birth is a blank slate – *tabula rasa* – that filled up with sense impressions mechanically associated into higher ideas. The mechanistic portion of the process Locke derived from post-Cartesian physiology, especially from Thomas Willis's brain theory, and iatromedicine. It amounted to the view that the impressions of all five senses are conducted by the animal spirits in neural pathways to the brain, where they are 'associated' into ideas before being sent back down those neural pathways (Rousseau 2004: 159–78). Locke's more abstract view was that mind is essentially consciousness, and 'consciousness alone maketh self' (Locke 1975: II, 35, referring to *Essay* II, 27, heading 23–5). But Sterne opined that his sequence of mind, consciousness, self was far too simplistic and mechanical to be credible. More recently in literary criticism several books followed John Traugott's study of Sterne's distrust of Locke's materialism (1954), most demonstrating Sterne's ambivalence, if not outright hostility, to Locke's mechanistic epistemology of cognition.

Sterne also explicates how Tristram, in contrast to any Lockean associationist puppet, was in no position to contest these distinctions, so confused is he. To the contrary, from the first sentence of Sterne's book Tristram maintains (to the degree Tristram can intelligibly iterate any idea without distorting its internal logic and then digressing from it) that his life has been wrecked by his biological origins; by the anatomic nerves and fibres he has inherited; by his parents' sperm and egg and the animal and vital spirits they gave rise to in Tristram's body; and by the particular brain and neurological pathways they passed on to him – all of which have conspired to forge the neuroanatomical-physiobiological anomaly he is. No other fiction written in English between 1700 and 1820 so vigorously taps into these concerns with such erudition and wit.

autopoiesis in the "invisible hand." This is the concept of the development of social order through the unplanned interactions of large numbers of individuals, each seeking their own gain through production and exchange, coordinated through the development of the system of relative prices. This is a considerable conceptual advance beyond the rather one-dimensional mechanics of Newton. I would even credit Adam Smith with having perceived the evolutionary significance of positive feedback [in Maturana's sense] in expanding "hypercycles" . . . It has taken two hundred and fifty years to perceive the extraordinary general implications for science of Adam Smith's insights.' Adam Smith and Laurence Sterne wrote their books within a decade of each other.

Sterne's famed opening vivifying this biological tour de force has been widely praised for its rhetorical bravura, learned wit and ingenious leap in which Tristram obsesses on his parents, Elizabeth and Walter, and their coitus inter- ruptus. The prevailing biological theory in Sterne's era was that any distraction of the mother's mental state at the moment of coition would be imprinted on the foetus's psyche, but the mechanics of the process were not explained other than in crude mechanical terms (see Landa 1963 for the biological details). Walter has been interrupted by his wife's disruptive question ('have you wound up the clock?'), which distracts his mind and enervates his animal and other vital spirits. Elizabeth pops the question at the very moment of coition, and her infelicitous interrogation devastatingly interrupts the flow of Walter's sperm. To her ill-timed inquiry Tristram attributes all his subsequent cognitive ills, especially his deficient sense of time. Yet the most advanced embryological theory of the 1760s confirms Tristram's terror despite Sterne's ridicule of it: the idea that the specific site of the mother's imagination imprints itself at the moment of coition on the developing homunculus.

Sterne's gargantuan pastiche is so permeated with Renaissance and Enlightenment biological content – mechanistic, vitalistic, holistic, atomistic, espe- cially in relation to reproductive preformationism, epigenesis and morphology, all the embryological debates about these topics raging during his adulthood – that biologists Maturana and Varela would have been delightfully piqued by Sterne's diabolical riddles if they could have read his book. But proof is beside the point when a great imaginative novelist's intuition is the issue. Modern biologists such as Maturana and Varela would have recognised how Sterne's text playfully anticipates neurocognitive questions: what are the springs of life? What is the unconscious? What is consciousness? How does one know what one knows? Although Tristram claims not to understand classical mechanics, not even 'to comprehend the princi- ples of motion of a squirrel cage' (Sterne 1978–84: II, 626), his maker Sterne taps into these topics in a chapter entitled 'Vexations' with an Enlightenment scientist's neurocognitive savvy, proffering them as fragments of random and self-organised structural plotting. If the genre of Sterne's book is doubtlessly a prose fiction, as well as metafiction (in the sense that the narrative never loses sight of the fact that it parodies other fictions), it is also autopoietic to the degree that its self-regulations appear more arbitrary than in any other canonical text of the long eighteenth cen- tury. This view of Sterne's literary genre suggests that arbitrariness of boundaries is a feature of autopoiesis. The opposite would seem to be the case in standard autopoietic philosophical thought and modern systems theory. Sterne's narrative inverts the dependability of autopoietic borders, especially as they pertain to his protagonist, but also in respect of genre development. Tristram's biographical rituals and psychological patterns of mind are no more capable of containment than the prose form of Sterne's book (however it may seem to emanate from the tradition of Renaissance prose satire). Competing books are descendants of Robert Burton's *Anatomy of Melancholy* (1621) and Rabelais's sprawling prose satires, yet one is hard pressed to name another prose satire of the early modern period with such a well-defined cognitive agenda. In part this can occur because *Tristram Shandy* has been constructed as an integral (autopoietic) system, with characters, plot, setting and time scheme integrated into an indivisible organic form.

Literary works, even early modern works, often form integrated systems. What is special about Sterne's case in *Tristram Shandy* is (1) that the integrated system (characters to organic prose form) has been constructed so effortlessly, and (2) that the author has made the work's cognitive concerns palpable. The latter do not merely rouse readers from page one – Tristram trying to figure out how his cognitive apparatus has stemmed from dysfunctional neural anatomy; these cognitive explorations also touch on embodiment, enactivism and extendedness to a degree that the biographical Sterne, uncannily, seems to have anticipated the concerns of recent distributed cognition.

Mind, Memory and Contingency

Tristram's 'story' is intelligible provided we configure it *apart from* himself as an unreliable narrator, unreliable because his self-regulating cognitive apparatus is dysfunctional. At forty-one when the narrative opens in 1759, he is unmarried, has no living relations, no girlfriend or boyfriend, still lives in Shandy Hall, Yorkshire, where he was born on 5 March 1718, and where he has been sequestered in a room writing out his 'life and opinions' in fragments and digressions because linear time has no place in his mental universe. He jolts ahead into *present* time (to 1762) in volumes 7 to 9 after Death appears to him in the form of tuberculosis (consumption). Standard medical theory of Sterne's era confirms the common cognitive lapse of consumptives but rarely comments on contrasting flickers of insight and impaired memory (Morton 1720: 26–9). Terrified, Tristram flees to France, where he encounters the peasant girl Maria, driven out of her senses by forbidden marriage. On the book's last page Tristram reappears disjointedly in France, time having digressed backward and progressed forward again to 1762, when he encounters Maria once more, and asks her whether she perceives any resemblances between himself and her favourite goat. The male goat's symbolic virility would not have escaped Sterne's readers; if Tristram resembles her favourite goat she might look genially upon him. It is as if Tristram's identification with the goat uncannily suggests his selfhood extends to *include* the goat, which amounts to an outright nonsense.

Oddly, the bewildering question about the goat also embeds the only memory Tristram has of himself as continuous over the years before volume 9 closes. Indeed, he has never construed himself as a single continuous self, and goats, like bulls, are complex animals, distributed in Tristram's almost anticipated Malafourian sense where cognition outside Tristram's head is as plausible as inside (Malafouris and Renfrew 2010, 2013; Shanahan 2010). Furthermore, Tristram does not classify patterns within his memory: what he knows is that his neuroanatomy is damaged, and if such bodily defect can seem to explain his recollective system he will succumb to the temptation – so porous is his sense of psychological borders. The goat question's tone, nuance and context further justify the modern reader's bewilderment at his cognitive confusion (whether induced neurologically, psychologically or some combination of these factors). And Tristram's question, placed at such a crucial point at the very end of the long narrative, also imposes hurdles about the phenomenological limits of Tristram's understanding. Adequate contexts for the book *Tristram Shandy*, more generally, are problematic because it is so tempting to conflate Sterne and Tristram, which I continue to resist. Yet Sterneans often concede that these contexts are exacerbated by Tristram's unreliable memory, which he seeks to retrieve in all nine volumes despite its stranglehold over him. And it also highlights Sterne's disgust with the era's prevailing notion, as Sutton noted, that memory is specifically formed, and then activated, in the fluid medium of the animal spirits (Sutton 1998: 213).

No matter how the conflation of author and protagonist is left, Tristram digresses yet again in the most extraordinary way before the book actually closes, this time speculating about the Widow Wadman's ulterior motive for pestering Uncle Toby about the wound in his groin; on this note, and his further comment that the Shandy bull is impotent, volume nine ends. But it is not to be missed that the ox and goat are further connected – as male animals, erotically, reproductively – and their yoking overlooks the far less far-fetched connection that Tristram's 'life and opinions' are – as our narrator will iterate in just a few lines – a 'cock-n-bull' story: hence the *double entendre* between narrative and protagonist's cognition as more noteworthy than any lascivious innuendos. No potted summary, of course, can do justice to a nine-volume narrative as dense as *Tristram Shandy*, yet it needs to be observed how many of Tristram's lapses stem from his defective sense of time. He distorts, mangles and butchers temporality as the result of cognitive impairment from the moment of birth. Ultimately, however, only Sterne's rhetorical bravura enables the attentive reader to come into such exquisite touch with Tristram's neuroanatomically driven cognitive defect. But we also need to understand why Maturana and Varela would have added autopoietic lapse to these cognitive lapses.

More consequentially for Sterne's intentions in adjudicating whether his sense of Tristram's confusions can be diagnosed from an autopoietic or enactive perspective, Tristram's impairment yokes life and mind. Not mind and *body*, because Tristram functions as if he were a committed monist regarding the mind-body cupola; but life and mind, or a type of Cartesian-based cognition and mind, because Tristram has persuaded himself that 'life' is prior to mind, this especially in light of the catastrophe Mrs Shandy has wreaked by her abortive question during coitus interruptus. Tristram, furthermore, like his maker Sterne, is committed to an anti-Lockean stance; the Locke who was a dualist despite whole patches of his writings making gestures in the direction of philosophical monism. Even Hume, about whose ideas Sterne appears to have known little or nothing,[10] remained a dualist despite the compatibility of many of his ideas about mind with unequivocal physicalism. Sterne-as-thinker harboured deep-seated caveats about mind-body

[10] Nuttall (1974: 45) contends that 'Hume passed Sterne by altogether'.

dualism and, as Nuttall suggests, was more comfortable with David Hartley's associationism than Hume's scepticism (Nuttall 1974: 49).

The lifelong tyranny of Tristram's biological defect is his overarching *cri de coeur*,
but it is a psychological angst that does not explain how the impairment enacts his
movements from moment to moment, or accounts for his troubled relation to his
environment at Shandy Hall. He cannot even explain how he came to be Walter's
biological son. He wonders how such a proto-rationalist as Walter could have
engendered a boy so confused as he is. Only Sterne's biting parody permits the
reader to understand how Walter himself was a hostage to fragmented memory.
He became a trapped pedantic martyr when his own animal spirits were dispersed and scattered at the moment of the ill-fated Tristram's conception. Walter's
Lamentation captures his profound tragic sense: 'the few animal spirits I [Walter]
was worth in the world, and with which memory, fancy, and quick parts should
have been convey'd, – were all dispersed, confused, and confounded, scattered and
sent to the devil' (Sterne 1978–84: I, 354). Such passages form the clearest parody
to be found in the century of the animal spirits as the vehicle of embodied memory.

Nor can Tristram elucidate his extremely recessive mother (in nine volumes
Elizabeth Shandy appears briefly only four times). Nor clarify why, at forty-one, he
is so obsessed with the Shandean pedigree (the ghost-like ancestors whose presence
lingers in the Shandy parlour), especially the impossibility of reproducing himself as the consequence of impotence caused by damaged genitals when the sash
window fell on them (few goats could ever have been damaged in such a way). Nor
expound his selective memory: the mangled threads of his narrative have been told
to him rather than recalled as lived experiences. What he knows is that his memory
differs from that of other Shandy family members – not friends, because Tristram
has no friends.

Tristram also idiosyncratically grapples with chance and random contingency.
He cannot understand why events have evolved as they have, yet he does not sus-
pect time – whether linear or of some other variety – to be complicit as a culprit.
The modern reader wonders how all these (often comic) confusions can have produced a functioning, breathing, organic system – Tristram – composed of defective
biological genes, a modicum of solipsistic fear that the external world might not
exist, and a distributed cognitive system struggling to get outside his own head.
Tristram's introspection is not the supreme impediment despite appearing so to
him on numerous occasions.[11] The last category involving his cognitive system,
whether distributed or not, is more troubling than the other two, although it is far
from clear to what degree Tristram sees matters this way. That is, Tristram's intro-
spective awareness revolves around his deep-seated notion that it is intracranial,
entirely within his skull; that he, Tristram, ceases to exist at the boundaries of his
anatomical skin. Yet if this is so, it ought to have occurred to him long before his
forty-first year that his cognition is not – in any sense considered today by philosophers and neuroscientists – distributed. It must be the opposite: undistributed.

[11] For insights into historical introspection and its dilemmas see Butler 2013.

However Tristram may wish to believe he interacts with a world beyond Shandy Hall, the logical consequence of his mindset is that he cannot because he does not possess a distributed system. His competing cognitive belief – that he can figure out who he is if he 'writes himself out' – is, alternatively, distinctly distributed. He functions as a storytelling system extending himself into the beyond, as in his frequent outreaching to unknown 'good sirs' and 'good madams'. Yet his 'writing himself out' embeds the very essence of philosophical distributed cognition in ways adumbrated by the authors of this book.

And yet, whether or not distributed, and in which specific aspects of Tristram's complex introspection, the system Sterne created in the living organism 'Tristram' was not induced by Hume's philosophy. And Nuttall, already mentioned, has begun to explain why:

> If we compare the view of the mind offered in *Tristram Shandy* with that bequeathed to us by Hume, we may well feel that it is Sterne's account which is friendlier to the great intellectual enterprise of the seventeenth century . . . Hume would have proved intellectually paralyzing to Sterne. (Nuttall 1974: 60, 72)

Centuries later, Nuttall has a point, and further textual inspection reveals why Tristram cannot distinguish the boundaries of his Shandean self in relation to the other Shandys. He knows that his difference from other persons – his 'troubles', as he terms them – arises from the interaction of four seemingly hardwired facts of his life: (1) disturbed genes, (2) mutilated body, (3) errant memory and (4) disordered time sense.

Tristram assumes his pathography ('writing himself out' of his confusion) will assuage his systemic – that is to say cognitive – difference: 'I am aware, that I have begun the history of myself in the way I have done; and that I am able to go on tracing every thing in it, as *Horace* says, *ab Ovo*, and shall never finish' (Sterne 1978–84: I, 5). That is, Tristram suggests a tautology between his cognition and sense of self as a system in just the way some enactivist accounts do. His foreknowledge is proof and a compelling reason to doubt the last page as the end of Tristram's narrative or Sterne's book. Tristram harbours some Procrustean sense he is a storytelling system – one without end so long as the system remains alive – but maintains no notion of his oblique picture of things nor where his cognition lies: whether inside his head, distributed within the Shandy household, in Coxwold, Yorkshire, England, or further afield in the wide world. Unable to understand his cognitive processes, Tristram compulsively recalls, recounts, retells, but has little, if any, notion of the nature of his mind's propensities vis-à-vis his preferences for mutation-and-selection and a strictly representational/computational picture of things. He senses that reality is otherwise, but he cannot fathom how to access it. Among literary critics only Swearingen, already cited, wrote without any intuition of these matters but he had no access to Maturana's theories and autopoiesis, or to systems theory as it was developing in the late 1970s (see the many books by Heinz von Foerster, Gregory Bateson and Ilya Prigogine). Swearingen would also have profited from knowledge of Zahavi's 'phenomenological we', which explores 'self/other' along phenomenological lines (Zahavi 2014). And it is precisely this nexus – Tristram's picture of things in relation to his mind's propensities – which renders him such a stunning fictional and Enlightenment nonpareil, the embodiment of the concerns of historical cognition.

Tristram's vexations offer further clues, as offshoots of his anxieties and having been generated by his defective genes, sense of time, and perception of body-mind borders with other persons. They perturb him because he intuitively recognises how solipsistically locked within narratives he is. Considered in perspective, are these concerns not proximate to Maturana and Varela's (1980: 76) 'perturbations' in living systems? The perturbations in Sterne's narrative number in the dozens and form a large part of the narrator's self-disclosure. They especially include Tristram's parents' weird marriage contract and Walter's embodiment of Locke's philosophical ratiocination:

> My father, who had an itch, in common with all philosophers, of reasoning upon every thing which happened, and accounting for it too – proposed infinite pleasure to himself in this, of the succession of ideas, and had not the least apprehension of having it snatch'd out of his hands by my uncle Toby, who (honest man!) generally took every thing as it happened; – and who, of all things in the world, troubled his brain the least with abstruse thinking; – the ideas of time and space – or how we came by those ideas – or of what stuff they were made – or whether they were born with us – or we picked them up afterwards as we went along – or whether we did it in frocks – or not till we had got into breeches – with a thousand other inquiries and disputes about Infinity, Prescience, Liberty, Necessity, and so forth, upon whose desperate and unconquerable theories so many fine heads have been turned and cracked. (Sterne 1978–84: I, 175–6)

Walter mistrusts the subrational mind, and while Tristram has tried to emulate his father for forty-one years, he cannot: he is more Sternean in his zest for sentiment however damaged his mental apparatus may be. He writes pages overturning his father's arid syllogisms that have isolated him from his fellow men. He ridicules Walter's obsessive compulsions and theory of breech births (crushing the infant's soul in parturition); his 'Tristrapaedia', or treatise on the education of his son, causing further perturbations to Tristram's memory because Walter could not write it as quickly as Tristram grew up; Walter's belief that the secret of life lies in the auxiliary verbs; his risible, even hilarious, Germanic 'Beds of Justice' (as Walter has named them) in which every controversy is debated twice, once sober and once drunk, to ensure authenticity; Walter's inflicting ultimate doubt on Tristram whether Uncle Toby knew he was in love with the Widow Wadman at the moment the blister broke in his genital region, and other similarly embodied mockeries. Nonsense and sentiment inform these perturbations in Tristram's breast, but their cupola does not reduce Tristram's disgust for the degree of his father's endless Lockean onslaughts. Sterne's sense of organic form requires that no part of the

'Shandean system' can be altered without repercussions for every other part, as in modern systems theory. His notion reflected a crucial component of the mid-Georgian theory of medical sympathy (see Csengei 2011). One consequence for the larger autopoietic environment of *Tristram Shandy* is that all Tristram's cognitive confusions impact on others, as well as alter the temperature, as it were, of his constant perturbations (see Rousseau 1972 for the implications here of organic form).

Autopoietic, Enactive and Embodied Confusions

To perceive the effect of Walter's incursions we need to decide whether Tristram's confusions are best understood from autopoietic, enactive or embodied perspectives, particularly if we can determine whether Tristram's predicament arises from a particular type of aberrant cognition. That is, not merely to make sufficiently rigorous analyses of Sterne's text, which anticipates twenty-first-century cognitive theory, but also to shed light on Tristram's mid-eighteenth-century disorientation. The clarity brought to these cognitive approaches by Michael Wheeler's epitome of the alternatives helps (2010b: 33–6). Wheeler commences with an analysis of the potter at her wheel: the idea that 'we should replace our view of cognition as residing inside the potter's head, with that of cognition as spatially distributed over brain, body, and world' (2010b: 34). Yet Malafouris believes 'cognition is *enacted* at the potter's wheel' (2004: 59) rather than being spatially distributed there. Uncle Toby's maps, fortifications and hobby horses endorse the latter view. Uncle Toby knows himself through his maps, carries his fortifications in his mind night and day, comes to life when his finger alights on a particular city where he remembers the siege to have occurred. A further example might be the concert pianist's cognition distributed over brain, body and world versus enacted at the intersection where fingertip meets ivory keyboard. For the fictional figure Tristram Shandy these theories suggest – by analogy – the convergence of Tristram's memory of his past with selective aspects of a present he can neither recognise nor name.[12] This solution, however, is unsatisfactory for reasons Wheeler explains: '*cognition enacted cannot be cognition extended*' and he clarifies why: 'the theory of autopoiesis . . . is a non-negotiable component of enactivism' (2010b: 34).

Tristram is incapable of the distinction, of course, but sufficiently intuitive to sense the chasm between '*enacted* and *extended*'. In this entangled gorge even our experts tread lightly. Wheeler thinks 'this [non-negotiability] might come as a surprise to some fans of the enactivist "bible" *The Embodied Mind* [Varela et al. 1991] since that text doesn't foreground autopoiesis as a term' and, more pressingly, even though Evan Thompson's *Mind in Life* considers autopoiesis a keystone of the enactivist position (Wheeler 2005, 2010b: 34). These necessary distinctions are

---

[12] The goal is not to medicalise Tristram's situation but to explain it in the light of contemporary cognitive theory capable of shedding further light on Sterne's book. Put otherwise, there is no attempt here to situate Tristram as some type of demented figure suffering at forty-one from an early-onset Alzheimer's condition.

placed in the face of incommensurability, even existing 'triple E contradictions' enduring among doyens of cognitive distribution. Yet how do these caveats help those of us more historically invested to determine whether Tristram is embodied or extended? Wheeler further explains: 'cognition enacted *cannot* be cognition extended' (2010b: 34), and, as Maturana claimed four decades ago, 'living systems are cognitive systems, and living as a process is a process of cognition'.[13] The logical sequence would seem to be this: Tristram lives, Tristram thinks, Tristram is a cognitive system; his living *is* his cognition, all the more so as Tristram does nothing except cogitate on the past. But what about the equally crucial logical incommensurability Wheeler has identified, namely that 'cognition enacted *cannot* be cognition extended'? Is Tristram enacted or extended? Wheeler masterfully cuts to the quick by demonstrating how we must penetrate to the 'enactivist's core commitment' if we hope to understand how enactivism and embodiment *differ*. According to Wheeler, 'the bad news' for the uninitiated (and perhaps the initiated too?) is that they must clear their heads about autopoiesis; and getting autopoiesis right entails understanding how autopoietic systems – manifested even in literary figures such as Tristram Shandy – must, as Wheeler indicates, 'produce and maintain a physical boundary that distinguishes that system as a material unity' that 'withstands physical perturbations' (Wheeler 2010b: 34). Put otherwise, Tristram must be different from the other Shandys (the border at the end of the system), and Tristram needs to encounter his environment while maintaining his own self-organisation. Yet he cannot enact either, a dilemma cutting to the centre of his being; he cannot situate his bounded identity, bordered selfhood, unique personhood, while concurrently coping with Shandy nonsense and without losing that very self-organising identity and disintegrating in the ways we witness him narrating.

Even this is not the whole story. As Wheeler purports (building on Varela and Di Paolo), autopoietic systems 'form a subset of autonomous self-organizing systems': namely, '*a self-organizing system is one in which the intra-systemic components* ... *interact with each other* in *non-linear ways* to produce the emergence and maintenance of structured global order' (Wheeler 2010b: 34). What are these non-linear ways? The non-linear system appears when the output is not directly proportional to the input. Typically, self-organising systems involve non-linearity in terms of circular feedback between the intra-systemic elements. Oddly, Sterne's book abounds with these non-linear systems. A lucid example is found in Tristram's parents, Walter and Elizabeth. Elizabeth has been called the most inconsequential absent mother in canonical eighteenth-century fiction (Zunshine 2010: 193), and (as noted earlier) she appears only four times in nine volumes. But Walter is the domineering father *ne plus ultra* who seeks to predetermine every characteristic (in the evolutionary sense) of his son: body formation, ideas, beliefs, sentiments, view of reality. During Tristram's early years he unwittingly submits to his father's rules (how the child

---

[13] Cited in Wheeler (2010b: 34) in reference to Maturana and Varela (1980: 13) and the reprint of Maturana's 1970 essay on 'The Biology of Cognition'.

must be raised), and at each turning point of growth he fails to move forward; Sterne found some of these up-to-the-minute views in his wide reading on the management of children in such self-help manuals as those by John Hill (1754).

Something is logically askew: when Walter decrees that a child's baptismal name determines its personality, Tristram, reflecting on this phase of his childhood, accepts the edict. But having acceded to his father's baptismal decree, he rebels against it as an adult, as he does to all other critical junctures. In cognitive terms, Tristram's autopoietic system produces a runaway explosion resulting in his huge digression on how a child may be baptised before it is born by means of a squirt inserted *in utero*, to the extent that Tristram wants the whole faculty at the Sorbonne to be consulted on the veracity of this preposterous possibility. Note: the squirt *in utero* is Tristram's idea, not Walter's.

More globally in Sterne's sprawling text, Tristram's 'Walterian' increments – 'Walterian' in the son's being cognitively programmed to become a copy of his father – reach saturation points. But by his adolescence it is impossible to know what effect any Walterian cause has produced in light of Tristram's feedback mechanism, that is, memory, as he 'writes out' his life in relation to actuality. One might generalise that Tristram's non-linear self-organisation incrementally builds on his father's *positive* feedback. Yet by adolescence it seems apparent – if anything disclosed in Tristram's narrative is reliable – that the interaction of father and son, of input and output, cause and effect, has resulted in radically different self-organised systems. The evolving Tristram fundamentally differs from his father, so radically that his life has evolved into an autopoietic menace. Sterne even imagines the point of origination of self-organised systems, suggesting that in non-linear autopoietic systems this self-organisation starts with a phase of positive feedback. He therefore takes care to demonstrate how Tristram's negative and positive feedbacks have run amok, the son no longer capable of being recognised as his father's son either by father or by son. Oddly, with the passing of each year Walter recognises his boy less and less. The sense conveyed to modern readers is that this is a narrative constructed to demonstrate a strictly conceived autopoiesis.[14]

Autopoiesis and Perturbation

Influences other than Walterian logic feed Tristram's perturbations of the mind. As already indicated, he is acutely aware he is organised around defective neural pathways amounting to a damaged 'nervous system', of which Sterne was well aware.[15] Tristram is equally vexed by his environment's circular loop, especially

---

[14] Sterne satirically refers to Julien La Mettrie's radical materialism, especially the idea of the organic body as a 'machine', in both his letters and his novels, and historian Jonathan Israel (2010) has traced philosophical systems built on the first principle of anti-materialism during Sterne's lifetime. But Sterne may have also been stirred to imagine Tristram as a strictly conceived autopoietical system by immersion in Locke.

[15] In Sterne's adulthood, discussion of the nervous system as an organic body was widespread in Britain; see, for example, Monro 1783 and Rousseau 2004. It was unnecessary to know that

the circle of kinship from father to son. This intra-systemic Shandean loop produces the feverish perturbations spilling into Tristram's grotesque and gargantuan
digressions, such as the 'Tale of Diego's Nose' where the organic nose and penis are
so analogously interchangeable that Tristram's cognitive awareness is called into
question. In Tristram's words, 'so intense was the desire of the city's [Strasbourg,
France] matrons to touch Diego's huge nose that Diego mounted his mule and
rode on towards *Frankfort*' (Sterne 1978–84: I, 323). Readers have repeatedly commented on the comic effect of such incongruity, but Tristram's mind becomes further unhinged by the event. Each of these 'perturbations' contains representational
content (strangers, mules, noses, women), yet Tristram processes them computationally. For instance, it was Tristram's crushed nose at birth that led to Walter's
obsession with noses, about which Tristram learned later; this obsession in turn
caused Walter to assemble a library of books about noses, which Tristram discovered years after his father's death; this library contained the seminal book Tristram
discovered years later by Slawkenbergius recounting the stranger's nose as being
six times the length of a normal nose. In each sequence, representations of events
are processed computationally, each string giving rise to further perturbation. And
they are computational in the sense that Tristram perceives reality as embedded in
computation's numbered sequences: four deriving from three, three from two, two
from one and so forth, but never four having developed from one without the inter-
stices. The narrative unfolds displaying a Tristram who processes experience along
the lines of logical sequelae: every consequence deriving from its predecessor that
never could have arisen without it, and each condition producing heightened emotional perturbation. Perhaps this is also why Tristram cannot distinguish runaway
digression from the next psychological plateau he has reached . . . until he arrives
at the next perturbation. Nor does it disturb Sterne's calculated narrative flow to
view these computational moments as the feedbacks of a loop involved in a series
of ongoing structural couplings. They are strikingly proximate to the inputs and
outputs of non-linear systems in Ezequiel Di Paolo's formulation of self-organising
systems: 'Structural coupling refers to the mutual perturbation between organism
and environment and this exchange may or may not subserve a tendency towards
the conservation of autopoiesis' (2005: 443). Tristram's rhetoric provides the surest
clue to the inputs and outputs, yet his collective experience, memory and especially
the memories of childhood trauma best substantiate the claim.

So idiosyncratic is Tristram's computational mind it is challenging to attempt its
categorisation in terms of Enlightenment neurological, medical or even philosophical models. His so-called 'opinions', whether offered rhetorically as part of his main
thread or as digressions, appear to be the products of an information-processing
system rather than the iterations of a person with recognisable selfhood, social class

---

nervous systems are composed of neurons and that neurons are cells, and sufficient to understand
that the brain and nerves worked in tandem to create an organically integrated 'nervous system'
whose components were unified. Development of the cell theory after Sterne's lifetime is irrelevant
to this discussion.

and life goals. The only consistent pattern in his mental universe presents 'thinking' as a form of 'computing', as when Tristram reels off the types of auxiliary verbs or lists the number of 'matrons' in his tale about Diego in the 'promontory of NOSES' (Sterne 1978–84: I, 289). Such instances are not the product of Lockean associations but representations impinging on Tristram's mind as he spews them in numerical order, his narrative cascades flowing effortlessly without further self-reflection. His 'opinions' invoke the word 'brain' several dozen times yet are devoid of any sense of this anatomic organ as a computing machine. The representations encroaching on his mind's surface appear as fair game for computational treatment, and Tristram – like Walter – would have concurred with Hobbes in the *De corpore* that 'by Reasoning, I understand computation . . . to compute is to collect the sum of many things added together at the same time, or to know the remainder when one thing has been taken from another' (1655: 147). Indeed, Tristram considers his magnum opus as a study in 'close reasoning' and this type of exegesis is what he professes to be 'engaged in'. This 'reasoning' is proximate to counting in Hobbes, who concluded in the passage just cited that reasoning – which is to say understanding of the world around us and its reality – 'is the same as to add or to subtract' (1655: 162). Tristram's mind also functions in this proximate way because he has no other means to access the world: he can wax irrational or emotional but harbours no sense that things are *otherwise*. Walter's 'Tristrapaedia', even if not routinely administered to his son, has turned Tristram into a type of contemporary computational apparatus, anticipating nineteenth-century mathematician Charles Babbage's analytical engine that effectively counts, enumerates and classifies. A computing engine even when it dawns on Tristram that things might have been different.[16]

Even weirder is Tristram's anti-mutation, anti-selection view of things, anti-evolutionary in an era before evolution had been described, this notion to the extent that all things Shandean have grown worse: the generations of Shandys, his parents and Tristram himself, who will be the end of a line. It derives, in part, from his ingrained computational experience of accessing reality. But his misfortune, he thinks, is also attributable to a rotten world ruled by Fortune:

> for I can truly say, that from the first hour I drew my breath in it, to this, that I can now scarce draw it at all, for an asthma I got in skating against the wind in *Flanders*; – I have been the continual sport of what the world calls Fortune; and though I will not wrong her by saying, She has ever made me feel the weight of any great or signal evil; – yet with all the good temper in the world I affirm it of her, That in every stage of my life, and at every turn and corner where she could get fairly at me, the ungracious Duchess has pelted me with a set of as pitiful misadventures and cross accidents as ever small HERO sustained. (Sterne 1978–84: I, 8–9)

---

[16] There is a delicate balance between maker (Sterne) and fictional creation (Tristram), and it should not be overlooked that the biographical Sterne was invested in the nonsensical view of life as fervidly as the irrational (Bertelsen 1986).

Even in a small, close-knit society like Shandy Hall in remote Yorkshire this degeneration of an already 'rotten world' is palpable, and Tristram expends much energy pronouncing on how poorly the Shandy generations have evolved. Whatever selfhood he perceives in the recess of his mind – more Houyhnhnm than Yahoo (Swift, incidentally, was Sterne's favourite prose writer) – he never flexes from this staunchly anti-selection view of things. Ever-closer inspection of his mental processes suggests a vehicle, or instrument, steeped in computational predisposition.

Autopoiesis Extended

It is not superfluous to these concerns that there has not been a major reinterpretation of *Tristram Shandy* in three decades. Excellent textual, philological and historical commentaries have advanced understanding of Sterne's great masterpiece, as well as the sound prevailing view that, generically speaking, *Tristram Shandy* is a satire rather than a novel, plus recognition that it is one of the first, if not *the* first, metafictions in European literature (Waugh 1984: 13). Swearingen had tried to alter the tide of critical attention during the 1970s but had not done so: subdisciplines such as literature and neuroscience, or literature and cognition, held too little sway then. Set the chronological dials to circa 1980 and many dix-huitièmistes were awaiting a book hypothetically titled *Tristram Shandy and the Life Sciences*, which would have made a dent. But it was never written. Nearly four decades later the state of affairs has changed, strengthened in part by external developments in systems theory, artificial intelligence and neuroscience. Most contemporary literary critics are au fait with such views, as most living organisms are autopoietic systems, even if not all living systems are cognitive systems. But few would cavil that these developments are irrelevant for understanding a work as perplexing as *Tristram Shandy*. More locally, riddles about autopoietic and cognition systems vex wide camps of philosophers and scientists, particularly those who (like Maturana and Varela and their heirs) have demonstrated how structural coupling – the systems we have just seen encountering perturbations from the environment – constitutes a basis for enaction. Wheeler has explained why:

> The idea . . . is that the autopoietic organization, in establishing the distinction between the self-maintenance and the collapse of the system as a material unity, institutes a norm of survival, and thereby the significance or relevance of certain environmental perturbations as either leaving the system organizationally intact or resulting in its disintegration. (2010b: 35)

Leaving the system intact or disintegrated, however, the implication stands that the triple-E cognate amounts to the view that life and cognition are identical, or, at least, that living systems are subsets of cognitive systems. The logical qualification to this position is, of course, the reverse: that cognitive systems are subsets of living systems. The sequence marks a difference but, in whichever order, the implications for Sterne's book are multiple and revert, once again, to Tristram's mind-body conundrum. For however embodied he may be, his mind cannot become extended. He will not, or he cannot, be bounded by his skin because each perturbation radically further disturbs his self-organisation. Literary critics do not invoke a vocabulary of perturbations, self-organisation, autopoietic boundaries and borders; their concerns are ordinarily narrated in more conventional critical categories of character, plot, time scheme, narrative voice and genre (Traugott 1954; Lanham 1973; Iser 1988). The linguistic variance may herald the start of a new line of enquiry into Sterne's tour de force for a great canonical text that has been called the most important metafiction of the eighteenth century (Waugh 1984).

The matter of boundaries and perturbations merits further comment. Tristram tries to traverse his own autopoietic border, and – when he does – becomes progressively disturbed, even cognitively mutilated when aiming to blend into it, by the narrative's ending ruminating about his resemblance to Maria's goat. This final potshot – do I resemble your goat? – is not intended sentimentally (however charming it may seem to those wishing to read it affectively) but as further evidence of Tristram's cognitive impairment. His eccentric Shandean environment has 'perturbed' him in ways that deranged both mind and body. Perhaps this distortion of reality explains why he has no close friend, no wife, no profession, no home of his own, only fragmentary and mutant hallucinatory memories of his life before the Shandys died. All of which 'reflections' (if they can be called that) propel him to his fevered perturbation of 1762, 'Death in the form of Tuberculosis'.[17]

The pertinent question, in conclusion, probes whether Tristram's confusions are autopoietic, embodied or more generally enactive; and if one or the other, or a blend, or none, whether what drives the narrative forward is autopoiesis strictly conceived (as a particular mode of biological, material self-organisation) or a broader enactivist or embodied perspective. I have been suggesting that Sterne, in an idiosyncratic way, anticipated – stimulated by the mechanist-vitalist biological debates raging in his maturity – and intuited the view that cognition *enacted* cannot be cognition *extended*. Definitive proof cannot be given, certainly not as biographical or historical evidence of the origin of his impulse. Yet we would be hard pressed to identify another narrative in the epoch so ripe with these anticipations. And if the search were extended to non-fictional works of the same time frame, the pre-eminent candidate, Locke's *Essay*, is the very magisterial work Sterne has set himself up to counter:

Pray, Sir, in all the reading which you have ever read, did you ever read such a book as *Locke's* Essay upon the Human Understanding? – Don't answer me

---

[17] Tristram's digressions can seem to be interior monologues with himself: ruminative, fantastic, hallucinatory. Cognitively they can be interpreted in diverse ways, including impairment to his attentive capacity. Psychological *attention* became a topic of major concern to Sterne's contemporaries during the 1740s (see Crawford 2015). A more psychoanalytic approach to Tristram pursues his inability to separate himself from his parents long after their demise and builds on British psychologist John Bowlby's detachment theory.

rashly, – because many, I know, quote the book, who have not read it, – and many have read it who understand it not: – If either of these is your case, as I write to instruct, I will tell you in three words what the book is. – It is a history. – A history! Of who? what? where? when? Don't hurry yourself. – It is a history-book, Sir, (which may possibly recommend it to the world) of what passes in a man's own mind. (Sterne 1978–84: I, 98)

Tristram Shandy's metafictional status gains energy from the cognitive content its author has foregrounded, especially the relation of Tristram's self-consciousness to his versions of self-reflexivity. For yoking the two so robustly Sterne deserves a place in the Enlightenment's history of distributed cognition. But when situating Sterne within this historical genealogy of cognition, care should be taken not to conflate Sterne-the-author with Tristram-the-fictional-figure, for the biographical Sterne was not committed to the computational picture of things Tristram so tenaciously holds. Historically put, the biographical Sterne was not autopoietically invested in the ways this chapter has sketched autopoiesis, however prone Sterne was to 'Nonsense Clubs' and other cults of absurdity: he well knew that in reality things are otherwise than the runaway digressive loops of positive feedback driving Tristram, who cannot cross over the border. Tristram remains an inhabitant of the country Autopoiesis; a card-carrying citizen committed to a mutation-and-selection picture of things captured in his representational-computational passport to the real world. The two – autopoiesis versus mutation-and-selection – are set against each other in much cognitive theory. Yet Sterne wittily juxtaposes them as if to lodge the possibility of compatibility without logical impasse, or, at least, suggest some type of accommodation. Alternatively, literary critics claim that this picture of reality is precisely what is to be expected from an author so immersed in self-reflection, self-referencing, self-disclosure, self-exposure and the further deconstructions of self (Swearingen 1977). Perhaps another of Wheeler's admonishments, in addition to those already mentioned, is as pertinent here as can be found to clinch the distinction necessary for Tristram's version of cognition: 'Since autopoietic theory and (therefore) enactivism are committed to identifying the cognition system *with* the living system, the enactivist simply *cannot* endorse extended mind' (Wheeler 2010b: 35). It is a sobering thought not intended for the faint-hearted.

Computation and Mental Confusion

Wheeler's contradiction is intentional: it would indeed be more convenient to conflate these views and rest satisfied with the outcome that Tristram's mental confusions are merely cognitive. That to diagnose and anatomise these vexations and perturbations more exquisitely than this is folly, and that it does not matter, except to philosophers and historians of extended cognition, whether Sterne's protagonist is embodied, enacted or cognitively distributed. Perhaps so, but to leave the matter there insufficiently finesses Tristram's plight as well as circumvents the current state of thinking about distributed cognition. Nor would termination of our exploration so far short of the mark bode well for the future direction of literary analysis and cognitive studies, and at a moment when their connections are already advanced. Besides, it is not ancillary to these concerns that Sterne's genius in *Tristram Shandy* thrives on the philosopher's zest for debunking the very same academic ratiocination he has erected, as Nuttall has claimed, on 'the juggling of philosophical systems' (1974: 55). And in other quarters the student of distributed cognition is curious to speculate whether Sterne was committed, however Procrustean his engagement may have been, to a particular type of autopoiesis. For some it may be insufficient to claim Sterne deserves an accolade for admission to the pantheon of historical cognition – they want more. And they notice, for instance, that Tristram's aberrant computational mindset never teaches him his environment cannot be swallowed into his cognitive system as it is among ordinary folk. That 'environment', moreover, or perpetually *positive* feedback, remains foreign to Tristram. I have been using the term 'positive', here as well as earlier, along the lines of Wheeler's non-linear systems (2010b: 34). Its import for Tristram's cognition is that it is feedback incapable of becoming compatible with the pertinent aspects of his own autopoietic system, and – more broadly – to his life as a living organism. You might say Tristram's embodied mind depended on his autopoietic system long before it ought to have developmentally. His existence as an autonomous self-organised autopoietic system antedated his enacted or extended cognition. This is why he constantly tells himself tales proving his resistance to other environments. In some fundamentally rudimentary way he knows that an aspect of his confusion prevents him from becoming an 'extended mind'. And again, here's the rub, as Wheeler admonishes: 'Since autopoietic theory and (therefore) enactivism are committed to identifying the cognition system *with* the living system, the enactivist simply *cannot* endorse extended mind' (2010b: 35). Nor can Tristram endorse it because his sense-making occasionally amounts to a raw autopoietic system ('raw' is Wheeler's term rather than Di Paolo's or Thompson's). In 'raw systems' the organism either survives or dies, and *faute de mieux* Tristram has survived – just.[18]

---

[18] Tristram's survival is errantly mutant despite Sterne's comic mirth, and indeed raw too because Tristram cannot alter his behaviour despite constant environmental perturbations – that is, he is stuck. His survival is locked, as it were, without the prospect of alteration and he is so unaccustomed to different states of being as the result of his mutant nervous apparatus that he cannot change. He is Walter's son, programmed to engage in as much ratiocination as his father, yet forever rebelling against it. Here enter Evan Thompson, Canadian cognitive philosopher and collaborator of Varela, and his explications of autopoietic sense-making in terms of graded nuances and the organism's ability to regulate its behaviour in order to improve its prospects for a better survival; see Thompson 2007. But Tristram cannot *improve*: cannot monitor his progress, cannot adapt, can only keep telling 'cock-and-bull' stories. Put crudely, he is a raw system lacking the adaptation necessary to become a sense-making extended mind; as such, he is *enacted* but not *extended*. Naively, he thinks his pedigree wholly Shandean (although his Maker Sterne knew better when inserting the material about Yorick as his possible biological father). Tristram descends from a lineage of raw enacted autopoiesis rather than the pedigree of extended minds.

Literary critics may retort that Sterne's genius captured the conversational side of human life for literature: the idea that writing itself was another form of conversation, and that Sterne's enduring achievement was the identification of a genetic vehicle (prose satire) and rhetorical form embedded, as Sterne himself wrote, in 'that ornamental figure in oratory, which Rhetoricians style the Aposiopesis' (Sterne 1978–84: I, 115), a form capable of containing these confusions.[19] It may be true and no critic or scholar would wish to detract from Sterne's enduring achievement. But Sterne also shuffled cognitive systems as proficiently as he enshrined himself in metafiction's pedigree from Homer and Cervantes to John Barth and Thomas Pynchon. No less than these metafictionalists he expended attention on Tristram's subjective experience: how Tristram feels as a boy of five when his genitals are injured by the window sash; how it 'feels like' to him to be writing out his life and opinions; his fear of 'Death' when it visits him in the form of consumption; how he grows romantically excited by watching Janatone, the innkeeper's pretty daughter, as she knits a white-thread stocking in the sun; how he imagines he has known the peasant girl Nanette for many years after the knot in her hair clumsily falls down. Sterne takes care precisely to describe how each of these moments 'actually seems' to Tristram. But these are also the *qualia* of contemporary philosophers, ranging from David Chalmers (pro) to Daniel Dennett (con), who considers qualia to be 'an unfamiliar term for something that could not be more familiar to each of us: the ways things seem to us' (Dennett 1988). Reality's semblances to Tristram are vital to the anti-materialist Sterne, who was persuaded of the empiricists' (the Lockes, Humes and company) limitations in explicating his protagonist's consciousness. Sterne would have taken heart from the writings of Erwin Schrödinger, the celebrated Austrian physicist and Nobel Laureate in physics, who put forward his anti-materialist cards less satirically than Sterne did:

> The sensation of color cannot be accounted for by the physicist's objective picture of light-waves. Could the physiologist account for it, if he had fuller knowledge than he has of the processes in the retina and the nervous processes set up by them in the optical nerve bundles and in the brain? I do not think so. (Schrödinger 1944: 37)

Perhaps we ought to retain a semblance of doubt. For example, Sterne had never heard of 'qualia', yet he could have told us that the Latin word was derived from the Latin plural adjective *qualis*, meaning 'of what sort' or 'of what kind'. And Sterne would have concurred that questions such as how it feels to be Tristram, or the 'what it is like' character of his mental states, are legitimate interrogations. An approach to Tristram's cognition through qualia might probe his moods for what they indicate about his experience of pain, engaging through memory in particular mental associations, and even speculate about his response, for instance,

---

[19] A brief history of the figure is found in Sterne 1978–84: III, 146. For such a predominantly rhetorical approach to Sterne's achievement see Lanham 1973.

to 'inverted spectrums', the correlative of our physical responses to John Locke's thought experiment that the colours of the world have been inverted (Locke 1975: II, 32). Further pursuit of Tristram and qualia might well pay for Sterne's niche in the history of distributed cognition even if it did not alter the cognitive turn taken here: to diagnose Tristram's confusions from an autopoietic or enactive perspective. For the present it seems more pressing – especially through the absence of recent phenomenological approaches to Sterne's great masterpiece – to probe which type of cognitive model drives the narrative: an autopoiesis strictly conceived as an Enlightenment model of bio-material self-organisation, or a broader, and possibly looser, enactivist or embodied perspective.

Moreover, future inquiry into Sterne and qualia may buttress my developing sense that Tristram's confusions arise from a more or less narrowly construed autopoiesis. Analysis from the qualia, furthermore, would confirm the distance between the biographical Sterne and the fictional Tristram, a divide I have bookmarked from the start. A strictly configured autopoiesis combined with qualia would demonstrate that the complex states of 'what it feels like to be Tristram' are as inherently constitutive of Sterne's genius as his narrative brilliance in the discovery of a rhetorical vehicle for his conversational mode. Such an approach to this cornerstone of metafiction will require a robust sense of autopoiesis and qualia, which, in turn, would demonstrate more emphatically than I have been able to here that what 'Tristram thinks and feels' is rarely what 'Sterne thinks and feels'. Unless the difference is held in mind, Sterne's literary achievement is diminished.

7

Enacting the Absolute:
Subject-Object Relations in Samuel Taylor Coleridge's Theory of Knowledge

Lisa Ann Robertson

Identity and knowledge stand in relation to each other as two sides of a single process . . .

Francisco Varela

Truth is the correlative of Being.

Samuel Taylor Coleridge

Written in 1816, a year before the *Biographia Literaria* was published, Coleridge's 'Theory of life' (pub. 1848) advances a hypothesis that explains the relationship between the transient world and the absolute. Dissatisfied with Cartesian dualism that, in his view, 'made nature utterly lifeless and Godless' (Coleridge 2000: 565) and with materialist theories that attempted to solve dualist problems by reducing the world to a single substance, Coleridge advanced an alternative ontological system based on his reading in German *Naturphilosophie*. Initially, the essay was meant to form the first half of a lecture on scrofula that James Gillman, the physician who helped him get his opium use under control, intended to submit to a competition sponsored by the Royal College of Surgeons. As he wrote, however, it grew. Rather than detailing the history of scrofula, it answered the question 'What is life?' (Coleridge 1995: 506). While the essay responds to the debate of 1816–19 between John Abernethy and William Lawrence about the Hunterian theory of life, I argue that Coleridge's answer to this question provides a model to explain his claim in the *Biographia* that knowledge emerges from the coalescence of the subject and the object.[1]

Coleridge was a theoretical vitalist, who used the experiments of others to support his theory. According to Robert Mitchell, who coined the term, theoretical vitalists are interested in vitalism 'as an aid not to investigation but to interpretation' (2013: 8). As such, Coleridge uses other thinkers' work to investigate human cognition as a function of life. In Mitchell's view, 'Theory of life' is an abandoned experiment that enables a critical reorientation of Coleridge's turn away from

[1] See Jacyna 1983.

poetry to the genre of 'the life-manual' (2013: 103).[2] His analysis looks forward
to Coleridge's later work by focusing on how the broad principles outlined in the
theory, particularly individuation, animate his writing from 1817 on. In a similar
spirit, I contend that the essay can reorient our understanding of the discussion of
subject-object relations in *Biographia Literaria*. Once Coleridge worked out an ontological relationship between the subject, the object and the absolute in 'Theory of
life', he could answer the epistemological questions raised in *Biographia*.

In addition to situating these two texts within contemporary vitalist and
mind-matter debates of the period, I also look to their continued relevance within
twenty-first-century discussions about cognition. Mitchell characterises Coleridge's
concept of life as 'a power that intensified itself by generating new forms of unity'
(2013: 91), a definition that, in my view, aligns it with modern autopoietic theory. I
argue that reading Coleridge's 'Theory of life' and *Biographia* alongside current theories of autopoietic enaction demonstrates the importance of his cognitive theory
stripped of its theological baggage. Such a reading also pushes past the limitations
of Romantic organicism as an attempt to reconcile 'the diversity and seeming
dissonance of materials . . . into unity' (Abrams 1974: 221). Many scholars understand Coleridge's theories in 'the more transcendental guise of a form or a law that
is the grounds of possibility for the very life of living beings' (Armstrong 2003: 184).
What that approach misses, and one significant reason to examine Coleridge's
texts alongside autopoietic enaction, is that he was not merely concerned with a
theory of organic form. 'Theory of life' and the *Biographia* launch an investigation
into the complex connection between individuation and cognition that extends
beyond how parts and wholes, or subjects and objects, co-exist. He was interested
in how individuals acquire knowledge of and understand themselves as part of the
whole they comprise.

In both texts, Coleridge counters eighteenth- and nineteenth-century accounts
of the mind, which he deemed unsatisfactory because they relied on problematic
ontological claims. 'Theory of life' provides an ontological basis for the relationship
between the subject, the object and the absolute by conceiving of the eternal (God,
the absolute) and the transient (nature, human beings) as existing in a recursive,
mutually constitutive relationship. Coleridge advances a concept of an eternal God
that co-exists with the transient world in an infinite loop. This only becomes apparent, however, when we interrogate his theories of life and knowledge together.
Elsewhere in this volume, John Savarese asserts that Coleridge's notion that autonomy can exist within the scaffolding of distributed cognition is not as paradoxical as
it might seem. Likewise, I maintain that his idea that the subjective mind emerges
from objective nature is equally plausible. Applying the lens of autopoietic enaction, which positions the subject and the object similarly to Coleridge, in order to
theorise emergent knowledge, illuminates the relationship of his two theories.

---

[2] Mitchell categorises Coleridge's later work as 'life-manuals', including *The Statesman's Manual*
(1816), *A Lay Sermon* (1817), the revision of *The Friend* (1818), *Aids to Reflection* (1825), *The Constitution
of Church and State* (1829) and the unfinished *Logosophia*.

A cognitive theory based on biological systems theory, autopoietic enaction maintains that knowledge (and the mind it comprises) emerges from the interaction of an organism and its environment. Enaction is based on autopoiesis, which posits an interdependent relationship between what Coleridge would call the subject (percipient organism) and the object (the organism's milieu).[3] Uninterested in theological concerns, autopoietic enaction attributes both the subject and the object to the physical or, in Coleridge's terms, transient world. It eschews the concept of the absolute because by definition something is 'absolute only if it does not depend on anything else; it must have an identity that transcends all relations' (Varela et al. 1991: 224). Despite their differences, the scientific concepts on which the enactive approach relies – autopoiesis, structural coupling, dynamic co-emergence – help articulate what Coleridge was trying to convey before the advent of cell theory and systems theory. Looking at enaction as a reaction against contemporary theories of cognition allows us to see how Coleridge's theory of knowledge serves as an alternative to Cartesian, materialist and idealist accounts of mind. It also enables us to see the value of Coleridge's ideas stripped of their metaphysics and highlights their importance in a history of non-Cartesian accounts of cognition. Where Savarese's contribution explores the relationship between the mind and its products – thought and language – in the development of autonomy, this chapter examines the relationship between the mind and nature in terms other than organicism, as it is typically understood.

Coleridge was not alone in his dissatisfaction with Descartes's concept of a mind that exists discretely from the material world. Over the centuries, philosophers have wrestled with the 'explanatory gap between mind and matter, consciousness and nature' (Thompson 2007: 6), or the mind-body problem. They wondered how the material body transmits sensory information to an immaterial substance and, conversely, how the mind acts on the body. Despite the nearly insurmountable difficulties answering these questions, Descartes's *cogito ergo sum* gained ascendency during the seventeenth century and was widely accepted for nearly two hundred years until, ostensibly, it was overturned by scientific accounts of cognition advanced in the 1940s and 1950s. According to commonly received histories of cognitive science, the rise of cognitivism – the theory that the brain functions like an organic computer – finally purged the ghost from the machine.[4] This narrative, however, has recently been disputed by advocates of the 4E approach to the mind. The 4E approach is a 'new way of thinking about the mind . . . inspired by, and organised around, not the brain, but some combination of the ideas that mental processes are (1) *embodied*, (2) *embedded*, (3) *enacted*, and (4) *extended*' (Rowlands 2010:

---

[3] Since its inception in the late 1990s, enaction has branched into two trajectories. Autopoietic enaction takes a 'biologically-inspired approach to understanding cognition', while sensorimotor enaction focuses on 'a skillful grasp of patterns linking sensory stimulation and movement' (Ward 2014). The former is associated with Varela, Thompson and Rosch, while the latter has been developed by thinkers such as Alva Noë.

[4] Gilbert Ryle used this phrase to describe Cartesian mind-body dualism in *The Concept of Mind* (1949).

3).[5] Scholars in this multidisciplinary group reject cognitivism because, they claim, it rests on unacknowledged Cartesian assumptions about the mind and its relationship to the world.

When proponents of the 4E view of cognition ask 'Where does the mind stop and the rest of the world begin?' (Clark and Chalmers 1998: 7), they are, in essence, posing a question about the relationship between the subject and the object. Seeing the mind as embodied in a particular subject, embedded in a concrete environment, enacted through the coupling of a subject with its surroundings, and extended beyond the boundaries of skull and skin into the environment, 4E advocates study cognition in context. While not all 4E theorists agree that each of these Es accurately characterises the mind, they all consider the subject and the object together. This, in my estimation, is strikingly similar to Coleridge's project in the *Biographia*. Coleridge struggled to theorise the relationship between the subject and the object (human beings and nature) and their relationship to the absolute (God) for most of his life. The *Biographia* represents one historical attempt to solve the epistemological dimensions of this problem, while 'Theory of life' works through it ontologically.

This chapter takes up Coleridge's mid-career forays into the mind-matter and vitalism debates, which are informed by the British empiricist context of his youth and his reading in German transcendentalism. I apply a contemporary theoretical lens to provide a better sense of how Coleridge wrestled with embodiment when theorising subject-object relations. His goal was to avoid positing a world that is wholly matter or wholly mind and to circumvent the Cartesian trap of making them discrete substances. I argue that these theories stand in a recursive relationship to each other. 'Theory of life' proposes an ontological solution for Coleridge's epistemological challenges, but this solution entails knowing as a correlative of being and vice versa. When we consider his abstract account of life and his disembodied account of knowledge-production in conjunction with autopoietic enaction, it reveals how these theories might function on an embodied level.

C. Smith notes an 'increasing interest in the problem that "consciousness," [and] "mind," poses to the essentially Cartesian world-view of natural science' and expresses the hope that this will lead to 'a renewed interest in Coleridge's philosophy (shorn of its metaphysics)' (1999: 46). Coleridge's work warrants attention because it challenges empirical science's unacknowledged philosophical assumptions. Ironically, though Descartes rejected the evidence of the senses, dualism laid the groundwork for the rise of science as we know it. With a 'mind infinitely separated from a world which is matter', declares F. E. Sutcliffe, 'the role of man can only be that of dominating his surroundings' (1971: 21). Yet, even though empirical science eventually rejected substance dualism, Cartesian models of mind remain, according to Francisco Varela, 'the dominant core of modern neuroscience and in the public's understanding' (Varela et al. 1991: 44). Read through the lens of autopoietic enaction, Coleridge provides an alternative philosophical model

[5] Shaun Gallagher coined the term '4E' (Rowlands 2010: 219 n. 4).

for thinking about how we orient ourselves toward the world we inhabit that can provide a corrective to the pernicious effects of Cartesianism on the way human beings relate to the natural world.

The Cartesian Conundrum

In *Discourse on Method* (1637) and *Meditations on First Philosophy* (1641), Descartes set out to discover 'the true method of arriving at knowledge of everything the mind was capable of grasping' (1971: 40). In order to solve this epistemological problem, he advanced a new ontological system that divided the world into two substances. Having 'observed that there are very few things one can know with certainty about corporeal objects, [and] that there are many more things which are known to us about the human mind' (1971: 132), he concluded that the evidence of his senses was less reliable than knowledge of his own mind. Privileging mind over matter, Descartes determined that the mind 'needs no place and depends on no material thing' (1971: 54). As a discrete substance, it does not require materiality but can exist 'independently of physical instantiation' (Jackendoff 1987: 15), a claim that twentieth-century cognitivists such as Ray Jackendoff also made not about the mind, but about the information that it processes. Descartes's *cogito* represents an influential moment in the history of mind science because it posed ontological and epistemological quandaries about how two fundamentally different substances interact and how the mind comes to know its surroundings, questions that occupied natural philosophers for at least two centuries. Furthermore, according to 4E theorists the Cartesian model of mind provides the foundations of cognitivism.[6]

Despite critique, Descartes denied there was any 'reason to think heterogeneity renders mind-body interaction incoherent' (Richardson 1982: 22).[7] Regardless of the difficulties inherent in interactionism, Cartesian ontology appealed to many thinkers because by 'rejecting . . . attempts to link thought with matter' they believed they were 'undermining the grounds for atheism' by separating the immortal soul from a substance that decays and dies (Yolton 1983: 8). For dualists, matter comprises the transient, or object, world that stands in contradistinction to the eternal, unchanging immaterial realm. In this system, subjects are eternal since the soul or mind is immaterial and immortal. Some of Descartes's contemporaries attempted to resolve the problems of interactionism by proposing solutions such as occasionalism or pre-established harmony.[8] Others, however, found dualist

---

[6] For early expressions of this critique see Dreyfus and Haugeland 1978; Dreyfus 1979; Varela et al. 1991. Michael Wheeler synthesises these claims and shows the similarities between cognitivism and Cartesian dualism in *Reconstructing the Cognitive World* (2005).

[7] Princess Elisabeth of Bohemia, in her correspondence with Descartes, and Pierre Gassendi, in his critique of *Meditations*, raised this question. See Richardson 1982 for a history of the interactionism 'scandal' and a defence of Descartes's response.

[8] Occasionalism, advanced by Louis de la Forge and Nicolas Malebranche in the 1660s, is the idea that God is the only true cause of mental or physical action. Leibniz's early-eighteenth-century

explanations implausible and endeavoured to solve the problem with materialist theories of mind.[9] Of particular interest to Coleridge, who experimented with materialism early in his career before deeming it heretical, were David Hartley and Joseph Priestley, who tried to solve the mind-body problem by advancing theories of embodied cognition.

Hartley, who had observed the effects of alcohol and head injuries on cognitive ability, claimed that the 'Brain is . . . the Seat of the rational Soul' (1749: 81). Hartley's language is intentionally equivocal as he carefully positions himself as neither materialist nor dualist. Nonetheless, his *Observations on Man* outlines one of the first detailed physiological accounts of cognition, advancing the hypothesis that external objects transmit sensory information via vibrations that travel along the nerves to the brain.[10] Scientist and dissenting theologian Joseph Priestley adopted Hartley's theory and argued for a materialist concept of the mind by proposing an alternative to the Cartesian view of matter. In *Disquisitions Relating to Matter and Spirit* (1777), he asserts that matter is neither inert nor extended, but composed of powers that attract and repel each other. Extension, along with solidity, divisibility and inertness, is one of the properties that Descartes attributed to matter. He and later dualists used these properties to argue against materialist accounts of mind because, they claimed, it was an immaterial substance that took up no space and, most importantly, exhibited the active property of self-motivation. According to Priestley, matter inherently possesses the active forces of attraction and repulsion that enable objects in the world to cohere. What a subject 'senses' in perception 'is the complex action of varying forces' (Schofield 1978: 351), which Priestley thought could very well be Hartley's vibrations. Reformulating matter as active, Priestley challenged dualist objections that an inert substance could sustain consciousness.[11]

The primary problem with these theories is that they make thought a passive process in which the external world inscribes sensations, perceptions and experiences onto the subject. Just as a billiard ball cannot resist being moved when it's struck by a pool cue, neither can the embodied mind avoid being imprinted by the sensory data it encounters. Matter may be active, but it is still governed by physical

theory of pre-established harmony asserts that at the time of creation everything is programmed to act in concert with each other.

[9] See Yolton 1983 for a detailed history of the mind-matter debates in the eighteenth century.

[10] Though Hartley refrains from making ontological claims, asserting that 'it is all one to the Purpose of the foregoing Theory, whether the Motions in the medullary Substance be the physical Cause of the Sensations . . . or the occasional Cause, according to *Malebranche*; or only an Adjunct, according to *Leibnizt* [*sic*]' (1749: 5), I read his theory as materialist; see Robertson 2011. For other views, see Marsh 1959; Haven 1959; Christensen 1981.

[11] According to Alan Beretta, Priestley is the only historical figure that recognised the implications for the mind-matter debate when Newton 'proposed action-at-a-distance, or gravity, to account for planetary motion' (2014: 77). In the wake of Newtonian physics and later developments pioneered by James Maxwell, Werner Heisenberg and Richard Feynman, Beretta argues, no serviceable definition of the 'physical' exists that justifies privileging it over the abstract as do contemporary cognitive scientists and neurobiologists committed to physicalist explanations. For this reason, Priestley's insight continues to be relevant to contemporary cognitive science.

laws. Hartley's and Priestley's theories deny the existence of free will; human character, they maintain, is environmentally determined. The mind becomes, in Coleridge's terms, 'a lazy Lookeron on an external World' (Coleridge 1956–71: I, 709).

In addition to eliminating autonomy, materialist theories of cognition threaten to eradicate the subject altogether. By ontologically conflating the subject and the object in order to overcome the mind-body problem, they objectify the subject. Priestley tries to account for the phenomenological 'I' by defining the '*Self*' as 'that substance which is the seat of a particular set of sensations and ideas' (2005: 88). Identifying the self as a 'substance' blurs the line that demarcates the percipient from the perceived. These materialist approaches flatten the subject into a caus-ally determined being that is, potentially, indistinguishable from its surroundings. They make the subject part of the transient world without explaining, at least to Coleridge's satisfaction, how it might participate in eternity. Ontological idealism presents the opposite problem by making the world a product of thought, thus sub-jectifying the object and failing to adequately account for transience in the physical realm. The difficulty for Coleridge was how to separate the mind from its environ-ment without imposing an ontological rupture between the two. He wrangled with these problems in *Biographia* and 'Theory of life', positing recursion and mutual co-dependence, to use the idiom of autopoietic enaction.

Despite its detractors, Cartesianism remained the dominant paradigm into the twentieth century. By the mid-twentieth century, however, it became, according to Mark Rowlands, 'one of the most reviled philosophical views ever invented' (2010: 12). The 'popularity of the mind-brain identity/exclusive neural realization combination [cognitivism] stemmed, in large part, from the belief that to deny it was to be committed to dualism of a broadly Cartesian sort' (12). Cognitivism came into being in the 1940s and 1950s as part of the Macy Conferences on cybernetics in an attempt to bring scientific rigour to the study of the mind, which its founders believed 'had been far too long in the hands of psychologists and philosophers' (Varela et al. 1991: 38).[12] As part of the study of communication systems, it advanced a computer model of cognition whereby the brain transduces sensory input into mental representations, or symbols.

This understanding of cognition relies on objectivism, which prioritises the object by 'taking idealized formulations of mathematical physics as descriptions of the way the world really is' (Varela et al. 1991: 17). In this view, the brain pro-cesses information that exists independently of the perceiving mind. Conflating the mind with brain-based procedures, cognitivism reduces it to a series of subpersonal neural processes that occur beyond the pale of consciousness. Epistemologically, cognitivism drives a wedge between the subject and the object, while ontolog-ically it objectifies the subject by trying to understand it through an objectivist lens. Claiming that information exists objectively, it divorces cognitive processes

---

[12] For brief histories of cognitivism, see Varela et al. 1991: chapter 3; Thompson 2007: 4–8.

from actual, embodied subjects in specific, concrete environments.[13] Despite its materialist orientation, cognitivism replicates the core Cartesian assumption that cognition is a disembodied process. All the action occurs in the head.

Cognitivism also ignores the phenomenological aspects of cognition. Disregarding what phenomenologists call the life-world, it deems consciousness an epiphenomenon, an unnecessary by-product of real cognition. Failing to see subjectivity as an unavoidable screen through which human beings perceive and know the world, cognitivism perpetuates the Cartesian explanatory gap 'in a materialist form by opening up a new gap between subpersonal, computational cognition and subjective mental phenomena' (Thompson 2007: 6). This perceived gap – whether materialist or dualist in its perpetration – has had inimical consequences for the way that people in Euro-Western traditions conceive of themselves in relation to the natural world and to their own bodies. First it disconnects human beings from nature, then it separates the mind from its physical container, viewing subjectivity as unrelated to embodiment and embeddedness.[14]

Enter Enaction

Though it has not gained widespread acceptance, the enactive approach to cognition offers an important alternative to Cartesian and cognitivist theories. It does not separate the percipient from its milieu with respect to cognitive processes, but sees the mind as enacted. That is, knowledge of the world emerges from an organism's interactions with its environment through structural coupling. Taking the autopoietic definition of life as its starting point, the enactive approach defines organisms as autonomous systems that produce and reproduce themselves through endogenous activity. In autopoiesis, this activity serves to demarcate the living from the non-living. Accordingly, the most minimally self-replicating systems – a single-celled bacterium, for example – meet the criteria for life. An organism's boundary emerges from the activity of maintaining itself as a discrete, unified entity.

---

[13] V. S. Ramachandran's (2006) version of the 'brain in a vat' thought experiment exemplifies this contradiction. In this scenario, neuroscientists can keep a disembodied brain alive in a vat and it will 'think and feel that it's experiencing actual life events'. The subject can choose to be 'deliriously happy' indefinitely in the vat or to live an embodied, mortal life. The driving assumption is that human consciousness arises from 'a brain in a vat (the cranial cavity) nurtured by cerebrospinal fluid and blood and bombarded by photons'. In this view, besides the head, the body plays no role in cognition. 'We are', Ramachandran asserts, 'nothing but a pack of neurons.' To further highlight the problems of this disembodied approach, it is worth noting that Ramachandran sweetens the pot by offering the knowledge and experience of five other minds. His choice aptly demonstrates the dangers of divorcing cognition from embodiment. All male and mostly Euro-Western (Albert Einstein, Mahatma Gandhi, Mark Spitz, Bill Gates and Hugh Heffner), these brains underscore questions of race, sex and other cultural factors that significantly affect 'the "I" who experiences the world' based on an embodiment that is bracketed by cognitivism.

[14] Recall Ralph Waldo Emerson's mid-nineteenth-century division of 'Nature and the soul', with the former consisting of 'all that is separate from us, all that which Philosophy distinguishes as not me, that is, both nature and art, all other men and my own body' (2003: 36).

In short, the boundary between inner and outer is not fixed, as in Cartesian dualism, but flexibly defined by various organisms' life-producing activities. According to Varela, one of the co-founders of the enactive approach, in 'defining what it is as unity, in the very same movement it defines what remains exterior to it, that is to say, its surrounding environment' (1991: 85). Savarese, in this volume, claims that for Coleridge the outer becomes inner through appropriation. In biological terms, this refers to the process by which an organism assimilates aspects of the environment to maintain its autonomous self-organisation. This process is known as structural coupling.

Structural coupling refers to the relationship between the subject and the object, based on the kinds of actions the former takes within its environment. According to the enactive approach, these actions are structurally determined by the subject's material instantiation and by the physical features of its habitat. Though autonomous, organisms are in a constant exchange with their surroundings. According to enaction, an organism is 'always structurally coupled to its environment' such that 'the conduct of each is a function of the conduct of the other' (Thompson 2007: 45). As an organism moves through its environment, it encounters perturbations that trigger internal processes that enable it to keep its boundaries intact and to maintain its unified state. Another way to think about perturbations is as sensory stimuli. The kind of sensations that register for an organism is based on its physiological structure, but the kind of sensations that are available is delimited by its surroundings. Self-production and boundary maintenance in response to external stimuli lead to a spatiotemporal history of interaction between an organism and its environment. In this way, structural coupling enables and delimits cognitive activity.

Through structural coupling, embodiment and environment provide affordances and constraints that determine how an organism senses and perceives the world and what kind of knowledge it constructs about its surroundings. What a subject notices is a function of the structurally determined relationship between its body and its milieu.[15] From this interaction, the subject brings 'forth a domain of significance', or relevant knowledge (Varela et al. 1991: 156). The prototypical example is a bacterium in a gradient of sugar. The sugar is part of its environment, and it physiologically requires sugar to survive. Thus sucrose becomes meaningful to the bacterium such that it will actively seek it out, moving to areas with greater concentrations. As Evan Thompson explains, 'although sucrose is a real and present condition of the physiochemical environment, its status as food is not' (2007: 158; see also Varela 1991: 85–6). The value of sugar as food is not inherent but relational, just as bacteria's recognition and knowledge (or subjects'

---

[15] Enactive psychologist Ralph D. Ellis claims that consciousness is not only enacted but emotionally driven. He argues that 'our emotions gear us up for action, and then we search and scan the environment for relevant perceptual cues, which become conscious to the extent that they resonate with image schemas' (2005: 169). In his view, all organisms are subjects, from the most basic to human beings, because they have emotion, agency and core selves.

knowledge, broadly defined) of it depends on its significance as food. Subjects, as it were, 'constantly confront the encounters (perturbations, shocks, coupling) with [their] environment and treat them from a perspective which is not intrinsic to the encounters themselves' (Varela 1991: 86). They come to know their environments by attending to those things that are most relevant to them and that they are capable of perceiving. This, according to the enactive approach, is cognition.

Coleridge suggests a similar relationship between life and cognition in 'Theory of life', and enaction also characterises his understanding of the body's role in knowledge-production. For example, in the *Biographia* he imagines that 'the delicious melodies of Purcell or Cimarosa might be disjointed stammerings to a hearer, whose partition of time should be a thousand times subtler than ours' (Coleridge 1983: 118). This exhibits awareness that differently embodied organisms construe the world differently. Implied in his description of these melodies, which are 'delicious' and therefore meaningful to him, is the understanding that they would not be meaningful to 'a hearer' for whom they 'might be disjointed stammerings'. Pushing this analogy further, the enactive idea that the mind is a product of the spatiotemporal history of interactions between a body and its surroundings resembles Coleridge's assertion that knowledge transpires in the coalescence of the subject and the object. In the *Biographia*, he envisions the percipient and the perceived in a mutually co-dependent relationship.

In trying to conceptualise a subject that is both related to and separate from the world, Coleridge faced epistemological and ontological problems. He wanted to understand 'the mode in which our perceptions originated', or how perception occurs, and 'the natural differences of *things* and *thoughts*' (1983: 90). Of the extant theories, he found the formulations of 'the dogmatic materialist' as absurd as that of 'the common rank of *soul-and-bodyists*' (1983: 135). A second difficulty involves the relationship between freedom and necessity. While he wanted to believe that 'Every man is the maker of his own fortune', he recognised that human 'nature appears conditioned & determined by an outward Nature' (1957–2002: III.1, 4109). As materialist theories of the mind aptly demonstrate, humans are subject to the laws that govern the physical world even as they seem to exhibit free will.

Coleridge conceived of this problem as a 'Skein of necessities' from which, he sometimes despaired, he might never 'disentangle himself' (1957–2002: III.1, 4109). Refusing to split the subject from the object, as in Cartesian ontology, it becomes difficult, almost impossible, to tease out the boundary that separates the two. Like a tangled skein of yarn, subject and object loop round each other until, if yanked hard enough to untangle the knot, it becomes a single thread. They are intertwined in such a way that, as it unravels, so does the clear distinction between them. This Gordian dilemma of how to distinguish between '*things* and *thoughts*' was Coleridge's third problem (1983: 90). It was an ontological problem involving not just the relationship between the subject and the object, but also how they relate to the absolute. Despite his attraction to Spinoza's ideas and to *Naturphilosophie*, Coleridge recognised in the underlying pantheism 'a worldview [that] deeply problematizes the status and identity of both finite individuals and God' (Berkeley 2006:

458).[16] Though he draws on the work of Friedrich Schelling and Henrik Steffens in 'Theory of life', he attempts to advance an ontological alternative to substance dualism and to materialism that avoids the problems of idealism.[17]

This reading stands in contrast to criticism that interprets 'Theory of life' as an articulation of Coleridge's mature transcendentalism that substantiates his repudiation of Hartleyan associationism in the *Biographia*. In his analysis of 'The Eolian Harp', M. H. Abrams argues that the 'powers and forces' described in the treatise 'are not physical or phenomenal, but metascientific and pre-phenomenal elements . . ., hence they cannot be pictured, but only imagined'; they do not exist 'within the phenomenal world', but 'bring [it] into being, [and] have especially close and revealing analogues' (1984: 171). Likewise, Smith claims that Coleridge 'sees through the veil in moments of inspiration to the underlying non-material reality' (1999: 36), and David Vallins asserts that he outlines a 'Plotinian theory of evolution', though he borrows from 'contemporary scientific theory' (2000: 135). For these critics, Coleridge posits an ideal world that exists independently of the phenomenal world that is accessible to the mind, but not the body. Thus many scholars contend that he sets 'Reason and Imagination above the mind of the flesh' (Willey 1946: 11). These critics see Coleridge as an idealist, espousing the sort of vitalist position held by his German influences.

In my reading, 'Theory of life' represents Coleridge's attempt to disrupt 'the traditional opposition between the mechanistic/reductionists on the one hand and holist/vitalists on the other', which defined the 'biological problem-space of the 19th century' (Varela 1991: 84). The ontological propositions that he puts forward in 'Theory of life' make the claims in the *Biographia* possible on a physical level. His proposal that the subject and the object emerge from the absolute serves as a prerequisite for human perception of the absolute. 'Theory of life' allows Coleridge to explain how human beings can apprehend 'a God not visible, audible, or tangible' (1983: 121), a feat that is inexplicable under dualism and impossible under materialism. Because his theory of knowledge hinges on his theory of life, it resembles the connection between enaction and autopoiesis. By interrogating its ontological claims using autopoietic enaction, we understand how an embodied subject and object might exist in relationship to the 'self-grounded, unconditional' (Coleridge 1983: 268).

---

[16] See also Thomas McFarland, *Coleridge and the Pantheist Tradition* (1969).

[17] Passages of 'Theory of life' are direct translations made by Coleridge from Schelling's *Ideen zu einer Philosophie der Natur* (1803) and *System des transcendentalen Idealismus* (1800), as well as Steffens's *Grundzüge der philosophischen Naturwissenschaft* (1806) and *Beyträge zut innern Naturegeschichte der Erde* (1801). Some critics view his use of these works as plagiarism, intentional or otherwise. René Wellek, for example, argues that in light of these borrowings, 'we must . . . come to a lower estimate of his significance' as a thinker (1981: 151). Conversely, Jackson and Jackson claim that Coleridge did not merely parrot *Naturphilosophie*, but 'differed from Schelling and Steffens in his conception of the beginning and end of the dynamic process' (1995: I, 483). In my view, Coleridge used other philosophers' work to help articulate his own position and to present his own ideas. See Berkeley's *Coleridge and the Crisis of Reason* (2007) for a nuanced analysis of Coleridge's borrowings that teases out his position in light of the debate about Spinoza amongst the German transcendentalists.

In 'Theory of life', Coleridge identifies the source of life, as he understood it at that period in his life. In a public debate, Abernethy championed John Hunter's theory that life is a vital principle that animates matter, while Lawrence claimed that life originates in the material substance that is organised to support it.[18] While Coleridge approved of Abernethy's position, he objected to the idea that the '*material vitae diffusa* ("the diffused matter of life") was something like electricity' (Jackson and Jackson 1995: I, 482), which Abernethy claimed was a subtle fluid. Attributing the power of life to a material phenomenon threatens hylozoism, the idea that every particle of matter is alive. Like Kant, whose work influenced the essay, Coleridge wanted to avoid 'the doctrine that all matter is endowed with life', but also saw 'the futility of appealing to any immaterial principle of vitality outside of nature' (Thompson 2007: 140). Where Kant refused to make ontological claims, advancing 'the position that self-organization can be only a regulative principle of our judgment, not a constitutive principle of nature' (Thompson 2007: 140), Coleridge replaces a world composed of substances – material or immaterial – with one made of self-organising energy. This, I argue, allowed him to explain how the eternal absolute can serve as substrate for transient nature.

In some respects, Coleridge's reconceptualisation of the material world is similar to Priestley's in that it 'consist[s] in the spiritualization of all the laws of nature' (Coleridge 1983: 256). However, where Priestley spiritualised matter by challenging accepted definitions, Coleridge eliminates matter by substituting it with 'laws of intuition and intellect' (Coleridge 1983: 256). For Coleridge, the world exists by means of a creative act of an intelligent and intelligible being. Influenced by *Naturphilosophie*, he conceived of life as an absolute law that has two poles, unity and individuality. Life's tendency toward union and its countermovement toward individuation are in constant tension. From this striving of opposites, the actual or real world emerges. According to Coleridge, this activity manifests as the laws of nature – gravity, electricity, magnetism and so forth – each with its own striving poles. As these energies synthesise, the transient world emerges and matter is reconceived 'as a fluxional antecedent' (Coleridge 1995: 523). In this view, it has no substance, only activity.

Coleridge advanced his idea before the advent of cell theory and dynamic systems theory. Yet examining his ideas in light of the contemporary concepts of autopoiesis and dynamic co-emergence makes them legible from a twenty-first-century perspective and provides a context for a more tangible understanding of his theory of knowledge. To distinguish living from non-living things, autopoiesis separates heteronomous from autonomous systems. The former is a system 'whose organization is defined by . . . external mechanisms of control', while an autonomous system 'is defined by its endogenous, self-organizing and self-controlling dynamics' (Thompson 2007: 43). In this view, heteronomous systems are determined by external circumstances, while autonomous systems are self-generating,

---

[18] Lawrence echoes John Thelwall's position, articulated nearly a quarter of a century earlier in *An Essay Towards a Definition of Animal Vitality* (1793).

self-maintaining and determined from within. In autopoiesis, the cell is the basic exemplar of a living system. It is self-organising and autonomous and, therefore, meets the two minimal conditions for life. This concept is similar to Coleridge's distinction between organisation *ab extra* (from without) and organisation *ab intra* (from within). He claims that the '*vis vitae vivida*', or life force, is 'contradistinguished from mechanism, *ab extra*, under the form of organization', and 'whatever is organized from without, is a product of mechanism; whatever is mechanised from within, is a production of organization' (Coleridge 1995: 511). That is, entities formed entirely by external forces – rocks, for example – are distinguished from living entities, which are organised from within.[19] For Coleridge, as for proponents of autopoiesis, living organisms exhibit self-organising tendencies that separate them from non-living things.

The autopoietic concept of self-organisation is comparable to Coleridge's claim that living things exhibit 'the tendency to individuation' (1995: 516). He defines individuation as the pole of life that strives to express itself as a singularity, or autonomous entity. In contemporary terms, we might call this an organism. Individuation opposes the tendency toward unity, which is the pole that strives to merge back into the universal life force. Striving, for Coleridge, expresses oppositional energies that move toward different states of being – existence as an individual entity or absorption into an undifferentiated whole. The former he called life; the latter is death. Thus Coleridge characterises living things by their ability to 'maintain for themselves a distinction from the universal life of the planet' (1995: 516). They are able to self-organise enough to differentiate themselves from the life force into an individuated being, and they remain alive as long as they are able to resist the pull of the other pole. When they can no longer maintain themselves, they dissolve and merge back into the life force. In autopoiesis, this 'tendency to individuate' is described in terms of cell theory, whereby 'a cell stands out of a molecular soup by creating the boundaries that set it apart from what it is not' (Thompson 2007: 99). As long as the cell is able to maintain and reproduce its boundaries, it resists dissolution and death. What Coleridge calls the law of life, autopoiesis calls a molecular soup. The law of life governs the life force's self-organising activity, whereas in autopoiesis cells emerge from their surround because they are a certain kind of self-organising system.[20] In both cases, however, the important point is the self-organising tendency because it is an example of dynamic co-emergence.

Coleridge's theory expresses an idea similar to the twenty-first-century concept of dynamic co-emergence that not only challenges Cartesian ontology but enables him to advance a theory of cognition that he hoped would solve the problems

---

[19] It is difficult to know what Coleridge saw as non-living entities because of his broad definition of life, a point I take up below.

[20] The relationship between the law of life and the life force in 'Theory of life' is complex. In a forthcoming work, I argue that their relation can be understood in terms of Coleridge's aesthetic concept of the symbol, whereby an object (or organism in this case) represents a concept that is greater than its instantiation but is also a manifestation of the concept: the life force both represents and manifests the law of life.

inherent in other accounts. In autopoiesis, organisms actively emerge and distinguish themselves from their environments. Dynamic co-emergence describes the relationship between the parts and the whole. It is a relationship that is active and reciprocal. The interaction of the parts creates a unified entity that is something more than the parts taken individually. The parts also become something more because they exist in connection to the whole, which gives them definition and purpose as part of a system. This definition and purpose is greater than each part would have on its own. Thompson explains that when a system dynamically co-emerges, the 'whole not only arises from its parts, but the parts also arise from that whole' such that they 'mutually specify each other' (2007: 38). Each part of the system, including the system itself, takes on new definitions and functions that only have meaning because they exist in relationship to each other. The system that emerges exhibits behaviours and properties beyond those displayed by its component parts separately.[21]

Coleridge postulates that 'a whole composed, *ab intra*, of different parts, so far interdependent that each is reciprocally means and ends, is an individual' (1995: 512). The threshold for being classed as a discrete, living entity in his theory depends on self-organisation. Furthermore, the parts that make up the entity create each other, or, in Thompson's words, 'mutually specify' each other, such that they function as both cause and effect within the relationship. They are 'so far interdependent that each is reciprocally means and end'. Not only does the interaction of the parts redefine them, but the 'relation which the parts have to the whole' is that 'their action extends more or less beyond themselves' (Coleridge 1995: 512). As a result of being part of a system, each component's function transforms into something more than it would have been on its own. In other words, something new emerges from the interdependent relationship between the parts and the whole in living systems. For Coleridge, as in autopoiesis, this something new is an autonomous, self-organising entity.

Coleridge calls the thing that emerges from the law of life's striving poles 'a tertium aliquid' or third thing (1983: 300). In terms of 'Theory of life', the *tertium aliquid* manifests as the world in which we live. In the *Biographia*, he calls it a 'finite generation' (Coleridge 1983: 300). Thus the transient world emerges from the absolute. In this way, Coleridge explains how the perishable subject and the impermanent object exist in relationship to the eternal. When they individuate from the life force, they differentiate not only from the absolute, but also from each other. This relationship is characterised by dynamic co-emergence. Viewed from an autopoietic perspective, Coleridge considers life as an emergent biotic system. He defines life more expansively than biologists do today. For example, he considers

---

[21] A useful example is Frankenstein's creature. From stitched-together body parts and electricity emerges something greater than either – life and intelligence in the form of an eloquent and tormented being. He demonstrates how a whole can be more than the sum of its parts and how each part can be transformed into something more than it was on its own. Thompson (2007: 38) cites tornadoes as an example of a non-living dynamically co-emergent system.

The absolute, or the law of life

Unity ← → Individuation

The

Sensible World

noble metals and crystalline formations as living systems.[22] For Coleridge, nearly everything in the sensible world is an expression of this law. His 'definition of a thing', or object, is 'the synthesis of opposing energies. That a thing *is*, is owing to the co-inherence therein of any two powers; but that it is *that* particular thing arises from the proportions in which these powers are co-present' (Coleridge 1995: 535). Objects exist because life's clashing poles manifest as various types of energy (gravity, magnetism, electricity) that combine to create a dynamic tension that allows 'a thing' to emerge. What makes it unique, or a 'particular thing', is the ratio of each kind of energy that comprises it. Objects differ because 'the proportions' of 'these powers' vary from thing to thing. By conceiving of life in this way, Coleridge subverts Cartesian dichotomies.

Coleridge's ontological claims attempt to solve the problem of interactionism by rendering the world perceptible. As the powers of nature strive, 'their interpenetration and co-inherence first constitute them sensible', or available to perception (Coleridge 1995: 524). The objects of nature, in this theory, must organise into individual entities so that subjects can sense and perceive them. The tendency to individuate is required for cognition. Coleridge asserts that 'divisibility, or *multeity*, . . . is the indispensable condition, under which alone anything can *appear* to us, or even be *thought* of, as a *thing*' (1995: 513). Through individuation the world becomes tangible. Proposing that everything is made of energy, Coleridge provides an explanation of how the mind, body and world interact. Consequently, although he does not explicitly address cognition in 'Theory of life', he clears the way for his treatment of it in the *Biographia*.

---

[22] While many biologists today and back then would disagree, his broad definition of life may be compared to the Gaia theory, which maintains that 'the material environment of life on Earth is in part a biological construction' (Thompson 2007: 119).

Coleridge's ontology lets him claim, in the *Biographia*, that the 'body and spirit are . . . no longer absolutely heterogeneous, but *may* without any *absurdity* be supposed to be different modes, or degrees in perfection, of a common substratum' (1983: 114). All things in the transient world, according to his theory of life, including human beings, are the same in kind though different in degree. Though neither text references the other, nor makes an overt connection between the ontological and epistemological claims laid out in each, their relationship becomes apparent as we examine his theories in conjunction with autopoietic enaction.

Coleridge's theory of knowledge, though highly abstract, hypostatises when we examine it in light of his ontological claims. As in enaction, Coleridge refuses to privilege either the subject or the object: 'During the act of knowledge itself, the objective and the subjective are so instantly united, that we cannot determine to which of the two priority belongs' (1983: 255). He places them in a reciprocal relationship that is analogous to the law of life's striving poles. One cannot exist without the other, for 'an object is inconceivable without a subject as its antithesis' (Coleridge 1983: 271). Conversely, the subject is 'the necessary correlative of the object' (1983: 254). This mutually co-dependent relationship implies that the 'mind or sentient being' cannot exist unless there is an object to specify it (1983: 253). Knowledge, then, is not something that the subject imposes on the object or that the object impresses on the subject. Rather, 'in all acts of positive knowledge there is required a reciprocal concurrence of both' (1983: 255). It emerges from the interaction of subject and object, and, for Coleridge, knowledge extends beyond the natural and social worlds to encompass the absolute.

When we look at the *Biographia* and 'Theory of life' together, we see that knowledge of the absolute emerges from the intersection of the subject and the object in much the same way as they emerge from the absolute. The relationship is recursive. Just as the sensible world emerges from the law of life as a third thing, knowledge of

The enacted mind

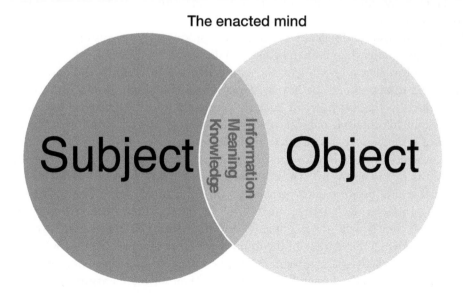

the law emerges as the *tertium aliquid* of interaction with the world. Coleridge's philosophical discussion of cognition assumes embodiment and embeddedness as he draws together strands from the dualist, materialist, transcendentalist and mystical authors he had read. By shifting the ontological ground, he can accept as 'true . . . the assertion of Hobbes, of Hartley, and of their masters in ancient Greece, that all real knowledge supposes a prior sensation' (Coleridge 1983: 285–86). His acknowledgement that sensation is a precondition of knowledge implies that the subject has a body with which to sense the world. It further suggests that this embodied subject is embedded in a real environment that affords sensory stimuli. Coleridge can accept this materialist tenet because he, at least provisionally, worked out a theory of life that did not equate sensation and thought. '[S]ensation', he explains, 'is a vision nascent, not the cause of intelligence, but intelligence itself revealed' (Coleridge 1983: 286). Through embodied interaction with the environment, the subject gains knowledge of the entity that makes being and knowing possible – the absolute.

If we consider this idea in terms of structural coupling, it becomes apparent that organisation – the literal fact of having organs with which to see, hear, taste, smell and feel – is necessary in Coleridge's theory of cognition. In 'Theory of life', he asserts that living things individuate in increasingly complex structures, finding highest expression in humankind, particularly the human mind. Humans are 'the apex of the living pyramid' (Coleridge 1995: 550), in which 'the centripetal and individualizing tendency of all Nature is itself concentred and individualized' (1995: 551). In human beings, dynamic co-emergence manifests most perfectly because the reciprocity between the parts and the whole is in greatest balance. Thus the particular organisation of the human body enables knowledge of the absolute. Nature, likewise, provides the right kinds of affordances. Coleridge states that 'all the organs of sense are framed for a corresponding world of sense' (1983: 242). Here, he postulates that human cognitive apparatus enacts knowledge of the absolute in conjunction with the natural world.

Despite his abstract discussion of knowledge-production in terms of the subject and the object rather than human beings and the natural world, Coleridge's theory assumes and implies embodiment and embeddedness because the human body is organised to apprehend the law of life as it moves through an external world equally fitted to that purpose. In enactive terms, the idea of structural coupling suggests that information qua information exists neither subjectively nor objectively, but is defined by the interaction of the two and only becomes meaningful as it is enacted by a subject for self-organising ends: 'what is meaningful for an organism is precisely given by its constitution as a distributed process, with an indissociable link between local processes where an interaction occurs' (Varela 1991: 86). In Coleridge's terms, 'quantities', or data, acquire meaning 'only in the relations they bear to the percipient', and that 'reality, in the external world' cannot be known 'independent of the mind that perceives them' (1995: 506). Like contemporary enactivists, he recognises the phenomenological aspect of cognition, that is, that objects have no significance in and of themselves, but assume meaning based on how they are perceived. Subjects construct the world subjectively because their perceptual and cognitive apparatuses and their physiological requirements as autonomous systems make certain aspects of their environments meaningful. Subjects do not construct it solipsistically because the object-world exists independently of them.

While the absolute composes both the subject and the object, it is apprehensible only when they are taken together. Coleridge claims that the absolute 'is to be found . . . neither in subject or object taken separately, . . . [but] must be found in that which is neither subject nor object exclusively, but which is the identity of both' (1983: 271). As with the enactive idea of structural coupling, it is a product of a history of spatiotemporal interactions between the percipient and the perceived through which the former gains knowledge both of the world and of the absolute.

One final ingredient is required, though, to make perception of the absolute possible: self-consciousness. In autopoietic enaction, consciousness is the condition under which human beings obtain all knowledge. Phenomenologically, it is 'a form or structure of comportment, a perceptual and motor attunement to the world' that shapes and defines our understanding of it (Thompson 2007: 80). Coleridge claims that 'self-consciousness is for *us* the source and principle of all *our* possible knowledge' (1983: 284). The use of the adjective 'possible' indicates that it demarcates what we can and cannot know about the world, the absolute, and even ourselves. Refuting both the sceptical and idealist positions, Coleridge attempts to explain how we can know 'the existence of things without us' (1983: 260), or that the world is not a mere projection of the human mind. For him, self-consciousness assures us that we live in a real, rather than ideal, world because in self-consciousness the sensible world and our perception of it coincide. Unlike other sensate creatures, it is characteristic of human beings alone because of our anatomical organisation.

In the concept of self-consciousness, the recursive nature of Coleridge's theory of life and theory of knowledge becomes apparent. He asserts that in self-consciousness 'the realism of man properly consist[s]' (1983: 261). Realism, as 'Theory of life' explains, refers to the sensible world as distinguished from the absolute. In the act of perception, the absolute and the transient meet and mutually specify each other. Also, according to 'Theory of life', the absolute manifests as autonomous self-organisation, reaching its pinnacle in self-consciousness, which, according to *Biographia Literaria*, is the basis of human cognition. These two processes necessitate each other. They intersect in the actual world, beginning with sensation, which Coleridge defines as 'an earlier power in the process of self-construction' (1983: 286). Sensation, as noted earlier, is the means by which we begin to apprehend the world and the life force that generates it.

Life in the sensate human body is, by nature, characterised by cognition. The very act of sensing and perceiving the world, which is contingent upon action and motor skills, results in intelligence. This, I contend, is what Coleridge means when he asserts that 'Truth is correlative of being' (1983: 264). To live in the world is to interact with it. To interact with the world is to come to know it. 'To know', he claims, 'is in its very essence a verb active' (1983: 264). Cognition is an act that defines human existence, and through embodied, embedded action emerges intelligence, both human and divine: 'in the absolute identity of subject and object . . . is nothing else but self-conscious will or intelligence' (1983: 285). Human life and the absolute law of life are expressions of a creative, intelligent act.

Being and knowing exist in an endless, reciprocal, mutually constitutive relationship, like Coleridge's knotted skein of yarn. In enactive terms, 'we find ourselves in a circle: we are in a world that seems to be there before reflection [cognition] begins, but that world is not separate from us' (Varela et al. 1991: 3). Epistemology and ontology are recursive in Coleridge's system because knowledge of the world emerges from subject-object interaction while, simultaneously, the subject and the object come into being through the striving poles of the law of life. This law is the 'actuating principle of all other truths, whether physical or intellectual' (Coleridge 1995: 534), and cognition is 'the action of enacting a law' (Thompson 2007: 13). In Coleridge's theories, the act of knowing is, quite literally, the implementation and manifestation of the law. Thus the absolute and the transient world are brought into being through the cognitive act.

The absolute, the subject and the object dynamically co-emerge from each other, each making the others possible in an infinitely repeating loop. For Coleridge, this relationship 'may be described as a perpetual self-duplication of one and the same power into object and subject, which presupposes each other, and can only exist as antithesis' (1983: 273). The poles of life, unity and individuation, synthesise to create the sensible world, and the interaction of subject and object synthesises into knowledge. These processes, in Thompson's terms, 'recursively depend on each other for their own generation and realization' (2007: 67). Just as life is 'the copula or unity of thesis and antithesis' (Coleridge 1995: 518–19), so knowledge of the absolute emerges as a copula of the subject and the object. Coleridge's antithesis can be understood in terms of mutual co-dependence and co-origination because

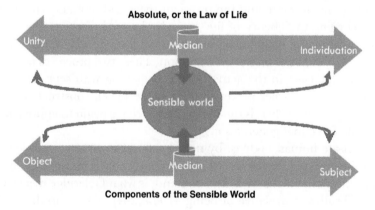

Recursive relationship between life and cognition

Absolute, or the Law of Life

Unity   Median   Individuation

Sensible world

Object   Median   Subject

Components of the Sensible World

knowledge, in enactive terms, comes into being through an emergent process that occurs in a system of 'interrelated components' (Thompson 2007: 418). In Coleridge's case, the interrelated components are the subject, the object and the absolute.

Conclusion

While applying the lens of autopoietic enaction allows us to understand the problems that Coleridge was trying to solve, ultimately he was dissatisfied with the theories that he advanced in these works. According to Jackson and Jackson, 'Theory of life' was never published during Coleridge's lifetime because his 'views on the German philosophers who provided some of the materials for the work altered rapidly' (1995: I, 481). Likewise, editors James Engell and W. Jackson Bate note that he changed his mind about some of the views expressed in *Biographia*. Perhaps Coleridge recognised that no matter the ontology, conflating the subject and the object always raises the question about how to distinguish between the two. Indeed, the originators of enaction claim that 'grasping after a[n absolute] ground, whether inner or outer, is the deep source of frustration and anxiety' (Varela et al. 1991: 143). Scholars such as N. Katherine Hayles are sceptical that theories such as autopoietic enaction solve the problems they say they do. In her view, these theories cling to the illusion of an autonomous subject even as they challenge the grounds for its existence by positing that organisms are 'fascinating meshworks of selfless selves' (Varela 1991: 104).[23] Regardless of these critiques, I maintain that the ideas advanced by contemporary theorists and by Coleridge offer productive ways of reconceptualising ourselves in relationship to the world.

The metaphors used to describe and understand cognition deeply affect the ways that human beings understand and relate to our surroundings and to other people. Moving away from a computational model, which analogises human beings to machines, toward a more inclusive model that not only defines cognition more broadly, but also sees it as an emergent process between percipients and their surroundings, can loosen the grip of Cartesian concepts of subject and object, or self and other. Understanding life as 'reciprocal causality' between living things and their environments has potential to change the way we understand ourselves, our world and the relationship between the two. If we no longer see nature as mechanistic or animated by a vital principle, but as dependent on us as we are on it, perhaps it would obviate the need to act as the 'master and possessor of Nature' (Sutcliffe 1971: 21). According to the concept of structural coupling the environment evolves in response to actions taken by organisms just as much as organisms adapt to their surroundings. Adopting such an understanding seems to be what environmental groups advocate, and the enactive approach could enable this epistemic shift. Of course, this worldview is not new; many of the peoples who inhabited what is now called North America understood, and continue to understand,

---

[23] See Hayles's discussion of autopoiesis in *How We Became Posthuman* (1999).

relationships between humans, animals and the land in terms that theorists of enaction label mutual co-dependence.[24]

For Coleridge, ontology and epistemology had an ethical imperative. Indeed, I contend that our ingrained understanding of what the world is, and how we come to know it, affects the rightness or wrongness of our relationships. For this reason, Coleridge's ideas merit renewed attention because his theories of life and of knowledge 'force us to revise how we think about matter, life, and mind' (Thompson 2007: 67).[25] Coleridge's 'ambition [was] to find a way of healing the Cartesian divide' (Smith 1999: 31) because it drives a detrimental wedge between the subject and the object. Though he did not find a satisfactory landing place in the theories advanced in these texts, he continued to seek resolution for the philosophical and theological quandary of how the many relate to the one. Coleridge's notebooks make clear that he was never satisfied with his efforts to synthesise ontology, epistemology, ethics and theology. Nonetheless, he continued to try. Mitchell's analysis of the life manuals demonstrates that Coleridge's abiding pursuit was not just finding answers, but 'providing readers with protocols for disorienting themselves' (Mitchell 2013: 99). Coleridge saw this as a process of engaging mindfully with life rather than relying on mindless habit.[26]

Coleridge continued to participate in this struggle even though he could not ultimately solve the problem. In this respect, his efforts were successful, and his work invites us to do the same – to continuously engage in the difficult task of considering whether we are in the right relationship with ourselves, our surroundings, our community, and with the ground of being.[27] His theory, like autopoietic enaction, enables us to come to 'the inevitable conclusion [which] is that knower and known, mind and world, stand in relation to each other through mutual specification' (Varela et al. 1991: 150). This is more important than finding ultimate answers. Coleridge's writings on ontology and epistemology from this period stand as an important challenge to the Cartesian dichotomy between mind and matter and present a meaningful attempt to close the gap between consciousness and nature. He participates in a history that sought to repair the Cartesian split between the subject and the object by resituating nature in a meaningful relationship with humanity.[28] His work, in conjunction with contemporary 4E theories, encourages us to continue to engage with these questions and to muddle through the answers.

---

[24] I owe the inspiration for this comparison to Audra Simpson's Joseph Harper Cash Memorial Lecture '"We are not Red Indians" (We might all be Red Indians): Anticolonial sovereignty across the borders of time, place and sentiment', delivered on 17 March 2016 at the University of South Dakota.

[25] Thompson says this about Maurice Merleau-Ponty, but it applies equally to Coleridge.

[26] Richard Sha also argues that in the *Biographia* Coleridge 'demands readers to think about their own methods as they think about the imagination' (2013: 412).

[27] For Coleridge, God is the ground of being, but for us it might be something like 'society' or 'the environment'.

[28] See Nicholas Halmi, 'Mind as microcosm' (2001: 48).

8

Cognitive Scaffolding, *Aids to Reflection*

John Savarese

This chapter takes Coleridge's *Aids to Reflection* (1825) as a case study in how Coleridge pictured thinking as distributed. While he developed *Aids to Reflection* as a handbook that would help young adults grapple with difficult religious questions, it ultimately models 'reflection' as a process that took place between an individual mind and its assistive apparatuses, the textual 'aids' of the title. Coleridge was consistently committed to a picture of mental life that exceeded the bounds of the individual, and that depended on a set of external props and supports. This chapter's premise is that we might usefully read this aspect of Coleridge's thought in light of the notion of 'scaffolding' in embedded and extended accounts of cognition. 'Scaffolding', in this more recent sense, derives from the tradition of Soviet psychologist Lev Vygotsky, who emphasised the ways that structures of a learning environment shape and change a learner's mental processing. Vygotsky offered an account of language itself as a scaffolding structure of this sort, and his resulting picture of 'inner' thought as deriving from a social and environmental apparatus has been influential both in pedagogical theory and more recently in a number of approaches to distributed cognition. I invoke scaffolding here as a general term, rather than affiliating Coleridge with a particular embedded or extended position. First, there is significant overlap in the ways that different approaches to distributed cognition use scaffolding as a concept, with ample room as well for hybrid crossings. Second, and perhaps more importantly, Coleridge's own theories of cognitive 'aids', in *Aids to Reflection* and elsewhere, gesture alternately toward the way minds internalise their learning apparatuses and the way they continue to depend on external props, or create what Clark and Chalmers (in Clark 2008: 222) call a 'coupled system'. In other words, this chapter argues that Coleridge belongs in the history of distributed cognition precisely because he restlessly experimented with different ways of understanding the relationships among mind, language and information technology.

We are accustomed to a different picture of Coleridge's philosophy of mind, one centred on the individual mind's autonomy or organic unity and its capacity for transcendental deduction. This Coleridge appears most clearly in his repudiation of David Hartley's association psychology, which on Coleridge's argument made the mind too thoroughly dependent upon the external world. Hartley, like Locke, saw the mind as furnished with ideas by sensory impressions (though Hartley specified that this happened by producing a particular vibrational pattern in the nerves), and held that impressions themselves developed those ideas into an organised neural network by virtue of the association of ideas.[1] Coleridge offered a systematic refutation of Hartley's system in his 1817 *Biographia Literaria*, in which he argued that the mind must stand apart from its environment, form its own, internal organisational architecture, and, perhaps most famously, exert a creative and shaping force in the form of a transcendental power of imagination.

Over the past decades, however, an increased attention to Coleridge's scientific imagination – and to the intimacy between Romantic literature and science more broadly – has recovered a different Coleridge with a more complex relationship to physiological psychology. Richardson (2001: 9) has gone so far as to argue that Coleridge's attack on Hartley was an act of intellectual bad faith, since Hartley posed an easier target than the more nuanced and challenging physiological accounts of the mind on offer by the second decade of the nineteenth century.[2] At the same time, a renewed interest in Scottish Enlightenment figures like Thomas Reid has made it increasingly easy to see beyond Coleridge's German-influenced transcendental philosophy to his affinities with other anti-Cartesian impulses at work in Romantic-era philosophy.[3]

Shifting the focus from Romantic organicism (focused on minds as bounded, autonomous wholes) to Romantic anti-Cartesianism makes Romanticism's place in the history of distributed cognition seem somewhat closer to common sense.[4] The idea that William Blake, William Wordsworth and others saw cognition as the shared product of mind, body and world has been a critical commonplace at least since M. H. Abrams (1971: 28) described the Romantics as reconciling 'the awesome depths and height of the human mind, and of the power of that mind as in itself inadequate, by consummating a holy marriage with the external universe'. Romantic writers' hopes for a mind wedded to the external world bear some of the same anti-Cartesian exuberance as Clark and Chalmers (Clark 2008: 232), who announce that an 'extended' account of cognition will enable us 'to see ourselves more truly as creatures of the world'.

Coleridge was no stranger to the high-stakes, theologically invested language of Abrams's 'holy marriage'. The prospect that minds were constitutively linked to the world outside the head was never far from his theology, from his early sub-

---

[1] On Hartley's associationism as a 'distributed model of memory' see Sutton 1998: 248–59.

[2] Richardson was an early contributor to a sharp increase in studies of Coleridge and the science of the mind, including among others McLane 2000, Vallins 2000, Levere 2002, Vickers 2004 and Ford 2005. For a response to Richardson on the subject of Romantic materialism and identity theory, see Jager 2011.

[3] For readings of Coleridge, and Romanticism more broadly, at the intersection of science and 'common sense' philosophy, see especially Jackson 2003 and Budge 2007.

[4] For more on Coleridge's anti-Cartesianism in light of distributed cognition, see Robertson's chapter in this volume.

scription to the Unitarian idea of the 'one life' (that all beings partook of the same essence, which was God's) to his later theological handbooks. Yet as he renounced his Unitarianism and turned to defences of more orthodox Christian doctrine, what persisted was his conviction that thinking is not the inner business of enclosed individual minds, but a networked process that took place between an embodied mind and various linguistic and technological aids. Coleridge makes several explicit disavowals of the 'one life' in *Aids to Reflection* itself, warning readers against 'reducing the Creator to a mere Anima Mundi' (1993: 403).[5] Yet in its very framing *Aids to Reflection* is Coleridge's clearest assertion that an individual's spiritual life and moments of reflective meditation – apparently the most private aspects of inner life – are actually heavily mediated and depend upon assistive scaffolds.

In her chapter in this volume, Lisa Ann Robertson convincingly argues that Coleridge's theories of life, the organism and the absolute can helpfully be read in light of autopoietic enactivism. In this chapter, I am more interested in how Coleridge framed the individual process of philosophical reflection *about* those subjects, which more often emphasises aspects of the mind we would now call embedded or extended. Reading Coleridge's spiritual guidebook alongside a text like Clark and Chalmers' 'The extended mind' makes clear that Romantic-era claims about the marriage of mind and world are not always claims about the nature of spirit, and that the inner and outer do not always link up into a feedback loop or organic system. Instead, *Aids to Reflection* models the way thinking depends upon assistive devices, and demonstrates how manipulating texts can supplement internal processes. In that respect, my argument shares with Elspeth Jajdelska's chapter in this volume a focus on the way that writing systems come to serve as an environmental support for individual thought.

In what follows, I argue that even in Coleridge's most overtly spiritual 'transcendentalist' works he frames 'first philosophy' as an activity to be pursued by the individual in collaboration with environmental props. Reflection is both an inner activity and a skilled interaction with a set of external tools. The first part of the chapter examines how that way of understanding philosophical reflection – as an interaction between inner and outer – endures throughout Coleridge's long career. The second section shows how he framed individual development (and *Aids to Reflection*'s project of education) as the process of leaning upon and, in most cases, internalising scaffolding technologies like language. I conclude by turning to Coleridge's anxieties about information management systems, note-taking

---

[5] On Coleridge's relationship to Christian doctrine see Barth 2003. On his relationship to Unitarianism see White 2006: 119ff. On *Aids to Reflection*'s relationship to the 'one life' argument in particular, see Perry 1999: 69. The classic account of Coleridge's relationship to pantheism is McFarland 1969. For an alternative reading, see Hamilton's (2007: 97) argument that Coleridge is not resistant to pantheism's material implications but to the way its impersonal picture of the deity risked losing the 'communicability of knowledge, including the communication of its grounding in an Absolute or God'. This chapter's interest is less in the 'absolute' than in the model of communication it engenders, which may bring its argument closer to Haney's (2001) reading of Coleridge in terms of communicative reason.

practices and memory loss, which gave him something of a divided legacy later in the nineteenth century, and made him at once a sage in the transcendentalist tradition and a more empirical, eclectic figure of materially and textually mediated thinking.

Leaning on Philosophy

Coleridge's abiding theme was the difficulty of the kind of thinking that higher philosophy demanded, especially as it bore upon the mysteries of the Christian faith. While *Aids to Reflection* aimed to complete a young person's apprenticeship years by encouraging the development of mature, autonomous, deliberative action grounded in first philosophy, Coleridge thought of such autonomy in a nuanced way that never quite left the scaffolding embrace that initially supports it. The volume's full title – *Aids to Reflection in the Formation of a Manly Character on the Several Grounds of Prudence, Morality, and Religion: Illustrated by Select Passages from our Elder Divines, Especially from Archbishop Leighton* – registers several of the main factors that place Coleridge in the history of distributed cognition. As a book geared toward character formation, specifically promoting the arrival of young minds at a position of maturity with respect to spiritual matters, it sets up the book's focus on autonomy, self-direction and introspection, yet it bookends that independent position with scaffolds on both sides. The main title first and foremost posits 'reflection', which means both thought-fulness in general and inward-directed or self-contemplative thinking, as a project that requires 'aids'. In that sense, the volume is positioned as a vehicle of enlightenment that would promote intellectual autonomy: to think for oneself, to become a reflecting person. However, Coleridge's emphasis falls not on a Kantian ([1784] 1985a: 54) injunction to 'have courage to use your *own* understanding', but on the process of developing that understanding through the use of external scaffolds.

In Kantian terms, that is, the emphasis is less on maturity than tutelage. Siskin and Warner (2010: 3–4) have recently described this tension within theories of 'enlightenment', in terms that apply equally to Coleridge, as an equivocation between Kant's focus on the autonomous use of the understanding and a more Baconian conviction that 'you should *not* depend on your own understanding'. They cite Bacon's ([1620] 2000: 28) assertion that 'from the very start, the mind should not be left to itself, but be constantly controlled; and the business done (if I may put it this way) by machines', the latter being a term for which Bacon often substitutes 'aids', 'assistance', 'means', 'instruments' and 'tools' (Siskin and Warner 2010: 4). Siskin and Warner's reframing of enlightenment in terms of the history of 'mediation', and related work on a more media- or technology-focused linkage between Baconian enlightenment and Romanticism, makes it easier to see how Coleridge's resistance to Lockean empiricism continues working within the broad contours of enlightenment and improvement by tools.[6] Indeed, Coleridge thought

---

[6] On Romanticism's continuation of this enlightenment focus on media and mediation see especially Goodman 2005.

of his own approach to method as retaining a Baconian focus on the mind's direction of outer circumstances. In his treatment of method in the 1818 reissue of *The Friend*, he affiliates himself with 'Lord Bacon', who he claims also, like himself, 'demands . . . the intellectual or mental initiative, as the motive and guide of every philosophical experiment', such that 'an experiment is an idea realised' (1969: 489–90). *Aids to Reflection* points toward a similar use of method as the cultivation of an 'inner' guidance of the external world, but its method shifts from 'reflection' to 'aids', the means by which method disciplines and guides the intellect from without. The enlightenment had expended much effort to reframe this paradox of subject formation as a linear process of development from guidance to self-reliance. Coleridge would have found the roots of that argument in Bacon's (2000: 28) young mind that 'from the very start . . . should not be left to itself', which he would have heard echoed in Kant's (1985a: 54) account of enlightenment as coming 'to use your *own* understanding' after a period of 'immaturity' or 'guidance'. That use of the apprenticeship model has at present become more pointed in studies of mind and intelligence by way of Vygotsky's ([1930] 1978: 73) children who 'master their own behaviour, at first by external means and later by more complex inner operations'.

Coleridge's decision to produce a book of philosophical aphorisms was Baconian at the level of form, too, and underscores that developing minds found supports and scaffolds in a mediated relationship to stylised texts. The continuation of the subtitle, with its focus on 'passages from our elder divines', signals the book's still more pronounced relationship to a mode of textually mediated reflection. *Aids to Reflection* was originally conceived, after all, not as a series of Coleridgean aphorisms, but as an experiment in guided or scaffolded reading. The germ of the plan was initially for Coleridge to produce an edition of his favourite passages from the writings of Robert Leighton, Principal of the University of Edinburgh from 1653 to 1662 and Archbishop of Glasgow from 1670 to 1674, whose aphorisms he thought to be particularly helpful. Coleridge's role was to be less author than editor, almost as if offering the public his commonplace book.[7] His voice would primarily come through in an editorial apparatus. As plans progressed, Coleridge's annotations and glosses began to overtake Leighton's aphorisms, and the volume ultimately published was in good part Coleridge's own prose.[8] Its apparatus, though, often makes it fairly difficult for readers to parse Leighton's from Coleridge's voice, the 'authorial' from 'editorial' hand. As the voices blended, so too did the relationship between the text and its assistive apparatus, between the reflections Leighton was to have prompted and the reflections upon Leighton which its humble editor was to have aided. It would seem, then, that it was not enough to offer Leighton's aphorisms as 'aids to reflection': those aids required aids of their own. Over the course

---

[7] On commonplacing in light of distributed cognition see below, as well as Jajdelska's chapter in this volume and Anderson 2015b.

[8] For a detailed overview of *Aids to Reflection*'s editorial history, see Beer's introduction in Coleridge 1993: cxxxi.

of the title alone, what begins as a set of scaffolded mental exercises to promote autonomy gradually comes to appear more dispersed, an increasingly intricate series of texts about texts.

This was hardly the first time Coleridge framed philosophical reflection as a process to be guided or mediated by textual apparatuses. That orientation dates back at least to February 1801, when he wrote a letter to Josiah Wedgewood lamenting the 'pernicious custom begun', no less, 'by the great Bacon, & in no small degree fostered by Des Cartes [*sic*], of neglecting to make ourselves accurately acquainted with the opinions of those who have gone before us' (1956–71: II, 700–1). As an antidote, Coleridge urges young would-be philosophers to read widely in previous philosophy, which will make sure they 'lose no time in superfluous Discoveries of Truths long before discovered' (2, 701). Coleridge is not just advising wide reading, but is specifically accusing proponents of the British empiricist tradition (in context, primarily Locke) of pushing aside previously established knowledge in favour of an enlightened self-reliance on one's own reason and the evidence of the senses. Coleridge's aim, too, is ultimately for the individual to arrive at a position of mature, autonomous thinking. However, for him the process of cultivating that autonomy is fundamentally collaborative rather than individual.

Of particular interest for historians of distributed cognition is the way that Coleridge emphasises this scaffolded thinking's ability to accelerate the process of thinking – it is better to stand on the shoulders of giants than to waste time – and especially the way he goes on to analogise the process of collective philosophical memory with biological memory:

> That periodical Forgetfulness, which would be a shocking Disease in the mind of an Individual relatively to its own Discoveries, must be pernicious in the Species. For I would believe there is more than a metaphor in the affirmation, that the whole human Species from Adam to Bonaparte, from China to Peru, may be considered as one Individual Mind. (1956–71: II, 701)

The idea of the species as 'one Individual Mind', if 'more than a metaphor', is still something less than a literal account of a group mind. This could mean that the Unitarian 'one life' is beginning to become metaphorical for Coleridge, but it could also mean that he sees a way in which the whole species could 'be considered as' a single mind in a more modest sense, if we are willing to entertain the notion that important parts of our cognitive apparatus exist in a shared storehouse of arguments and 'truths'. Milnes (2010: 181) is surely correct to find traces in this passage of Coleridge's Kantian tendency toward absolutes, and his conviction in 'truth as the *presupposition* of communication'. Yet the letter's main thrust is as much that there is a truth of the matter – about which Locke and his followers are wrong – as that modern-day thinkers should make use of available, textual aids rather than thinking by the force of their own intellects alone.

For my purposes here, the letter's most relevant detail is not its hint at a vast spiritual community, or a set of established and orthodox truths, which should be inculcated into the rising generation, but the way it makes philosophical reflection an activity that occurs in real time, with the same immediacy as working out a particularly complex mathematical equation or logical proof. Philosophy generates a common stock of knowledge and texts that can help individual thinkers 'lose no time'. Thinking with philosophical history behind you, to use the example Clark and Chalmers (in Clark 2008: 221) cite, is like solving an equation with the aid of pen and paper, or reaching for the best word to play in Scrabble by rearranging the tiles. Coleridge's language is still, to be sure, that of a grand narrative of philosophical progress, but his language of fast and slow thinking, and above all his analogy between philosophical precedent and biological memory, make his gesture toward a group mind seem less invested in the group or species than in the individual thinker and in the resources available to that thinker. In other words, books of philosophy are already cognitive scaffolding for Coleridge in 1801. The language of the species as one mind may even move Coleridge into the territory of the extended mind, insofar as he pictures the scaffolded thought process as taking place outside the individual. The 'one mind' argument is here 'more than a metaphor' perhaps because of a real sense in which Coleridge wanted to see the cognitive labour here as performed, at least in part, by the scaffolding apparatus rather than the individual alone.

Coleridge remained interested in these collective repositories of knowledge. Long after he disowned the 'one life' argument and gestures toward the species mind, he retained a similar focus on the way that collective life depended upon the development of better tools, both in the form of particular texts or philosophical systems and by the broader, more dispersed mediation of cultural institutions. Books of philosophy were not the only location of these artefacts, which also included the more diffuse way in which ideological assumptions existed in common life; features of ordinary language, which Coleridge thought changed over time to reflect a society's increasing intellectual cultivation; and the establishment of political and religious institutions that had a constant though frequently unnoticed effect on the British population of all ranks.

Aids to Reflection begins by gesturing explicitly toward the affordances of life in a society that has been set up, at the structural rather than individual level, to foster a particular, Christian mode of thinking. The volume's very first words, in the 'Address to the Reader' (1993: 9), hail that reader energetically as 'FELLOW CHRISTIAN!' not just because it is a book on Christian doctrine (meant to be read in good faith by co-religionists), but because the material and ideological apparatus of Christianity is central to the process Coleridge envisioned for his audience. He continues:

READER! – You have been bred in a land abounding with men, able in arts, learning, and knowledges manifold, this man in one, this in another, few in many, none in all. But there is one art, of which every man should be master, the art of REFLECTION. (1993: 9)

This sounds like the classic definition of reflection as introspection. On this initial account, reflection is the sole exception to the logic of the division of labour. While modern subjects depend on various trades and disciplinary 'knowledges', reflection is an internal activity that simply cannot be performed by another.

Yet this begs the question of the entire volume of *Aids to Reflection*, and so Coleridge immediately goes on to suggest that this type of reflection is, in some important ways, subject to the division of labour after all: 'But you are likewise born in a CHRISTIAN land, and Revelation has provided for you new subjects for reflection, and new treasures of knowledge, never to be unlocked by him who remains self-ignorant' (1993: 10). The broadest framework here is the idea of a history of revelation that supplements natural religion and the corporeal understanding. Living 'in a CHRISTIAN land' means having access, in the world-historical sense, to these aids that come from outside the human thought process altogether. The geographical situation of the reader in a Christian land is a geographical designation that also tracks a temporal progress within a grand providential narrative: living in the age of Christian revelation meant, for a guardian of orthodoxy like Coleridge, having access to means or mediations (the revelation of the Gospels, or the mediating action of Christ) simply not available to earlier ages, or in any age to the merely corporeal understanding. Yet it also tracks temporal progress within a more material narrative of social development, namely the Scottish Enlightenment 'stage theory' typified by Adam Smith's ([1762] 1978: 14) identification of 'four distinct states which mankind pass thro' (hunting, pastoral life, agriculture and commerce). As societies develop in economic and technological complexity (via, for example, the increased division of labour or the development of irrigation systems), individuals in those societies find their own labour lightened.

The analogy between those two models of social development – one calibrated to the supernatural supplement of divine action and the other to the society's material base – meant, for Coleridge, that claims about providential history needed to be rearticulated as claims about a particular society's material infrastructure. He frequently supplemented the sheer force of revelation with a number of more concrete, material sites for the support and cultivation of life in 'a Christian land', from the practice of living in parishes in an established Christian state, which he thought offered particular affordances to parishioners, to the provision of what he termed 'the Clerisy', a secular learned class continuing the work originally assigned to religious clergy. Coleridge describes the clerisy as curators of the domains of knowledge that had previously fallen under the rubric of theology, above all 'the ground-knowledge, the prima scientia as it was named, – PHILOSOPHY, or the doctrine and discipline of *ideas*' ([1830] 1976: 46–7). The idea of the clerisy might be understood as another way Coleridge thought higher philosophical thinking (and specifically Baconian 'first philosophy') could be built into social institutions rather than leaving them to private study or an inward model of spiritual reflection.[9]

While Coleridge's main point of reference here is cultivation, civilisation and

---

[9] On Coleridge's idea of 'the clerisy' see Prickett 1979 and Knights 2010.

providential history, it might be fruitful to read his account of structured institutions alongside what Wheeler and Clark (2008: 3564) call 'cognitive niche construction': the way that 'the cultural transmission of knowledge and practices resulting from individual lifetime learning, when combined with the physical persistence of artefacts', affects the environment in which selection and adaptation occur. The examples of group practices Wheeler and Clark cite – a bartender who 'inherits an array of differently shaped glassware' that helps keep track of recipes and orders, beavers' process of dam building, or methods for domesticating cattle and producing milk – would for Coleridge also include living in a society organised into parishes, or where various features of civic life were structured and shaped by a nationally provisioned, learned class. Not least among these reshaped artefacts of inherited thinking was language, which Coleridge explicitly framed as a socially derived tool that improved over time. Indeed, in a more famous (1983: 114) gesture toward a group mind, he coins the term 'collective unconscious' to refer to 'an instinct of growth, a certain collective, unconscious good sense' that operates 'in all societies' to make a language's vocabulary increasingly precise, and thus make language a better tool to think with.[10] Coleridge's account of ordinary language thus resembles Richard Gregory's (1993: 48) description of language as the most important kind of 'mind tool', or Andy Clark's (1998) more recent suggestion that, besides its communicative function, language also serves as a world-changing artefact that simplifies problems and aids in their solution.[11] While Coleridge had conflicting opinions about whether language should be viewed as a tool in this way, he frequently frames ordinary language as a feature of a local, culturally specific environment that assists thinking.

Coupled Systems and the 'Net-Work' of Thought

Aids to Reflection hinges on Coleridge's technological account of language. 'Self-knowledge' can be gleaned 'by reflection alone', according to Coleridge, but reflection is as much a process of introspection as a more skilful use of linguistic tools. As he writes:

> Forming a *habit* of reflection requires one to reflect on the words you use, hear, or read, their birth, derivation, and history. For if words are not THINGS, they are LIVING POWERS, by which the things of most importance to mankind are actuated, combined and humanised. (1993: 10)

---

[10] For a reading of this theory of 'desynonymisation' in terms of radical theories of language, see Hamilton 1983: 58–134.

[11] For an extension of Gregory on 'mind tools' see Dennett 2008: 100ff. For a critique of Clark's argument for language as an artefact – hinging on the question of whether language actually is and remains an external tool, or whether it reshapes the mind in the process of internalisation – see Wheeler 2004.

This claim for the external powers that words propagate on their own is particularly intriguing given that just a few pages earlier Coleridge had set his approach against that of Horne Tooke, a former associate whose conventionalist, materialist theory of language he had once endorsed.

The arbitrariness of the linguistic sign, the core of Tooke's system, eventually became one of Coleridge's biggest anxieties. As Keach (2010: 119) notes, Coleridge eventually 'repudiates the cardinal principle of the Lockean tradition, that language is the arbitrarily and historically contingent "workmanship" of the human mind'. He sought instead to draw a more essential connection between word and referent by grounding language in the mind's transcendental operations, and ultimately in the divine Logos. Nevertheless, as McKusick (1986) has argued, Tooke's philosophy continued to hold attractions for Coleridge. Above all, by attending to language as a constructed tool – arbitrarily instituted, but historically rooted – Tooke emphasised that language is a feature of the built environment. In that respect, Tooke was an important touchstone for the eighteenth-century interest in what we would now call semantic externalism: that the meaning of at least some words inheres not in an individual's sense of what that word means, but in properties external to the individual: either the natural properties to which the word refers, or its conventional histories of use in particular social institutions.[12]

Coleridge's treatment of Tooke in *Aids to Reflection* retains that sense that words have lives of their own. He writes:

> Horne Tooke entitled his celebrated work, Ἔπεα πτερόεντα, winged words: or language, not only the vehicle of thought but the wheels. With my convictions and views, for ἔπεα I should substitute λόγοι, that is, words select and determinate, and for πτερόεντα ζώοντες, that is, living words. The wheels of the intellect I admit them to be: but such as Ezekiel beheld in the visions of God as he sate among the captives by the river of Chebar. *Withersoever the Spirit was to go, the wheels went, and thither was the Spirit to go: for the Spirit of the living creature was in the wheels also.* (1993: 7)

As this passage from *Aids to Reflection* makes clear, Coleridge retains that conviction about the close relation between words and things with some qualification. His correction of Tooke, like many of Coleridge's gestures toward the transcendental basis of knowledge, has two very different results. First, it posits that words are 'living' because they are not mechanical after all, but tap into the life of the Logos. We should thus not understand words as being like mechanical tools. Yet the metaphor also suggests almost precisely the opposite: because Coleridge asserted that language had a divine basis in 'truth', he could continue with a practical approach to language that looked very much like Tooke's externalism. He simply replaced Tooke's social and conventional account of meaning with one rooted in the tran-

---

[12] For classic arguments in favour of externalism, see Kripke 1972 on the socially instituted use of proper nouns, Putnam 1975 on natural kinds, and Burge 1979 on social institutions.

scendental. Language reformers, or creators of philosophical neologisms, only needed to be reframed as bringing language closer to truth, rather than as creating new social contexts for language use. Accordingly, the emphasis in the passage equivocates between 'the Spirit of the living creature' and the weirdly spirited wheels; between words as divinely grounded symbols, and words as possessing a life of their own. If the metaphor is to hold, then mind, or spirit, must be a property that circulates throughout the entire system of words.

In practical terms, from the point of view of an individual language user, this would still imply that language developed, improved and changed as societies progressed, and that words performed intellectual labour by dint of their external properties. A word's meaning inheres not in the speaker's intentions, but in the word's socially and conventionally determined meanings, of which speakers may not even be aware. One way to put this is that Coleridge's transcendentalism commits him to an extreme (indeed supernatural) form of content externalism, but that very process makes possible what sounds, in this passage, like the '*active externalism*' proposed by Clark and Chalmers (1998: 7), 'based on the active role of the environment in driving cognitive processes'. Attending to a word's 'birth, derivation' and 'history' will reveal to the reader that those words had been doing intellectual work all along, probably without that reader's knowledge (Coleridge 1993: 10). On the face of it, Coleridge is attempting to reframe these pre-loaded words as a set of tools the reader might use more efficiently, through a skilled interaction with the environment similar to the way Wheeler and Clark's (2008: 3564) bartender uses glasses lined up along a bar rather than relying solely on biological memory. One way of reading Coleridge's advice to reflect on the origin and derivation of words, then, is that it enables the reader to use words more deliberatively: to internalise that scaffolding more fully, and to leave less to the automatic work of convention, association or habit. Yet the result is precisely something Coleridge wants to understand in terms of habit and not deliberative action: learning more about words will enable readers to cultivate 'the habit of using them appropriately' (Coleridge 1993: 10). *Aids to Reflection* is not a catechism focused on doctrine but a practical guide to thinking over the course of one's life, which has led Mitchell (2013: 99) to call it a 'life-manual', 'a text less interested in asserting a series of truths than in providing readers with protocols for disorienting themselves, for changing their lives'. 'Life-manual' is a useful term insofar as it captures the ambition, aims and practical orientation of many of Coleridge's later-career works. The reflective praxis they encourage is as much about developing an 'inner' moral and intellectual centre and internalising scaffolding (like the external or 'mechanical' aspects of language) as it is about fostering the mastery and appropriation of a scaffolding that remains, at least in part, external. The very idea of a 'manual' nicely captures, too, the sense that the work of formation is never quite complete, but might continue to depend on external props for future recalibration or 'disorientation'. Rather than a fully internalised apparatus, what Coleridge proposes makes language, guidebooks and their users look more like coupled systems.

Coleridge develops this line of thought later in *Aids to Reflection* when he draws a 'similitude' between the flowering of charity in people of the 'strongest and best balanced natures' and the biological 'ascent of life':

> The lowest class of Animals or Protozoa, the Polypi for instance, have neither brain nor nerves. Their motive powers are all from without. The Sun, Light, the Warmth, the Air are their Nerves and Brain. As life ascends, nerves appear; but still only as the conductors of an *external* Influence. (1993: 7–8)

This 'ascent' of life continues until 'the Reservoir of Sensibility and the imitative power that actuates the Organs of Motion (the Muscles) with the net-work of conductors, are all taken inward and appropriated' and, finally, the fully internalised organism is 'prepared for the manifestation of a Free Will'. Coleridge is once more, as in the letter to Wedgewood, speaking in that mode between the literal and the metaphorical. According to this account of polyps, which Coleridge probably found in Lamarck, in lower forms of life it is difficult to distinguish the inner from the outer in the first place, and only gradually does a central, superintending power develop to reel in the elements of sensation and the impulses of external influences. It is fascinating that 'a Free Will', that highest of Coleridgean values, correlates here with an originally external apparatus being 'taken inward and appropriated'. The picture of early, bare life as quite literally distributed in its local environment matches his usual discomfort with involuntary motion ('sensibility' or 'irritability'), despite his admission that they were very real parts of living organisms' embodied nature.[13] More importantly, the metaphor of the polyp here serves to depict the process of education and maturation as moving on a trajectory from dependency upon external scaffolds to the internalisation of those scaffolds, an internalisation that for Coleridge marked mastery over one's environment by 'appropriating' it.[14]

'Thinking Connectedly'

That sense of maturation as mastery of an internalised apparatus, especially in terms of how best to navigate a life mediated by texts, is reflected in one of Coleridge's favourite passages from Leighton, which he includes in *Aids to Reflection*:

> He (says Archbishop Leighton) who teaches men the principles and precepts of spiritual wisdom, before their minds are called off from foreign objects, and turned inward upon themselves, might as well write his instructions, as the sibyl wrote her prophecies, on the loose leaves of trees, and commit them to the mercy of the inconstant winds. (1993: 13)

---

[13] For a different and more object-centred role of the polyp in Coleridge's writing see Perry (1999: 94), who places the polyp's 'divisible life' in the context of Coleridge on the '"independence" of things from the mind's ambitions'.

[14] I am thinking here of Clark's (2003: 198) argument that 'it is our basic *human* nature to annex, exploit and incorporate nonbiological stuff deep into our mental profiles'.

The developing mind turns inward upon itself, and this could mean obtaining powers of self-contemplation, wholeness, self-determination or free agency. It also refers to the process of ordering and organising those scattered leaves, and bringing them under a coherent plan, in which *Aids to Reflection* trades. If we lack this fixing power, we are left with sibylline leaves.

In this final section I want to turn to those sibylline leaves, which provided Coleridge with one of his favourite images and the title of his 1817 collected poems (suggesting, in that case, both a scattered or fragmentary corpus and his aspiration to bring them together in one volume, however disconnected). In *Aids to Reflection* (1993: 13) Leighton describes as sibylline leaves the ephemeral and intractable 'precepts' taught to those who are not yet able to retain them and incorporate or assimilate them under an organised and reasoned rubric. As I will discuss below, that is something Coleridge frequently felt unable to do for his own works in progress. Crucially, though, it is precisely the work that Coleridge saw *Aids* as assisting, in the sense that he is organising for the reader what might have appeared, in Leighton's original, too diffuse or sibylline.

In the book's opening address 'To the reader', Coleridge offers himself as a humble assistive device, caring less about his own voice than his usefulness as an editor and a philosophical and spiritual mediator. After having read the volume, he implores the reader, 'compare the state of your mind, with the state in which your mind was, when you first opened the Book'. The series of questions he asks – has the volume prompted reflection, has it 'removed any obstacle' to faith, and so on – suggestively concludes, 'Lastly, has it increased your power of thinking connectedly?' (1993: 3). On the face of it, 'thinking connectedly' most likely means synthesising different areas of knowledge and grasping the connections between apparently unconnected concepts. However, that phrase also seems to point toward the collaborative nature of reflection as this patchwork volume will have redefined it for the reader. Coleridge's language here suggests an image of organised or systematised knowledge. It is probably no accident that he sounds like he could be describing computer networks, or in his own metaphor the nervous system's 'net-work of conductors' (1993: 98). On my argument, 'thinking connectedly' here also does some of the same work as the term 'connectionist' in more recent accounts that picture cognition as an emergent property of networked systems and thus issue a challenge to 'classical models of internal representation and of computational process' (Clark 1997: 185). 'Connectedly' works two ways, pointing both to a heightened connectivity of the ideas Coleridge's reader is processing, and to the way that such connectivity can be increased by linking up to an assistive system like *Aids to Reflection* itself.

'To the reader' (1993: 3) ends by underscoring the relationship between those two types of connectivity, as the language of connection shifts to the language of extension in its closing request, that the reader 'endeavour to extend my utility'. Thinking connectedly, that is, in a more organic, inwardly focused way, also implies a networked activity that depends on connections between systems, and Coleridge envisions such connections multiplying and extending in turn. King

(2012: 49) offers a useful reminder that *Aids to Reflection* was above all a corrective to the scattered, distracting or unmanageable aspects of early-nineteenth-century print culture and the 'mental passivity encouraged by the print market'. Cultivating reflective, fully formed, autonomous mental subjects was crucial to counteract that passivity. Yet the book's goal was ultimately to use print culture, not to avoid it: by creating readers and future writers able to reflect, and thus 'to affirm truths of morality and Christianity as necessary and derived from the indwelling Logos', *Aids to Reflection* would promote the 'diffusion of these principles through the print network' (King 2012: 44). *Aids to Reflection* is thus largely concerned with prescribing a healthy and functional use of print technologies, as opposed to the dependent, passive relation to print that Coleridge considered unhealthy or dysfunctional.

The same principle holds for Coleridge's approach to the information management systems that could promote 'thinking connectedly' in one's private study. His main paradigm for information management would have been the commonplace book, a form which was still employed as a means for linking detached fragments of text into a connected 'net-work', though as Jajdelska notes the practice had changed significantly during the eighteenth century.[15] Commonplace books facilitated connectivity at the textual level, usually by using headings and indexes to turn detached quotations or even scraps of paper and notebook entries into an information retrieval system. The organisational structure of *Aids to Reflection*, which brings Leighton's aphorisms under three main headings (as the book's title indicates, 'Prudence, Morality, and Religion'), resembles the heading system that might appear in a commonplace book. We might, following Jajdelska's work on the interplay between public and private textuality, read the very form of *Aids to Reflection* as a way to publicly model a private practice of thinking-with-texts. If commonplacing was losing currency as a practice, that would be in keeping with Coleridge's professed traditionalism.

From very early on, commonplacing and related methods had been linked to information overload. Blair and Stallybrass (2010: 139, 148), for example, trace the practice roughly to the middle of the fifteenth century, during which 'information began to be stockpiled in Europe on a radically new scale', as a result of which 'abundant stockpiles of notes posed new problems of information management'. For some, commonplacing and indexing offered antidotes to the frailty of the mind's inward organisational powers. For others – though not, as Miranda Anderson (2016) notes, for Francis Bacon – commonplace books (like calculators, search engines and mobile devices of later centuries) were bad influences that allowed biological memory to deteriorate, or else risked promoting further disorganisation among their users.[16]

Coleridge's own textual practice was notoriously disorganised, and he frequently

---

[15] On Coleridge's adaptation of the commonplace book see Hess 2012.

[16] Anderson (2016) notes that Francis Bacon defended commonplace books against the charge that they led to the atrophy of the memory. On Coleridge's usual resistance to 'artificial memory schemes' see Sutton 1998: 272.

fantasised about a mode of information management that would subject his scattered notes and fragments into fully formed works, as if by some process of automatic writing. In an 1820 letter to Thomas Allsop, he lists, in addition to the *opus maximum* he referred to as, among other titles, the 'Logosophia' or 'Assertion of Religion', four other major works in progress: one on Shakespeare, and one each on broader histories of literature, philosophy and theology. He adds:

> To the completion of these four Works I have literally nothing more to do, than *to transcribe*; but, as I before hinted, from so many scraps & *sibylline* leaves, including Margins of Books & blank Pages, that unfortunately I must be my own Scribe – & not done by myself, they will be all but lost – or perhaps (as has been too often the case already) furnish feathers in the caps of others – some for this purpose, and some to plume the arrows of detraction to be let fly against the luckless Bird, from whom they had been plucked or moulted! (1956–71: V, 27)

The 'sibylline leaves' are here, as in Leighton's aphorism about teaching spiritual wisdom to those whose minds had not yet been 'called off from foreign objects', a stand-in for fragmentary or ephemeral bits of wisdom that lack a central organising principle or superintending power (Coleridge 1993: 13). He is performatively confessing to an extreme disorganisation – bringing together his disjoined fragments is extremely slow, difficult labour unassisted by a proper management system – and suggesting at the same time that the truly hard thinking is already done. As a result, this letter can also be read as a fantasy of writing reduced to mere transcription, and authorship reduced to being one's own scribe. Even if his worry at having feathers plucked to furnish the caps of others registers Coleridge's anxiety about failed information management and plagiarism, his sense of being his own scribe indicates a close connection between philosophical writing in general (as a presentation of his own thought) and the curation and arrangement of other people's writing, such as *Aids to Reflections'* processing of Leighton to create a guided or scaffolded reading experience.

Christensen (1981: 96–117) has argued that many of Coleridge's published works, and his notorious plagiarisms, blend these authorial and scribal functions in what he calls Coleridge's 'marginal method': his tendency to merge between his roles as author, commentator and editor.[17] Even texts that were not (like *Aids to Reflection*) intended as editions or anthologies, notably *Biographia Literaria* or *The Friend*, became patchworks of quoted, summarised and sometimes plagiarised texts that obscure the boundary between writing and glossing, creation and mere arrangement. From the vantage point of deconstructive theory, Christensen's argument pointed to the way Coleridge's obsession with the free will (or with the creative 'imagination' as opposed to the mechanical, merely reorganising 'fancy') sometimes only barely repressed an anxiety about writing as an automatic,

---

[17] On Coleridge's plagiarisms see McFarland 1969: 1–52 and, more recently, Mazzeo 2013: 17–48. On connections to the 'myth of solitary genius' see Stillinger 1991: 96–120.

involuntary or passive engagement with knowledge. From the vantage point of distributed cognition, on the other hand, that 'marginal method' appears in a somewhat different light, since Coleridge was actually very comfortable with thinking as a process of curating and arranging external materials, or (as in that 1820 letter) with marginalia as a mode of writing that equivocated between commentary and original composition.[18] For Coleridge, thinking simply was, at some level, information management. It was not something that happened alone, in the head, to be subsequently expressed via writing, but an activity that took place in language, on paper, and in the extended textual apparatus formed by commonplace books, quotations, marginalia upon other people's works, and the resulting mess of 'scraps & *sibylline* leaves'.

Coleridge's sense of being his 'own scribe' subsequently became important to his reputation across the Atlantic. Edgar Allan Poe (1836: 451) reprints that 1820 letter in a review of Coleridge's posthumous table talk and letters in the *Southern Literary Messenger*, and glosses it as offering 'a picture, never surpassed, of great mental power conscious of its greatness, and tranquilly submitting to the indignities of the world'. Poe goes on to assert that publishing an American edition of *Biographia Literaria* would offer

> an important service to the cause of psychological science in America, by introducing a work of great scope and power in itself, and well calculated to do away with the generally received impression here entertained of the *mysticism* of the writer. (Poe 1836: 453)

It is intriguing that Poe finds in *Biographia Literaria*, but also presumably in the letter he has just quoted at great length, a less 'mystical' Coleridge than the one that had been popularly received. More recent readers of *Biographia Literaria* are more likely to focus on its 'ill-fated' attempt at a transcendental deduction of the imagination (Hamilton 1983: 67). Poe's suggestion of a shift from *Aids to Reflection*'s religious prescriptions to the *Biographia*'s detailed engagement with 'psychological science' matches Coleridge's legacy in nineteenth-century Britain, which after the adoption of his political theology by John Stuart Mill and 'Cambridge Apostles' like F. D. Maurice shifted almost wholly to the *Biographia*.[19] If Coleridge's legacy across the Atlantic appeared more 'mystical', via important inheritors like Emerson, Poe's less mystical, more scattered Coleridge is in one sense truer to *Aids to Reflection*, too.[20] As King (2012: 44) has demonstrated, *Aids to Reflection* itself was premised

---

[18] On marginalia in *Aids to Reflection* see Murley 1998; on Coleridge's marginalia in general see Jackson 2001: 149–65.

[19] On this shift see King 2012: 56–60.

[20] On the early history of Coleridge's transatlantic reception, see Duffy 1970 and Dameron 1985; on Emerson's Coleridgean influences see Walls 2008 and Follett 2015. On connections between Bacon, Coleridge and Emerson on the hierarchy of knowledge, including the poet's role as mediating figure, see Harvey 2013: 14. For echoes of *Aids to Reflection* in Emerson's *Nature*, see Harvey 2013: 123. For a Coleridgean reading of Emerson and science see Wilson 1999.

on the idea of 'a spiritual republic of letters' that offered 'a way of adapting to the matrix of print into which [Coleridge] felt the minds of the nation were being rapidly absorbed'. It modelled a thinking process firmly tethered to the mind's material apparatus and extended, via print, out into the 'minds of the nation'.

Coleridge's approach to the transcendental toggled between privileging, on the one hand, the individual mind's subterranean access to its own divine origins, and, on the other hand, the dependency of corporeal understanding on supplements that came from without. Sometimes those supplements were clearly supernatural in nature for Coleridge. At other times they came in a form that looks more like an empirical account of cognition taking place between mind and world – a legacy that could also be traced forward through William James and Wittgenstein, who retain the broader anti-Cartesian impulses present in Coleridge's political theology and 'life-manuals' as well as his psychological writings (Mitchell 2013: 99).

Aids to Reflection may aim for transcendental truths, but one of its pay-offs, at least, is a more modest model of private thought scaffolded not by divine action but by an integrated network of texts and information management systems. While 'Germano-Coleridgean' becomes for Mill ([1840] 1969: 125) synonymous with the method of transcendental deduction, for another set of inheritors Coleridgean thinking looked more like a skilled interaction with social, linguistic and textual scaffolds. This suggests that what Mill and many since him have understood as Coleridge's political and intellectual conservatism drew not just on his Christian orthodoxy or his defence of traditional social practices, but also on his physiologically attuned study of the mind and his commitment to something like a distributed account of cognition. It is a conservatism often less intent on suturing individuals to tradition than on opening the mind up to the world.

9

The Self in the History of Distributed Cognition: A View from the History of Reading

Elspeth Jajdelska

Introduction

How do we come to have a sense of self, and tacit beliefs about our particular selves? In cognitive science, a view has emerged of the self as dynamic and malleable rather than fixed. The philosopher Daniel Dennett has characterised the self as 'a centre of narrative gravity', comparing selves to the physical centre of gravity, 'a purely abstract object', 'if you like, a theorist's fiction', but with the potential for a 'well delineated and well behaved role within physics' (Dennett 1992: 104–5). In this formulation, the self is subject to constraints, but not the clearly identifiable and comparatively fixed constraints of, for example, the field of vision afforded by retinal cells. The cognitive psychologist Martin Conway has identified a 'Self-Memory System' (Conway et al. 2004) in which memory is motivated by sometimes conflicting needs for accurate knowledge of the world on the one hand, and a coherent, though dynamically changing, set of beliefs about the self on the other. For example, 'an individual who recalls a memory of a happy experience from a period of their life they evaluate as unhappy, might categorise the dissonant happy memory as being an exception in a period of otherwise unhappy experiences', one of a range of possible 'cognitive reactions to dissonant memories'. Another possible reaction to dissonant memories of this kind might be an alteration to the belief about the self through a re-evaluation of the period in question (Conway 2005: 595).

In what follows I identify new eighteenth-century relationships with the cognitive scaffolding provided by ink and paper that have potential consequences for this process of dynamic self-formation. The technologies of writing and print themselves were not new, though they were extended to new users, in particular among women and the lower ranks. Furthermore, they were reconceptualised in ways that allowed at least two important developments in self-formation. First, a new model of written texts as utterances by an absent author to a silent hearer, rather than scripts for performance by an oral reader to a live audience, created new possibilities for life writing, especially diaries and letters, as a way to externalise the self. The process of writing then becomes a looped and extended process of self-formation, in which the writing body can oscillate rapidly between *addressing* a notional audience and *being* that notional audience. Second, a split emerges in the eighteenth century between the social norms governing speech and those governing print, writing and reading. While social inferiors were still broadly proscribed from addressing their superiors in speech without invitation, they were no longer barred from reading and writing on topics previously reserved for the higher ranks. This had the potential to create dissonant embodied experiences of the self. In reading and writing, both silent and shared, the lower ranks could embody a model of the self in which both real and notional participants were social equals, while in face-to-face interactions with superiors they embodied another model, through the obligation to avoid initiating speech, to stand rather than sit, or to avoid eye contact. As we shall see, this dissonance may have had the potential to undermine the legitimacy of social hierarchy, even if the content of the texts they read and approved was socially conformist (Ross 1996; Mee 2011: 30–1; Jajdelska 2007, 2016).

I begin with an introduction to the history of reading in general, and of the eighteenth century in particular, pointing out ways in which the material organisation of texts and their environment allowed readers embedded in that environment to relate to knowledge in more flexible ways, accelerating the generation of new kinds of knowledge. I go on to identify less visible changes in the relationship between readers and material objects, arising from changing conceptions of what writing represents in relation to speech. I then discuss how these new conceptions could support new developments in extended cognition in a selection of seventeenth- and eighteenth-century life writings: the diary of John Courtney of Beverley in the 1760s (Courtney 2001); the diaries of Alexander and James Brodie in the late seventeenth century (Brodie and Brodie 1863); the late-eighteenth-century diary of wealthy socialite Frances Anne Crewe (Crewe 2006); the diary of a provincial eighteenth-century draper, Thomas Turner (Turner 1984); and the diary of Sarah Hurst of Horsham in the 1760s (Hurst 2003). These diaries are interesting comparators for the paradigm case of extension, the relationship between Otto and his notebook, outlined in the paper which first introduced the 'extended mind' thesis (Clark and Chalmers 1998). Otto suffers from Alzheimer's disease and carries a notebook wherever he goes to note down new information and look up old information. In this way he is able to accomplish some of the same goals as his cognitively unimpaired counterpart Inga. When they both wish to go to the museum, she consults her organic memory and Otto consults his notebook and they both manage to get there. Otto's notebook illustrates the extension of semantic memory. With eighteenth-century diaries, new conceptualisations of writing supported the extension of dynamic self-formation. I then outline changing social norms around printed versus spoken communication between different ranks, and illustrate their potential for dissonant embodied experiences of the self.

The History of Reading

This field has emerged during the last thirty years from the disciplines of bibliography (McKenzie 1969; McKitterick 2003), anthropology and sociology (Radway 1984) and economic, social and cultural history (Spufford 1981; Raven 1988; Darnton 1990). Interpreting the historical evidence for reading requires particular care and sensitivity, due to the piecemeal, fragmented nature of the historical record and to high levels of variation between individuals (see Bannet 2013 for a useful review of scholarship on eighteenth-century reading). With this caveat in mind, the history of reading is a valuable resource for historians of distributed cognition. Reading is central to the paradigm case of extended cognition, that of Otto, and books are also good analogues for the barman's glasses in another paradigm example in the philosophy literature, this time of embedded cognition. Here we are invited to imagine a novice bartender charged with serving different drinks in differently shaped glasses. As he grows expert he learns to line the different glasses up to match the sequence of drinks orders, thus turning a problem of memory into one of recognising the drink from the glass by constructing a 'cognitive niche' (Clark 2008: 62–3). Counterparts of the glasses in this case could include the arrival of hymn-books in eighteenth-century pews (Rivers and Wykes 2011), and the arrangement of Bibles on eighteenth-century lecterns and prayer books in eighteenth-century hands (Bradshaw 2005). These books embedded worship in the environment by offloading memory tasks for when, where and what to sing or speak.

In the eighteenth century there were important transitions in the way books and writing extended, embedded and embodied cognition. The intimate, one-to-one relationship between user and document exemplified by Otto was common in the Renaissance, and continued in some eighteenth-century contexts. But it was no longer ubiquitous; commonplace books and annotated volumes were less often used to support memorisation and artful speech (Jajdelska 2016; Allan 2010). New kinds of cognitive scaffolding emerged instead, allowing readers to identify flexible, individualised and spontaneous routes to knowledge. Within documents, for example, footnotes began to distinguish the text's content from the editors' or author's beliefs about that content, enabling readers to adopt a sceptical stance to either (Grafton 2003: 23; Walsh 2009: 687–98). Indexes changed their function so that readers could develop personalised paths through knowledge to suit their own interests (Bell 2008: 37). Ever-longer encyclopaedias used the value-neutral sequence of the alphabet as an organisational tool, rather than traditional and hierarchically organised domains such as 'theology' or 'philosophy' (Burke 2000: 115; Blom 2004: 43; Roche 2006: 173–4). Library catalogues began to organise texts by author as well as the more traditional book size and shelf mark, and the books themselves were more widely circulated, again creating new pathways to and through the environment to support cognition (Simpson 2012: 325, 327; Manley 2012: 344). Books themselves were more systematically distinguished from other rare and valuable objects, as libraries became distinct from museums, so that cognitive scaffolding was divided into verbal and non-verbal categories (Simpson

2012: 326). And changes in prose style and domestic architecture supported silent and solitary reading alongside sociable oral reading, providing more varied pathways through books' content (Jajdelska 2007, 2016; Williams 2016).

Alongside these comparatively visible developments in distributed cognition came tacit changes in the ways documents were conceptualised in relation to socially embodied speech. Where Renaissance readers and writers easily conceived of letters as representing speech, recording it or providing a support for new speech, their eighteenth-century counterparts began to think of print and writing as kinds of reified utterance which were independent of speech and of their authors' and readers' bodies (Jajdelska 2016). These implicit, rather abstract changes in the conceptual framework for books and the written word had the potential for momentous social and cognitive effects, coordinating widening and recurrent cognitive loops between books, readers' selves and their interactions with other people.

Diary Writing as Gesture in a Cognitive Loop

On Sunday, 9 March 1662, Alexander Brodie, laird of Brodie in Scotland, wrote as follows in his diary:

> 9. – Die Dom. I declind to goe to the Quakers to diner. But I found the euel spirit within me, which turnd me from the servic of God. This indisposd, and I had much drowsines and indisposdnes, and noe delight in the drauing neir unto him. Lorn, his brother, and I, din'd with Eglingtoun. Our discours was litl savourie, and smelt litl of grac. Let not the Lord charg this upon me. (Brodie and Brodie 1863: 244)

To us, Brodie's diary might at first seem confessional, admitting to his diary what he might hide from friends and neighbours, such as his conquest by the 'evil spirit' which turns him from the service of God, or his 'little savoury' and ungodly conversation. But Brodie wrote within a long tradition of using diaries for data collection, observing, as a meteorologist does the weather, the workings of God in his soul at various points of the day. This allowed him, and those who read and used his diary, including his son, to improve their spiritual knowledge and keep an eye on their spiritual credit and debit accounts. Hence its publication in 1740, as a work by 'a gentleman of shining piety' to encourage the godly. Pious diaries like Brodie's were frequently circulated among friends and families to allow as many as possible to learn the method, observe the workings of grace in the human soul, and encourage them to do the same (Jajdelska 2007: 133–41).

Brodie's son continued the tradition of diary writing as a shared family practice rather than a variety of private storytelling:

> 13 [May 1680] – I read in the morning Calvin on Math. And on Isai . . . Grant cam here from Forres, and expressed his sence of his loss in my Father, professd kindnes and affection to his hous and famely. I desir to be taught of God in evrie

thing that conerns dutie to himself and to al relations. Calder went by and cam not in. I desyr to affoord no ground or occasion to anie friend to draw away. *Diary of James Brodie of Brodie* (Brodie and Brodie 1863: 429)

Like his father, young Brodie documents those actions (reading Calvin, praying for God's teaching) and responses (wishing to welcome friends) which are relevant to his pursuit of salvation, as well as events which are relevant to assessing his family's local standing (visits and opinions of neighbours). This latter goal – assessing the family standing – also illustrates that assessing one's state of grace was not the only motivation for record-keeping. Diaries could be motivated by the pursuit of history, or science, or legal evidence in the future (Jajdelska 2007: 152–7). What these motivations have in common is utility, of keeping the diary for some observable and easily explicable end.

This utilitarian approach runs through almost all of the surviving diaries from the seventeenth century, and a great many from the eighteenth and nineteenth (Jajdelska 2007: 138–9; Aalders 2015). But an alternative approach was emerging, in which utility sat alongside or was replaced by less explicit motives for diary writing. Diary entries became micro-narratives, and diaries macro-narratives, of continuous personal experience (Jajdelska 2007: 157–65). In the diary of John Courtney, a gentleman living in the Yorkshire town of Beverley in the 1760s, we find utility and this rather more elusive motive side by side. Like many earlier diarists, Courtney records the financial and legal arrangements he or his heirs might need to check at a later date:

> *Wednesday Nov 27* [1765] I paid my mother her quarters annuity due 20th instant £25. This day my mother and I attended the court at Hall-Garth and took the oath of fealty to the lords on being admitted tenants.
> . . .
> *Tuesday Dec 3* Received a letter from Mr Stonestreet.
> . . .
> *Wednesday Dec 4* Paid my servant Richard one years wage due Martinmas last, nine pounds. (Courtney 2001: 113)

In some entries, however, these bare observations of events are embedded in a narrative of the diarist's *experience* of them:

> *Thursday Nov 7* [1765] In morning (with Mr Robarts) went to Mr Nelsons office. He seemed much cooler than before in his temper, and told me that he had searched the rolls but as only the sums paid are mentioned and not the rent of the land, they could give no satisfaction. This in great measure I admitted, he showed me a copy of some directions (from an old book which Dickinson has) about setting the fines and said it was customary to take 2 years and ½ rent for a life and a remainder; but that he thought 2 years a reasonable fine . . . He said that this was the first fine of this nature that had happened since Mr Dickinson

was steward and that he had a deal of business upon his hands etc but I insisted that when he made a demand upon me, it was reasonable I should know for what I paid my money. (Courtney 2001: 112)

The events Courtney records are still relevant to a legally motivated diary. But the observations now include personal experiences and impressions: 'he seemed much cooler than before'. The choice of verbs goes beyond the 'he said' and 'I said' required for a transcribed dialogue. One moment Courtney is on the back foot – 'This in great measure I *admitted*' – and the next he is on the attack again – 'I *insisted* . . . it was reasonable I should know for what I paid my money'.

In many entries the legalistic function yields altogether to experiential narrative. In this example the woman who would later agree to marry him calls:

Saturday Nov 9 [1765] Mr Robarts dined with us. In afternoon Mrs Goulton and Miss S---t [Smelt] called. We talked about indifferent subjects. The latter looked very well, and with a smiling countenance. She goes away on Monday or Tuesday next. I wished her health and a good journey. I feel not withstanding! NB I saw today in this town the most surprizing exploits of Price, who rode on 3 horses, mounted and dismounted on full gallop, rode with his head upon the saddle and his feet in the air making the horse gallop etc. etc. It was the most curious thing I have seen a long time. (Courtney 2001: 112)

None of the information here has obvious utility for Courtney or anyone else; that he talked with a woman who interested him on 'indifferent subjects' is not a fact with an obvious future use. But it *is* relevant to giving a third party an account of the diarist's experience of Miss Smelt's visit. Such a third party could infer, for example, that Courtney's Miss Smelt disturbs his feelings independently of anything she does or tells him, that he is minutely concerned with her health (she 'looked very well') and with how she feels about being with him ('with a smiling countenance'). The information that she will depart on Monday or Tuesday, and that he, unremarkably, 'wished her health and a good journey', again are significant only because the very fact of his recording them reveals his state at the time. Only if these inferences are assumed can his conclusion – 'I feel not withstanding' – make sense. Otherwise we might ask, 'Notwithstanding what?'

Letter writing too moves from the goal of clear utility to a narrative of the writer's direct or inferred experiences, to the point where some groups of letters to a single correspondent can be treated as a diary, such as the letters written by the wealthy socialite Frances Anne Crewe during a three-month stay in Paris to a friend in England. Here, she describes a night at the opera in 1786:

It was a very fine Spectacle. Gluck and Piccini are now the favourite Composers here. Their Taste in Music is, I think, much improved within these ten or twelve Years, and their Theatres on that Account much worth going to. ~ I still think, however, one may trace a great deal of the abominable French Stile of Composition. (Crewe 2006: 93)

As with Courtney's diary, Crewe provides information which may be valued in its own right, independently of what it reveals of the writer's experience: the favourite composers of Paris are Gluck and Piccini, supplanting older French styles. But this information is embedded in an experiential account both explicit ('It was a very fine Spectacle') and implicit ('one may trace a great deal of the abominable French Stile', implying that she has experienced the music as having this style).

One way to describe these changes in letter and diary writing is novelisation. The emergence of the novel in the eighteenth century also requires the reader to infer that information is selected in a narrative with the indirect goal of conveying a trajectory of experience. Indeed, it has been argued that the eighteenth-century novel is inextricably involved with eighteenth-century letter writing (Whyman 2009: 161–90). But diaries and letters have a much more direct relationship with the writer's memory, and therefore self, than novels do. A substantial body of research shows that, like readers, writers regularly pause as they produce text. In the past, these pauses were interpreted as time for deciding what to write next (Flower and Hayes 1981). However, new methods relating writers' eye movements to key strokes confirm an alternative, more complex account:

> Pausing is often accompanied by directed eye movements within the text produced so far. Some of this eye activity seems to be similar to that which would be observed if a participant were reading an experimenter-provided text for comprehension. However, our preliminary analyses suggest other recurring patterns, including repeated backward and forward saccades within the sentence that is being composed, multiple well-spaced glances across several sentences or paragraphs, and a 'reverse-reading' pattern involving series of fixations separated by two- or three-word right-to-left saccades. More than one of these or other patterns may occur within a single pause. (Wengelin et al. 2009: 349)

Writing, it would appear, is determined in part by processing what has been written, and not only at the level of conscious access – when we proofread or edit text, for example – but through a much faster oscillation that blurs processing with production. In this respect, the act of writing recalls the role of gesture in thought, researched by the psychologist Susan Goldin-Meadow (Goldin-Meadow 2005; Goldin-Meadow and Wagner 2005) and discussed by Clark (2006):

> It does not seem to be the case that our ongoing gestures during problem-solving merely express ideas that are fully present to our verbal reasoning. Rather, the gestures are themselves elements in a loose-knit, distributed representational economy . . . The wrong image here . . . is that of a single central reasoning engine that uses gesture to clothe pre-formed ideas for expressive purposes. Instead, gesture and (overt or covert) speech emerge as interacting parts of the overall reasoning machinery itself. (Clark 2006: 373)

If, as Clark argues, overt or covert speech are analogous to gesture, if they collaborate in cognition rather than simply communicating cognition's outcomes, then novelised diary writing extends that collaboration in a loop of rapid oscillations between: remembering recent personal experience; the comparatively short window of working memory for verbatim speech; the motor process of writing; the eye saccades of reading while writing; and the slower process of rereading on completion.

Neither writing nor diary writing were new practices in the eighteenth century. But diary writing with the goal of turning experience, rather than just events, into a narrative was new, and had implications for the dynamic creation of the self. Conway (2005) describes how each act of autobiographical memory is a rebalancing of beliefs about the self and the need for accurate knowledge of the world. New ways to write about the self can turn such comparatively disparate incidents of autobiographical memory into sustained and repeatable trains of experience. And while this repeatability might point towards a more reified, fixed model of the self, the narrative shape of the experience in fact points towards greater flexibility. Narratives are often durable precisely because they are ambiguous and flexible enough to be adapted to new circumstances (see for example Trompf et al. 1988).

Reading and Speaking: Dissonant Embodiments of the Self

Humans often, perhaps always, experience their social world as stratified; they have lower or higher status than some or most of the other humans they encounter (Santamaria-Garcia et al. 2015). However, one difference between present-day liberal democracies and the British Isles in the eighteenth century is that hierarchy then was not analysed primarily as an expression of economic and social class stratification. Instead it was underpinned by an explicit ideology of hierarchy by birth and rank (Davidson 2009: 53–7).

The prominence of the Enlightenment and of the French Revolution mean that popular accounts of the eighteenth century are associated with landmark steps towards an alternative ideology: that of human rights and equality before the law. But eighteenth-century Britain was still a place defined by institutionally sanctioned deference to social superiors (Clark 2000; Pocock 1976). Social deference by lower ranks to higher – by servants to masters, women to men, merchants to gentlemen, gentlemen to lords – was not just a side effect of economic stratification but an ideology. It was explicitly, rather than implicitly, embodied and embedded in the environment. Servants and children lived in the extremes of buildings, at the top and the bottom. The bars of law courts separated judges from lawyers as the positioning of galleries and pews in churches separated gentry from artisans (Marsh 2002). Inferiors were expected to stand while their betters sat, to be silent while they spoke, to avoid eye contact, to be insulted without answering, and, on occasion, to submit to violence without recourse to the law (Jajdelska 2016: chapter 2; Bryson 1998; Hay 2000).

What was more novel in the eighteenth century was the way these embodied and embedded social relationships included speech but, increasingly, not print. In the seventeenth and eighteenth centuries alike, there was a widely accepted social norm that speech from inferiors that was uninvited, or on topics improper to their rank, was impertinent (literally 'irrelevant'; Jajdelska 2016: chapter 2). This is not to say that no such speech happened; breaches of this social norm were common, just as breaches of social norms today (cutting into traffic, say, or not tipping in restaurants) are common (Colclough 2005; Cressy 2010). But frequent breaches should not distract us from the ubiquity of a norm.

In this respect, eighteenth-century practice was continuous with the seventeenth century (Jajdelska 2016: chapter 2). But the implications for print were different. Late-seventeenth-century readers were more likely than their eighteenth-century counterparts to conceptualise print and writing as representations of speech, and books and documents as proxies for their authors' speech (Hope 2010: 5, 39; Jajdelska 2016: chapter 3). One consequence of this in the seventeenth century is that where a lower-ranking author published on a topic proper to the higher ranks – such as policy or speculative thought – he (or sometimes she) was potentially viewed as impertinent or, even worse, as an inferior speaking uninvited to superiors. In October 1662, for example, the gentlemanly Samuel Pepys wrote of a work on trade by a fisherman that it had 'some things good' but was 'very impertinent' (Pepys 1971–83: III, 214). The quality of the good things was irrelevant because the author had breached the social norms prohibiting uninvited address to superiors by publishing on a topic (government policy) proper only to elites.

In the eighteenth century, under pressure from the more open social networks of growing towns and cities, and higher financial rewards for at least some authors, this changed. As the aristocratic propagandist James Hervey put it in a political rebuke to the House of Lords in 1740:

> I hope it will not be thought too presuming in me . . . for as it is to be concluded that every thing from the Press is design'd for the use of the Publick, so the Publick, in my opinion, has an undoubted Right to discuss the Validity & Strength of all Arguments so transmitted to them. (Halsband 1973: 92–3)

This split between the norms governing speech and those governing print also extended to reading. On the one hand, appreciation for elite literary forms, like lyric poetry, was associated with taste, acquirable through sociability among men of breeding and rank (Patey 1997). On the other hand, the influential critic Joseph Addison advocated the democratisation of speculative thought and literature alongside gentlemanly good taste, aiming through his periodical *The Spectator* to bring 'Philosophy out of Closets and Libraries, Schools and Colleges, to dwell in Clubs and Assemblies, at Tea-Tables, and in Coffee-Houses' (Addison [1711] 1965: I, 44). Eighteenth-century readers of all ranks could legitimately read, write and share with one another texts which had once been the proper reserve of gentry and nobility alone. But they could not necessarily share speech with their superiors in the same way.

Plate 1 'London', *Songs of Innocence and Experience,* by William Blake. Lessing J. Rosenwald Collection, Library of Congress, © 2016 William Blake Archive. Used with permission.

ARCHAEOPHILORVM . SODALITIO . LONDINENSI .
GVGL . HAMILTONVS . BAL . . ORD . EQVES .
D.D.D.

Plate 2 Frontispiece to Tischbein, *Collection of Engravings*, © The Trustees of the British Museum. All rights reserved.

Plate 3 The Meidias Hydria, © The Trustees of the British Museum. All rights reserved.

Plate 4 Emma Hamilton as Niobe, © The Trustees of the British Museum. All rights reserved.

Plate 5 The Belvedere Apollo. Vatican, Museo Pio-Clementino. © 2018. Photo Scala, Florence.

Sarah Hurst (1736–1808) was one enthusiastic writer and reader who experienced this contrast. Hurst was the daughter of a tailor in the East Sussex town of Horsham, and she kept a diary between 1759 and 1762 (Hurst 2003). The diaries show how her social life around books and reading was determined by different principles from other social encounters. Hurst was an intelligent reader and a competent poet. She could not afford many books herself, but she found patrons among the local elites, including clergy, gentry and minor nobility, who lent her books and took an interest in her education (Hurst 2003: xxvii). She also had access to journals like *The Monthly Review* through a group of readers of her own rank who pooled costs (Hurst 2003: 85).

The evidence of her diary suggests that in exchanges relating to reading, she could speak with comparative freedom to her social superiors: 'I go with Sally Sheppard to Bet Cook to drink a Sillibub, then walk in the Park. Meet Sir Charles who treats us with Apricocks, & chat on various subjects' (Hurst 2003: 103). Sally Sheppard and Bet Cook were close friends and family belonging to her own tradesman's rank. Sir Charles Everard was a local landowner who often flirted with the young women, and also lent Hurst books. The encounter here, then, is one of condescension; Everard could choose not to invite the women, to shun them indeed, without breaching decorum. He is 'treating' them, not fulfilling an obligation. But the conversation is not, as far as we can tell, constrained by the topics proper to different ranks – they 'chat on various subjects'.

Hurst's couple of encounters with a much greater man, the Duke of Richmond, are again occasioned by her literary expertise and again show condescension and comparative freedom of speech: 'Lord Irwin sees my verses on Mrs Shelley, praises them much, wants to see the Sermon I wrote so long ago, I refuse it' (Hurst 2003: 48). On another occasion, Hurst's friendship with the socially superior Miss Gittins, daughter of a clergyman, prompts the Irwins' condescension to Hurst:

> Go to see Goodwood, the Duke of Richmond's seat. View the Hermitage the shell house, & the gardens which are of a prodigious extent, & delightfully situated. The Duke & Duchess knowing Miss Gittins send for us in, & behave very polite. (Hurst 2003: 52–3)

A love of reading and writing has both enabled a friendship with a woman somewhat her superior, Miss Gittins, and brought her to the favourable attention of a Duke and Duchess. The foundation of this acquaintance in reading and writing again seems to have made it one of comparably free speech for Sarah; she refuses, after all, Lord Irwin's request to see her verses, adopting a traditionally elite writer's stance of keeping poetry within a coterie, at least if her name is attached to it.

For other readers of tradesman's rank, there was no such condescension from local patrons. Thomas Turner was a draper in the nearby town of East Hoathly. Like Hurst, Turner was a diarist and a reader: 'Reading . . . seems to be the only diversion that I have any appetite for. Reading and study would in a manner be both meat and drink to me, were my circumstances but independent' (Turner 1984:

143). Turner's experiences of reading, however, were shared not with patrons but with his own rank, and he bought many of his own books.

As readers, both Turner and Hurst, whether reading with friends of their own rank or, in Hurst's case, talking about her reading and writing with superiors, enjoyed a sense of entitlement and legitimacy in reading works by elites on topics that were still largely reserved for elites in speech. Hurst's learning in particular attracted some hostility from her own rank. Here she sends a friend one of her own poems, who shares it with another friend, a tanner, 'who approves, several more hear it & guess the Author, which will I suppose excite Malice & envy, whose keen fangs I have so often experience'd' (Hurst 2003: 132). On writing a letter to Miss Gittins, the clergyman's daughter, Hurst notes that her father 'does not love to see me thus employed . . . I wou'd not disoblige him, yet cannot quit this favourite amusement' (Hurst 2003: 122). Elsewhere, Hurst regrets that 'this propensity to writing creates me more enemies than friends, because . . . we are more prone to envy than admire' (Hurst 2003: 30). Turner meanwhile experienced hostility for socialising with those beneath him on the pretext of shared reading; some thought it 'odd and profuse or extravagant' of him to spend time with Thomas Davy, the village shoemaker, a humbler man than Turner but 'a very sober man and one who has read a great deal, by which I oftentimes learned something' (Turner 1984: 82–3).

Both Turner and Hurst, then, experienced social encounters around reading which were outside of their usual social experiences and which attracted some hostility from their social peers. As readers, they felt fully confident about evaluating works by writers at or above the rank of gentleman (or sometimes gentlewoman) on elite topics. Their predecessors may well have reached comparable conclusions. But they could not have felt sanctioned in the same way as eighteenth-century readers schooled by the influential critic Addison and *The Spectator* could (Jajdelska 2016: 146–7, 167). Turner developed many of his critical approaches from periodicals, including *The Spectator* and *The Gentleman's Magazine*, praising the last book of *Paradise Lost*, for example, as exceeding 'anything I ever read for sublimity of language and beauty of similes' (Turner 1984: 153). Hurst, too, shared many of the judgements of the periodicals she read: 'read *The Monthly Review*, the[y] condemn *Tristram Shandy* which please[s] me extreamly as it entirely corresponds with my own sentiments' (Hurst 2003: 98). But she also strikes out some opinions of her own: 'I read *The Monthly Review*, they find great faults & very few perfections in most performances; grant all their remarks are just, it only shews, what all must be well acquainted with, that Human Nature is incapable of perfection' (Hurst 2003: 87). Yet the content of their critical opinions is not so important as the cognitive experience of forming and expressing them externally. In forming a view on the works of Laurence Sterne, or of Milton, or on the critics of the review, Hurst and Turner had first to conceive of themselves as being addressed by these men as equals. It is one thing to observe two superiors exchanging views. But in their diaries, and in speech among friends, Courtney and Hurst too pass judgement on the work of their superiors.

Although knowledge of the brain areas and processes implicated in language has advanced rapidly (Price 2012) we still know surprisingly little about how far our behaviour as readers and writers is modelled on our face-to-face experience of language in social encounters. But emerging accounts of language production and comprehension as symbiotic, with hearers simulating and predicting the speech of interlocutors in order to time and coordinate their contributions as speakers (Pickering and Garrod 2013), suggest that Hurst and Turner could successfully understand these texts and produce apt responses of their own by simulating the freedom of speech proper to elites.

Their embodied encounters with social superiors may have conflicted with these reading experiences. Turner suffered repeated personal humiliations at the hands of his village rector, including verbal abuse and being forced to dance for the (drunk) rector's amusement early in the morning (Turner 1984: 138–9). Hurst experienced social hierarchy in rejection and exclusion from physical spaces:

Make a visit at Tanbridge, but the Miss Ellis's have so much pride & reserve they are excessive disagreeable, but I suppose they think it right to keep people in trade at a distance (2003: 31)

Mrs. Tredcroft . . . says that trade people going to the Assembly at Brighthelmstone has spoilt it, for people of Quality don't chuse to be in company with them. (2003: 38)

[Mr Willes] presses me to go to the Assembly. I tell him am afraid it will be dislik'd, as I am the daughter of a person in trade. (2003: 150)

Insofar as their diary entries involved simulating a social status higher than their own, Hurst and Turner were likely to experience dissonance between reading, writing and talking about elite texts and meeting social superiors. There is evidence to suggest that identification of social hierarchies is a very rapid cognitive process, one that is not easily overridden at the level of conscious thought (Santamaria-Garcia et al. 2015). We can only speculate on the potential effects of this dissonance, but one possibility is that it prepared receptive ground for challenges to the legitimacy of hierarchy by birth and occupation (Pocock 1976). Historians of reading, when they have considered the relationship of books to politics and social change, have tended to focus on the contents of the books, assuming a model of dissemination of ideas usually associated with the work of Eisenstein, who argued that the intellectual revolutions of Copernicus and Luther in the sixteenth century were possible only because of the invention of moveable type in the fifteenth (Darnton 1996; Eisenstein 1980). But it may be that revolutionary or dissident content would not have spread far without an audience of readers already accustomed to the embodied experience of social equality through reading and social hierarchy through speech with superiors.

Conclusion

Some eighteenth-century changes to the way cognition was entangled with books and writing are comparatively visible. An eighteenth-century commonplace book, or an annotated eighteenth-century printed book, can often be distinguished fairly swiftly in content and style from a seventeenth-century one (Jackson 2001; Allan 2010). A reader of Gibbon's *Decline and Fall* can identify with comparative ease that footnotes have acquired a new use since, say, John Donne's *Pseudomartyr* (Grafton 2003), and that these new ways of organising books, internally and, in the case of libraries, externally, allow the new, more flexible pathways through knowledge exemplified by Diderot's *Encyclopédie* (Blom 2004). This flexibility suggests in itself a possible route from changes in the distribution of cognition to the liberty of thought associated with this century, allowing different readers to follow trains of thought and evidence which were less accessible when negotiating Medieval and Renaissance hierarchies of knowledge, such as the trivium (grammar, rhetoric and logic) and quadrivium (music, astronomy, geometry and arithmetic), divisions of the seven liberal arts which were once considered to distinguish men from beasts (McKeon 1942).

Powerful as these changes may have been, the less visible changes in the way cognition was embodied, embedded and extended may have been just as important, though with effects more difficult to track. The semantic memory downloaded by Otto and by some Renaissance commonplacers – addresses on the one hand, fixed sequences of words and ideas on the other – can be broken down into discrete, malleable chunks of information. But the eighteenth-century diarist does not simply download or upload chunks of autobiographical memory on to the text. She or he interacts with the diary in what could be described as a continuous and rapidly oscillating loop. The work of generating a coherent self is shared with the environment through the gesture of writing and the act of reading. And although not every eighteenth-century reader or writer kept a diary, a very large number of eighteenth-century readers were exposed to novelised narratives of character. Again, the effect of reading these on the process of forming a narrative of the self is impossible to measure but potentially powerful. One possible outcome is that novelised narratives of the self could increase belief in one's uniqueness, and the interest of that uniqueness to third parties, since narrative implies audience. Like the new flexible pathways available to different individuals through existing knowledge, this sense of a unique self of interest to others could have added leverage to an emerging politics of equality of rights.

The same is true of the changing relationship between areas of knowledge and rank. As speech norms split from print norms at the start of the century, a powerful tension was created between embodied experiences of reading, alone or with social peers, and embodied experiences of sharing a social space with higher ranks. Again, the embodied experience of reading is hard for us to capture; we do not necessarily learn much from simply watching silent readers. But we can capture some of the ways in which the freedom to read on what had once been elite topics could, in some circumstances, blend into conversations across ranks which were unavailable without reference to reading. This was a patchy business. Sarah Hurst enjoyed patronage, and therefore conversation, in support of her reading. Thomas Turner did not. But both read, wrote and spoke with social peers in ways that involved simulating the authority of high status, and then engaged with social superiors and enacted low status. Again, the cognitive effects of this kind of reading are not identifiable as chunks of knowledge and information. They form a widely extended loop between readers, peers and texts, one whose workings were influenced by the common knowledge of distant and unknown readers and writers having comparable experiences. The history of distributed cognition and reading in the eighteenth century, then, illustrates the power that comparatively small changes in the environment – cheaper paper, more books, more reading instruction – could have on social, political and cultural history. But it also shows that these comparatively small changes sometimes need to be accompanied by less visible changes in the conceptual framework around them, in this case conceptual changes around the diary's function, and around the relationship of print norms and speech norms.

10

Distributed Cognition and Women Writers' Representation of Theatre in Eighteenth-Century England: 'Thoroughly to unfold the labyrinths of the human mind'

Ros Ballaster

Eighteenth-century Britain appears to be a culture rich in sites and practices of distributed cognition. At the heart of its new philosophies and textual practices is an ethic of 'sociability', a conception of subjectivity as compulsively driven to engage with other minds from first formation through attachments to family and kin through to a later extension of loyalties to civil society (see in particular Mullan 1990; Ahnert and Manning 2011; Russell 2007). The establishment and expansion of engines of trade and communication, such as the General Post Office, the Bank of England, the Royal Exchange and coffee-houses, are all indicators of this heightened attention to sociability and a sense of need for institutions that promote and regulate virtuous sociability. Collaboration is the norm in the production and reception of sociable literary forms, such as the familiar letters or satires, as for example with the works produced under the signature of Martinus Scriblerus by Alexander Pope, Jonathan Swift, John Gay and John Arbuthnot. Increasingly, something that we might now call 'group mind' (see Brooks 1986; Rupert 2011) is ascribed to these art forms and the institutions of sociability they represent and in which they circulated. Group mind involves a shared intention and set of values beyond acts of collaboration in which individual minds complete tasks to produce a shared outcome. Shaun Gallagher argues that what he calls the 'socially extended mind' is constituted not only through social interactions between people but through 'mental institutions' such as 'legal systems, research practices and cultural institutions' (2013: 6). A mental institution includes 'cognitive practices that are produced in specific times and places' and these are 'activated in ways that extend our cognitive processes when we engage with them' (ibid.). I suggest that genre systems extend to accommodate new ways of thinking about cognition. In the mid-eighteenth century not only do traditional genres – tragedy, comedy, epic, lyric – extend their repertoire and practices to promote the value of sociable connection with others, but the mental institutions of culture develop new generic forms designed to extend the cognitive processes of the audience/reader.

In this chapter, I speculate that a form of 'group mind' is figured in those literary genres which emerge to express the new culture of sociability; the periodical press and the novel are modes that promote a sense of community and shared participation, a common knowledge or commonality of knowledge, which are markedly different from the elite forms of prose writing (the private dispatch, the news sheet, romance fiction) that had preceded them. The experience of regular theatre-going of the urban population who were the main target of novel publishing was one of sociable interaction with others in relation to a shared object or objects (the whole show of the theatrical night out) and that experience, I suggest, served as a model for aesthetic experience beyond the theatre walls. Theatrical criticism and reference is a recurrent topic within both the novel and the periodical. Not only are the individual cognitive ecologies of genres changed in this process but the genre-system and the values ascribed to particular elements within it shift. The story told in this chapter is also one of the novel's increasing claims to pre-eminence as a means of connecting minds to other minds, a claim founded precisely on the *absence* of body in the experience of reading as opposed to the *presence* of body in dramatic performance.

Accounts of distributed cognition in the theatre have to date largely been confined to discussions of its explanatory power in accounting for the extraordinary feats of memory demanded of actors in the early modern period: stage doors, the apprentice system and written 'plots' are all technologies and systems designed to support a repertory of six different plays each week at a minimum. Evelyn Tribble and John Sutton describe the early modern theatre as a 'cognitive ecology' which is

> a distributed but interconnected system or assemblage of social, material, bodily, and psychological resources and mechanisms which work together in mutually dependent, context-sensitive ways to enact some shared, flexible practice or activity. (2012: 592)

Miranda Anderson (2015b) points to a direction that has informed my own here: an attention to the ways in which early modern concepts of mind can be paralleled with recent philosophical theories of extended mind. In particular, an essay on Shakespeare's *Julius Caesar* understands the play as narrating a process of fusion and fission with other minds – between stage characters and between stage characters and the audience; the conspirators in Caesar's murder experience both fission and fusion of mind in contemplating and performing their act:

> Shakespeare deploys the affordance of the dramatic form to extend the collective mind from the characters to the audience, with *Julius Caesar* representing and playing upon notions of both the intramental and intermental as social and multiple. (Anderson 2015a: 166)

In this chapter I explore how two narrative modes – the mimetic (showing) of drama in performance and the diegetic (telling) of printed prose – are put into relations of fission and fusion in the eighteenth century. The so-called 'rise' of the novel stages a challenge to the dominance of stage performance as a means of representing the sociable value that is the product of putting minds into relation with other minds. My interest here is in exploring how understanding of the theatre is not only 'distributed' across other non-theatrical forms but also informs the shaping of those forms; newer sociable genres come to measure their own ecologies of production and personhood against the dominant norms of the theatre. Cognitive theory here allows us to think about the history of genre through a history of figuring mind. We need to acknowledge, of course, that cognitive theory may prove less an enabling strategy than a form of misdirection. When we begin to categorise genres and cultural institutions as forms of cognitive activity, it is arguable that we lose sight of any meaningful delimitation of 'mind' itself. Equally, literary historians may feel that we have an adequate vocabulary to describe genre and its transformations without recourse to the philosophy of mind. However, it is the working proposition of this chapter that conceiving of the eighteenth-century 'turn' to mental schemas that mediate persons (and relations between persons) through fictions of print rather than performance allows us to look differently at how aesthetic cultures past and present operate. Rather than a rule-governed system of representation open to limited adaptation in order to refresh its attraction to audiences, we conceive of genres as collaborative participants with authors and audiences in the production of knowledge, meaning and aesthetic experience.

The periodical and the novel both seek to shape their own cognitive ecologies as forms of sociable exchange rather than isolated modes of knowledge acquisition, despite the (apparently) solitary conditions of their consumption. The experience of silent reading, even if carried out in company (in a coffee-house or a parlour), remains a solitary interaction with a story, especially by comparison with the communal experience of watching a play. However, the image of silent immersion in story and character can also lay claim to providing enhanced opportunities for shaping the collective mind. The dominance of theatrical conventions of performing mind through the body (gesture and voice) comes under question with the rise of forms of prose that seek to render plausible being through text. Disguise and performance feature in established pre-Enlightenment prose fictional forms, such as romance, picaresque fiction and the short novella, and these are often represented through reference to theatrical performances, such as masques, masquerades and via analogy with theatrical characters. However, new forms of hybrid writing which make explicit reference to the particularity of the eighteenth-century playhouses and performances instead begin to shape competing forms of character grounded in the new potentialities and peculiarities of print personae.

Distinctive to eighteenth-century culture is the emergence of a number of new genres; the best known is the novel. Another new kind of extended prose writing closely related to the novel and equally concerned with the power of fiction to render or represent consciousness is that of theatrical criticism. And it is striking that women who wrote for, performed in, or wrote about the theatre were also responsible for some of the most hybrid and experimental forms of the novel in the period: Eliza Haywood, Sarah Fielding, Charlotte Lennox, Frances Brooke. Each of these writers is preoccupied with the ways in which 'mind' and its variation through the passions is signified in embodied form in the theatre. In this chapter, I consider

Eliza Haywood's series of plot summaries and critical insights into the major plays of the Renaissance to her present day, *The Dramatic Historiographer* (1735); Sarah Fielding and Jane Collier's part-fiction-part-philosophical tract *The Cry: A New Dramatic Fable* (1754); Charlotte Lennox's account of and energetic defence of the aesthetic superiority of Shakespeare's prose narrative sources, *Shakespear Illustrated* (1753–4); and Frances Brooke's periodical *The Old Maid* (published in 1755–6). These printed prose works invoke memories of performance – the co-presence of the real bodies of audience and actors. But they often do so to make the case for the superior cognitive experience of the reader's engagement through print with a fictional persona in the 'mind'. While play texts are also published forms of fiction, theatrical criticism of the eighteenth century tends to recall the experience of spectatorial presence in the theatre or to imagine the text in performance. Conjuring the 'lost' or 'absent' or 'imagined' presence of theatrical performance provides a means of bringing to life new kinds of (dis)embodied personae in the new hybrid diegetic modes of print.

Recent cognitive accounts of theatre in the early modern period have tended to focus on actors and memory (Tribble 2011; Tribble and Sutton 2012). Tribble and Sutton argue that distributed cognition of performance lies in the architectural and bodily geographies, as well as the prompt copy, that help to recall the part and performance. Many changes are introduced to the infrastructure of theatre in the century after the Restoration of 1660 (for example, female actors, indoor theatres seating several thousand, forestage and flats, etc.) which make a difference to the ways that dramatic performance is distributed. However, that knowledge is also distributed in new ways by the production of new genres with their own discourses and techniques of representing consciousness (for example, the periodical 'eidolon', the narrator of a fiction and the historiographer). These new genres distribute to a reading audience an understanding of the theatrical repertory and ways of judging the aesthetic and affective achievements of theatrical performance. Tobin Nellhaus (2006) sketches the emergence in the eighteenth century of a new 'image schema' for cognition modelled on the written line rather than the action and points structure of the traditional theatre. Print is increasingly the medium of understanding of 'practical life' (for example, the almanac, the conduct book and the legal contract), while the theatre, Nellhaus argues, responds with sentimental drama which offers an account of character developed on a sequential line of response which is replicated in the mind of the spectator. In *Novel Minds: Philosophers and Romance Readers, 1680–1740*, Rebecca Tierney-Hynes argues for a similar paradigm shift or new image schema founded in the vision of text in the mind, in place of the sight of the body in performance. In other words, the increasing significance of prose renderings of character produces a necessary shift in the cognitive ecology of the (previously) dominant mode of performing personhood: the theatre.

An image schema responds to changes in the material sociopolitical conditions of cultural production and both men and women found ways to capitalise on the profitability of theatre through 'spin-off' print forms. Women were not alone in turning to theatrical criticism; ever since Richard Steele's regular discussions of the playhouse and plays in the periodicals he co-authored with Joseph Addison in the first two decades of the eighteenth century, *The Tatler* and *The Spectator*, the experience of theatre-going – suitably distanced through the medium of prose recall – had served as a measure of polite cultural metropolitanism. However, there are practical commercial reasons why women writers may have found prose writing a particularly congenial means of reflecting on the ways in which theatre embodies mind, as well as seeking to find new markets for works experienced only through print publication: even before the passing of the Licensing Act in 1737 and the legislative confinement of spoken drama to two patent theatres in London (at least until the Act of 1788 extended patents to regional theatres), playwriting was a minority occupation for those seeking to make a living through writing. And typically women were rarely among the few who saw their plays into production, although they frequently recount their ambitions to see their work staged (Frances Brooke's 1777 *The Excursion* is perhaps the best-known fictional rendering of this struggle in its transparent attack on the Drury Lane manager, David Garrick, who had rejected Brooke's manuscript of a tragedy). Each of the patent theatres rarely produced more than a handful of new plays each season and relied on a familiar and already licensed repertoire from the Renaissance and Restoration.

One of the most famous female proponents of theatrical criticism is, of course, a fictional persona. In the second part of Samuel Richardson's *Pamela*, entitled *Pamela in her Exalted Condition* (1741), a rehearsal of John Locke's theory of mind is explicitly linked to a body of theatrical criticism. To pass the time late in her pregnancy and as she muses on her new role as model of virtue to her children, Pamela composes two 'little books', one for her sister-in-law, Lady Davers, and one for her new husband, Mr. B. The former is her thoughts on the dramatic entertainments she has seen in London the previous winter reconstructed from the pencil notes she made in the margins of the play texts she bought after having seen the performances. The second little book contains her sentiments on reading John Locke's *Some Thoughts Concerning Education* (1693); Pamela leaves each opposite page blank for her husband to add his comments as he reads. *Pamela*'s success as a novel lies, of course, in its claim to 'write to the moment' and Pamela's writing activity is an attempt to reconstitute and memorialise the moment of reception: the immediacy of moral response in the playhouse and in the solitary reading of an instructional book. In both works she sets her own responses against the environment of collective response and received wisdom, proving unafraid to challenge but also engaging in acts of sociable communication about her understanding (Richardson 2012: Letter XVIII, 369–71; Letter L, 493–501; Letter LI, 501–4). Pamela's prose writing remediates her immediate response to works with a powerful affective charge, providing an opportunity to compose a structured and judicious recollection. Here, what seem to be very different cognitive experiences – attending a theatrical performance and thinking through a set of ethical propositions made in print – are equivalent under the transforming power of Pamela's pen. Again, the theatre is the starting point for a 'reflection' on how the mind can best be trained to bring about the moral reform of the self and others. But it must also be left behind, its bodily affect overcome, for a true meeting of minds (that of Pamela and readers) to take place.

I focus in this chapter on similar acts of female authorship which invoke a moment of peculiar affect in theatrical mimetic performance – the appearance of the ghost in Shakespeare's *Hamlet* is particularly resonant – and then reflect on the superior capacity of a diegetic mode to contain the undisciplined power of embodiment and promote faculties of judgement and reflection. I am particularly interested in the recurrence of ideas of 'group mind', often feminised, in arriving at judgement, whether fair or unjust: compare the Old Maid's 'little court of female criticism, consisting of myself, and six virgins of my own age' proposed in number 4 of the periodical (Brooke 1764: Saturday, 6 December 1755, 29) and its obverse, the (largely female) partial and prejudiced 'Cry' who seek to shout down the virtuous narrator Portia and her ally, Una, in Fielding and Collier's fable. The absence of the body in fiction (character is an effect of print rather than performance) is here precisely the ground for a claim of a peculiar richness of and accessibility to 'mind'. The proposition seems to be that print 'type' can provide an unmediated access to 'mind', an access which is impeded, rather than fulfilled, by the imperfections of actorly embodiment. That Pamela annotates Locke alongside stage plays to write her own little books illustrates this new argument for the power of written text to bring the mind of the audience into a deeper contemplation with its object, the artwork.

In the Prologue to the third of the five parts of *The Cry*, Fielding and Collier differentiate between our willingness to correct our sense perception and our unwillingness to seek forms of assistance, such as their fable, to ensure we arrive at intellectual truth:

> Invention then is truth pretty much the same with having eyes and opening them in order to discern the objects which are placed before us. But the eye here made use of must be the mind's eye (as *Shakespear*, with his peculiar aptness of expression, calls it) and so strictly used is this metaphor, that nothing is apparently more frequent than a perverse shutting of this mental eye when we have not an inclination to perceive the things offered to our internal view. I know not likewise, why a short-sighted mind's eye should not be as good an expression as a short-sighted body's eye. But in this we are much kinder to our sense than to our intellect; for in order to assist the former we use glasses and spectacles of all kinds adapted to our deficiency of sight, whereas in the latter we are so far from accepting the assistance of mental glasses or spectacles, that we often strain our mind's eye, even to blindness, and at the same time affirm that our sight is nothing less than perfect. ('Prologue to Part the Third', Fielding and Collier 2018: 133)

The book is here represented as a tool, in analogy with a pair of spectacles; it serves as a substitute for the deficiencies of the cognitive activity in the 'mind's eye'. Perhaps it should not surprise us that the metaphor is attributed to Shakespeare and that it originates in *Hamlet* and refers specifically to the dead father's supernatural manifestation in that play. When Hamlet returns to Denmark from Wittenberg, he expresses his regret that his mother has so swiftly remarried after his father's death and to that father's brother. Hamlet comments, 'My father, methinks I see my father' (1.2.183). Horatio asks, 'Where, my lord?' (1.2.184), to which Hamlet responds, 'In my mind's eye' (1.2.185), providing Horatio with his opening to report the visitation of the ghost the night before.[1] Here, Fielding and Collier suggest an analogy between theatrical embodiment (the actor makes Old Hamlet flesh) and textual presence (the book); both concretise and externalise our longing to make 'solid' those truths that we often prefer not to see.

Fielding and Collier's interest in a version of what we might now think of as a group mind seems to stem from the work's engagement with the philosophy of Anthony Ashley Cooper, Earl of Shaftesbury, and his argument in the 1711 *Characteristics of Men, Manners, Opinions, Times* for the inherent virtue of the whole organism despite what appears to be apparent vice and weakness in its individual parts. Indeed, the flawed anti-heroine Cylinda, foil to the virtuous speaker Portia, is a neophyte philosopher who slavishly attempts to live by Shaftesbury's principles to disastrous effect. Like many other works of the mid-eighteenth century among which we might include Voltaire's *Candide* (1759), Laurence Sterne's *Tristram Shandy* (1759–67) and Samuel Johnson's *Rasselas* (1759), *The Cry* is deeply critical of such individual submission to a totalising theoretical system. Individuals who espouse a system to live by fail to live at all. However, *The Cry* is equally sceptical about submission to a collective will or thinking. If a lonely pursuit through reading of a single philosophy is criticised, so too is the unthinking conformity to majority 'opinion'. Here, too, the fictional work or the theatrical experience – and *The Cry* proffers itself to its readers as a hybrid mixture of both – can offer a relatively secure cognitive scaffold shared by an audience, and one that falls between extreme individualism and extreme totalitarianism. Readers of *The Cry* are invited to compare themselves favourably with the intradiegetic audience, the fictional Cry.

We have already noticed the ghostly presence and resonance of Shakespeare's *Hamlet* in *The Cry*. Hamlet appears to have been a touchstone for the 'awfulness' of embodiment of the past or hidden truth in physical form in the work of those who travelled productively between the sociable forms of theatre, periodical and novel. Look for example at Eliza Haywood's venture into theatrical criticism in the mid-1730s, a period in her own career when the acting parts seem to have run dry and the writing of fiction was proving less lucrative than it had been in previous decades. Haywood penned for publication a series of plot summaries of plays from the sixteenth to the early eighteenth centuries. *Hamlet* was one of the forty-five plays whose plots Eliza Haywood selected for summary in her 1735 *The*

---

[1] In the first scene, Horatio tells Barnardo that the armed figure like the king is 'A mote . . . to trouble the mind's eye' (1.1.111): in other words, a premonition that is there to disturb the inner sense of order (although note that the mote might blind as well as act as a marker).

Dramatic Historiographer. Half of her account of *Hamlet* is dedicated to the fate of Old Hamlet, and the historiographer is hugely impressed by this 'amazing Fantom', 'tremendous Shade' and 'awful Form' (Haywood 2001: 91).[2] Haywood's work was dedicated to Charles Fleetwood who had just acquired the patent to Drury Lane, a theatre in the doldrums after an actors' walkout in 1733, and clearly Haywood was seeking his patronage as a playwright. Drury Lane famously stuck to established plays, and the historiographer's preference for summaries of plays from the sixteenth- and seventeenth-century repertoire suggests Haywood's attempt to support this conservative culture at the patent playhouse.

Haywood appears to have been unsuccessful in seeking patronage for her own writing since one year later we find her working with Henry Fielding at the Little Theatre in the Haymarket. Fielding was the brother of Sarah Fielding and went on to provide a memorable scene of the affective power of theatrical embodiment in an account of a theatre trip to see *Hamlet* in his 1748 novel *The History of Tom Jones* (book 16, chapter 5). Tom and his tutor, the unworldly Benjamin Partridge, attend a performance of Hamlet in which David Garrick takes the lead part. Partridge is transfixed and moved by the sight of Garrick's portrayal of Hamlet's fear when he first encounters his father's ghost. Garrick had a mechanical fright wig he wore to play Hamlet, which allowed him to make his hair stand on end at the sight of the ghost: a literal interpretation of Old Hamlet's promise that his 'tale' will make 'each particular hair' 'stand on end / Like quills upon the fearful porpentine' (1.5.15–20). Partridge 'fell into so violent a Trembling, that his Knees knocked against each other' and 'during the whole Speech of the Ghost, he sat with his Eyes fixed partly on the Ghost and partly on *Hamlet*, and with his Mouth open; the same Passions which succeeded each other in *Hamlet*, succeeding likewise in him' (Fielding 1974: II, 853, 854). Partridge mirrors the performance he watches on stage. So convinced, however, is Partridge of the authenticity of Garrick's performance that he expresses contempt for his acting powers, arguing that this is nothing more than what is to be expected from an ordinary person at the sight of such a revenant parent. Here, too, Henry Fielding, like his female counterparts, suggests that the diegetic treatment of plot provides a less compromised sense of engaging with the 'minds' of characters than theatrical performance allows. Tom's own fatherless condition and his usurpation by an undeserving, guileful brother (Blifil/Claudius) is referenced in the choice of play, but we can be confident of a comic rather than tragic resolution as well as convinced of the 'realness' of the cast of novelistic characters in the prose fiction as opposed to the play precisely because of the *absence* of embodiment. And so too the novel audience has more capacity to arrive at measured judgement guided by a narrating hand than the theatrical audience pushed and pulled by mere bodily affect.

Charlotte Lennox, like Eliza Haywood, turned to a work that summarised play plots after she had enjoyed some success in the novel and a brief career as an

---

[2] The other plays by Shakespeare that Haywood selects are *King Lear, Macbeth, Othello, Timon of Athens, Julius Caesar* and *The Merry Wives of Windsor* (the only comedy).

actress. Her *The Life of Harriot Stuart* and *The Female Quixote, or the Adventures of Arabella* had appeared in 1751 and 1752 respectively, the latter to considerable acclaim. *Shakespear Illustrated* was published in three volumes in 1753–4 and advertised as by the author of *The Female Quixote*. Lennox summarised the sources from which Shakespeare had worked and then provided short comments on the 'Use' the play-wright had made of those sources in adapting them for the stage. A discussion of *Hamlet* and Shakespeare's treatment of 'the Story of *Amleth* from the *Danish* History of *Saxo-Grammaticus*' features in the second volume. Lennox's judgement of the source associates it with the Quixotic whimsicality of her last heroine, Arabella: 'the Story itself is full of ridiculous Fancies, wild and Improbable Circumstances, and as it is conducted, has more the Appearance of a Romance than an Historical Fact' (II, 267). She comments that it is not known whether Shakespeare encoun-tered the work already novelised or adapted it from the original. As elsewhere in the three volumes, Lennox is largely critical of the changes Shakespeare makes to his source, seeing them as undermining the force and focus of the story. The invention of Laertes, she complains, 'lessens' the importance of our hero and 'almost divides our Attention and Concern' (271). Hamlet's pretended madness, she complains, is essential to the plot in the source but in Shakespeare's play 'is of no other Use than to enliven the Dialogue' (272). Lennox is not especially interested in the affective power of the Ghost, observing only that 'The Ghost is wholly the Invention of *Shakespear*' (269). The superiority of the prose narrative, she argues, originates in more probable and concentrated renderings of character. She concludes by complaining that Shakespeare makes the death of his hero attendant on his act of revenge, whereas the Danish history simply reports his death in battle some time after the successful completion of his revenge:

> The Violation of poetical Justice is not the only Fault that arises from the Death of *Hamlet* [because Hamlet, justified in his revenge, nonetheless dies in its execu-tion]; the revenging his Father's Murder is the sole End of all his Designs, and the great Business of the Play, and the noble and fixed Resolution of *Hamlet* to accomplish it, makes up the most shining Part of his Character; yet this great End is delayed till after *Hamlet* is mortally wounded: He stabs the King imme-diately upon the Information of his Treachery to himself! thus his Revenge becomes interested, and he seems to punish his Uncle rather for his own Death, than the Murder of the King, his Father. (Lennox 1753–4: II, 274)

Hamlet's 'shining' and visible virtue is made murky through the concatenation of action in the drama's conclusion, according to Lennox. Ethics are wrongly subor-dinated to the pressure for a cathartic denouement.

In the same year as Lennox published the third volume of her *Shakespear Illustrated*, Sarah Fielding and Jane Collier produced a strange hybrid work some way between a summary of a (non-existent) stage performance, a novel and a work of moral philosophy. *The Cry: A New Dramatic Fable* plays with the mutual depend-ence of the mimetic and diegetic, performance and narration. Its virtuous heroine,

Portia, is called before the Cry, a large audience wedded to error; Portia's sole ally is the one virtuous auditor, an allegorical figure named Una (who stands for simplicity or truth). Over the course of five parts in three volumes, Portia counters the Cry's attempt – aided by Una's nemesis, Duessa – to ridicule and denigrate her. Along the way she delivers the story of her love for Ferdinand, his twin sister, Cordelia, and sufferings at the hands of their evil elder brother, Oliver, their foolish father, Nicanor, his conflicted mistress, Cylinda, and her jealous friend, Melantha. Fielding and Collier reanimate here in their modern hybrid novel not only the characters of Shakespeare's romance dramas – Portia from *The Merchant of Venice*, twins named Ferdinand (*The Tempest*) and Cordelia (*King Lear*) and Oliver from *As You Like It* – but also Edmund Spenser's Elizabethan romance epic *The Faerie Queene*, in which Una is the virtuous lady and allegorical embodiment of the Christian Church whom the Knight of the Redcrosse protects, while Duessa is the witch who adopts Una's form to seduce and distract the Knight from his purpose. Portia's truth telling is contrasted with the error into which her opposite, Cylinda, is led as a result of her intellectual vainglory. In *The Faerie Queene* Una represents the Protestant Church and the authority of the Bible, whereas Duessa represents the Catholic Church and its reliance on sensory entrainment, affective imagery and idolatry. We might recall Henry Fielding's ascription of Partridge's affective vulnerability as a member of the theatre audience to his superstitious temperament. A known tension in Christianity between sensory affective stimulus and textual authority is repurposed to draw a contrast between theatrical and printed prose narrative.

The *Cry* turns not just stage plots but also theatrical conventions and the cognitive ecology of the stage into prose fictional form. If the 1737 stage Licensing Act was designed to silence the stage's habit of putting political error on trial, prose fiction offers new consolations. In the world of *The Cry*, a single, virtuous member of the audience (Una) can resist the majority verdict more effectively than in the playhouse. Plays, after all, were only guaranteed a continuing life if the audience clapped sufficiently to secure a further performance the following night. So too a single, apparently errant interpretation can, through diegetic narration, have authority conferred upon it. This experiment in fiction assesses, addresses and attempts to bridge the gap between the stage play's cognitive advantage (real bodies represent personages) over that of the prose fiction (print is the medium that conjures the impression of character). Portia, true to her namesake, the legal cross-dresser of Shakespeare's *Merchant of Venice*, speaks truth to power but has more success in converting her extradiegetic than her intradiegetic audience. *The Cry*'s Portia is also the voice of a resistance to the imitative reproduction of familiar meanings. She coins new words – 'turba' for disturbance of mind and 'sinistra' for deviance of mind by comparison with 'dextra', the pursuit of the good but also a 'dextrous' management of speech. And she resists lazy use of quotation or instrumental treatments of allegory.

Words in *The Cry* have the capacity to be experienced through the body. See, for example, the fourth scene of Part III, where Portia warns the Cry not to indulge in angry feelings and to try to be 'agreeable'. Do not, she warns, 'invite into your breasts such evil passions as are, according to *Shakespear* in his *Winter's Tale, – Goads, thorns, nettles, tails of wasps*'; Portia refers to the pangs of jealousy that torment Leontes when he suspects Hermione of infidelity. We are told that

> The *Cry*, conscious of the force of Portia's quotation by the pains they felt within, yet resolutely bent on not confessing their folly in being thus their own tormentors, with lowering brows, with raised voices, and every technical mark of anger, declared that Portia was to them the highest object of contempt, and that they despised her from their very souls. (Fielding and Collier 2018: 153)

Later, in the sixth scene of Part III, Portia tells the Cry about a proposal she received from a sly and self-interested suitor, Oliver, brother to the man she really loves, Ferdinand (their names recall the violent brother of Orlando in *As You Like It* and Miranda's devoted suitor in *The Tempest*). Oliver depends on the 'force of his wise maxims' to pursue his amours:

> He had invented and remember'd political maxims enough to have filled a large volume on the methods of gaining women's hearts. The difference of their positions he never consulted; for he had read, *That women have no characters at all:* and no sooner had he read this assertion than the truth of it gained in his mind an unlimited credit. For that the author of the above verse confessed an exception to his own general rule, by addressing the poem to a lady, was an observation that could never enter into the head of such characters as *Oliver*. (Fielding and Collier 2018: 157–8)

Portia both resists Oliver's application of a quotation to her case and proves its appropriateness in ways he and the Cry fail to understand. She demonstrates to Una and her extradiegetic audience her superior understanding of its place in the work from which it comes, Alexander Pope's 'Epistle to a Lady' (1735), a poem addressed to Martha Blount in which Pope is in fact praising his female friend for her exceptionality to this 'rule'. Further irony missed by Oliver is that the statement is in fact the lady's and quoted by Pope, who then proceeds to delineate the different 'characters' of those women from whom she differs. Portia puts herself in sociable alliance with an audience absent – with the honourable exception of Una – from the stage on which she is performing. *The Cry* stages a series of such disputes about the inappropriate 'relocation' of elements from one work to another (quotation used out of context) within a work which operates by just such a process (taking names, words, elements from dramatic works and repurposing them for a printed prose fiction). The distinction is however presented as one between a mechanical application of terms to fulfil a collective intention and what the 'Cry' often represents as a 'candid' openness to pursue meaning for its own sake and in sympathetic alliance with the terms of the advocate (Portia).

    The Cry proclaims itself a new form of allegory. It provides a fiction of an animated mind at work, in place of the theatrical or (old) romance actor whose psychological conflicts are depicted through action and allegorical embodiment. In their 'Introduction', Fielding and Collier reject the obvious allegory of the 'romance' for the new allegorical psychology of their work in which the authors themselves feature as the heroic protagonists who defend the mind from error in collaboration with their reader:

> If the heroine of a romance was to travel through countries, where the castles of giants rise to her view; through gloomy forests, amongst the dens of savage beasts, where at one time she is in danger of being torn and devoured, at another, retarded in her flight by puzzling mazes, and falls at last into the hands of a cruel giant; the reader's fears will be alarmed for her safety; his pleasure will arise on seeing her escape from the teeth of a lion, or the paws of a fierce tiger . . . But the puzzling mazes into which we shall throw our heroine, are the perverse interpretations made upon her words; the lions, tigers, and giants, from which we endeavour to rescue her, are the spiteful and malicious tongues of her enemies . . .
>
> Thoroughly to unfold the labyrinths of the human mind is an arduous task; and notwithstanding the many skilful and penetrating strokes which are to be found in the best authors, there seems yet to remain some intricate and unopened recesses in the heart of man. In order to dive into those recesses, and lay them open to the reader in a striking and intelligible manner, it is necessary to assume a certain freedom in writing, not strictly perhaps within the limits prescribed by rules. Yet we desire only to be free, and not licentious. We wish to give our imagination leave to play; but within such bounds as not to grow mad. And if we step into allegory, it shall not be out of sight of our reader. (Fielding and Collier 2018: 41–2)

Fielding and Collier here open the vein of analogy which runs throughout the work between the image schema of the eye that traces the written word across the page and the 'mind's eye' that is strengthened to recognise truths through the experience of reading (their fable). The prose work and the experience of its reading lays bare its mechanisms to the reader. They do nothing 'out of sight' of their reader. While the theatrical performance appears to give us a more powerful visual experience, it is also an act of concealment because it absents the narrating consciousness. Again, *Hamlet* seems to be evoked in the shadows here: a man driven mad by the visual proof of his father's murder through a ghostly visitation. Reason can be maintained if we can participate in the framing critical consciousness of the fable we are immersed in. The whole cognitive effort is, however, still designed for an ethical purpose: to lay open the hidden recesses of the 'hearts' of readers, to make us feel with a character in order to know better what the nature of character is in general.

Frances Brooke also imagines a prose fictional persona as a superior vehicle for ethical criticism than theatrical embodiment. And she also, like Portia, demonstrates that superiority through the persona's alliance with a select group of like

minds. Brooke edited and chiefly wrote thirty-seven numbers of a periodical entitled *The Old Maid* in the persona of an eidolon, Mary Singleton, between 15
November 1755 and 4 July 1756; the periodical was explicitly addressed to other
women in the same circumstances as its eidolon. In the first number, Mary promises 'just as the whim takes me' to 'animadvert upon fashions, plays, masquerades,
or whatever else happens to fall within my observation' (Brooke 1764: 11), and
adds,

> I have thoughts of taking the theatres in an especial manner into consideration,
> because they have been almost entirely neglected by the best of our late essay
> writers, and because the few things that have been published on that subject
> within these two or three years, have been neither wrote with judgement nor
> impartiality. (Brooke 1764: 12)

Mary constitutes 'a little court of female criticism', which consists of herself and
six virgins who will pass judgement on the contemporary stage, since there is no
objective academy to take on this role in England. In fact, the thirty-seven numbers
cover a variety of contemporary topics: the Seven Years War and a fantasy of a
female army of Amazons defending Britain from French invasion by their powers
of attraction; a proposal for taxation of the single to fund the Foundling Hospital
in London; a plea to raise a subscription for a new edition of the Cambridge
scholar Simon Ockley's *History of the Saracen Empire* by his impoverished spinster
daughter; attacks on the cowardice of Admiral Byng; a rational Anglican perspective on the arbitrariness of the Lisbon Earthquake. Alongside such commentary,
Mary sustains an account of the parallel affairs of the heart of the niece who is her
ward, Julia, and the latter's friend, Rosara. Numbers also incorporate letters from
supposed correspondents and Brooke included contributions from her husband
and friends such as the playwright Arthur Murphy, Richard Gifford and Lord
Orrery. Mary enjoys her own little community of virtuous men and women: Mr
Hartingley, a Berkshire clergyman, his wife, and their friend, Sir Harry Hyacinth,
as well as Julia's suitor, Bellville. However, most relevant to our discussion here are
Mary Singleton's acts of literary criticism which are deeply attentive to interpretive
ambiguity and to the powers of theatrical affect.

The eighth number of Saturday, 3 January 1756, penned by one of Brooke's
contributors, John Boyle, fifth earl of Cork and Orrery (1707–62),[3] concerns
Christopher Pitt's translation of Virgil's *Aeneid* in the 1753 joint translation by Pitt
and Joseph Warton of the *Works* of Virgil. And the focus is on a particular scene of

---

[3] Boyle annotated his issues of all numbers of *The Old Maid* indicating the different authors of the
numbers. Clergyman Richard Gifford, fellow periodical writer Arthur Murphy, Frances's clergyman husband John and the poet John Robertson also contributed material to issues. The annotated issues are bound in a volume inscribed 'Corke 1756' in the front inside cover, and are held in
the Thomas Fisher Rare Book Library of the University of Toronto. With thanks to Kathryn King
for sharing with me her table of the authorship of the issues and her essay about it; see King 2017.

ghostly visitation and obscurity of moral vision. Mary Singleton offers a conjecture on the silence of Dido at the sight of Aeneas in the Elysian fields. Dido's silence, she suggests, 'proceeded from shame' prompted not by the sight of Aeneas but rather the 'sight and presence of the most virtuous of all women the *Cumaean Sybil*' (Brooke 1764: 56). Dido at their last interview at Carthage had warned Aeneas that her ghost would wait on him after her death. The reproachful sight of the Cumaean Sybil holds her back from speaking to Aeneas in the regions of the dead (Dido is excluded from following him into the higher regions): 'Her conscience struck her, by seeing a chaste and most exemplary virgin, who had withstood the offers of a god' (57). Dido keeps her eyes fixed upon the ground, evidence, Mary insists, of conscious guilt which is 'upon all occasions . . . observed to be remarkably apparent by down-cast eyes, and by the silence of a distracted and uneasy mind, whose horrible sensations dread to give themselves utterance' (58). Mary Singleton is here invoking her readers' understanding of the attitudes adopted by eighteenth-century actors to signal the passions to an audience (see Roach 1993). She goes on to contrast the silence of Ajax, which is proud and sullen, with that of Dido, which is one of 'confusion and speechless horror' (58). Here, as in our other examples, it is the sight of the returned figure ambiguously placed between embodiment and visionary illusion that serves as the occasion for the prose writer to meditate on the superior powers of the diegetic texts – simultaneously engaged in an act of narration and interpretation – to render character plausible and understand its workings. Here, too, the critic-narrator represents the act of interpretation as both individual and autonomous (Mary is offering a 'new' but more true interpretation of this famous scene from the *Aeneid*) and carried out before an audience which participates in and confirms the legitimacy of her reading.

Other numbers (and these are the numbers that we know Frances Brooke herself wrote) are more directly concerned with the eighteenth-century stage and its powers of realising moral truth, historical veracity and character. Two in particular are concerned with the privileged vantage point of the virgin judge. Mary Singleton, like the Cumaean Sibyl, has the power to engender shame. Number 18 of Saturday, 13 March 1756 provides an account of a visit with Rosara, Julia and three of her six virgin council to see the famous Spranger Barry give his Lear at Covent Garden. The ladies are comfortably situated in

> a part of the house where we enjoyed the double advantage of seeing the play and observing upon the audience; and I had the satisfaction of finding we were accompanied in our tears by almost the whole house; the young people especially showing such a becoming sensibility, as gives me hopes virtue has a stronger party in the rising generation, than those of my age in general are inclined to allow. (Brooke 1764: 146)

Mary is very impressed with Spranger Barry's performance, which she speculates is better than David Garrick's rival performance even though she has not had the benefit of seeing the latter:

> I think it a great mark of judgment in Mr Barry, that he has thrown so strong and affecting a cast of tenderness into the character: he never loses sight of the Father, but in all his rage, even in the midst of his severest curses, you see that his heart, heavily injured as he is, and provoked to the last excess of fury, still owns the offenders for his children. (Brooke 1764: 146)

But Mary Singleton is nonetheless critical of the production and, significantly, on the grounds of its departure from the print source she knows. She complains that both houses (Covent Garden and Drury Lane) have chosen Nahum Tate's 1681 adaptation, *The History of King Lear* (which provides a happy and restorative conclusion reconciling Lear and Cordelia), over Shakespeare's 'excellent original' (Brooke 1764: 149). In her preference for Shakespeare's 'original' play only known to an eighteenth-century audience in print since Nahum Tate's reworking was the standard performance text, Brooke, like Lennox, insists on the superiority of print to performance. It both supports Spranger's interpretation of the part and is aesthetically superior. Here, as with *The Cry*, print criticism of the theatre can resituate the play in a context which makes its rendering of character and plot more coherent, affecting and consistent than the embodied performance of theatre.

It is a response to a Shakespeare play that provides one further illustration of Brooke's ethical criticism. Number 26 (Saturday, 8 May 1756) tells us that Mary Singleton attended a performance of Shakespeare's *Henry VIII* where she took particular pleasure in observing the responses of the Moroccan Ambassador in the King's Box (the play was performed at Drury Lane on 4 May 1756). Here, too, Mary is as interested in observing the way the play is received by audience members as the performance itself. The ambassador, she observes, is graceful and intelligent. Halfway through Harry's opening scene, however, 'he burst into a most immoderate fit of apparently contemptuous laughter, which he repeated very often through the whole playing of the part' (Brooke 1764: 221). Mary is inclined to agree with what she takes to be his judgement: that the actor Edward Berry (1706–60) burlesques the part and plays it as an 'impudent cobler' (223) rather than a justly angry king. The ambassador is also offended at the married king's noticing of Anna Bullen and she notices that the ambassador scans his fellow audience to see if others are similarly affected by such fecklessness in a king. At the play's close, he gets up to leave but is delighted to be detained to see the pantomime afterpiece. Not all of it pleases, however. Again, his moral sensibilities lead him to be 'surprised and disgusted' at the Harlequin and the genii flying across the stage. Mary Singleton concludes: 'I received so much pleasure from this specimen of mere natural wild taste in his Excellency of *Morocco*, that I am determined never to miss a play at which he is to be present' (224).

Mary Singleton here aligns herself with the response of an audience member whose taste confirms her own and is in turn to be shared with her like-minded readers. This projection of an imagined community through the sociable experience of theatre rests on the distancing effect of prose to discriminate between different forms of response to the performance of character. Does the collaborative nature of periodical composition gathered under the signature of an eidolon such as Mary Singleton support, then, the argument for group mind in the production of aesthetic forms? Or does it suggest, rather, the translation of the known forms of distributed cognition in one genre of literary production (the theatre) into other genres more often associated with more simple acts of communication of mind between a single author and reader?

Cognitive theorists are, with fair consistency, sceptical about the existence of group mind. Robert Rupert (2011) argues on Occam's razor grounds (no more assumptions should be made than are necessary to explain a thing) that if one can account for group-level phenomena in terms of the cognitive states of individuals and the interaction between those individuals, then there is no explanatory warrant for a group mind interpretation or ontology. It is not my purpose here to claim that the history of eighteenth-century cultural ecology – and the shift in its dynamics with the increasing significance of forms of prose renderings of character by contrast with theatrical ones – provides evidence of group mind. I am not here making an ontological claim but an epistemological one: that consumers of aesthetic experience in the mid-eighteenth century were increasingly invited to translate their knowledge about the social extension of mind learned in the experience of theatre to that of reading 'new' prose forms of the periodical and the novel. We can see in the prose works I have discussed evidence of a conscious promotion of something that we might best account for as distributed cognition: a form of understanding of genre-shift arrived at through the play of voices past and present with technologies of production and distribution (book, theatrical stage, periodical essay). The prose work is imagined as a repository of socially extended mind for its audience, an opportunity not only to recreate the experience of communal consumption of the artwork which theatre affords, but also to provide a more sophisticated form of narrative scaffolding. Distance and reflection are, according to the advocates of new sociable forms of prose, enabled by the absence of the performer's body and the judicious authority of a framing narrator.

Of course, the rationale for such distributed cognition is, for the eighteenth-century cultural projector, always one of ethical training. Well-regulated discursive exploration of the terms and conditions of past cultural objects results in a better-regulated social community, hence an attention to careful interpretation and the necessary distancing of immediate bodily affect from acts of mental judgement, and the resituation of literary quotation in its textual context before applying it to 'life'. As we have seen, women writers were especially interested in the role of women's voices in these acts of sociable cognitive negotiation, and found in prose fiction the opportunity to present women as cognitive agents rather than affective vehicles (arguably still the most frequent position of women in the theatre world).[4] For Sarah Fielding and Jane Collier this extends even to the attempt to make new 'terms' in the shape of Portia's coining of 'dextra' and 'turba' to name the forms of

---

[4] See, however, the lively debate about the agency of the actress in current theatre studies in F. Nussbaum 2010 and Brooks 2015.

virtuous agency and cognitive dissonance she identifies in modern culture. Acts of collaboration between women are central to the promotion of these kinds of sociable virtue, from Mary Singleton's imagined court of like-minded old maids casting judgement on the theatre to Sarah Fielding and Jane Collier's shared writing of their strange hybrid work *The Cry* (see Londry 2004). And the group of women writers I have discussed here are all, to varying degrees, associated with the mixed coterie close to the two male writers seen as the major protagonists in the 'elevation' of the mid-century novel: Samuel Richardson and Henry Fielding. The collaborative practices of composition and print in which Richardson engaged with his female correspondents, readers and cohabitants are becoming increasingly evident through the archive work of literary historians. Donatella Montini, for example, calls attention to a sketch by Susanna Highmore which depicts Richardson reading from the manuscript of *Sir Charles Grandison* to six of his correspondent admirers, three of whom are women (Montini 2014: 173).

Of course, to some extent the imagining of community may be a necessary ploy by writers struggling to create an audience for a new medium. Fielding and Collier open the 'Introduction' to *The Cry* with the assertion 'Our address is to the candid reader' (2018: 37). The plea for candour – the word derives from the Latin *candidus* ('white') and is defined by Samuel Johnson in his 1755 *Dictionary* as 'Without malice; without deceit; fair; open; ingenuous' – suggests this sense of the unknown nature of an audience not physically present at the point of production, a certain nervousness in trying to imagine one's reception in the mind of an absent reader. A 'candid' reader (unlike the Cry) reads with sympathy and openness according to the inferred spirit of the author rather than the letter of a work (see Reid 2005 and Ballaster 2010). He or she forms community with the author to arrive at a shared ethics of cognition. And this may explain why those moments of encounter between a human and a supernatural being are so often the sight or site of an exploration of the power of literary arts to conjure an impression of a 'real' being from feigned performance – whether impersonated on the stage or on the page. In the eighteenth century the growing competition between print and performed renderings of personhood, between dramatic mimesis and print diegesis is, as we have seen, often characterised in accounts of such ghostly returns. Print forms simultaneously conjure and lay to rest the ghost of dramatic renderings of 'mind', asserting the superior power of the framing narrator to ensure the moral affect of this shared experience.

11

The Literary Designer Environments of Eighteenth-Century Jesuit Poetics

Karin Kukkonen

This chapter proposes to extend the notion of 'designer environment', that is, spatial and procedural arrangements that scaffold and amplify cognition, beyond the usual focus on problem-solving and the immediate task at hand. As designer environments are embedded in linguistic, cultural and literary contexts, they take on more varied and complex capacities. In tracing these capacities, we will enlist the help of the Jesuits of eighteenth-century France, who had developed both a theory and a practice of what we could call 'literary designer environments'.[1]

Problem-Solving in the Globe

Evelyn Tribble's 'Distributing cognition in the Globe' (2005), as well as her monograph *Cognition in the Globe: Attention and Memory in Shakespeare's Theatre* (2011) which extends the original article, make a persuasive argument for 'distributed cognition' in the context of humanities research. 'Companies performed a staggering number of plays,' she writes, 'six different plays a week, with relatively infrequent repetition and with the additional demands of putting on a new play roughly every fortnight' (2005: 135–6). However, despite the rapid succession of plays in the repertory, it could not have taken superhuman memory to be an actor in the early modern theatre. How, then, did actors in Shakespeare's time manage to perform so many different roles in so many different plays?

In order to answer this question, Tribble draws on Edwin Hutchins's *Cognition in the Wild* (1995). Hutchins investigates how sailors steer the massive hulls of aircraft carriers into narrow harbours, and how they navigate the oceans with the help of relatively simple technical implements, by discussing the ship's functional environments and social interaction among the crew. No one from the crew, Hutchins demonstrates, could steer the ship by themselves. Instead, it is the complex cognitive ecology of machinery, instruments and interpersonal communication that makes these feats of seafaring possible. Just as Hutchins's sailors navigate vast

[1] This research was supported by TUCEMEMS and the Academy of Finland. Thanks are due to *Archives jésuites en France* (Vanves).

oceans, so do Tribble's actors find their way through the repertory with the help of spatial arrangements of the stage, interpersonal coordination and surprisingly simple implements, such as the so-called 'plots'. Tribble explains, 'These folio-sized sheets of paper contain scene-by-scene accounts of entrances and, some-times, exits; necessary properties; casting; and sound and music cues' (2005: 144). On these sheets of paper the skeleton of the entire play is laid out, broken down into scenes, entrances and exits. Actors, who know their part (but not the entire play), can find their place on this plot as they wait in the green room. They will know when to go on stage (from the cue words), by which stage door (left for the entrances and right for the exits), when to deliver their lines and when to leave again. The regular feet of blank verse, repetitions and the frequent use of tropes (2005: 149–50), as well as codified gestures (2011: 85–105), help actors to remem-ber their lines, and protocols of entrances, exits and addresses, often inscribed in the play text, serve to teach inexperienced actors how to move about the stage.

Tribble re-describes the practices of stage-craft in the 1590s, well documented in earlier historical research, in terms of distributed cognition, and this allows her to paint a full picture of how Shakespeare's players were able to put on a different play every night. The sheer cognitive demand of remembering all these lines is 'offloaded' into the environment of the layout of the stage, the 'diagram' of the 'plot' and the verbal design of the play texts themselves. Without being situated in the spaces and protocols of the Elizabethan stage, the Elizabethan actor could not perform such a remarkable mnemonic feat. Tribble describes it as 'a common strategy for human beings engaged in expert group cognition: They created a smart space that prompts and constrains activity within it' (2011: 20). Through her analysis of theatrical space and protocol, then, Tribble delineates the extent to which the Elizabethan stage is a 'designer environment'.

Such a 'designer environment', a spatial-procedural arrangement assembled to support cognitive processes, usually looks more mundane than the Globe theatre in the cognitive and philosophical work on distributed cognition. We read of Tetris players who use the affordances of the game to turn the stones while they fall so as to improve their chances of fitting a slot (Kirsh 1995), and we encounter bartenders who use the shape and the arrangement of the glasses in front of them to process complicated drinks orders (Beach 1988; cited in Wheeler and Clark 2008). What they have in common with the Shakespearean theatre is that we have a problem that needs to be solved: How do you fit as many stones as possible into one row? How do you prepare everyone the drink which they have ordered? How do you put on a different play every night? The designer environments of the Tetris game, the bar and the Globe theatre enable such problem-solving by supporting spatial imagination, pre-structuring the action sequence and prompting memory. In the complex case of the Globe theatre, we have aspects of all three modes of problem-solving combined.

Tribble's analysis is striking because it reveals how limited the perspective on individual agents is when considering cultural activities. If we discuss only the indi-vidual player, then the Shakespearean repertory seems impossible to sustain. If we see the player as embedded in the spatial environment of the stage and the practices of playacting, then the whole process suddenly becomes feasible. Hutchins's plea for a 'cognitive ethnography', in the final chapter of *Cognition in the Wild*, stresses that cognitive phenomena need to be analysed in their cultural and social context because that is how they occur. On the orthodox cognitive-scientific picture, the entire situation of the individual within the cultural environment is condensed and transplanted into the individual's brain, and this leads to the presumption that an individual could steer a ship or that Shakespearean actors need to have the entire play in mind to be able to perform it. In reality, the situation is extended into the spatial, procedural and social dimensions of the environment and this entire situation needs to be studied by the cognitive ethnographer (or, indeed, the humanities scholar).

Hutchins, like Tribble and others who have thought about distributed cognition, conceives of these processes in terms of problem-solving. He rejects the first-generation assumption that culture is 'simply a pool of ideas that are operated on by cognitive processes' (1995: 353). Rather, he suggests, 'Culture is an adaptive process that accumulates partial solutions to frequently encountered problems' (354), and these problems can include navigating a ship or staging a play. Clearly, however, the cognitive ecology of the Shakespearean theatre does more than solve problems. Tribble's accounts point towards the apprentice system of the actors that leads to the 'enskillment' that facilitates the performances of boy actors (not dissimilar from the 'dynamic learning environments' of the Protestant faith that she analyses with Nicholas Keene).[2] However, given the ambitious suggestions of how 'designer environments' and the cognitive niche have enabled human beings to evolve beyond the capacities of other animals (Sterelny 2003, 2014) and how cognitive niche construction supports the 'ratchet' between culture and cognition (Wheeler and Clark 2008), one is poised to ask how exactly these designer environments reach beyond the paradigm of the Tetris game.

Enter the Jesuits

In 1726, the pupils at the Collège Louis-le-Grand in Paris performed a ballet called *L'homme instruit par le spectacle, ou le théâtre changé en école de vertu*. It was written by

[2] Tribble and Keene's *Cognitive Ecologies and the History of Remembering* (2011) takes a step towards considering designer environments as more versatile and culturally specific, when they trace how Protestantism creates its own 'cognitive ecologies' in England in the sixteenth century. A new layout for the Bible and prayer books, iconoclasm, the dominance of the sermon and the joint singing of psalms are all part of a redesigning of sacred spaces and holy protocols, as the country turns its back on the Catholic Church. Tribble and Keene's account takes a global perspective on distributed cognition in Protestantism: 'English Protestant reformers attempted to establish a new cognitive ecology based upon reordering of mnemonic and attentional priorities' (2011: 19). As new cognitive ecologies are designed, cognitive processes (mostly, memory) are reconfigured, and new habits and group identities emerge. The basic perspective, however, is on the enculturation of practices, rather than specific extended practices as we shall discuss them in what follows.

their teacher, the Jesuit Charles Porée, and in the printed overture to the ballet we read:

> Des hommes des differens âges, et de differens conditions paroissent fatigués des Instructions sérieuses que leur donnent les Philosophes de differentes Sectes. Ils demandent à Jupiter du délassement. Ce dieu leur envoie la Tragédie, la Comédie, le Génie de la Danse et la Genie de la Musique, pour instruire les hommes en les divertissant. (Porée 1726: 2)

> Men of different epochs and different stations appear tired of the serious instructions that the different sects of philosophers have given to them. They demand reprieve from Jupiter. This god sends them tragedy, comedy, the genius of dance and the genius of music, so as to instruct mankind through entertainment.[3]

The arts were a key instrument in the elite education which the Jesuits offered in the eighteenth century. Plays and ballets were performed to show off the skills of the pupils in delivering a speech, to display the Catholics' supreme command of visual brilliance and to educate both pupils and audiences in moral and religious matters. The Jesuit intellectuals themselves reflected on the uses of the theatre within their educational treatises, such as Jouvancy's *Ratio discendi et docendi* (1703), and in public discourses, such as Porée's *De theatro*, delivered in Neo-Latin, but translated and published for the French public by Pierre Brumoy as *Sur les spectacles* in 1733.[4]

A religious order with a clear sense of purpose in the context of the Counter-Reformation, the Jesuits recognised the soft power of culture for their work as missionaries and educators. As we shall see, it is rooted in an understanding of the human mind as strongly embodied and embedded in designer environments, devised, for example, by 'tragedy, comedy, the genius of dance and the genius of music'. When we place the Jesuits into dialogue with today's proponents of distributed cognition, we see that their poetics, as it extends from the theatre to poetry and the novel, can offer an alternative perspective to the problem-solution paradigm.

In *De theatro*, Porée describes the great power of the theatre to excite the passions of its audience and to lead them on the road to virtue by presenting examples in a lively and immersive fashion.

> Hé! quel Spectateur ne croiroit, que par un enchantement subit les siècles retrogradent, les intervalles des lieux se resserrent; & que par ce double charme il est transporté dans les climats & les tems où l'action représentée sur la Scène s'est réellement jouée sur le Theatre du monde, que dis-je? Quelle se passe encore à ses yeux! (Porée 2000: 21)

---

[3] These and the following translations are my own.
[4] For an accessible overview of the role of theatrical performance in the Jesuits' educational programme in France, see Dainville 1978: 463–517.

I say, what spectator would not believe that an enchantment lets the centuries run backwards and that the gaps between the locations close themselves, and that through this two-fold magic he is transported into the climes and times where the action represented on the stage has really taken place in the great theatre of the world? An action which is still going on before his eyes.

The stage brings history and religious examples to life. Porée mentions explicitly the 'annales des Martyrs' here (2000: 23), which make a much greater impression on the hearts of the faithful when they are enacted on the stage.[5] At the same time, however, these immersive powers of the stage might be very easily abused with plays that inculcate the wrong kinds of values and actors who perform in an overly lascivious manner. Porée makes two suggestions for how the theatre can be saved: first, he calls on the contemporary French dramatists to live up to the example of Athenian tragedy (27), but then, perhaps rather surprisingly, he stresses in the powerful conclusion to the discourse that it is in fact the audience that can bring the theatre to its full potential as a 'school of virtue'.

C'est donc à vous, Messieurs (je parle aux Spectateurs, Censeurs nez des la plume des Poëtes, & du jeu des Acteurs) c'est à vous particulièrement & plus qu'à eux, d'employer vos soins à la réforme du Théâtre. Votre indulgence a fait le mal; c'est à votre juste sévérité de la réperer. (Porée 2000: 71)

Hence it is up to you, Sirs (I speak to the spectators, sagacious censors of the pen of poets and the play of actors), it is up to you in particular, and more so than to these, to apply yourself to bring about the reform of the theatre. Your indulgence has caused the problem, and your just strictness will repair the damage.

The audience, in other words, needs to reflect on their own response to what goes on on stage and to command the authors and players to produce the kinds of plays that will make their immersion most profitable.

The eighteenth-century Jesuit Porée conceives of the theatre as a cognitive ecology in which the plays, their performance and the audience engage in an act of distributed cognition. He identifies the cognitive processes within this ecology, such as the affordances of a stage performance to immerse its audience[6] in the events and to elicit immediate emotional reactions, as well as the audience's different motivations to attend the theatre (see 2000: 67–9). Porée clearly has an agenda in his *De theatro*, but the dynamics of these interactions in the cognitive ecology of the

[5] The Jesuits themselves often produced plays on the martyrdom of converts, not only the martyrs of ancient Rome (see Dainville 1978: 476), but also the recent converts of Japan and South America, where they had their missions. For an example set in Japan, see Johann Baptist Adolph and Johan Bernhardt Staudt's *Mulier Fortis* (1698).

[6] See also Brumoy's 'A discourse upon the original of tragedy' in *The Greek Theatre* (1759: xlv). The immersiveness of the stage performance is a key issue in the debate around the neoclassical dramatic unities to time, space and action both in France and in Britain; see Kukkonen 2017.

Jesuit theatre are complex, and he does not reduce them to an instance of problem-solving. The mechanics of the performance are certainly not at stake here (even though Jesuits elsewhere have a lot to say about how to deliver a speech, sermon or part in a play effectively). Rather, Porée foregrounds the kinds of thinking which the literary text and its performance enables within this cognitive ecology, that is, in what sense it is a 'literary designer environment'.

The state which Porée describes is located between enactment (experiencing the events and emotions represented on stage in our own bodies) and reflection (contemplating the moral implications of these plays and applying them to our own lives). The Jesuits were poised to think about such tension, because it lies at the root of Jesuit practice in Ignatius of Loyola's *Spiritual Exercises*, the founding text of the Jesuit order, where the exercitants are encouraged to experience the passion of Christ through their own bodies but at the same time he also wants them to reflect on these meditative states. Catholic church design similarly evokes this double state. When standing in front of Leonardo's *Last Supper*, which serves as an altar-piece in a chapel in Milan, observers are invited to situate themselves in relation to Jesus and the disciples, taking their place on the other side of the communion table. When standing in the church of St Ignatius in Rome, the observer looks up into the apse to see Loyola's ascension to heaven. The stone pillars of the church itself are extended in the *trompe l'œil* painting, taking the building to the unlikely heights where the founder of the Jesuit order enters the heavens. Observers are related, in a spatial and embodied fashion, to these events, and they might well experience a slight sense of vertigo looking up. At the same time, the artificial nature of the *trompe l'œil* painting invites them to reflect on the staggering nature of the exultation of the saint, evoking admiration and the hope to ascend to similar heights of beatitude one day themselves.

The real-world architecture of the church receives what we could call a 'fictional extension' in St Ignatius. Similarly the theatrical stage offers a 'fictional extension' to the everyday experience of the spectator, as part of the distributed cognition in these cognitive ecologies. But we do not need Leonardo's altarpiece to remind us that there was a last supper and we do not need the painting in St Ignatius to tell us that the saint went to heaven. These fictional extensions do not serve to 'offload' memory and they do not contribute to solving a particular problem. Rather, they allow for the state between immersion and reflection which Porée describes in *De theatro*.

The literature on designer environments and cognitive niche construction often points towards books, performance and the arts as something like the end point of the development of extended cognition. The accounts tell an evolutionary narra-tive: animals like the mole cricket make use of their environment to amplify their natural abilities (in this case, burrows to enhance the noise from their chirping; see Clark 2005), and animals like the leaf-cutter ant or the beaver engineer their own ecosystem to support their everyday activities (see Odling-Smee et al. 2003). Human beings obviously enhance their natural capacities and engineer their eco-system through their cultural and social environments. Kim Sterelny, in *Thought in a Hostile World* (2003), argues for example that the human capacity of theory of mind emerges from social scaffolding, observing and imitating the example of parents and friends, as well as cultural inventions such as narratives. These elements of our sociocultural environment are crucial supports for the development of this cognitive capacity. Literary narratives, encountered in books and presented with the inside views of omniscient narrators, seem to be something like a rarefied end point of the everyday narratives in Sterelny (2003) and Hutto (2008), the exograms in Merlin Donald's *A Mind So Rare* (2001) or the 'surrogate situations' in Clark (2005).

The particular nature of *linguistic* designer environments has been considered by Andy Clark. The 'surrogate situations' that language enables go beyond the basic capacities for memory-offload in designer environments (see Clark 2005: 236). Language, as Clark also suggests in *Supersizing the Mind* (2008), allows us to abstract from the real world. It parses and tags elements of the real world, reduces their complexity, and makes them more accessible to reorganisation and reasoning. Like the singing burrows of the mole cricket, language and its surrogate situations amplify human cognitive processes (Clark 2005: 241). Clark, however, is careful to distinguish language from other kinds of cognition. 'Language is like that [labelling, abstract, etc.] because thought (or rather, biologically basic thought) is *not* like that' (2008: 47). In that sense, language offers a complement to intuitive, embodied modes of thinking. It becomes a 'cognitive superniche' that allows us to construct further niches, such as particular cultural designer environments and 'special training regimes to install (and to make habitual) the complex skills such environments demand' (59). Clark refers to Tribble's work on Shakespearean theatre as a case in point. Even though Clark's linguistic perspective extends the notion of 'designer environment' considerably, he also thinks of the cognition which it enables in terms of 'high-level human problem solving' (2005: 234). In this category, he includes instances in which we 'plan for next year's family vacation, design a new 100-story building, or sit down and think about equality, freedom, and the bad effects of the "war on terrorism"' (234). Even though each of these processes can be broken down into smaller 'problems', overall, one would not necessarily tag them as 'problemsolving'. There must be something more to this 'surrogate situatedness' that language enables, and arguably this something more interested the Jesuits.

The designer environment of the plays by, say, Corneille, Racine and Molière, which Porée discusses, modify thought like language does in Clark's account. The play abstracts from the real world by presenting us with characters whose actions can be observed and isolated, which sometimes allows us to tag them (as, say, a 'misanthrope' or a 'bourgeois gentilhomme'), and it presents to us what happens with them when their actions and desires are manipulated in the imagination. In his 'Discours sur l'usage des mathématiques par rapport aux Belles-Lettres' (1741, first delivered in 1725), Brumoy claims that training in the abstraction of mathematics is necessary for the mastery of the literary arts. He says,

> Ce seroit peu pour les Mathématiques de donner à l'imagination la facon qu'elle exige, afin de réussir dans la Littérature, ce ne seroit perfectionner le genie qu'à

demi; elles donnent encore à l'esprit les qualités necessaires pour y exceller: et quelles qualités? L'attention qui l'applique à méditer longtems un sujet sans se distraire; la justesse qui l'accoûtume à discerner le vrai d'avec le faux, & à prendre en tout le parti du bon sens; l'étendue ou la capacité . . . qui lui fait envisager un grand nombre d'objets d'une seule vûë; la pénétration enfin & la délicatesse, dont l'une le rend capable de considerer son objet de toutes parts sans que rien échappe à ses lumières, & dont l'autre lui fournit ces traits déliés qui expriment finement ce qu'il a solidement concu. (Brumoy 1741b: 286)

It would be little if mathematics only gave the imagination the form which it demands, with the goal to succeed in literature, but this means just leaving the genius half-way from perfection. Mathematics also gives the mind the necessary qualities to excel. What qualities? Attention, which the mind applies to consider a subject for a long time without distraction; the exactitude that makes it used to discern the right from the wrong and to join the party of common sense in everything; the understanding or capacity . . . which allows it to grasp a great number of objects with a single glace; finally, penetration and tact, where the first renders it capable of considering all aspects of a matter without a single one escaping from its insight, and the second gives it the fine features that express delicately what it has profoundly understood.

The Jesuit sounds not too different from the philosopher of extended cognition here: discernment, mastery of complexity and attention to detail are all linguistic capacities that contribute to the construction of the cognitive superniche in Clark's account. In light of Stanislas Dehaene's suggestion that exact calculation is language-based (Dehaene 1997; also cited in Clark 2005), Brumoy's attention to mathematics as a complement to the imaginative and immersive features of literature suggests the close connection between the abstract reasoning of mathematics (in geometry and calculation) and human linguistic capacities already present in the 1720s.

At the same time, however, the Jesuits were very aware that the performance of a play in the theatre has a strong element of embodiment, which is very different from the linguistic features which Clark describes. The 'fictional extensions' of the designer environment of the stage (and, arguably, also of the church, since in mass and prayer verbal processes are combined with the visual situation) seem to rely, at the same time, on an immediate appeal to our embodied, immersive meaning-making and more abstract modes of language-based manipulation of these elements. The 'fictional extensions' which these designer environments open combine immersive and reflective modes of thinking and hence go beyond immediate problem-solving.

Immersion and Reflection

When reading through these treatises from the eighteenth century, one is struck by the liveliness of the language of Porée in *De theatro* and Brumoy in 'Discours sur l'usage des mathématiques'. These discourses were first delivered orally (in Neo-Latin), and they are well stocked with the kinds of rhetorical tropes which the Jesuits would also teach to their students. For example, Porée addresses his audience as the audience that also goes to the theatre ('C'est donc à vous, Messieurs'). Brumoy makes Virgil himself speak in his *Discours* (in citing the *Georgics*) in order to underline his point (1741b: 284) and then goes on to discuss 'le témoinage de Virgile' ('the testimony of Virgil', 286). These speeches strike a balance between arguing a case and inviting listeners and readers to feel the force of this argument in an embodied, immersive fashion.

This is a strategy which the Jesuits also employ in their writings in the first half of the eighteenth century. In the didactic poem *De motibus animi*, Brumoy gives his readers an introduction to the emotions, the role they play both in mundane and in religious life, and how to gain control over them.[7] The second book of the poem introduces the different kinds of love to the reader: 'Iam levis ingenium populi moresque superbos disce memor. / Titulos et singula nomina pandam' ('Now learn (so that you remember) the disposition and haughty manners of this light tribe. / I will unfold the titles and individual names', 1741a: 88). What seems to begin as a dry list soon turns into an engaging tour of the passions. We get an animated allegory of the sneakiness of Amor, as well as retellings of Petronius's 'Matron of Ephesus', of the story of Psyche and Amor and of Homer's *Odyssey*, in which the Jesuit speaks for a while in the voice of Circe (98).

Brumoy's version of the 'Matron of Ephesus', for example, is billed as an 'Imitation de la Fontaine' in the French translation of *De motibus animi* (1741a: 91),[8] referring to La Fontaine's 'Fable XXVI'. Like La Fontaine, Brumoy introduces the god of Love as an agent in the narrative. Whereas there is no supernatural intervention in Petronius, La Fontaine has Amor shoot arrows at the hearts of the matron and the soldier (1991: 511), and Brumoy has him in addition lend eloquence to the soldier when he tries to win the heart of the matron: 'Ingeniosus amor facundum fecit' ('Ingenious love made him eloquent', 1741a: 92). In La Fontaine, the soldier has no verbal skills ('Encore que le Soldat fût mauvais Orateur', 1991: 511), and the matron's sadness is ridiculed as superficial ('La douleur est toujours moins forte que la plainte', 1991: 509). Brumoy, on the other hand, foregrounds the intensity of grief which then yields to an intensity of passion in the matron: 'Res dolor est violenta' ('Grief is a violent affair', 1741a: 90). He also speaks in the voice of the soldier seducing the matron. The soldier's strategy

---

[7] See Haskell 2003 for a detailed discussion of Jesuit didactic poetry.

[8] In the collection *Recueil des divers ouvrages* (1741), Brumoy's Neo-Latin poem is published with the French translation on the opposite page. When I cite the poem in what follows, even page numbers refer to the Latin and odd page numbers refer to the French.

in Brumoy[9] could be described as a picture book illustration of the working of embodied cognition: he wants the matron to watch him eat, in order to draw her out from her desire to starve herself to death: 'ecquid spectasse nocebit?' ('Is there anyone who will sin by having watched?', 1741a: 92), and then points out that her husband, reduced to ashes,[10] is not capable of a similar embodied action any more. The soldier invites an embodied simulation in the matron, which then leads to her copying his actions, first eating the supplies and then giving in to his passion. The narrative is retold to illustrate the strength of our emotions, but also to show how easily rhetorical skill and the embodied appeal of another person can turn a highly virtuous emotion (grief for the husband) into a highly amoral emotion (passion for a lover next to the husband's remains). Brumoy explicates the emotional process through the narrative, and at the same time he uses the narrative to enact these emotions and to demonstrate the guiding power of rhetoric, inviting readers to move between immersion and reflection.

'Quae me autem species tremebundum visa repente / Terruit?' ('But what aspect that I suddenly perceive with trembling alarms me?', 1741a: 108). About halfway through the second book of *De motibus animi*, Brumoy interrupts his flow of speech, as Apollo grants him a vision of the hidden kinds of passion, and as the Greek god also addresses the Jesuit directly (108). Apollo, the god of the Muses, gives Brumoy insights into the hidden motives of man and the space to reflect on these insights, and Brumoy reproduces this effect in the rhetorical set-up of his poem. He concludes the book by expressing his delight of being thus favoured by the gods of creativity and culture, and he realises that simply listing the different kinds of 'amor' is not the best way of approaching them. Rather, one needs to trace the ways in which they work and play their roles. Brumoy expresses this insight in clearly theatrical terms:

> Non aliter tenues proscenia formae / Parva ineunt, dictisque addunt scurrilibus artem. . . . Haec avidae spectacula plebi. / Verum occulta manus regit apto examine fila / Indeprensa oculis, pictoque ligata tigillo. (1741a: 116–18)

> In no other way do the slight forms enter the little stage, and add ridiculous words to their art. . . . Such a spectacle for the eager audience! In truth, a hand hidden from proper examination controls threads that are undetected by the eyes and connected with painted machines.

As Yasmin Haskell similarly proposes in her discussion of the poem, *De motibus animi* 'is marked by variety, visuality, and above all, *spectacularity*' (Haskell 2019: 59).
Jesuit intellectuals like Porée or Brumoy considered the theatre an art form well

---

[9] We do not find this strategy in Petronius or in La Fontaine.

[10] Brumoy does not mention that the soldier was guarding crucified criminals and he leaves out the retrospectively blasphemous conclusion to Petronius's narrative, in which the matron volunteers her husband's body to be mounted on a cross when the original corpse goes missing.

suited for moral and spiritual edification. While Porée's *De theatro* defends the theatre against accusations of immorality and dangerous seduction by pointing out that
it can in fact serve as a 'school of virtue' (if done right), he does not extend the same
courtesy to the new form of the novel. Several paragraphs in *De theatro* expound on
the influence of the novel on the theatre, concluding: 'Tout s'attendrit, tout soup-
ire: oiseaux, zephyr, ruisseaux, rochers même, tout apprend à aimer' ('Everything
softens, everything sighs: birds, zephyrs, brooks, even the rocks – everything learns
to love', 2000: 59). This is not what Porée has in mind for the theatre as 'school
of virtue'. In a later discourse, *De libris qui vulgo dicuntur romanenses* (1736),[11] Porée
attacks the novel as a genre which is only good for amorous discourse, but not for
the elevating emotions of the theatre.[12]

A year before Porée's *De libris*, Guillaume-Hyacinthe Bougeant published perhaps the most successful Jesuit attack on the novel – in the form of a novel: *Voyage
merveilleux du Prince Fan-Férédin dans la Romancie* (1735).[13] Prince Fan-Férédin travels
through the lands of the novel ('la Romancie'), encountering the conventional set-
tings, characters and plot events of the genre. With 'Romancie', Bougeant brings
together several of the textual traditions that would be associated with the term
'roman' at the time: the historical romances of Scudéry, La Calprenède and others,
which would tell the stories of highly virtuous women and the men who perform
heroic deeds for them at great length (also called the 'grand roman'), the *contes des
fées* of Perrault, d'Aulnoy and others, the oriental tales, such as *Arabian Nights*, as
well as the first-person memoir narratives of Marivaux, Prévost, Crébillon and
Mouhy that had taken the literary stage with great éclat in the 1730s. As Jean
Sgard and Geraldine Sheridan point out in their preface to *Voyage merveilleux*, the
Jesuits promoted a 'lecture guidée' in their colleges (1992: 16), where texts would
be read out aloud and where students would only encounter expurgated versions
of the classics and tailor-made didactic dramas.

The novel in the 1730s was different, however, not least because readers were
assumed to read these slim volumes in private without the supervision of an instruc-
tor.[14] As he trains his satiric artillery on them, Bougeant presents these books as
pervaded by the light touch of amorous, gallant emotions. Just as in Porée's *De
theatro*, even the rocks are feeling things in Bougeant's 'Romancie': 'son récit était
si touchant, ses accents douloureux si pitoyables, que les rochers n'avaient pu y

[11] Porée's complete discourse in *De libris* was published in Neo-Latin only, but the Jesuit journal
    Mémoires de Trévoux prints a condensed French translation, thus making the discourse accessible to
    a much wider readership.
[12] Novelists like Crébillon and Marivaux might have well agreed with the assessment that the emo-
    tions in the novel are lighter than those in the tragedies of Corneille or Racine, and much more
    geared towards pleasure. See Stewart 1973 for an overview of the development of the libertine
    novel in the eighteenth century.
[13] Bougeant's book went through three editions in the eighteenth century, and it was translated into
    German in 1736 and into English in 1789 (see Sgard and Sheridan 1992: 23–6).
[14] See Sgard and Sheridan 1992: 16; see also Ferrand 2002 for the history of reading in
    eighteenth-century France more generally.

résister malgré toute leur dureté naturelle' ('His narrative was so touching, his tear-ful speech so pitiful that the rocks could not resist it despite their natural hardness', 1992: 47). Just as the amorous narratives in *Voyage merveilleux* are able to soften the rocks, so, too, do they soften readers' hearts and make them vulnerable to sin. In the novel of the 1730s, with its emphasis on the emotional experience (that is not inscribed into a dramatic scheme of punishing and redeemable passions), its talkative first-person narrators that invite readers to sympathise with them, and its frequent elopements, secret marriages and proposals for prostitution, we have something different from the well-controlled designer environments that the Jesuits created with their plays, ballets and didactic poems like Brumoy's. Bougeant's *Voyage merveilleux* can be read as the attempt to bring such control into the novel too.[15]

In his guided tour of the lands of 'Romancie', Bougeant foregrounds and sat-irises the emotionally immersive experience of reading a novel to such an extent that readers are quite likely to reflect on these immersive strategies. He creates a fictional extension with the written text that uses the principles of novel-writing in order to create an explicit trade-off between immersive and reflective states of response that we have already observed for the Jesuit theatre and the didactic poem.

Like many of the novels from the 1730s, *Voyage merveilleux* is written as a first-person narrative told by the hero himself, Prince Fan-Férédin. When he enters 'Romancie', he falls down a mountain ridge and into a black hole:

> Mais avouerai-je ici ma faiblesse, ou ne l'avouerai-je pas? Faut-il parler ou me taire? Voilà une de ces situations difficiles, où j'ai souvent vu dans les romans les héros qui racontent leurs aventures, et dont on ne connaît bien l'embarras que lorsqu'on l'éprouve soi-même. (1992: 40–1)

> But should I admit here my weakness, or do I not admit it? Do I have to speak or fall silent? Here we have one of these difficult situations, which I have often seen in the novels where heroes narrate their own adventures, and one does not properly understand such embarrassment until one experiences it oneself.

The self-reflective discourse typical of Marivaux's Marianne (in *La Vie de Marianne*), Prévost's Grieux (in *Manon Lescaut*), Prévost's Cleveland (in *Le Philosophe anglois*) or Mouhy's Jeannette (in *La Paysanne parvenue*) is here taken to the point where the nar-rator reflects on whether he should stop narrating so as not to endanger his status as the hero. We find several instances in Marivaux and Mouhy where the narrator apologises for having spoken too much about her own feelings and promises to get

---

[15] There were also novels written by Jesuits in seventeenth-century Germany, such as Jakob Bidermann's *Utopia* (1640). These novels take the mode of the 'grand roman' (also popular in the German-speaking lands at the time), but they do not consider it necessary to react against the genre in the way that Bougeant does.

on with the tale. Bougeant's hero, however, reflects on whether he should even admit to these feelings in the first place. As the passage continues, he remembers that Prévost's protagonist Cleveland, in a similar situation, had fallen asleep and sets about to do the same thing (1992: 41).[16] But when he recalls the situation in the bottom of the dark pit, he is so taken by the memory of his own fear that he stops narrating: 'Le souvenir de cette aventure me fait encore tant d'horreur, que j'en abrège le récit' ('The remembrance of this adventure still horrifies me to such an extent that I'll stop narrating here', 1992: 41). Bougeant here takes up the tensions between the experiencing self and its (sometimes) moral judgement from hindsight by the narrating self in the novels of Marivaux, Prévost and others. Fan-Férédin's narrating self, which should have the distance of hindsight, feels overwhelmed by the intensity of the experience. His experiencing self, which is present as the story unfolds, consciously imitates other characters, reflecting on other experiential selves which it has read about. Tensions between narrating and experiencing self can create an interplay between immersive and reflective states in the novels by Prévost and Marivaux, but Bougeant's designer environment intensifies them to such a degree that he forces readers to reflect on their own immersion in the narrative discourse of the first-person narrator, as well as the danger of following their (perhaps) compromised moral compass.

Everything that happens in 'Romancie' follows very clear conventions and repetitive patterns of interaction. Prince Zazaraph, who serves as a guide to Fan-Férédin after he enters the lands of the novel, for example, explains to him that it is not necessary to eavesdrop on the lovers in the forest, because their discourse is so conventional and predictable that a look on the tablets at the entrance of the forest suffices to know what sweet nothings they might whisper (1992: 79). Furthermore, one can learn the language of 'Romancie' very easily by expressing oneself metaphorically and in a proliferation of epithets, such as *'l'amour tendre et passionné'* (instead of simply 'love', 1992: 67). By foregrounding all these conventional aspects of the novel, Bougeant indicates that their subject matter and psychological depths are slight and easy to appropriate (but not exactly worth the effort).

When Zazaraph tells his own narrative to Fan-Férédin, Bougeant uses the opportunity to demonstrate how easily readers fall prey to the novel's immersive power, even if they think they master its conventions. Zazaraph had fallen in love with the princess Anémone, and he is travelling across 'Romancie' in order to find her again. His only consolation during her absence is her portrait, which he duly shows to Fan-Férédin. Fan-Férédin immediately recognises his sister. 'Dieux! quel fut mon étonnement,' exclaims Fan-Férédin in the stock phrase of the mémoir novel, 'ami lecteur, je ne vous ai pas trop préparé à cet incident; mais il est vrai qu'alors je ne m'y attendais pas non plus moi-même; ainsi votre surprise ne sera pas plus grande que la mienne' ('Good God, I was astonished! My dear reader, I have not overprepared you for this incident, but it is true that I had not expected it either.

---

[16] The entire passage in Bougeant, as Sgard and Sheridan inform us in a footnote, is built around a scene in Prévost's novel.

Your surprise will be thus not greater than mine', 1992: 95). The reader's surprise is just as great as the character's, even though they both should be well prepared for the event. On the one hand, it is very common in novels of this kind that two characters who encounter each other on the road soon turn out to share emotional bonds and that, whenever a portrait is mentioned, one can expect a recognition scene. The very conventionality of the novel should make it entirely predictable for characters and readers. Moreover, the chapter heading, 'Des grands épreuves; et resemblance singulière qui fera soupçonner aux lecteurs le dénouement de cette histoire' ('Of great proofs; and a special resemblance which will indicate the outcome of this narrative to readers', 1992: 91), indicates the coming recognition to readers (at least those who have a smattering of Aristotle). On the other hand, however, there is a moment of surprise in reading the scene. We have moved away from the beginning of the chapter (and its heading) by several pages, and we have come to accept Fan-Férédin as a character guided through 'Romancie' but not as part of its stories. The recognition scene makes Fan-Férédin realise that he, too, is involved in the narratives whose principles he had dissected with Zazaraph just before. Arguably, this scene is designed to make readers realise that (despite their awareness of these principles) they are still immersed enough in the narrative to feel surprise at this moment. Bougeant uses the convention of the recognition scene and redoubles it, as he turns his own novel into a Jesuit designer environment.

In the afterword to the novel, Bougeant reveals that Prince Fan-Férédin is in fact a 'gentilhomme' called M. de la Brosse, who marries the sister of this brother-in-law and dreams up the whole narrative of *Voyage merveilleux*. A footnote by Sgard and Sheridan informs us that there are several novels in which 'le retour aux noms bourgeois marque l'écart entre le rêve romanesque et la réalité' ('The return to the bourgeois names marks the distance between the novelistic dream and reality', 1992: 124). However, M. de la Brosse is not described as a 'bourgeois' but as a 'gentilhomme' in Bougeant's text. It seems to me that Bougeant points here towards Molière's *Bourgeois-gentilhomme*, a play in which the delusional bourgeois M. Jourdain is led to believe that he will be ennobled by the Turkish sultan. Molière, a playwright much commended by Porée, for example, shows us a single man who is deluded, and the play foregrounds the process of his delusion and how others take advantage of it. In *Voyage merveilleux*, the delusion is turned into an evening's entertainment for M. de la Brosse and his family. Bougeant hints again at the slightness of the novel as a genre when compared to the theatre. He underlines the ridiculousness of its conventions one final time when he concludes his novel by echoing stock phrases from the prefaces in Prévost, Marivaux and others: 'On a de plus exigé de moi que je misse mon histoire par écrit. Ami lecteur, vous venez de la lire. Je souhaite qu'elle vous ait fait plaisir' ('Moreover, I have been beseeched to write down my narrative. My dear reader, you have just read it. I hope it has given you pleasure', 1992: 124).

The literary designer environment of *Voyage merveilleux* foregrounds the conventions of the novel. On the one hand, it allows Bougeant's readers to become aware of these conventions. On the other hand, it also immerses them in the flow of the narrative. Bougeant takes the elements of the 'roman' at his time (which in fact comprises many different genres) and arranges them in such a way that they serve as a literary designer environment that invites the interaction between immersion and reflection that is typical of the Jesuit theatre and didactic poetry.

Culture and Cognition

Literary designer environments like *Voyage merveilleux* depend on language for abstraction, but the fictional extensions which they create bring together reflective manipulation with immersion. My discussion of distributed cognition has moved a long way from Shakespeare's players solving the problem of their rapidly changing repertoire. Even though what I have called the 'literary designer environment' shares features with the traditional designer environments in the sense that it provides affordances for extended cognition, its primary focus is not problem-solving. The Shakespearean actors in Tribble's Globe theatre, the bartenders and Tetris players are solving a specific problem by drawing on the affordances of the environment (or manipulating them in such a way that extended cognition contributes to the procedure of problem-solving). In the literary designer environment, on the other hand, there is rarely a specific problem to be solved for which you need the elements of the environment.[17] Rather, we find manipulations of readers' expectations that make their responses discernible to us (such as the double recognition in Bougeant) or we find narratives told in different ways such as to enliven an idea and make it graspable for discussion (such as in Brumoy's version of the 'Matron of Ephesus'). These are ways in which the fictional extensions of the literary designer environment enhance human cognitive processes without being limited to problem-solving.

Literary designer environments have various kinds of material supports, such as the stage (for Porée's *L'homme instruit par le spectacle*) or a book (for Brumoy's *De motibus animi* and for Bougeant's *Voyage merveilleux*), which serve as the starting point for their fictional extension. In the designer environment of the Globe the material components, such as the plots and the stage doors, are necessary for the performance of the cognitive feat. For the literary designer environment, one needs to have the material support of the text in order to prompt the movement of cognition and to sustain a fully complex process of engagement. However, especially for the literature of the eighteenth century, which aims to delight and instruct, the question arises of how far the material support is necessary to support the outcome of the learning process of reading. One does not need to have *De motibus animi* to hand

---

[17] The detective story might serve as an exception. Critics like Noël Carroll (2007) have suggested that the detective story is the general paradigm of how we read narrative (looking for the answer to a narrative problem). However, arguably, there is no specific problem in *Voyage merveilleux*. Rather, Fan-Férédin travels to 'Romancie' in order to learn more about this world. As I have argued elsewhere, narrative is perhaps better understood as a process of modifying predictions (see Kukkonen 2014).

to remember that one strong emotion (such as grief) can easily turn into another strong emotion (such as passion) once one has read the second book of Brumoy's poem. Part of the thinking process elicited by the literary designer environment does not need the material support of the book. Instead, these leave their traces in our memory.[18]

Literature, of course, extends beyond the individual text and these memory traces of earlier experiences can then also be taken up in new literary designer environments. This does not simply amount to repeating a very similar process in a different setting, as it would if the Shakespearean actors moved to a different playhouse or if the bartender started to specialise in a different line of cocktails. Rather, it can serve as a second-order interaction between immersion and meta-reflection. Loyola's *Spiritual Exercises,* as we have seen, depend on the same kind of trade-off between immersion and reflection in the literary designer environment as Brumoy's *De motibus animi* or Bougeant's *Voyage merveilleux.* Yet once one looks into the texts that had influenced Loyola's thinking before he wrote the *Exercises,* one finds, perhaps surprisingly, the favourite reading matter of Don Quixote: the chivalric novel *Amadis de Gaula.* Already Câmara's *Autobiography of Saint Ignatius Loyola,* written on dictation from Loyola's deathbed, mentions his reading of *Amadis* (see Conrod 2008: 34). When Loyola set out to found the 'Company of Jesus' and became its first 'General', he took up elements from the chivalric world, where 'Amadis represented the Christian soldier *par excellence*' (33), but he also learned to distance himself from it. Later centuries, however, would compare Loyola himself to Don Quixote, that other immersed reader of *Amadis.* Frédéric Conrod discusses at some length how far Loyola (and his *Exercises*) can be considered as an inspiration for Cervantes' novel. The French debates of the 1730s were less considerate in exploiting the connection: in 1736, Pierre Quesnel published *Histoire de l'Admirable Dom Inigo de Guipuscoa, Chevalier de la Vierge, et Fontateur de la Monarchie des Inighistes,* which parodies Loyola's life-narrative so that he appears, as the English translation of Quesnel is titled, *The Spiritual Quixote* (1755). On the one hand, the literary designer environment comprises individual texts that extend thinking in an immersive and reflective way. On the other hand, the literary designer environment more generally also enables larger cross-connections between earlier instantiations in texts, as, for example, when Quesnel's *Spiritual Quixote* mocks Loyola's saint's life while at the same time aligning it more closely with its origins in *Amadis de Gaula.* The question arises whether more purpose-driven designer environments are capable of similar second-order instantiations (beyond the learning scaffolds of the linguistic 'superniche'; see Clark 2008).

Certainly, literary designer environments can be considered as part of the larger evolutionary narrative of how culture and cognition support and enhance each

---

[18] This observation is not intended to divide the extended mind into an interior and an exterior component. Rather, the question is one of timescales: the extended process of having read a book can have long-lasting effects without the material support being present. See Sterelny 2010 and Sutton 2006 for divergent opinions on different dimensions of the extended mind.

other. Michael Wheeler and Andy Clark have discussed the connections between embodied cognition, cognitive niche construction (which also includes designer environments) and human evolution. Human language is introduced in terms of the 'reduction of descriptive complexity' which it enables (2008: 3564). The 'open-ended expressive power' of language is only mentioned in passing (ibid.). However, in light of the Jesuits' 'literary designer environments', it seems to be necessary to explore this second aspect of language further for the contribution which it makes to different kinds of designer environments. Kim Sterelny (2003: 223) and Daniel Hutto (2008: 185) both suggest that narratives (and by extension their formalisation in prose fiction) support the development of the human ability to relate to and communicate with others. According to Hutto, folk narratives are crucial for this development: 'In the process, children are shown not only how the propositional and psychological attitudes operate in relation to one another; they are also prompted at crucial points to offer their own explanations using these terms.' Quite similar to the literary designer environment of the book, these folk narratives do not need their material, contextual support any more, once the learning process of how to interact with others (and how to explain these interactions) is completed. New folk narratives might have to be designed to solve new problems or puzzling misreadings, if we follow Hutto's account, but it does not seem that they would play out the 'open-ended expressive power' of language to the same extent as the permutations between *Amadis de Gaula*, the *Spiritual Exercises*, *Don Quixote* and *The Spiritual Quixote* suggest. Because these literary designer environments are not tied to problem-solving (be it spatial or psychological), they move more easily between immersion and meta-reflection in the first and second order.

In many ways, I have made a conventional argument about the capacities of literature to immerse its readers and to lead them to meta-reflection. Conceived as the defining feature of the 'literary designer environment', however, this argument invites the debate around extended cognition and the enculturation in the cognitive niche to revisit the premises on which standard accounts of the designer environment (or cognitive ecology) are based and to consider whether there might not be other features of designer environments that have similarly powerful cognitive effects but are not usually discussed. The 'massively self-engineered minds' of the human species (see Sterelny 2003: 178) can easily change the direction of their thoughts through the scaffolding provided by literary designer environments.

12

Blake and the Mark of the Cognitive: Notes Towards the Appearance of the Sceptical Subject

Richard C. Sha

Distributed cognition envisions a cognitive system that crosses what it defines as the arbitrary boundary of skull and skin into the environment so that cognition can be partly offloaded on to the environment. In this chapter, I seek to understand the implications of such a theory. I aim to open up new areas of inquiry for distributed cognition such as subject/object relations and scepticism, and I reframe William Blake's poem 'London' so that we can look afresh at his speaker. Blake's simultaneous commitment to the imagination as transformative and to the embodied materiality of perception makes him an ideal candidate for such an inquiry. Because Blake blurs where the inputs and outputs begin and end, cognition is distributed across brain and environment. What Blake adds to the debate is whether there are forms of distribution that should be encouraged or avoided. There may be a stiff price to be paid for all this cognitive efficiency, and that price may be the inability to distinguish between affordances and ideology.[1]

Where does cognition begin and end, and why does this question matter? To arrive at an answer, I compare here two historical moments when this question acquired salience. The second is today. The first is in the Romantic period where, despite robust criticism that touts a Romantic insistence on individuality, writers believed in either neural contextualism, where neural content is not autonomous with respect to the environment, or a panpsychism that, with the exception of David Chalmers, extends cognition even beyond the distributed cognition of today.[2] Panpsychists consider consciousness to be a feature of all things. Wordsworth famously claimed 'a motion and a spirit / that impels all thinking things / all objects of all thought', and his concept of 'thinking things', like Spinoza's *conatus* (the innate inclination of a thing to continue its existence), suggests both that

---

[1] For extremely helpful comments, I thank George Rousseau, Michael Wheeler and Miranda Anderson.

[2] Distributed cognition has the potential to challenge a number of still standard Romanticist assumptions about the relation of consciousness to nature and the self. The essays in *Romanticism and Consciousness* (Bloom 1970), for instance, assume an autotelism to consciousness and to self-consciousness, and that consciousness is necessarily about the division of the self from nature. Distributed cognition asks where this border really is.

consciousness inheres in at least some matter and, because motion impels all, that there are limits to autonomy.

Why does distributed cognition, a movement that extends the mind into the environment, matter to both the study of Romanticism and our thinking today? Distributed cognition demands an intimacy, and in some of the theories an integration, between mind and world, one that challenges both where we mark the boundaries and why and when we feel the need to mark them. In short, it challenges our very definitions of cognition. In the Romantic period, there were key reasons why such an intimacy was a necessary ground of intelligibility. First, building upon Jonathan Kramnick, action in the world helped shape how mental action could be thought about, and both idealism and internalism were tempered by a physical nervous system that was understood to be the locus of the processing of experience. Kramnick shows how Enlightenment ideas of mental causation were shaped by thinking about how physical objects in the world moved. Mental causation and states of mind could not come into being without those objects, and without a physics that explained their movement so that mental causality could be theorised as a supplement to physics. Charles Babbage's invention of the difference engine in 1832, a proto-computer which simulated human cognition, further strained any clear boundaries between mind and world because mechanism now could take the place of certain kinds of human thought.

Second, there was a fundamental need to understand how mind interacts with matter, and this meant that Cartesianism was believed to be in error when it stipulated two different kinds of matter, *res extensa* and *res cogitans*. Joseph Priestley, for instance, gets rid of impenetrability as the essence of matter precisely to do away with 'an immaterial thinking principle in man' (1778: 23). How would such an immaterial principle interact with a material one, Priestley wonders? Within the body, the spinal cord was seen as a continuation of the brain, but by the 1840s the brain was understood as the culmination of the spinal cord (Clarke and Jacyna 1987: 30–1). Both models highlight an embodied cognition and a continuum between brain and body that is achieved through the nervous system. The extension of the brain into the body prepares the way for the more radical extension of cognition into the environment. Without the former extension, the gap between the brain and the environment might seem insurmountable.

Third, the relationality of subject to object in Romanticism is stipulated by a nervous sensibility that demanded the existence of emotions even within matter. In this view, sensibility permitted what Heidegger would call dwelling in the world because feeling was on both sides of the subject and object. For example, the concept of chemical affinity portrays elements as longing for combinations, leading historian of chemistry Trevor Levere to detail the 'emotions of matter' (1971: 3). Chemical elements were virtually personified so that one could explain how and why they combined with other elements; Goethe called these elective affinities. It was hard to imagine matter as being indifferent to human beings.

Finally, when Kant made imagination necessary to the self and to the experience of the world because the synthesis of the manifold of presentations was the blind work of imagination that could not happen without a unified self, he made imagination a necessary avenue through to the world. If the imagination's synthesis of the manifold of presentations enables a unified view to appear of the external world, the stances of both the subject and the object require imagination. Again and again we find ideas about intimacy between mind and its surround, which makes it possible to ask where does cognition begin and end? In the study of Romanticism, poststructuralist approaches have emphasised the gap between mind and world, with an aporia where there is relationality.

Today, pushing a line in modern thought that begins with Spinoza and then Romanticism and then continues through Heidegger, proponents of distributed cognition argue that the environment and objects are not just tools for thought; rather, cognition occurs through an ecological assembly of problem-solving resources that are both brainbound and environmental (Clark 2008: 81, 2010a: 84, 2010b). Cognition thereby extends beyond embodiment and even occurs outside the head. The extension of the cognitive has led to debates about what counts as the mark of the cognitive, and growing dissatisfaction with cortical localisation as a tool of thought about thought manifests itself in the idea that the external can constitute a location where the processes of cognition take place so long as the external is 'integrated' into the cognitive system (Clark 2010a: 84).[3] Some versions of distributed cognition further allow cognition to happen either without demanding mental representation as a necessary step, or by conceiving of such representations not as detailed inner mirrors of a context-dependent world, but as control programmes for generating context-dependent embodied actions, so-called action-oriented representations (Wheeler 2005: 197).[4] In this view, the environment provides affordances that cognition can exploit directly and the mirror-like notion of mental representations adds an unnecessary layer of complication.

Within the extended mind debate, a mark of the cognitive is a scientifically informed account of what it is to be a proper part of a cognitive system that, so as not to beg any crucial questions, is fundamentally independent of where any candidate element happens to be spatially located. Once some candidate mark of the cognitive has been placed on the table, we need to find out (1) whether that account of cognition is independently plausible, and (2) just where cognition (so conceived) falls – in the brain and the non-neural body, or in a system that extends across the brain, body and world.

In comparing these two moments when the idea of distributed cognition becomes salient, I want to think about what such a theory enables and requires.

---

[3] Evan Thompson likewise insists upon integration for an autopoietic system to have autonomy: 'the physical boundary of a cell should not be confused with its organizational boundary' (2011: 37). A molecule that is inside the boundary but not integrated into the molecular processes is not part of the autopoietic system.

[4] This foreclosing of representation is ironic given that in the history of cognition itself, cognition, because it cannot be seen, was first represented by machines. As Harré queries, 'is it likely that any inorganic machine and the way it runs will be an adequate explanatory model of the brain and its workings?' (2002: 111).

Does attunement with the environment become an integral part of Romantic intelligence or genius? Since 'genius' is a concept that begins as an external force as in the idea of 'genius loci', or genius of the place, and remains so throughout the Renaissance, the fact that it is only gradually internalised over time reminds us that the internal brain-bound mind is a recent invention and not a transhistorical given. Yet if representation helps make a sceptical remove of the subject possible so that the 'given' can be a subject of debate, I ask what resources distributed cognition might have for scepticism, especially if the environment plays a constitutive role in the cognitive system, and thus the ability to distance oneself from such affordances seems impossible. The very vocabulary of affordances makes it difficult to think about why one would not want to embrace them. Such resources for scepticism are all the more necessary when the environment that is part of the cognitive system is also part of an ideological system, as it is in William Blake's 'London':

I wander thro' each charter'd street,
Near where the charter'd Thames does flow.
And mark in every face I meet
Marks of weakness, marks of woe.

In every cry of every Man,
In every Infants cry of fear,
In every voice: in every ban,
The mind-forg'd manacles I hear

How the Chimney-Sweepers cry
Every blackning Church appalls,
And the hapless Soldiers sigh
Runs in blood down Palace walls

But most thro' midnight streets I hear
How the youthful Harlots curse
Blasts the new-born Infants tear
And blights with plagues the Marriage hearse

Blake's 'London' provides an especially appropriate venue for thinking about the environment as part of a cognitive system because it highlights the process of cognitive mapping, where the urban environment functions as cognitive extensions so that one can think not only about how power and ideology work, but also whether the subject can disentangle him or herself from them.[5] The poem insists on experience and cognition as processes, and the short rapid-fire lines along with the puns underscore the dynamic interplay between what are traditionally considered

---

[5] See Makdisi 2015: 5. Makdisi reminds us of the London Blake walked through: 'the conjuncture of commerce, state, and religious power all in a single glance'.

internal or external. Indeed, the poem is structured on a dialectic between world and mind. The urban environment, moreover, helps Blake make sense of otherwise abstract social institutions like the church, King, the military, prostitution and the family. One might argue that Blake is after the feel of how these institutions come to embody power over pleasure, because his rhymes induce the sense of sclerosis. His repetition of 'charter', for instance, suggests that the granting of rights entails the taking-away of the rights of others, and this feeling underwrites the reader's growing sense of injustice. The poem opens: 'I wander thro' each charter'd street, / Near where the charter'd Thames does flow.' All this chartering negates the opening verb 'wander', a negation that is underscored by the full stop at the end of the first line. The speaker does not get to wander far until he or she bumps against a caesura. Because the very 'ban' the speaker hears is yet another restriction, the public proclamation of the intent to marry that is needed for a marriage licence becomes another means of societal discipline, falsely narrowing pleasure into sanctioned forms. Blake's pun on a marriage bann that bans is telling. This idea of rights that cancel out rights returns in the word 'charter'd' since the very word for giving rights is itself contracted and limited to the line's syllable count. Insofar as the poet maintains a dual commitment to the transformative imagination and the embodied materiality of perception, he considers where cognition and imagination begin and end. In the process, he asks what is the difference between cognition and ideology, and one question that remains is whether distributed cognition has the tools for working through the difference between these two. One wrinkle Blake adds is that active effort does not necessarily rescue cognition from ideology.[6]

Blake's speaker claims to 'mark in every face I meet / Marks of weakness, marks of woe'. On the one hand, Blake's play on 'marks' that are 'marked' by the subject blurs distinctions between subject and environment, thereby distributing cognition between them. At once passive and active, these marks collapse subject and object, and perception and action become entangled. On the other hand, the speaker insists that the marks he hears are 'mind-forg'd manacles'. But how might he claim to know that, especially if marking itself is distributed across the environment? The oscillation of 'mark' from verb to noun raises precisely the question of epistemology and ties it to agency: is mind the doer of the marking, or is it merely passively receiving the marks? In Blake's original manuscript, he had written 'german forged links I hear', and we should note the otherness of 'german' is replaced by 'mind', making the problem not so much about xenophobia and the German king foisting ideology upon the speaker, but about how the mind imposes and creates its own manacles.

Blake's process of relief-etching only compounds the problem of how to mark inside from outside insofar as the poet's marks on the copper plate are written with

---

[6] Rowlands can be helpful here. He argues that agency is often understood as an experience of effort. The problem is that 'in the normal contexts of activity, there is no sense of agency. This is not because we experience our actions as effortless. Rather we do not experience them at all' (2010: 158).

a burin and with acid-resist ink, only then to have the recesses bitten by an acid (Plate 1). Toggling between activeness and passivity, the active energy of evil and the passive obedience of the good, Blake's marks, like the marks of cognition within distributed cognition, are a system that defies the boundaries of agent and environment. The acid actively eats away at the copper plate, revealing the raised letters that are its new ground even as the burin, instead of digging into the plate, protects the surfaces of writing with acid-resist ink. In Blake's process, surfaces are depth, and the acid bath environment is an agent, bringing the noun mark even closer to its verbal mode. Given that Locke in his *Essay Concerning Human Understanding* had imaged the mind as a white paper to be written on by experience (1969: II, 205), Blake's combined play on marks and the making of marks challenges nothing less than Locke's account of how the mind and cognition work. For Blake, the mind was ideally no such passive object of inscription. And given the poet's wariness of how a 'system' can be enslaving – his famous remark is that he must 'Create a system, or be enslav'd by another Mans' (Blake 1988: 20) – it is important to note that Blake's system is emergent, with creative powers of self-organisation that have the capacity to be their own ends. The process insists upon accident and contingency: the marks are the work of the poet and the acid bath, and the bite of the acid has an intentionality all its own. Visually, if the diagonal constricting light showing an old man being passively led by a young boy also directs us to the fire below – the diagonal of the light points the way to a fire that may consume all – then all this constriction can be melted away. Blake thought of acid as fire and here the flames literally force his words to cower to the side of the plate. In the fourth chamber of his printing house in hell he described 'Lions of flaming fire raging around & melting the metals into living fluids'.[7] Thus his art strives to lead us away from the constrictions we have unknowingly embraced and towards freedom.

What does distributed cognition enable?[8] Distributed cognition overturns Cartesianism by allowing the costs of the mind's isolation from the world to be calculated. Lost to Cartesianism is the possibility of cognition as an intimate ecology, an interaction between mind and world that is rendered much more difficult by the two kinds of matter. In 'London' Blake's image of the old man's cane functions both as a prosthesis and as a cognitive extension, providing sensory information about his surroundings. Moreover, the young boy and, by implication, innocence become cognitive extensions, and one question is what happens when innocence is a vehicle of cognition? The dramatic use of lighting underscores the boy's constitutive role in the elder man's enlightenment.

Distributed cognition also helps eliminate the input/output picture of perception

[7] See Blake's *Marriage of Heaven and Hell*, plate 15 (1988: 40).
[8] For an overview of distributed cognition, see <http://www.hdc.ed.ac.uk> (last accessed 27 February 2019). Neuroscientist Rodolfo Llinás argues, by contrast, that the brain is a closed system, with a majority of internalist neurons that do not connect to the senses but rather with each other. That these neurons can set off their own activation patterns supports his claims, and suggests that distributed cognition tells only part of the story.

and action. Philosopher Susan Hurley explains: 'on this conception, perception is a matter of input from world to mind, and action a matter of output from mind to world' (1998: 247). The Romantic period could not see perception and action in terms of inputs and outputs. Perception is not just the passive registering of world; it requires imaginative action in Blake, as in his concept of fourfold vision. Perception is action, something which Blake here underscores with his infinitive verbs (meet, mark, hear, cry) that resist closure. To credit mind or world is what Edwin Hutchins called the attribution problem of cognitive science because we cannot generally observe cognition directly (1995: 355). In Blake, we do not know what is input and output, and the marks are hopelessly entangled from the act of marking. In *The Marriage of Heaven and Hell*, Blake argues that cleansing the 'doors of perception' will lead to infinity. These doors are only as good as the active cleansing that is maintained, and here the moment of active perception is not so much at the time of input, it is at the time of evaluating the inputs one wants to hold on to, and what will be cleansed away. Enactivist philosopher Evan Thompson argues that the organism's 'structural coupling with its environment' is where sense-making occurs (2007: 58) – sense-making is how he understands cognition – and major Romantic writers would at the very least assent to the coupling, if not the structural modifier. For Blake, changes in perception do indeed lead to structural changes: the doors are altered. The poem presents wandering our way through London as a way of feeling our way through the mind. Yet if this coupling is structural, it is also meandering, thus making it possible to detach oneself from the environment when necessary.

More radically, distributed cognition allows Hurley to name the 'magic membrane' problem. The membrane in question is the boundary between the internal matter (the brain etc.) and the external (beyond the skull and skin) matter. The received idea is that the internal matter has the power of creating consciousness while the external matter does not. But since we do not have an account of what is different about the internal matter that allows it to create consciousness, this is an appeal to magic. So the membrane divides the magical bits of the world from the non-magical bits. Hurley maintains, 'brains are in continuous causal interaction with their bodies and environments' (2010: 116). Percy Shelley similarly describes the dynamic between mind and environment in 'Mont Blanc' as an 'unremitting interchange'. In Blake's powerful image, the fact that the arms of the young boy mimic the plane of how the light falls moves any such membrane into the world. Of course, this leads to the problem of how to achieve epistemic closure, and without such closure, the issues of whether there can be transparency of either the self or the world arises (Metzinger 2004: 194); perhaps both forms of transparency are necessary in order to function within the world.

For Romanticists, distributed cognition undermines the powers of speculation and abstraction to guarantee the rigour of thought. To the extent interactions between organism and environment constitute cognition, the ability to stand above materiality is no longer a necessary good. It is now phenomenologically impossible to boot, since the world constitutes consciousness. Blake anticipates phenomenology when he underscores the world as it is experienced, and when he refuses to divide the world into subjects and objects. For instance, he connects the 'charter'd street' to the Thames whose 'charter'd flow' explains the speaker's marks of woe. Rhyme hints at a correlation if not causal link between chartering and woe. In Romanticism, irony functions to intensify scepticism about the given, and Blake highlights irony through his verb, 'appalls', which indicates an intensity of feeling that not only enables a subject to appear out from the environment but also incentivises it to question givenness. But with regard to distributed cognition, to the extent that the environment conditions and enables thought, attachment to the world will not so easily be severed. Perhaps the most important contribution distributed cognition potentially makes to the study of Romanticism is that it reminds us that Romantic writers were far more circumspect about individuality and far more invested in neural contexts because those neural contexts made the stakes of their claims social instead of personal happiness. The vital spirits of imagination, Blake's poet figure Los says, live in the brain and nerves. Los insists: 'Tho in the Brain of Man we live, & in his circling Nerves. / Tho' this bright world of all our joy is in the Human Brain' (1988: chapter 11, 15–16).[9] Blake thus grounds the imagination within a distributed nervous network across bodies because his circling nerves symbolise infinity; moreover, he insists upon a nervous physiology that makes one available to sympathy with another.

What needs to be in place for cognition to be thought about as distributed? Cognition must be defined in such a way as to allow bio-external elements to play a role in its processes. But here's the rub: the mark of the cognitive in both Romanticism and within enactive accounts of cognition rely upon life.[10] Like today's enactivists who tie cognition to autopoiesis, a term that Maturana and Varela define as 'the relations of a system in terms of a unity, [which] determines the dynamics of interaction and transformation which it may undergo as a unity' (1980: 137), Romanticism is when thought becomes tied to life and vitality.[11] Robert Richards has shown how Kant and his concept of purposiveness enabled biologists to think in terms of a plan without having to specify one (2002: 70–1). Jennifer Mensch has recently eloquently described Kant's 'epigenesist conception of mind' whereby its unity is its own cause and effect (2013: 9), and thought is its own cause. In this view, spontaneity of thought replaces preformed taxonomy. As thought is tied to epigenesis, it is tied to life and to process and thereby granted its own telos: such immanent teleology is necessary for both life and autopoiesis (Wheeler 2011: 160). In Blake's 'London', if the poet opens with distributed cognition, he closes the poem by insisting on life. He writes, 'But most thro' midnight

[9] For a suggestive reading of Blake's nerves, see Hilton 1983: chapter 5.

[10] Thompson defines 'the mark of the cognitive' in terms of 'sense making'. He argues that 'autopoiesis and adaptivity are jointly sufficient for immanent purposiveness and sense making' (2011: 36).

[11] Varela, Maturana and Uribe describe that 'an autopoietic system has a domain in which it can compensate for perturbations through the realization of its autopoiesis, and in this domain, it remains a unity' (1981: 9).

streets I hear / How the youthful Harlots curse / Blasts the new-born Infants tear / And blights with plagues the Marriage hearse.' In tracing the ways in which political power in the twentieth century attaches itself to the sacredness of life, and thus allows 'all politics [to] become the exception' (1998: 148), Giorgio Agamben allows us to think about how vitalism in the nineteenth century masks a politics that appears when life is construed as the beyond to politics. For our purposes here, Agamben demands that we consider the potential costs of autopoiesis, and the extent to which it is good to rely upon an automatic coupling of life and cognition. Agamben, moreover, challenges the idea that autopoiesis is necessarily a form of autonomy, thereby helping us to see that for Blake modesty pollutes desire, which in turn makes children blind.

If cognition requires autopoiesis, I wonder if some enactivist versions of distributed cognition can afford to distribute cognition to bio-external elements because life is the origin of cognition. Clark and Chalmers invent a parity principle to undermine biochauvinism, what Clark calls 'distractions of skin and skull' (2008: 114). However, autopoiesis runs this danger by relying upon life as the engine and teleology of cognition. The argument of the parity principle is that

> If, as we confront some task, a part of the world functions as a process which, *were it done in the head*, we would have no hesitation in recognizing as part of the cognitive process, then that part of the world *is* . . . part of the cognitive process. (Clark and Chalmers 1998: 8)

Clark reminds us that the parity principle never stipulated 'fine-grained sameness of processing and storage' (2008: 115), and as Richard Menary helps clarify, distributed cognition does not deny the differences between external and internal modes of cognition, but rather insists that similar functionality allows processes to be cognitive regardless of their location (2010: 6). To the degree that life explains cognition's causes and effects in terms of the unity of the organism, and that this explanation ties together cognition and the self, can the two have different boundaries?

Does the fact that enactivist theories place life at the root of cognition mask a prior biochauvinism surrounding enactive forms of cognition? And does this masking of biochauvinism instantiate a transparency of the self that would otherwise provide the very phenomenological vantage point that is the very basis for a self? I here build on Thomas Metzinger's idea that the self is something we see through and not with and Evan Thompson's insistence that the self is a process that enacts an I (2015: chapter 10).[12] I read 'functionality' as a metonymy for autopoiesis, itself

---

[12] Thompson chides Metzinger for his neuronihilism (2015: 322). For Thompson, the self is a process, and not a thing, but that does not mean it does not exist. Thompson turns to the hypnagogic state – the zone between waking and sleeping – to think about the relation of consciousness to materiality. This state collapses the two because it blurs the boundaries between inside and outside.

a metonymy for life. Our reliance upon life must be masked to create a space for a purposive self to appear, a self who is no one's end but its own, and for whom thought must be its own end. That is, if the autonomy critics generally attribute to the self is actually the work of life, then what does autonomy mean?[13] Clark recognises this problem when he invents a distinction between 'organism centred' and 'organism bound', and yet claims that human beings are organism centred and not bound (2008: 123, 139). The problem is that if life is the driver of cognition, the difference between centred and bound loses salience because one is now bound to an idea of an organism without borders. As Michael Wheeler points out, one cannot have autopoiesis without borders:

> to be autopoietic, an autonomous system must, through its own endogenous self-organizing dynamics, produce and maintain a material (or physical) boundary which distinguishes the system as a material (or physical) unity in the space in which it exists. (2011: 151)

And although Clark insists that the extended mind applies to vehicles and not contents (2008: 76), if life allows the vehicle to be a vehicle, the vehicle is hardly contentless.

This reliance of cognition on autopoiesis is not without further risk. The danger is that autopoiesis both makes the meaningful self unnecessary, because life itself is the ground zero of cognition, and minimises what is necessary for cognition without acknowledging the reduction in scale. I mean by this that the processes of an organism, which Antonio Damasio calls the proto-self, and the processes of what he calls an 'autobiographical self' are levelled so that differences in the scale of cognition grow invisible, and the difference between how an organism or even cell 'thinks' and how an autobiographical person thinks is more than the nominal difference between biology and psychology. Perhaps for this reason Clark looks for the 'problem solving agent' when looking for cognition (2008: 118): agent floats between the scales of the cell and personhood. If the good news is that this floating scale allows the sidestepping of what Fodor calls 'homuncular explanation' – the tendency to imagine a little man in charge inside the head – the not-so-good news is that metonymy is at work to distract us from how distributed cognition minimises what counts as cognition because life counters the problem of death, and in so doing generally requires an adaptive autopoiesis that is the basis of sense-making.[14]

I want, by contrast, a definition of cognition that earns its keep, and if 'adaptive' stretches from cell to person, I'm not sure that cognition always does. In a similar

---

[13] Nancy Yousef examines how in the Romantic period, on the one hand, autonomy is bound to ideas of self-sufficiency, and yet that self-sufficiency cannot come into being without going through childhood dependency (2004: 19).

[14] See Wheeler 2005: 218–19. Wheeler endorses homuncularity so long as 'the subsystems involved [are] responsive to the information that the elements carry' (219). In this view, homuncularity is a way of conceptualising architectural behavioural systems. Wheeler warns of the need to avoid the traditional homuncular fallacy that understands it as a literal understander of information.

move, Giovanna Colombetti creates the category of 'primordial affectivity' and even organisms that lack a nervous system can have it; Colombetti argues that affectivity is inextricable from cognition (2014: 19, 21). Perhaps it is. However, to the extent that it replaces the self with a life drive, autopoiesis makes fungible any first-person description, and explanation of phenomenal consciousness – and this loss of the first-person point of view perhaps marks the very essence of consciousness, if that is to be the subjective sense of self – becomes unavailable (Revonsuo 2000: 59). Jay Rosenberg reminds us that even magnets discriminate, and therefore cognition must be more than the mere exercise of discrimination capacity (1997: 297). Finally, Cowley and Gahrn-Andersen worry that by reducing cognition to a synchronic process or a kind of functionalism, even Andy Clark and David Chalmers have unwittingly short-circuited interactions between self and environment; autopoiesis, furthermore, can specify a closed system that is ironically antithetical to such interaction. At stake here is nothing less than a capitalist redefinition of intelligence and cognition, one that is not representationally driven (Wheeler 2005: 63), but instead highlights the efficient management of cognitive load. And yet without the ability of neural encoding to specify cognition, all we are left with is efficiency as the mark of cognition.[15] Evan Thompson turns to Merleau-Ponty's idea that the actualisation of the organism allows environment to emerge from the world (2007: 59), but this in my view runs the danger of making environment an extension of solipsism.[16] The question is how to have a deep continuity between life and mind that allows for the possibility of significant difference between them, and for cognition to be more than the demands of life? Such difference is needed because it questions what counts as cognitive development instead of presuming it as its opening premise.

Blake's 'London', and in particular his modulation of 'mark' from a verb meaning 'to notice' to 'mark' as something to be noticed, allows us to think about what the distribution of cognition between marks means and does. Both 'weakness' and 'woe' highlight affective cognition, and the processing of information. In Blake's view, what we call a self is some kind of feedback loop between the remarking and the marks. But given his insistence on the creative imagination, is it more than this efficient feedback loop? Here, affect marks cognition and suggests that affect is the occurrence of evaluation. Cabanis shares Blake's view; he argued that the brain 'digests' impressions (Richardson 2001: 17). Implicitly, some forms of digestion are more thorough than others. Shelley recalls Cabanis in his 'Defence of poetry' when he writes 'we have eaten more than we digest'. What have we lost when affordances prompt actions, and the quality of digestion no longer matters, as some forms of distributed cognition suggest?

Allow me to elaborate on this problem. If the environment functions directly as

---

[15] On this, see Fodor and Pylyshyn 1997: 314. For an indictment of how neural plasticity is commodified, see Malabou 2008. She stresses a version of plasticity that requires death to pre-empt arguments about efficiency.

[16] Miranda Anderson arrives separately at a similar concern (2015b: 13–14).

an affordance, or even a solicitation, how does one break the arc from cognition to action? I sidestep here Gibsonian arguments about how direct perception is grounded in ecological law and therefore is always accurate. Under this view, there would be no reason to break it. The breaking of an arc between cognition to action is actually an issue of both agency and ethics: how does one build agency and ethics upon cognition that is driven, on the one hand, by life and, on the other hand, by affordances? The passivity entailed in this version of agency seems dangerous: the agent begins to look like an object. According to Susan Hurley, we need to get rid of an input and output model because perception is active and is tied to outputs, and because mind is rarely isolated from a dynamic interrelationship with the world. What does this way of thinking do to our concepts of agency, especially if agency and action are the necessary mere follow-throughs of perception? Is the price of these kinds of automaticity an inability to distinguish between cognition and ideology?

Blake's 'London' ponders precisely how to arrest the arc from cognition to action. His speaker famously insists, 'In every cry of every Man . . . / The mind-forg'd manacles I hear' (ll. 5, 8). From Blake's perspective, 'mind-forged' means there is active sense-making insofar as the mind is forging, but perception does not lead to an output beyond man's cry. Blake's speaker, furthermore, limits action to the registration of the outputs surrounding him. In fact, the asymmetry between the marking subject and the plural marks that surround him raises the issue of the mark of cognition: what belongs to the cognising subject, what belongs to the cognising system, and is the subject the system? Blake further short-circuits a direct connection between active perception and action because 'London' makes perception as action incomplete when it leaves the results of the speaker's perceptions unsaid. Finally, when he connects cognition back to the 'marriage hearse', Blake questions how our concepts of life become a kind of bio-power, whereby the social institutions surrounding life dictate a politics that cannot be seen as a politics because they have the omnipresence of life. Marriage becomes a hearse when modesty demands prostitution, which leads to syphilis and blindness and death. When marriage is a hearse, life is perverted into the very death of autonomy, a perversion which takes the form of venereal disease. This trajectory towards the grave becomes the incentive to do something about it.

To what extent is the Romantic imagination – the gateway from the mind to the world – a name for 'actively embodied and situated brains' or distributed cognition (Hurley 2010: 130)? Blake of course depicts situatedness, but suspends judgement about what to do next. For example, 'midnight streets' insists on a fairly narrow window of time. Adding to this possibility, psychologist Ruth Byrne studies how people imagine alternatives to reality, and finds that these alternatives are surprisingly rational. She shows, for instance, how people turn to counterfactuals to work out causality (2005: 198), and thus the world intrudes on imagination. However, for Blake, the imaginative gap between mind and world is necessary for thinking about ideology, the ways in which social institutions impose themselves and become reality. What ideology shares with cognition is the immersive feeling of a reality, and the feeling of coherence enables this immersion. But Blake here considers a lively imagination to enable detachment from the appearance of the given or ideology, in part by asking what is the price of coherence and integration, and in part by offering an alternative position through which to imagine the world. He writes:

> In every cry of every Man,
> In every Infants cry of fear,
> In every voice: in every ban,
> The mind-forg'd manacles I hear.

The poet's insistent repetition of 'every', five times in three lines, further helps calculate the cost of coherence – note that coherence flattens and renders mono-chromatic the world – even as it demands the need for a creative imagination to individuate itself beyond those manacles. Insistence upon coherence allows it to feel like claustrophobia. To think of ideology as being 'mind-forged', then, is the throwing down of a gauntlet to the imagination to say are there not any better forms of mind than ideological manacles? And are there more important crite-ria for cognition than efficiency since repetition defies efficiency? Furthermore, Blake's claim to 'hear' the manacles invites synaesthesia, and the turn away from sense to imagination, since manacles are not ordinarily heard. This active unifica-tion of different senses through the imagination creates the space for representation to enable the subject to question the current world. The poet's 'midnight streets' intensifies such synaesthesia even as it signals the need for transition.[17]

Blake also helps us consider the degree to which cognition can be owned, especially when the environment becomes responsible for causal spread, archi-tectures whose 'behavior generating activities . . . are partially offloaded onto the non-neural body and the environment' (Wheeler 2005: 206). At the start of the poem, the speaker is acutely aware of ownership by others, and how ownership is translated into rights, which is itself translated into a legal notion of selfhood. He wanders through 'charter'd street[s]' 'near where the charter'd Thames does flow' (ll. 1, 2). The speaker, by contrast, is almost agnostic about his or her own ownership. This lack of felt ownership undermines the legal model of selfhood that turns to property as a way of conceiving the self because that model is simply not at that time open to most people. This idea allows us to infer a causal connection between the granting of rights to others, 'chartering', and the marks of woe, and not until this causal inference do we have a way of connecting lines 1 and 2 with 3 and 4 and thus coming up with the potential basis for action. The flattening of the subject and environment demands that we ask what allows the cognising subject to appear? The only clues Blake gives us are the 'weakness' and 'woe' added by the cogniser, which suggests that affect is a form of evaluation or what philosopher

---

[17] Paul Miner reminds us that midnight in Matthew 25 is when Heaven is imaged as the virgin going to holy consummation (2002: 288).

Robert Solomon calls a 'judgment'. Solomon considers all emotions to be judgements, and considers judgements to be engagements with the world, but at the cost of allowing them to be unconscious and automatic. And yet if this affect is also seepage from the world, can it mark ownership? I therefore question the degree to which ownership can be defined in terms of integration, as Rupert does, since that integration would seem to require a simultaneous extension and transparency of the self. Can one extend the borders of the self and promote the self's transparency at once, or do these two cancel each other out?

And yet perhaps in the end we can turn to Blake to understand that the best use of distributed cognition might be to make us wary, on the one hand, of vaunting both the independence and effectivity of internal powers. Internalism might hereafter be branded cognitive solipsism. On the other hand, without a means of disengaging cognition from both the environmental surround and the social body, Blake's speaker is reduced to ideology or a version of group mind. For a self to appear, personal experience had to be seen as personal, requiring some withdrawal from the world, but there never could be total transcendence if we take the Romantic investment in Spinoza's *conatus* seriously. Blake captures this problem by, on the one hand, giving us a lyric speaker whose experiences can be bracketed as not the reader's, and, on the other hand, making the reader feel the speaker's constrictions through metre and rhyme. Blake further invites readers to think about how the Romantic imagination constantly moves the boundary between mind and world to encourage either detachment from or attachment to the environment, and to find a way to incorporate this moving boundary into the process of distributed cognition. On the one hand, he confuses what belongs to mind and world – all is 'mind-forg'd' and at the same time a result of what he hears – but on the other hand, the devolution of 'hear' into 'hearse' in the final stanza implies that cognition might need to detach itself from the world. Notice how 'hearse' brilliantly blends 'hear' with 'curse', and in the process shows the building-up of cognition from elements in the world. Accordingly, his version of the Romantic imagination has the capacity to evaluate the kinds of distribution that are possible, as well as the capacity to avoid forms of cognition that are ideology. In short, the movability of the boundary means that it functions as representation, and thus one can distance oneself from it with scepticism and irony.

In closing, given fairly widespread recognition of the problems with Cartesianism, why do some scholars still feel the need to go after Descartes centuries later with such fervour? I want to suggest that when Descartes made selfhood contingent upon cognition in his famous 'I think, therefore, I am' (2013: 47), he relied upon a homology between cognition and the self insofar as cognition enacts the self. Of course, his distinction between thinking matter and extended matter placed clear boundaries around cognition and the self. Although when considering the borders of cognition we can be generous about cognitive extensions into the environment, when thinking about the borders of the self such extension defies the borders necessary to the self even as the environment becomes the necessary backdrop against which the self appears to itself. And to the extent that autonomy is based on a life drive, is that truly autonomous, or has the autonomy just been moved to another system? Here, Harry Frankfurt's reminder that the self is contingent, and that therefore any version of autonomy must come to grips with necessity and contingency, perhaps invites us to lower the stakes of autonomy. Finally, if autonomy and autopoiesis require the generation of a border so that inside can be separated from the outside, can that border be fungible and moveable, especially if it is material and structural, and does the border that corresponds to cognition necessarily correspond to the self? Kant's retort to Descartes was to claim 'I am therefore I think', which is to say that the concept of a unified self was *a priori* because it was necessary to thought (1996a: B135). Such reversal nonetheless relies upon the same homology between self and cognition. In his concept of self-annihilation and its ethical form of forgiveness, Blake, by contrast, not only demands a concept of cognition beyond the borders of the self, but also insists that the self might get in the way of cognition.

13

Eighteenth-Century Antiquity: Extended, Embodied, Enacted

Helen Slaney

In 1790 or thereabouts, near a settlement called Nola, not far inland from Naples, an ancient tomb is being excavated, containing numerous examples of Greek fig-ured pottery (Plate 2). A man cradles a heavy amphora between his hands, gazing at it intently. Beside him, a woman grasps one small jug but is already looking greedily beyond it, index finger extended towards the other vessels, perhaps point-ing out to the servant who kneels to wipe them with a cloth, 'You missed a bit!' In the background, another worker wields a pickaxe, smashing open another cache. This scene, the frontispiece to Tischbein's catalogue of Sir William Hamilton's second vase collection, compresses and idealises the process of comprehension into a moment of discovery which is also a moment of acquisition: Hamilton, face to face with the artefact, at once relishing its beauty, scrutinising its iconography, and appraising its value. The image captures not a documentary incident but a mode of interaction. It is a reflexive meditation on the same cognitive process to be facilitated by the catalogue, namely the recruitment of material objects into knowledge-production.

Hamilton, his collections, and their circulation in catalogue form played a cru-cial role in the contemporary reconceptualisation of classical antiquity.[1] As Noah Heringman (2013) has shown, activity such as Hamilton's in the Neapolitan region stimulated the development of antiquarianism into a science, as opposed to a rec-reational diversion. While excavation methods admittedly remained crude, the artefacts themselves were meticulously recorded and classified. Transformed from curiosities into specimens, they became devices for conducting systematic investi-gation into the ancient societies that produced them. As such, they provide a case study in what could be identified as extended cognition. This operates in two ways: firstly, knowledge or apprehension (cognisance) of the ancient world – a state of affairs no longer sensorially accessible – was developed in conjunction with these surviving objects. The idea of 'ancient Greece' was extrapolated from their attrib-utes. Secondly, such cognisance derived from the way the objects were arranged,

---

[1] On the importance of Naples and Hamilton as its intellectual broker, see Jenkins and Sloan 1996; Constantine 2001; Schnapp 2013; Heringman 2013.

presented and conveyed; the organisation of any collection, as much as its components, determines what it can transmit (Gould 1996; Pearce 1992). Rather than 'cognition', then, I will be referring more narrowly here to 'cognisance' or the apprehension of knowledge in one form or another. The term will be used interchangeably with *connaissance*,[2] with the intention of retaining its overtones of realisation, recognition and coming-to-know.

William Hamilton, however, is only half the story. The woman in the Tischbein engraving is Sir William's wife, Emma, whose alternative mode of engagement with the vase collection provides a second case study, this time of embodied cognition (or, to be precise, kinaesthetic cognisance, coming-to-know through movement). In response to the abundance of ancient material culture surrounding her in Naples, Emma developed a genre of performance art, the 'Attitudes', solo *tableaux vivants* drawing on imagery from Sir William's collection. Dressed in costumes based on the vase-figures, and often handling the vases themselves in her tableaux, she posed as a succession of characters from classical mythology. A former artist's model, Emma applied her knowledge of postural and gestural convention to this new form of plastic performance art.[3] Her poses, however, were anything but static. Their stillness was an illusion, supported not only by concentrated muscular activity in the moment of execution, but also by the hours of rehearsal necessary to perfect the dramatic compressions and fluid transitions that were her hallmark. Emma's experience, I argue, demonstrates the contribution made by kinaesthesia or the sense of self-movement to gaining personal *connaissance* of an imagined past. Kinaesthesia has been recognised as an important aspect of embodied cognition more generally. Maxine Sheets-Johnstone (2011), for example, points out that it is self-movement which enables embodied brains to discover and interact with their environment. It is not simply 'the body' which comes to know, but the body in motion. Unlike Sir William's catalogue, however, the Attitudes were neither portable nor reproducible: their kinaesthetic mode of apprehension was confined to the cognitive circuit of Emma's own body. Although her terpsichoreal talent was widely recognised at the time, it was not in any way regarded as an intellectually sophisticated instance of classical reception. I argue here that, on the contrary, if redefined as cognitive activity that requires the vehicle of the performing body in order to take place, the Attitudes can be recuperated as a conceptualisation of classical antiquity equal (if alternative) to Sir William's.

They were certainly not regarded as such by contemporary philosopher Johann Gottfried Herder, who visited the Hamiltons at Naples in 1789. Herder's somewhat idiosyncratic aesthetic response to ancient art has much in common with the principles of enactivism, and as such provides my final case study. Preferring the implicit simulation of movement to its explicit performance, Herder proposes a method for suspending corporeal gratification in order to prolong communion with the artwork. The artwork's presence is vital as an ongoing stimulus to the

---

[2] *Connaissance* is the term used by d'Hancarville. For discussion, see below.

[3] Barnett (1987) shows how eighteenth-century painting and theatre shared a gestural iconography pertaining to character and emotion.

beholder's imagination but its cognitive contribution is neither semiotic, as for Sir William, nor sensorimotor, as for Emma; rather, Herder's version of ancient Greece is predicated on a quest for the purely aesthetic. All three approaches – the catalogue, the dance and the simulation – required the interaction of subject and matter for knowledge of antiquity to be formulated. Their co-existence in this heady, pre-disciplinary period (Most 2002; Calè and Craciun 2011; Heringman 2013), when the ground around Naples seemed to be sprouting antiquities like exotic mushrooms, suggests constituent (not merely causal) dependence of these ideas on the unprecedented emergence of material artefacts.

Collected Works

Arriving in Naples as the British envoy in 1764, William Hamilton began accumulating the collection of Greek ceramics that became his most notable contribution to classical scholarship. His activities as a collector and antiquarian have been well documented.[4] Fascinated by both the volcanology of the region and the recent excavations of Pompeii and Herculaneum, Hamilton began to build up his own private stash of ancient artefacts: not the imposing marble sculpture favoured by connoisseurial Grand Tourists like Charles Townley, but a cornucopia of smaller items such as coins, bronze miniatures, engraved signets, geological specimens and, above all, the 'vases'.[5] These came primarily from tomb deposits in the Neapolitan hinterland around Nola and Caserta, and were acquired by Hamilton either directly from local landowners or from intermediary dealers.[6] The vessels themselves, ceremonial grave-goods for the most part but fashioned like the pottery of everyday (Sparkes 1996: 68–72), consist mainly of red-figure ware dating from the fifth and fourth centuries BCE (Schütze and Gisler-Huwiler 2004; Sparkes 1996; Higginson 2011). Preservation in tombs meant they were unearthed for the most part fully intact, an uncanny survival comparable to the later entombment of the Roman cities beneath Vesuvius.

The dating and cultural attribution of these vessels were crucial in determining their position in the history of ancient art that was emerging at the time. J. J. Winckelmann's philhellenic *Geschichte der Kunst des Altertums* had been published in 1764, the year of Hamilton's arrival, and indeed Winckelmann himself would also have been involved in cataloguing the Hamilton vases but for his untimely death (Jenkins 1996: 46, 48; Schütze 2004: 21–2). Originally identified as 'Etruscan' on the basis of their Italian provenance, Hamilton's vases were later redefined as ethnically Greek.[7] For champions of Roman design like Piranesi, however, who

---

[4] Jenkins and Sloan 1996; Lyons 1997; Constantine 2001; Coltman 2001; Schütze 2004; Higginson 2011; Heringman 2013.

[5] On the problematic use of the term 'vase', see Higginson 2011: 5.

[6] Schütze 2004: 21–2; Constantine 2001: 32; Lyons 1997; Sparkes 1996: 48.

[7] Winckelmann was the first to claim the figured vases as Greek due to the presence of Greek script in some images, but it did not become generally accepted until the same type of pottery was discovered on the Greek mainland in the early nineteenth century. In the introduction to his 1779

argued in an essay of 1769 that their shapes derived from natural phenomena such as seashells, these vessels remained unequivocally local and Italian, that is, natively pre-Roman, or 'Etruscan' (Lyons 1997; Higginson 2011; Burn 1997). Their classification was a live political and intellectual issue, with implications for evaluating the relative aesthetic precedence of ancient cultures on which contemporary art theory was founded. Hamilton's decision to catalogue and publish his acquisitions, then, in addition to selling the vases themselves to the recently established British Museum, represented an intervention into current art-historical and antiquarian debate. Ancient vases, like shells and mineral samples, could be treated as scientific specimens, representative of human as opposed to natural history but nevertheless equally capable of conveying information both as individual units and as components of a sequence. The baroque cabinet of curiosities had given way to the encyclopaedic collection which encoded knowledge – in this case, knowledge of the ancient past – in its very arrangement, in its taxonomic structure and its aspirations to comprehensiveness (Arnold 2006: esp. 242; Hooper-Greenhill 1992). The very possibility of a catalogue stemmed from this principle of encoding, which enabled the structure to part company with the objects themselves and to circulate independently while still claiming to retain and convey their essential properties.

In this way, the published collection came to participate in a circuit of what has been termed 'extended cognition'. Theories of extended cognition propose that the mind or mental activity consists not merely of neurochemical signals but can also involve the outsourcing of information to transferable repositories in the world outside the body (Clark 2008; Rowlands 2010). The map, the shopping list, the minutes of the meeting – and, it could be argued, the poem, the book, the relic, the landscape, even language itself [8] – facilitate cognitive transactions more complex than the isolated brain could accomplish alone. Memory, speculation and abstract reasoning can all be augmented by assimilating external mechanisms. It could be objected that defining interactions with the catalogue or collection as a form of extended cognition falls into what Adams and Aizawa (2010) term the 'coupling-constitution fallacy': in other words, the mere 'coupling' of a material phenomenon (such as a vase) with intelligent perception does not entail the constituent dependence of that perception on its object. As Wheeler (2010a: 246) puts it, 'causal dependence of mentality [i.e. thought] on external factors . . . is simply not enough for genuine cognitive extension'. The cognitive act – in this case, the act of formulating knowledge of antiquity – may be causally embedded in material circumstances without extending to encompass them; they are simply, inertly, the context in which people have ideas. This restriction of agency to the perceiving subject, however, does not account for the two-way traffic of (classical)

---

catalogue, Wedgwood could blithely elide the categories, stating that 'it is evident the finer sort of Etruscan vases, found in Magna Graecia, are truly Grecian workmanship'. Higginson 2011: 23–6, 35, 49–52; see also Burn 1997 on the progressive recognition of the vases as Greek.

[8] 'Language, which appears to be a central means by which cognitive processes are extended into the world' (Clark and Chalmers 1998: 11).

reception.[9] Artists and antiquarians did not regard themselves as fabricating new ideas of the past *ex nihilo*. Rather, they experienced the vases as informing, instructing and, in some extreme cases, initiating them into sacred mysteries, behaving as bearers of knowledge which it was the antiquarian's humble duty to transcribe.

Objects, then, can function as repositories of information, or can be treated as such. Hamilton's vases, like other artefacts subject to analytical scrutiny, contained latent data about the distant past ostensibly capable of being transmitted to modern observers. The assumption behind their cataloguing was that such information could be extracted – abstracted – and reformulated in different media without changing its salient properties. Having extrapolated 'what System the Ancients followed to give their Vases, that elegance which all the World acknowledge in them', Hamilton's catalogue promises to confer upon its readers all the advantages of virtual ownership: 'Artists of every country will have these fine forms under their eyes, almost as if they were in the very Cabinet which contains the originals.'[10] The preface implies that each vase functions as an ambassador from the past, conveying knowledge or *connaissance* which exists independently and transcends the direct encounter between artefact and individual. The success of the catalogue as a communicative device relied on this knowledge-content remaining stable. Similarly, the meaning of each artefact adhered to the vessel itself, not (as in twenty-first-century archaeology) to the context of its discovery. The vases' primary divulgences were the chronology of ancient art and the imitable technique of their manufacture; they were the loci of these ideas, the materials around which these ideas coalesced, but once interrogated could be re-presented in such a way as to extend the apprehension of these ideas into 'every country'. Cognisance of antiquity, in this model, is borne through time preserved objectively in fired clay.

Hamilton's first vase collection, comprising 730 separate items,[11] arrived at the British Museum in 1772, where it was displayed among the coins and curiosities and stuffed giraffes to members of the public fortunate or tenacious enough to gain admittance.[12] Mass British reproduction of Hamilton-style vases, however, had already begun with the opening of Wedgwood's ceramics factory, named 'Etruria', in 1769. Wedgwood's designs for 'black basalt' (imitation red-figure) vessels were based not on the Hamilton collection itself, which was still in Italy, but on the first volume of its catalogue, which was published in 1767.[13] In this respect, the

---

[9] Bennett (2010) distributes agency, or what she terms 'material vitality' (55), among non-human and inanimate actors in any given system.

[10] D'Hancarville 1767–76: I, vi and xvi. Translations are from the parallel English text supplied in the first two volumes. The translators are anonymous.

[11] Of these, only 184 can now be securely identified remaining in the British Museum, with another twenty identified elsewhere in Europe; see Gisler-Huwiler 2004: 34–6.

[12] On contemporary admission requirements for the British Museum, see Candlin 2010: 72–8.

[13] Coltman 2001; Brylowe 2008: 38. Wedgwood's signature blue and white jasperware did draw directly on a material source, the 'Portland' or 'Barberini' vase, a rare Roman cameo glass vessel which Hamilton sold to the Duchess of Portland in 1784. Wedgwood produced a version of the vase in jasper, and it remains the company's logo.

catalogue had achieved its stated aim of availing contemporary artisans of otherwise inaccessible ancient models. As Thora Brylowe (2008: 24) remarks, 'it was
the idea of the collection as represented in print, and not the collection of things,
that was so important to the English imagination' (cf. Coltman 2001). Following
the British Museum sale, Hamilton began building up a second collection along
similar lines. This was exported from Naples during the French invasion in 1798,
but the ship carrying the majority of the vases was wrecked en route to England
and the entire cargo lost.[14] This second collection, then, remained extant only in
the publication superintended by German artist Johann Tischbein in the 1790s.

The catalogue of the earlier collection had been released in four increasingly
swollen and recondite volumes by rogue scholar Pierre-François Hugues, self-
styled 'Baron' d'Hancarville. D'Hancarville was engaged by Hamilton in 1766
and duly completed the first two volumes, but in 1770 he fled from debts accrued
in Naples and proceeded to pawn the remainder of the plates (Haskell 1987: 38).
Following outraged negotiations over the spiralling costs of production (Jenkins
1996: 48–9), volumes 3 and 4 of *Greek, Roman, and Etruscan Antiquities from the Cabinet
of the Honourable William Hamilton* finally appeared in 1776. Tischbein proved a
considerably more reliable, not to mention economical mediator of material culture, and his *Collection of engravings from ancient vases, mostly of pure Grecian workmanship*
(1791–5) continued the project of dissemination in a more accessible and systematic fashion than that of the flamboyant d'Hancarville.

In both cases, while they purported to avail readers of a cognitive experience
equivalent to the collector's, the sensory parameters of this experience were altogether altered. For one thing, the transposition of three-dimensional objects into
flattened panels disrupted their formal properties. According to Sebastian Schütze,
'the projection of the paintings from the curved vase onto the flat paper, together
with framing and other pictorial presentation devices, altered the aesthetic effect,
in some cases considerably . . . The engraved vase-pictures came across as paintings, and ultimately even more "classical" than their classical originals' (Schütze
2004: 29–30; cf. Brylowe 2008: 28). The painted scenes are artificially separated
from their material ground, a process intensified, as Schütze (2004: 33) notes,
in Tischbein's catalogue of the second collection. Tischbein groups his images
according to the painted subjects: a flurry of maenads, a run of Amazons, Hercules'
labours, battle scenes, banquets. Unlike d'Hancarville, Tischbein had no preten-
sions to a grand narrative, content merely to satisfy his commission of transcribing
Hamilton's vase-paintings as line drawings of figures altogether detached from
material context.

D'Hancarville performs a prestidigitatory correlation between the painted vases
of the catalogue and the paintings of Renaissance artists in volume 2's 'Preliminary
remarks on painting, &c', asserting that

---

[14] Jenkins 1996: 58–9; connoisseur and designer Thomas Hope later purchased some surviving
specimens. Fragments were recovered from the wreck site in the 1970s (Sparkes 1996: 55).

Painting . . . has not only, like writing, preserved the Thoughts of men; but, has found the means of fixing the Lineaments of their Figures . . . of their Passions, which from their nature are of short duration; of their Actions, which time buries . . . and of perpetuating even the Affections, and the smallest Emotions of the soul . . . By Painting, we live in the times, and with the men themselves, who have preceded us; By her, whole Countries enclosed in the narrow compass of a Picture, are traced to our Eye. (D'Hancarville 1767–76: II, 6)

In order to consolidate the comparison, d'Hancarville's collaborating artist Pécheux renders a scene from the 'Meidias' hydria (Plate 3) in the style of Raphael.[15] By comparing the painters of vases to Raphael, d'Hancarville is again emulating Winckelmann (2006: 177–8), but goes further in his conclusions regarding both the function of the vases and their hermeneutic value. Vase-painting is made to seem a purely visual medium, equivalent to fine art,[16] and as such appreciably independent of its material context. It provides a window through which the ancient world can be viewed, preserving an accurate record of emotion, behaviour and physique. The 'narrow compass of a picture' brings Greek customs in microcosm under the scrutiny of the modern gaze, sealing the temporal rift as we find ourselves apparently co-existent with these 'fixed' representations.

Moreover, as presented by d'Hancarville, the plates of the vases themselves are deeply embedded in introductory matter, reburied beneath essays on the history of ancient art that become ever more esoteric and disconnected from the catalogues' ostensible subject over the course of each volume.[17] The most pertinent of d'Hancarville's prefaces, in volume 2, outlines the circumstances in which Hamilton's vases were discovered and discusses their use and manufacture in antiquity. 'The surest method of acquiring knowledge [*connaissance*], relative to the Vases of the Ancients', d'Hancarville states, 'is to compare in a methodical manner [*avec méthode*] what the Authors have said upon them with the Monuments that remain' (D'Hancarville 1767–76: II, 84). The vases function as reference points in an emergent chronology. By volume 3, the plates have come to serve as illustrations of d'Hancarville's theories, rather than the prefaces providing a frame for the collection. Volume 4 makes this transition explicit: although initially intended to display Hamilton's vases to the reading public, 'the desire of rendering it [the publication] more useful made the plan be changed, it is now the History of Art from its birth to the times that the Greeks brought it to it's [*sic*] perfection' (D'Hancarville 1767–76: IV, iii).

This *méthode*, this 'plan', endows otherwise disparate objects with an imagined

---

[15] Coltman 2001: 3–4; cf. Brylowe 2008: 33–4; Jenkins and Sloan 1996: 50, 180–1; Schütze 2004: 28–9.

[16] Not the case in antiquity, as Sparkes (1996: esp. 32) points out. See also Schnapp 1992: 213.

[17] On the progressive decoupling of text from plates, see Schütze 2004: 25; Brylowe 2008: 26–8. It should also be noted that not all of Hamilton's vases are depicted, and d'Hancarville also includes items from other collections in support of his theories.

underlying significance, from which infrastructure it is afterwards difficult to disinter them. In attempting to establish himself as a rival to Winckelmann, d'Hancarville draws unwary readers into a (meticulously footnoted) labyrinth of speculation concerning the religious origins of sculpture in archaic Greece. As Alain Schnapp (1992: 214) shows, he treats the iconography of vase-painting as discursive, 'une sorte d'écriture'.[18] Its images are esoteric symbols or signs, visible indices of hidden patterns of thought. Schnapp proposes that d'Hancarville's approach might be seen as a 'pre-structuralist' application of a linguistic method to archaeological material (Schnapp 1992: 216). It seeks a deep structure operating behind or beneath or beyond the objects themselves, these mere cracked utterances of a *système* it is the antiquarian's intellectual duty to reconstruct.

The work's dual epistemological objectives, that of classification and that of reverse engineering, mean that the vases are taken as 'examples' of 'principles' either formal-aesthetic or historical-teleological (D'Hancarville 1767–76: I, xii–xiii). The collection claims to be arranged in such a way as to demonstrate 'the infancy, the perfection, and the Sublime' stages of painting and design, in order that, 'in this collection, one may see the Stiles of the different periods in the Art of the Ancients' (ibid. I, 168). 'On s'est efforcé de lier la connaissance d'Antiquités, à celle de l'Art qui les a produites,' states d'Hancarville ('Effort has been made to connect knowledge of each period in Antiquity to the type of Art which produced it', ibid. IV, 5).[19] This insistence that Hamilton's vases, if correctly assembled, will function as indices of artistic periodisation, as purveyors of a particular kind of connoisseurial *connaissance*, is the underlying assumption of d'Hancarville's catalogue and publications like it.

In one sense, then, Hamilton's vases could be approached as capsules of information, vessels in which *connaissance des Antiquités* was preserved in underground chambers, unaffected by the passage of time. They are storage devices, but instead of storing wine or grain or ashes, they store data. If decrypted in the right way, these data can be recovered and repurposed as legible, moveable, saleable knowledge, a cosmopolitan commodity. The cognitive transaction which the vases broker – modern comprehension of ancient practices – is certainly a prerogative of the receiving individual, but it is borne to him by vessels brimming with semiotic cargo undischarged for two millennia.

[18] On d'Hancarville's theory of signs, see also Haskell 1987: 39–40 and Heringman 2013: 183–218. Later, under the patronage of Richard Payne Knight, d'Hancarville explored comparative religion more fully in *Recherches sur l'origine, l'esprit et les progrès des arts de la Grèce* (1785), which inspired Payne Knight's own *Discourse on the Worship of Priapus* (1786) and the somewhat less jocular *Symbolical Language of Ancient Art* (1818). On this phase of d'Hancarville's career, see Haskell 1987: 41–4 and Funnell 1982.

[19] The parallel English translation in this case is slightly misleading: 'We have strove every where to connect the knowledge of Antiquity [singular] with that of the Art that produced it.' The idea of multiple successive periods is vital, however, to d'Hancarville's teleological thinking.

Grecian Attitudes

While Sir William was collating, classifying and redistributing samples of ancient pottery, his wife Emma cultivated an alternative mode of response. Having formerly worked as a model for artist George Romney, Emma was already accustomed to composing her body in such a way as to express the narratives associated with numerous classical figures. She developed a form of performance in Naples which derived its inspiration in part from her husband's collection. Costumed in a custom-made 'Grecian' gown with two or more floor-length shawls as drapery, hair loose and feet bare or sandalled, Emma moved through a series of poses depicting heroines from ancient tragedy or history. Moments of high emotion were favoured, interspersed with contrasting studies of ebullient bacchantes or pensive nymphs. Emma's antiquity was absorbed not through the eyes, but through the skin. Executing these 'Attitudes' required acute proprioceptive sensitivity in order not only to craft a recognisable pose, one which would immediately convey to spectators both the character's identity and her emotional condition, but also to arrive in this pose precisely and repeatedly. Aristocratic diarist Adèle de Boigne, who attended one of Emma's performances as a child in 1792, unexpectedly found herself involved as a participant:

> One day she had placed me on my knees before an urn, hands joined in an attitude of pleading. Bending over me, she seemed lost in her grief, [and] both of us were dishevelled. All at once, straightening herself up and withdrawing a little, she seized me by the hair in a movement so abrupt that I recoiled in surprise and also in some fear, that made me enter into the spirit of my role, because in her hand she was brandishing a dagger. The passionate applause of the watching artists made themselves heard with exclamations of 'Bravo Medea!' Then drawing me to her, clutching me to her breast and having the air of disputing me with the wrath of heaven, she received from the same voices the cry of 'Viva Niobe!' (Plate 4)[20]

The swiftness of the transitions and the iconicity of the images were both integral components. Moreover, although comprising a montage of motionless tableaux, the Attitudes were evidently vigorous and impassioned rather than static or ethereal. Seizing, brandishing, clutching, disputing with heaven: these actions, the repertoire of melodrama, admit no half measures. The body is fully, actively

---

[20] 'Un jour elle m'avait placée à genoux devant une urne, les mains jointés dans l'attitude de la prière. Penchée sur moi, elle semblait abîmée dans sa douleur, toutes deux nous étions échevelées. Tout à coup, se redressant et s'éloignant un peu, elle me saisit par les cheveux d'un mouvement si brusque, que je me retournai avec surprise et même un peu d'effroi, ce qui me fit entrer dans l'esprit de mon rôle, car elle brandissait un poignard. Les applaudissements passionées des spectateurs artistes se firent entendre avec les exclamations de: Bravo la Médéa! Puis m'attirant à elle, me serrant sur son sein en ayant l'air de me disputer à la colère du ciel, elle arracha aux mêmes voix le cri de: Viva la Niobé!' French quoted in Chard 2000: 164–5; translation mine.

committed to their realisation, even – especially – when suspended mid-strike like the frozen frame of a film, every activated sinew straining to hold the resulting composition in place.

Emma performed her Attitudes throughout the 1790s, her recitals becoming as much of a Neapolitan must-see Grand Tourist attraction as Vesuvius, Pompeii and Virgil's tomb (Touchette 2000: 123). Typically, the critical literature has followed these contemporary evaluations of Emma as object of the (male) tourist gaze: part of Sir William's collection, his Galatea, his 'gallery of statues'.[21] This has tended to overlook Emma's own agency, however, obscuring in the process the extent to which the Attitudes constituted not only an alternative sensory mode of receiving ancient culture but also, as I will argue here, an equally legitimate cognitive practice. The distinction between Sir William's antiquarianism and Emma's performativity corresponds to the epistemological distinction identified by Diana Taylor (2003: 19) between 'the *archive* of supposedly enduring materials (i.e. texts, documents, buildings, bones) and the so-called ephemeral *repertoire* of embodied/ practical knowledge (i.e. spoken language, dance, sports, ritual)'. Both of Taylor's categories comprise a number of means and/or media by which the past becomes manifest as knowledge in the present. In determining which media constitute the archive and which the repertoire, Taylor somewhat overstates the supposed fixity of the 'stable text' of a monument or an artefact and the supposed polyvalence of bodily (re)enactment. This incubates the misconception that an unbroken flow of body-to-body transmission is needed in order for the non-verbal repertoire to retain its integrity, its authenticity, and hence its claim to alternative authority. More common, in fact, is the invented tradition, the effort to recover what Marion Kant (2015) has called 'an embodied, albeit invented past' by means of actualising its imagined properties in living individuals.[22] Emma's dancing brought into being a version of antiquity which seemed as tangible as the vases around her, and perhaps even more so, as out of herself and her garments she constructed in three sculptural dimensions the forms that appeared on the vases' flanks in flat silhouette (see Petsalis-Diomidis 2014; Macintosh 2013).

Rather than any properties inherent in the media themselves, then, I suggest that the difference between archival practices such as Sir William's catalogue and practices of the repertoire such as the Attitudes consists in the type of cognitive circuit each establishes. The material source in each case remains the same, namely the figured vase. It is the transposition of selected features into print form that renders them ostensibly 'stable' units of cognisance: the implicit claim that a line drawing of a bacchante, for instance, encapsulates all the relevant information

---

[21] Touchette (2000: 132) quotes from Fraser's (1986) biography: "'Let us then assume that he coached her'"; Constantine (2001: 164) assures us that Sir William was 'very likely . . . the inventor of the art' but that 'the painter George Romney deserves some credit too'; Nolta (1997: 112) stresses Sir William's ownership of Emma-as-collected-object and claims that 'under [his] guidance she developed the performances'.

[22] Another comparandum might be the (re)invented traditions of classical Indian dance, on which see Sahai 2011: 106–8.

about the vessel on which it appears. Emma, on the other hand, utilises the field of her own physicality, her personal body schema, to attain physiological comprehension of an imagined ancient world. Such cognisance is neither more creative nor less intelligent than Sir William's, merely embodied as opposed to extended.

Proponents of embodied cognition or the 'embodied mind' thesis contend that so-called mental activity (such as interpreting an ancient artefact, forming conjectures about its value, meaning and use(s), or drawing conclusions about the society that produced it) not only occurs within the brain but is spread across the whole organism; that imagination and abstract thought are predicated upon sense perception (Gallese and Lakoff 2005), and sense perception operates not as simple input but in a constant feedback loop as it is filtered for utility, novelty and priority, reinforcing certain factors and disregarding others, determining and determined by the organism's fluctuating interests (Damasio 1999; Gallagher 2005). Thought is affected – indeed, produced – by the condition of the body. Reasoning is psychophysical. For Emma, then, corporeal repositioning vis-à-vis the vases and the images they showed, her repeated assumption of these particular roles and their associated postures, created a perceptual relationship very different from that experienced by her husband (and his readers).

As Rick Kemp (2012: 48) has argued in relation to acting generally, 'physical experience in the material world shapes conceptual thought'. Actors extend the range of states at their disposal by breaking habitual patterns of movement, increasing plasticity and responsiveness through exercises which may be purely technical but nevertheless consolidate links between motor schemas (also known as 'muscle memory') and imagined scenarios. Not only does this enable the performer to present her audience with more nuanced and varied personifications, but it also modifies the performer's own relationship to her body. Kemp points out that 'using postures and gestures that are different from those we employ in everyday life is likely to create an altered sense of self' (Kemp 2012: 138; cf. Thompson 2005: 416). If nothing else, it demonstrates the relativity of physicality, or the way one subjectively occupies the physiological confines of one's body.[23] That this experience *can* be altered, and indeed is irrevocably defamiliarised even by exposure to other, less automatic ways of moving, is central to the epistemological function of Emma's Attitudes. By accommodating her body to shapes, rhythms and mannerisms derived from ancient sources, she provided herself with an extended sensorimotor spectrum from which to assemble impressions of 'Grecian' femininity. Moreover, just as artists were expected to study anatomy in order to represent with verisimilitude the effect of the passions on the human body, Emma acquired an intimate working knowledge of these same anatomical processes from, as it were, the inside: how to encode in a single gesture *ēthos* (character) and *pathos* (emotion) to render it at once legible, believable and affective.

---

[23] See Thomspon 2005: 409 on the dichotomy of the biological and the phenomenological body, which he argues should replace the so-called mind-body problem with a 'body-body' problem. Sheets-Johnstone (2011) posits movement as the basis for a sense of self.

Sketches and engravings of Emma performing show multiple points of contact with images in Sir William's collections, although the correspondences are rarely absolute.[24] As Adèle de Boigne comments, 'she takes inspiration from antique statues, and brings them to mind without servile imitation';[25] sculpture, as well as frescoes and vase-paintings, contributed to the Attitudes' composition. Comparing drawings by Friedrich Rehberg and Pietro Novelli to the published plates of the Hamilton collection, it is evident that some of the poses they depict – Rehberg's seated Sibyl, for instance, the bacchante with a tambourine, the priestess bearing libations, the dancer caught mid-leap with her flying shawl – recur among the vases with sufficient frequency to be counted as probable resources.[26] More subtle elements, in particular the ways that female figures interact with their garments, wrapping them or plucking at them, also appear to have been incorporated, but it should be noted that the more dramatic scenes in which Emma lies full-length or kneels in supplication are not attested in any extant record of Sir William's collection. Occasionally, the posture of an emotionally uninflected painted figure has been modified to invest it with dramatic significance, such as the outflung arm of Rehberg's 'Sophonisba' or the soulful embraces addressed by Novelli's Emma to urns placed strategically on plinths.

It is not clear how far these drawings can be taken as reflecting Emma's actual use of props, but her use of the vases themselves to reproduce in her tableaux the scenes they depict is independently attested. In an anecdote from 1794, Emma reclines 'in the pose of a water nymph, her head resting on a Greek vase', cheerfully reassuring her anxious husband that she won't break his 'jug'.[27] To Emma, the vessels are not merely items for display; they are funeral urns, libations, jugs of wine, poisoned cups, opportunities for interaction. Similarly interactive are the women's painted garments. The innovation of performing in antique dress copied from ancient pictorial and plastic sources was relatively recent; the Galatea of Rousseau's 1775 *Pygmalion* stepped down from her pedestal in a stiff bodice, high wig and panniered skirts (Holmström 1967: 45). Emma's Grecian gown and copious shawls, however, according to Amelia Rauser (2015: 474), 'brought the neoclassical white chemise from the [painter's] studio into the salon', making available the unprecedented sensation of b(e)aring one's body uncorseted in public space.

---

[24] Touchette (2000: 127–8) argues that no precise correlations can be made; cf. Nolta 1997. There are numerous points of resemblance even if no figure is identical. It cannot be ruled out that the artists who engraved Emma were also referencing images in the catalogue.

[25] 'C'est ainsi qu'elle s'inspirait des statues antiques, et que, sans les copier servilement, elle les rappelait aux imaginations', Adèle de Boigne, quoted in Chard 2000: 152. Translation mine.

[26] Although Emma, like Wedgwood, could have consulted d'Hancarville's catalogue, she would never have seen the first vase collection, as it left Naples before her arrival. Nolta (1997: 112) makes the ingenious suggestion that Emma's poses as depicted by Rehberg and Novelli show figures from vases turned ninety degrees laterally (that is, facing frontally rather than in profile), but he gives only one example and may have done better to take it from the second collection, to which Emma had direct access.

[27] Elisabeth Holland, quoted in Fraser 1986: 207.

Emma's ancient Greece is a lifestyle reimagined through the tangible mediation and manipulation of clothing and objects. The resulting performances should not be regarded as an after-effect or a by-product of cognition so much as a cognitive process in their own right: the process of coming-to-know something intrinsically inaccessible, something no longer in existence, not through linguistic approximation but rather through haptic and kinetic representation to oneself. The drawback of kinaesthetic cognisance is that it remains essentially incommunicable. What Emma perceives from within the Attitudes differs qualitatively from what is perceived by her spectators, not least because for her these movements constitute the culmination of hours of practice and concentrated somatic attention.[28] Emma's gestures communicate emotional content but do not disclose the procedural knowledge of how to reproduce them; nor do they divulge how she has been reshaped from within by a willing assimilation of alien physicalities, rendering her own body foreign. This kinaesthetic construal – in other words, cognitive apprehension via self-movement – is what sets Emma's practice apart from other contemporary methods of accessing the past via its material remains.

To Dance or Not to Dance?[29]

One spectator who did not find Emma's Attitudes at all edifying was aesthetic philosopher Johann Gottfried Herder, who visited Naples in 1789. He 'teases' her ('ich sie neckte'), and she retaliates by directing some especially lewd *bacchantische* poses at him. 'She is fundamentally such a common person,' Herder afterwards writes indignantly, 'without finer feeling, I believe, for anything at all, anything beautiful that is sublime, great, and immortal; but rather she is an ape, and nothing like this at all.' He is angry, he explains, because she 'awakened me so rudely from my dream, and a large part of my ideas about artistic composition – which in all honesty had been somewhat exaggerated – she has positively ruined . . . Anyway, I came out of the land of Art as virtually an enemy of this ape-art.'[30] Although Herder himself claims to have been at best indifferent to, and in retrospect offended by, Emma's combination of sexual assertiveness and artistic pastiche, other accounts contradict his professed antipathy. One of Herder's companions describes him as

---

[28] Kinesic comprehension, or sensorimotor response to the movement of others, has been shown to depend on the expertise of the viewer themselves in performing the action witnessed; see Calvo-Merino et al. 2005.

[29] Some of this material is also covered in Slaney 2016 and 2017.

[30] 'Übrigens ist sie a fonds eine sehr gemeine Person in ihrem Innern, ohne feineres Gefühl wie ich glaube, für irgend etwas, was erhaben, groß u. ewig schön ist; eine Äffin aber, daß nichts drüber geht. Da alles vorbei war, bin ich über sie recht ergrimmt worden, daß sie mich so gewaltig aus dem Traum geweckt, u. einen großen teil meinter Ideen über die Kunstellungen, die freilich in aller Einfalt etwas übertrieben waren, ziemlich ruiniert hat. Ich sahe nämlich, wie entfernt man vom wahren Sentiment jeder edlen Art doch so ein glücklicher Affe sein könne. Überhaupt komme ich aus dem Lande der Kunst beinah als ein Feind der Affenkunst, oder wenigstens sehr gleichgültig gegen sie zurück', Herder, *Italienische Reise*, March 1789 (1989: 361). Translation mine.

captivated by 'one of [Parthenope's] magical Syrens, who, through shape, voice, and magical attitudes of the most beautiful Greek art, enraptured him';[31] another reports him as having discovered for the first time what the pantomime-dancing of the Romans had really been.[32]

Herder's intense ambivalence towards Emma's embodied reception of the artworks he revered has been interpreted by Amelia Rauser as fundamentally gendered:

> The performer switches poses at her own volition, not the viewer's, disrupting the process of contemplation and transcendence . . . Thus, the (male) viewer is not in complete control of the process of enlivening, as he is when in the presence of an actual statue; instead, the living sculpture herself directs the action and controls the pace . . . When the sculptural body being scrutinised is already alive, and when it moves, all of these processes [of sublimation] are disrupted. (Rauser 2015: 478)

For Herder, Emma's performance art lacks authenticity; merely an 'ape-art', it engages with ancient artworks by attempting to copy or imitate them, rather than through cultivating a more contemplative, interior response. While the gendered basis of Herder's attack is undeniable, Rauser demonstrating persuasively how Emma's deployment of her own sexualisation threatened to literalise the erotic foundations of masculine connoisseurship,[33] I wish to focus here instead on the difference in their respective modes of cognisance. Herder's own 'Ideen über die Kunstellungen' had been formed prior to his visit to Italy. His somewhat radical theory of haptic aesthetics, published in the essay *Plastik* or 'Sculpture', subtitled 'Some observations on shape and form from Pygmalion's creative dream' (1779), had been more fully developed a decade earlier in the more polemical *Fourth Critical Grove*.[34] Here, Herder had proposed that particular art forms appealed to particular human senses: painting to vision, music to hearing, and sculpture to touch ('Gefühl'). It is this last, least obvious correlation which informs *Plastik*, and which provoked both his fascination with and his condemnation of Emma Hamilton.

When Herder states that 'Sculpture – the fine art of bodies – is above all tangible' (*KW4* 2.1, 2006: 210),[35] he does not mean that it is necessary to run your hands over ancient statues, but rather that their three-dimensionality is appreciated as a haptic phenomenon. Although acknowledging that statues are visible, Herder argues that vision alone cannot communicate the type of beauty ('schöne

---

[31] Anna Amalia, quoted in Rauser 2015: 477.
[32] C. A. Böttiger, quoted in Lada-Richards 2003: 28–9.
[33] Rauser 2015: 478–82; see also Coltman 2009: esp. 159–90 on the erotic aspect of connoisseurship.
[34] *Kritische Wäldchen 4*, hereafter *KW4*, remained unpublished until after Herder's death. For Herder in the context of contemporary aesthetic philosophy, see Moore 2006; Norton 1991; Harloe 2013: 205–43. Other versions of the following discussion have appeared in *Deep Classics* (Slaney 2016) and *Touch and the Ancient Senses* (Slaney 2017).
[35] All translations of *KW4* are by Gregory Moore.

Form') inherent in the plastic arts because it is capable only of perceiving surfaces. 'The living, embodied truth of three-dimensional space, of angles, of form and volume, is not something we can learn through sight,' Herder writes ('Raum, Winkel, Form, Rundung lerne ich als solche in leibhafter Wahrheit nicht durch Gesicht erkennen', *Plastik* 1.3, 2002: 40–1).[36] We cannot properly come to know ('erkennen') that a statue is beautiful by seeing it in a picture or engraving, because this deprives it of the 'Innigkeit' (interiority), 'Fülle' (solidity) and 'Runde' (convexity) that can only be perceived in the material presence of the artwork. Perception of these qualities via what Herder calls 'the silent sense of touch that feels things in the dark' produces in us the recognition that the artwork in question satisfies the aesthetic criteria appropriate to its medium.[37]

The sculptures Herder refers to in *Plastik* are all Graeco-Roman antiquities in Italian collections such as the Farnese Hercules, Borghese Hermaphrodite and Belvedere Apollo (Plate 5), believed at the time to epitomise the perfection of Greek art.[38] Like Winckelmann and d'Hancarville, Herder treats them as representatives of a culture whose unparalleled achievement can be apprehended from its material remains, but unlike the chronology of d'Hancarville's catalogue, this cognisance of beauty cannot be abstracted from its source. According to Herder's epistemological paradigm, we know that Greek society was mature and wholesome because of the beauty of the artworks it produced; we come to know that the artworks are beautiful through the application of our sense of 'Gefühl'. Our cognisance of antiquity therefore depends on the haptic interaction of beholder and artefact, their evolving spatial relationship, and the manufacture of imaginary movement.

Herder's art-lover does also move in reality, at least initially. In order to arrive as what Rachel Zuckert (2009: 288) has termed a 'nonperspectival grasp' of the artwork, he 'circles restlessly' around it;[39] because sculpture, unlike painting, has no single frontal viewpoint, the beholder must approach it from every possible angle if he is fully to realise its multifaceted composition of depths, curves and hollows. He cannot *see* nor even *visualise* every configuration simultaneously, but he can build up a *feel* for the sculpture as a three-dimensional object rather than a flat plane. Once such a 'nonperspectival grasp' has been attained, the beholder can dispense with his preparatory circling and now stands motionless, 'sunk deep in silent contemplation':

He seems to stand in a fixed position, but nothing could be further from the truth. He adopts as many viewpoints as he can, changing his perspective from one moment to the next so that he avoids sharply defined surfaces. To this end he gently glides only around the contours of the body, changes his position,

---

[36] All translations of *Plastik* are by Jason Gaiger.

[37] Herder is at pains in *KW4* to demonstrate that beauty is an acquired taste, not an inherent property.

[38] These works are now identified as (Graeco-)Roman and dated to the first two centuries ce.

[39] This only works of course for sculpture in the round.

moves from one spot to another and then back again; he follows the line that unfolds and runs back on itself, the line that forms bodies and here, with its gentle declivities, forms the beauty of the body standing before him. (*KW4* 2.3, 2006: 218–19)[40]

Without performing any of these movements physically, Herder's art-lover experiences them with as much intensity as if they were indeed occurring: he 'glides' around the marble limbs, he 'follows' the body's smooth contours even as he remains in place. This simulation of motor activity corresponds to what Marc Jeannerod terms 'covert' movement, a preparatory motor schema which uses the same neural apparatus as actual, 'overt' movement but remains unrealised.[41] Covert schemas are based on the perceived affordances of the objects in question, or in other words their potential for haptic interaction:[42] whether they can be lifted, climbed on, hidden in, scrunched, stroked, smashed, embraced, and what type of muscular preparation would be necessary were any of these actions to be performed. Jeannerod further suggests that we become aware of these counterfactual possibilities only when they are not discharged through overt performance (1994: 190). One way of reading Herder's virtual glide around the Belvedere Apollo, then, is as the sustained pursuit of an unrealised affordance, perpetually anticipated and perpetually deferred.

The question is whether this counts as an embodied reception. In comparison with the type of cognisance furnished by d'Hancarville's catalogue, it certainly depends more profoundly on physical co-presence with an artefact and the ensuing sensorimotor response. On the other hand, unlike Emma's bodily reanimation of painted and sculptural figures, it does not involve – and in fact firmly suppresses – any literal physical action. The simulated glide is confined to the art-lover's brain, projected deliberately on to the artefact and reflected back again in a solipsistic loop. Although facilitated by awareness of the statue's polymorphism, incorporating its manifold alternative configurations or what Alva Noë would call its 'sensorimotor profile',[43] the rapport in which its beauty becomes apparent takes place within a mind that is running an avowedly disembodied simulation. Its very potency derives from its suspension of actual motion.

[40] 'Er scheint auf einem ewigen Punkte zu stehen, und nichts ist weniger; er nimmt sich eben so viel Gesichtspunkte, als er kann, und verändert jeden in jedem Augenblick, um sich gleichsam durchaus keine scharfe, bestimmte Fläche zu geben. Zu diesem Zweck gleitet er nur in der Umfläche des Körpers sanft umhin, verändert seine Stellung, geht und kommt wieder; er folgt der in sich selbst umherlaufenden Linie, die einen Körper und die hier mit ihren sanften Abfällen das Schöne des Körpers bildet.'

[41] 'Covert actions are in fact actions, except for the fact that they are not executed', Jeannerod 2001: 103. Gallese and Lakoff (2005) similarly argue for the use of the premotor cortex in imagined action.

[42] The theory of affordances was first proposed by Gibson (1977). See also Jeannerod 1994.

[43] 'The sensorimotor profile of an object is the way its appearance changes as you move with respect to it', Noë 2004: 78. Also on cognition as 'enactive', or a product of 'dynamic sensorimotor activity', see Thompson 2005: esp. 407–8.

Object affordances, however, constitute a crucial interface between the material world and its phenomenological import. 'When we perceive', according to Noë (2004: 105), 'we perceive in an idiom of possibilities for movement.' This 'enactive' or 'enactivist' approach to cognition has been critiqued for remaining essentially brain-based, in that its cognitive circuit is neither (properly speaking) embodied nor (properly speaking) extended (Rowlands 2010: 82–3), but its proponents would certainly count it among the challenges to a Cartesian model in that it posits an indispensable role for kinaesthesia in perceptual processing. Noë's (2004: 1) account of 'sensorimotor dependence' in object perception displays some striking points of convergence with Herder's (*KW4* 2.3, 2006: 220) account of the aesthetics of 'Gefühl' or 'fühlende Einbildungskraft' (the 'feeling' or 'haptic/tactile imagination'). As Noë (2004: 75–7) puts it:

Perceptual experience acquires spatial content due to the perceiver's implicit understanding of the way sensory stimulation varies as a result of movement . . . Despite the fact that you can only see part of the object's surface, in looking at it we enjoy an experience as of a voluminous solid.

The art-lover is able to predict not only how the sculpture's aspect would change if he were to move, but also how these aspects in turn might prompt further (and different) movements. The crucial cognitive difference between Emma and Herder is that Emma's performance commits her to a single kinaesthetic response. Pinned down in the denser medium of flesh, her motor impulses are selectively moulded and hardened into the resulting Attitude. Herder's simulation, on the other hand, keeps all the possibilities in play, whether physically plausible or not, as an endlessly proliferating act of speculation.

Cognition incorporates cognisance, or *connaissance*, the process of coming to know, of formulating a conception of some designated object of knowledge (such as classical antiquity). The acquisition, storage and retrieval of knowledge makes fundamental use of practices identified as involving distributed cognition. In this respect, the various mechanisms of cognitive distribution have epistemological ramifications: how do you know what it is that you think you know about an imagined past, a past which can only be 'known' from its traces in the present? *Connaissance* of antiquity has been discovered persisting in diverse media, among them the contours of marble and the archive of clay, and conceivably also the mutable repertoire of flesh. Different cognitive fields emerge from these interactions. For d'Hancarville, knowledge acquisition is a semiotic pursuit, a systematic decryption of images treated as ideograms which, when correctly de-cyphered, exhaust their function in delivering time capsules of information. For Herder, meanwhile, *connaissance* has a sensual basis. The enduring beauty of classical sculpture is accessed aesthetically, by communing in spatial proximity with the artefact itself. Perceived by the sense of 'Gefühl' as beautiful at the time of apprehension, such artworks enable Herder – like Winckelmann before him – to extrapolate, to 'dream', a beautiful society responsible for their creation. But Herder's dream is predicated, paradoxically enough, on a form of disembodiment, riding a constant wave of hypothetical movement that never collapses into realisation. Part of his shock when 'awakened' by Emma results from a confrontation with the coalescence of a swarm of affordances into one bodily incarnation. Herder might fantasise about feeling the weariness of Hercules or the Borghese Hermaphrodite's pleasure (*KW4* 2.3, 2006: 219; *Plastik* 4.1, 2002: 80–1), but Emma has developed the actual capacity for shaping herself into sculptural forms, the embodied knowledge necessary to perform as well as perceive. She has made herself a vessel. Vases hold ashes and signs, and sculpture holds Herder entranced, but Emma, in holding herself in the pose of the dancer, contains her cognisance of classical Greece in the field and the fact of her body.

Notes on Contributors

Miranda Anderson is an Honorary Fellow at the University of Edinburgh and an Anniversary Fellow at the University of Stirling. Her research focuses on cognitive approaches to literature and culture. She is the author of *The Renaissance Extended Mind* (2015) and she has recently published articles in *Narrative* and *Poetics Today*, among others.

Ros Ballaster is Professor of Eighteenth-Century Studies in the Faculty of English, Oxford University at Mansfield College. Her particular research interests are in oriental fiction, women's writing, drama and performance. She is author of two monographs, *Seductive Forms: Women's Amatory Fiction 1684–1740* (1992) and *Fabulous Orients: Fictions of the East in England 1662–1785* (2005), and a further is forthcoming: *Being There: Theatre and Novel in Eighteenth-Century England*.

Renee Harris is Assistant Professor of British Literature at Lewis-Clark State College in Lewiston, Idaho. Her research examines the physiology of sympathy in the writer-reader relationship by placing eighteenth-century medical knowledge alongside the moral philosophy of the Scottish Enlightenment. She seeks to understand how the circulation of affect is theorised and staged by Romantic narrative and how these poems become sites of shared feeling. She has published on materiality and social exchange in Romantic novels.

Elspeth Jajdelska has written two monographs on the history of reading in the seventeenth and eighteenth centuries, *Silent Reading and the Birth of the Narrator* and *Speech, Print and Decorum in Britain, 1600–1750*. In 2016 she completed a master's degree in Mind, Language and Embodied Cognition, and she has published on vividness in literary description, simulation and its limits in literary experience, and the literary representation of sex.

Karin Kukkonen is Associate Professor in Comparative Literature at the University of Oslo. She has published on neoclassical literary theory as a precursor of today's cognitive approaches to literature (*A Prehistory of Cognitive Poetics:*

Neoclassicism and the Novel, 2017). Currently, Kukkonen is working on a book-length study investigating the connections between literature, 4E cognition and predictive processing.

Charlotte Lee is University Lecturer in Modern German Studies at the University of Cambridge. She is the author of *The Very Late Goethe: Self-Consciousness and the Art of Ageing* (2014). She has published numerous articles on Goethe and his era, and has also co-edited a special number of *German Life and Letters*, published in 2017, which examines alignments between intellectual activity in the long eighteenth century and the findings of modern cognitive science.

Jennifer Mensch is a Kant specialist whose research lies at the intersection of philosophy and science during the long eighteenth century. In addition to numerous publications on Kant and the German Enlightenment, she has published a monograph entitled *Kant's Organicism: Epigenesis and the Development of Critical Philosophy* (2013). Her current projects focus on Kant's legacy in the history of comparative linguistics and physical anthropology.

Lisa Ann Robertson is an Assistant Professor of Nineteenth-Century British Literature at the University of South Dakota, where she teaches on British Romanticism, sensibility, the Gothic, eighteenth- and nineteenth-century Black Transatlantic writers, and representations of minds and bodies in literature and science. She researches and writes about theories of mind, the body and Romantic literary and scientific theories of imagination, as well as materialist theories of education and cognitive science, both historical and contemporary.

George Rousseau taught at Harvard, UCLA, King's College Aberdeen, and Oxford, where he was Co-Director of the Centre for the History of Childhood. In America he was formative in establishing the interdisciplinary subdisciplines of Literature and Science and the Medical Humanities. His publications emanate from an interest in the long eighteenth century viewed in historical and theoretical contexts. Rousseau is currently working on a study of old age that takes account of 4E cognition.

John Savarese is an Assistant Professor of English Language and Literature at the University of Waterloo. His current book project focuses on the prehistory of cognitive poetics and Romantic-era theories of the social mind. His articles on Romantic literature and science have appeared in *ELH*, *European Romantic Review*, *Literature Compass* and *Romantic Circles Praxis Series*.

Richard C. Sha is author of *Imagination and Science in Romanticism* (2018) and *Perverse Romanticism: Aesthetics and Sexuality in Britain, 1750–1850* (2009) and editor (with Joel Faflak) of *Romanticism and the Emotions* (2016). He is currently working on *Modelling*

Emotion: Romanticism and Beyond, which features chapters on Leopardi, Goethe, Wordsworth, Baillie and Voltaire.

Helen Slaney has been Research Coordinator for the Humanities Department and a member of the Classics faculty at Roehampton since 2016. Previously she held a Junior Research Fellowship and a British Academy Postdoctoral Fellowship at St Hilda's College, Oxford, where she also completed her DPhil in 2012. Her monograph *The Senecan Aesthetic: A Performance History* was published in 2015.

Mark Sprevak is a Senior Lecturer in Philosophy at the University of Edinburgh. His primary research interests are in philosophy of mind, philosophy of science and metaphysics, with particular focus on the cognitive sciences. He has published articles in, among other places, *The Journal of Philosophy*, *The British Journal for the Philosophy of Science*, *Synthese*, *Philosophy*, *Psychiatry & Psychology* and *Studies in History and Philosophy of Science*. His book *The Computational Mind* is forthcoming from Routledge.

Michael Wheeler is Professor of Philosophy at the University of Stirling. His primary research interests are in philosophy of science (especially cognitive science, psychology, biology and artificial intelligence) and philosophy of mind. He also works on Heidegger and on developing ideas at the interface between the analytic and the continental philosophical traditions. His book, *Reconstructing the Cognitive World: The Next Step*, was published by MIT Press in 2005.

Bibliography

Aalders, C. (2015), '"Your journal, my love": Constructing personal and religious bonds in eighteenth-century women's diaries', *Journal of Religious History* 39.3: 386–98.

Abrams, M. H. (1971), *Natural Supernaturalism: Tradition and Revolution in Romantic Literature*, New York: W. W. Norton.

Abrams, M. H. [1953] (1974), *The Mirror and the Lamp: Romantic Theory and the Critical Tradition*, Oxford: Oxford University Press.

Abrams, M. H. (1984), *The Correspondent Breeze: Essays on English Romanticism*, New York: W. W. Norton.

Ackerknecht, E. H. (1974), 'The history of the discovery of the vegetative (autonomic) nervous system', *Medical History* 18: 1–8.

Adams, F. and K. Aizawa (2008), *The Bounds of Cognition*, Malden, MA, and Oxford: Blackwell.

Adams, F. and K. Aizawa (2010), 'Defending the bounds of cognition', in R. Menary (ed.), *The Extended Mind*, Cambridge, MA: MIT Press, pp. 67–80.

Addison, J. [1711] (1965), *The Spectator*, ed. D. Bond, 5 vols, Oxford: Clarendon Press.

Agamben, G. (1998), *Homo Sacer*, Stanford: Stanford University Press.

Ahnert, T. (2003), 'De sympathia et antipathia rerum: Natural Law, religion and the rejection of mechanistic science in the works of Christian Thomasius', in T. J. Hochstrasser and P. Schröder (eds), *Early Modern Natural Law Theories: Contexts and Strategies in the Early Enlightenment*, Dordrecht and London: Kluwer, pp. 257–78.

Ahnert, T. and S. Manning (eds) (2011), *Character, Self and Sociability in the Scottish Enlightenment*, New York: Palgrave Macmillan.

Allan, D. (2010), *Commonplace Books and Reading in Georgian England*, Cambridge: Cambridge University Press.

Allison, H. (1973), 'Kant's critique of Berkeley', *Journal of the History of Philosophy* 11: 43–63.

Anderson, M. (2007), 'Chaucer and the subject of the mirror', in M. Anderson (ed.), *The Book of the Mirror: An Interdisciplinary Collection Exploring the Cultural Story of the Mirror*, Newcastle upon Tyne: Cambridge Scholars Publishing, pp. 70–9.

Anderson, M. (2015a), 'Fission-fusion cognition in Shakespearean drama: The case for *Julius Caesar*', *Narrative* 23.2: 154–68.

Anderson, M. (2015b), *The Renaissance Extended Mind*, Basingstoke and New York: Palgrave Macmillan.

Anderson, M. (2016), 'Francis Bacon's flux of the spirits and Renaissance paradigms of hybridity and adaptation', in G. Giglioni, J. A. T. Lancaster, S. Corneanu and D. Jalobeanu (eds), *Francis Bacon on Motion and Power*, Dordrecht: Springer, pp. 133–51.

Anon. [C. Garve] (1782), 'Kritic der reinen Vernunft. Von Imman. Kant. 1781', *Göttingen Anzeigen von gelehrten Sachen*, 19 January, 40–8.

Armstrong, C. I. (2003), *Romantic Organicism: From Idealist Origins to Ambivalent Afterlife*, New York: Palgrave Macmillan.

Armstrong, D. M. (1993), *A Materialist Theory of the Mind (International Library of Philosophy)*, rev. edn, London: Routledge.

Arnold, K. (2006), *Cabinets for the Curious: Looking Back at Early English Museums*, Aldershot: Ashgate.

Atherton, M. (2005), 'Berkeley's theory of vision and its reception', in K. Winkler (ed.), *The Cambridge Companion to Berkeley*, Cambridge: Cambridge University Press, pp. 94–124.

Bacon, F. [1620] (2000), *The New Organon*, ed. L. Jardine and M. Silverthorne, Cambridge: Cambridge University Press.

Ballaster, R. (2010), 'The eastern tale and the candid reader: Tristram Shandy, Candide, Rasselas', *L'attrait de l'Orient/The Call of the East*, special edn *RSEAA (Revue de la Société d'Etudes Anglo-Américaines des XVIIe et XVIIIe siècles)*, *Proceedings of Colloque tenu en Sorbonne – 22–23 janvier 2010* of *XVII–XVIII* 67: 109–26.

Bannet, E. T. (2013), 'History of reading: The long eighteenth century', *Literature Compass* 10.2: 122–33.

Barnett, D. (1987), *The Art of Gesture: The Practices and Principles of 18th Century Acting*, Heidelberg: Carl Winter.

Barth, J. R. (2003), *Romanticism and Transcendence: Wordsworth, Coleridge, and the Religious Imagination*, Columbia: University of Missouri Press.

Baynes, D. (1738), *A New Essay on the Nerves and the Doctrine of Animal Spirits*, London.

Beach, K. (1988), 'The role of external mnemonic symbols in acquiring an occupation', in M. M. Gruneberg and R. N. Sykes (eds), *Practical Aspects of Memory*, vol. 1, New York: Wiley, pp. 342–6.

Beer, J. (1989), 'Coleridge and Wordsworth on reflections', *The Wordsworth Circle* 20.1: 20–9.

Beer, J. B. (2003), *Romantic Consciousness: Blake to Mary Shelley*, Basingstoke: Palgrave Macmillan.

Bell, C. (1802), *The Anatomy of the Brain*, London: Longman.

Bell, H. K. (2008), *From Flock Beds to Professionalism: A History of Index-Makers*, New Castle, DE: Oak Knoll Press.

Bennett, A. (1994), *Keats, Narrative and Audience*, Cambridge: Cambridge University Press.

Bennett, A. (1999), *Romantic Poets and the Culture of Posterity*, Cambridge: Cambridge University Press.

Bennett, J. (2010), *Vibrant Matter: A Political Ecology of Things*, Durham, NC: Duke University Press.

Berchtold, J. and J.-L. Guichet (2010), *L'animal des Lumières*, Paris: Société française d'étude du 18e siècle.

Beretta, A. (ed.) (2014), 'Joseph Priestley: An instructive eighteenth-century perspective on the mind-body problem', in C. U. M. Smith and H. Whitaker (eds), *Brain, Mind and Consciousness in the History of Neuroscience*, New York: Springer, pp. 75–89.

Bergk, J. A. [1799] (1966), *Die Kunst Bücher zu lesen: Nebst Bemerkungen über Schriften und Schriftsteller*, Jena: In der Hempelschen Buchhandlung.

Berkeley, G. [1732] (1950), *Alciphron*, vol. 3 of *The Works of George Berkeley, Bishop of Cloyne*, ed. A. Luce and T. Jessop, 9 vols, London: Thomas Nelson and Sons, 1948–57.

Berkeley, G. (2000), *Philosophical Works Including the Works on Vision*, ed. M. Ayers, London: J. M. Dent.

Berkeley, R. (2006), 'The providential wreck: Coleridge and Spinoza's metaphysics', *European Romantic Review* 17.4: 457–75.

Berkeley, R. (2007), *Coleridge and the Crisis of Reason*, Basingstoke: Palgrave Macmillan.

Bertelsen, L. (1986), *The Nonsense Club: Literature and Popular Culture, 1749–1764*, Oxford and New York: Oxford University Press.

Berti, A. and F. Frassinetti (2000), 'When far becomes near: Re-mapping of space by tool use', *Journal of Cognitive Neuroscience* 12: 415–20.

Blair, A. and P. Stallybrass (2010), 'Mediating information', in C. Siskin and W. Warner (eds), *This Is Enlightenment*, Chicago: University of Chicago Press, pp. 139–63.

Blake, W. (1988), *The Complete Poetry and Prose of William Blake*, ed. D. Erdman, New York: Anchor Books.

Blom, P. (2004), *Encyclopédie: The Triumph of Reason in an Unreasonable Age*, London: Fourth Estate.

Bloom, H. (ed.) (1970), *Romanticism and Consciousness*, New York: Norton.

Bolens, G. (2017), 'Mind in movement', History of Distributed Cognition Project, <http://www.hdc.ed.ac.uk/lectures/mind-movement> (last accessed 31 January 2019).

Bougeant, G. H. [1735] (1992), *Voyage merveilleux du Prince Fan-Férédin dans la Romancie*, Saint-Étienne: Publications de l'Université de Saint-Étienne.

Bourdin, Jean-Claude (1996), *Les Matérialistes au xviiie Siècle, Petite Bibliothèque Payot Classiques*, Paris: Payot & Rivages.

Bracken, H. (1965), *The Early Reception of Berkeley's Immaterialism, 1710–1730*, The Hague: Martinus Nijhoff.

Bradshaw, P. F. (ed.) (2005), *New SCM Dictionary of Liturgy and Worship*, London: SCM Press.

Brockes, B. H. [1721–48] (1999), *Irdisches Vergnügen in Gott. Naturlyrik und Lehrdichtung*, ed. H. G. Kemper, Stuttgart: Reclam.

Brockes, B. H. [1721–48] (2012–16), *Werke: Irdisches Vergnügen in Gott* (5 vols to date), ed. J. Rathje, Göttingen: Wallstein.

Brodie, A. (1740), *Diary of Alexander Brodie*, Edinburgh: T. Lumisden and F. Robertson.

Brodie, A. and J. Brodie (1863), *The Diary of Alexander Brodie of Brodie 1662–1680. And of his Son, James Brodie of Brodie 1680–1685*, Aberdeen: Spalding Club.

Brooke, F. [née Moore] (1764), *The Old Maid. By Mary Singleton, Spinster. A new edition, revised and corrected by the Editor*, London.

Brooks, D. H. M. (1986), 'Group minds', *Australasian Journal of Philosophy*, 64.4: 457–70.

Brooks, H. (2015), *Actresses, Gender, and the Eighteenth-Century Stage*, Basingstoke: Palgrave Macmillan.

Brown, S., P. Clements and I. Grundy (eds) (2006), *Orlando: Women's Writing in the British Isles from the Beginnings to the Present*, Cambridge: Cambridge University Press.

Bruhn, M. J. (2011), 'Exchange values: Poetics and cognitive science', *Poetics Today* 32.3: 403–60.

Bruhn, M. J. and D. R. Wehrs (2013), *Cognition, Literature, and History*, New York: Routledge.

Brumoy, P. (1741a), 'De motibus animi: liber secundus', *Recueil des divers ouvrages en prose et en vers*, vol. 3, 88–119.

Brumoy, P. (1741b), 'Discours sur l'usage des mathématiques par rapport aux Belles-Lettres', *Recueil des divers ouvrages en prose et en vers*, vol. 2, 275–98.

Brumoy, P. (1759), *The Greek Theatre of Father Brumoy*, trans. C. Lennox, London.

Brylowe, T. (2008), 'Two kinds of collections: Sir William Hamilton's vases, real and represented', *Eighteenth-Century Life* 32.1: 23–56.

Bryson, A. (1998), *From Courtesy to Civility: Changing Codes of Conduct in Early Modern England*, Oxford: Clarendon Press.

Budge, G. (2007), *Romantic Empiricism: Poetics and the Philosophy of Common Sense, 1780–1830*, Lewisburg: Bucknell University Press.

Burge, T. (1979), 'Individualism and the mental', *Midwest Studies in Philosophy* 4: 73–122.

Burke, P. (2000), *A Social History of Knowledge: From Gutenberg to Diderot*, Cambridge: Polity.

Burn, L. (1997), 'Sir William Hamilton and the Greekness of Greek vases', *Journal of the History of Collections* 9.2: 241–52.

Buroker, J. V. (1981), *Space and Incongruence: The Origin of Kant's Idealism*, Dordrecht: Reidel Press.

Butler, J. (1997), *The Psychic Life of Power: Theories in Subjection*, Stanford: Stanford University Press.

Butler, J. (1998), 'Imitation and gender insubordination', in J. Rivkin and M. Ryan (eds), *Literary Theory: An Anthology*, Oxford: Blackwell Publishers, pp. 722–30.

Butler, J. (2013), *Rethinking Introspection: A Pluralist Approach to the First-Person Perspective*, Basingstoke: Palgrave Macmillan.

Byrne, R. M. J. (2005), *The Rational Imagination: How People Create Alternatives to Reality*, Cambridge, MA: MIT Press.

Calè, L. and A. Craciun (2011), 'The disorder of things', *Eighteenth-Century Studies* 45.1: 1–13.

Calvo-Merino, B., D. E. Glaser, J. Grèzes, R. E. Passingham and P. Haggard (2005), 'Action observation and acquired motor skills: An fMRI study with expert dancers', *Cerebral Cortex* 15.8: 1243–9.

Candlin, F. (2010), *Art, Museums and Touch*, Manchester: Manchester University Press.

Carroll, J. (1994), *Evolution and Literary Theory*, Columbia: University of Missouri Press.

Carroll, J. (2012), *Graphing Jane Austen: The Evolutionary Basis of Literary Meaning*, Basingstoke: Palgrave Macmillan.

Carroll, N. (2007), 'Narrative closure', *Philosophical Studies* 135: 1–15.

Carter, R. and C. D. Frith (1998), *Mapping the Mind*, London: Weidenfeld & Nicolson.

Cave, T. (2016), *Thinking with Literature: Towards a Cognitive Criticism*, Oxford: Oxford University Press.

Chard, C. (2000), 'Comedy, antiquity, the feminine, and the foreign: Emma Hamilton and *Corinne*', in C. Hornsby (ed.), *The Impact of Italy: The Grand Tour and Beyond*, London: British School at Rome, pp. 145–67.

Christensen, J. (1981), *Coleridge's Blessed Machine of Language*, Ithaca: Cornell University Press.

Clark, A. (1997), *Being There: Putting Brain, Body, and World Together Again*, Cambridge, MA: MIT Press.

Clark, A. (1998), 'Magic words: How language augments human computation', in P. Carruthers and J. Boucher (eds), *Language and Thought: Interdisciplinary Themes*, Oxford: Oxford University Press, pp. 162–83.

Clark, A. (2003), *Natural-Born Cyborgs: Minds, Technologies, and the Future of Human Intelligence*, Oxford: Oxford University Press.

Clark, A. (2005), 'Beyond the flesh: Some lessons from a mole cricket', *Artificial Life* 11.1–2: 233–44.

Clark, A. (2006), 'Language, embodiment, and the cognitive niche', *Trends in Cognitive Science* 10.8: 370–4.

Clark, A. (2008), *Supersizing the Mind: Embodiment, Action, and Cognitive Extension*, Oxford: Oxford University Press.

Clark, A. (2009), 'Spreading the joy? Why the machinery of consciousness is (probably) still in the head', *Mind* 118.472: 963–93.

Clark, A. (2010a), 'Coupling, constitution, and the cognitive kind: A reply to Adams and Aizawa', in R. Menary (ed.), *The Extended Mind*, Cambridge, MA: MIT Press, pp. 81–100.

Clark, A. (2010b), 'Memento's revenge: The extended mind, extended', in R. Menary (ed.), *The Extended Mind*, Cambridge, MA: MIT Press, pp. 43–66.

Clark, A. and D. Chalmers (1998), 'The extended mind', *Analysis* 58.1: 7–19.

Clark, J. C. D. [1985] (2000), *English Society 1660–1832: Religion, Ideology and Politics during the Ancien Regime*, 2nd edn, Cambridge: Cambridge University Press.

Clarke, E. and L. S. Jacyna (1987), *Nineteenth-Century Origins of Neuroscientific Concepts*, Berkeley: University of California Press.

Colclough, D. (2005), *Freedom of Speech in Early Stuart England*, Cambridge: Cambridge University Press.

Coleridge, S. T. (1817), *Biographia Literaria*, <http://www.gutenberg.org/files/6081/6081-h/6081-h.htm> (last accessed 31 January 2019).

Coleridge, S. T. (1956–71), *Collected Letters of Samuel Taylor Coleridge*, ed. E. L. Griggs, 6 vols, Oxford: Clarendon Press.

Coleridge, S. T. (1957–2002), *The Notebooks of Samuel Taylor Coleridge*, ed. K. Coburn, 5 vols, London: Routledge & Kegan Paul.

Coleridge, S. T. (1969), *The Friend*, ed. B. E. Rooke, vol. 1 of 2, vol. 4 of *The Collected Works of Samuel Taylor Coleridge*, Princeton: Princeton University Press.

Coleridge, S. T. (1976), *On the Constitution of Church and State*, ed. J. Colmer, vol. 10 of *The Collected Works of Samuel Taylor Coleridge*, Princeton: Princeton University Press.

Coleridge, S. T. (1983), *Biographia Literaria*, ed. J. Engell and W. J. Bate, vol. 1 of 2, vol. 7 of *The Collected Works of Samuel Taylor Coleridge*, Princeton: Princeton University Press.

Coleridge, S. T. (1993), *Aids to Reflection*, ed. J. Beer, vol. 9 of *The Collected Works of Samuel Taylor Coleridge*, Princeton: Princeton University Press.

Coleridge, S. T. (1995), 'Theory of life', in *Shorter Works and Fragments*, ed. H. J. Jackson and J. R. de J. Jackson, vol. 1 of 2, vol. 11 of *The Collected Works of Samuel Taylor Coleridge*, Princeton: Princeton University Press, pp. 481–557.

Coleridge, S. T. (2000), *Lectures 1818–1819: On the History of Philosophy*, ed. J. R. de J. Jackson, 2 vols, vol. 8 of *The Collected Works of Samuel Taylor Coleridge*, Princeton: Princeton University Press.

Collini, S. (2009), 'Impact on humanities: Researchers must take a stand now or be judged and rewarded as salesmen', *Times Literary Supplement*, 13 November 2009, pp. 18–19.

Colombetti, G. (2014), *The Feeling Body: Affective Science Meets the Enactive Mind*, Cambridge, MA: MIT Press.

Colombetti, G. and T. Roberts (2015), 'Extending the extended mind: The case for extended affectivity', *Philosophical Studies* 172.5: 1243–63.

Coltman, V. (2001), 'Sir William Hamilton's vase publications', *Journal of Design History* 14.1: 1–16.

Coltman, V. (2009), *Classical Sculpture and the Culture of Collecting in Britain since 1760*, Oxford: Oxford University Press.

Conrod, F. (2008), *Loyola's Greater Narrative: The Architecture of the Spiritual Exercises in Golden Age and Enlightenment Literature*, New York: Peter Lang.

Constantine, D. (2001), *Fields of Fire: A Life of Sir William Hamilton*, London: Weidenfeld & Nicolson.

Conway, A. M. and M. H. McMurran (2016), *Mind, Body, Motion, Matter: Eighteenth-Century British and French Literary Perspectives*, Toronto: University of Toronto Press.

Conway, M. (2005), 'Memory and the self', *Journal of Memory and Language* 53: 594–628.

Conway, M. A., J. A. Singer and A. Tagini (2004), 'The self and autobiographical memory: Correspondence and coherence', *Social Cognition* 22: 325–39.

Courtney, J. (2001), *The Diary of a Yorkshire Gentleman: John Courtney of Beverley, 1759–1768*, ed. S. and D. Neave, Otley: Smith Settle.

Cowley, S. and R. Gahrn-Andersen (forthcoming), 'Deflating autonomy: Human interactivity in the emerging social world', *Intellectica* 63.

Crane, T. and S. Patterson (2000), *History of the Mind-Body Problem*, London: Routledge.

Crary, J. (2001), *Suspensions of Perception: Attention, Spectacle, and Modern Culture*, Cambridge, MA: MIT Press.

Crawford, M. B. (2015), *The World Beyond Your Head: How to Flourish in an Age of Distraction*, London: Viking.

Cressy, D. (2010), *Dangerous Talk: Scandalous, Seditious and Treasonable Speech in Pre-Modern England*, Oxford: Oxford University Press.

Crewe, F. A. (2006), *An English Lady in Paris: The Diary of Frances Anne Crewe 1786*, ed. M. Allen, St Leonards: Oxford-Stockley Publications.

Csengei, I. (2011), *Sympathy, Sensibility and the Literature of Feeling in the Eighteenth Century*, Basingstoke: Palgrave Macmillan.

D'Hancarville, P. F. (1767–76), *Antiquités Etrusques, Grècques et Romaines, tirées du cabinet du M. William Hamilton, envoyé extraordinaire de S.M. Britanique en cour de Naples*, 4 vols, Naples: Morelli.

Dainville, F. de (1978), *L'éducation des jésuites (XVIe–XVIIIe siècles)*, Paris: Minuit.

Damasio, A. (1999), *The Feeling of What Happens: Body and Emotion in the Making of Consciousness*, New York: Harcourt Brace.

Dameron, J. L. (1985), 'Emerson and Fraser's on Coleridge's *Aids to Reflection*', *American Transcendental Quarterly* 57: 15–19.

Damrosch, D. and K. J. H. Dettmar (eds) (2006), *The Longman Anthology of British Literature*, vol. 2A, 3rd edn, New York: Pearson.

Danta, C. and H. Groth (2014), *Mindful Aesthetics: Literature and the Science of Mind*, New York: Bloomsbury.

Darnton, R. (1990), 'First steps towards a history of reading', in *Kiss of the Lamourette: Reflections in Cultural History*, London: Faber and Faber, pp. 154–90.

Darnton, R. (1996), *The Forbidden Bestsellers of Pre-Revolutionary France*, New York: Norton.

Daston, L. (2004), 'Attention and the values of nature in the Enlightenment', in F. Vidal (ed.), *The Moral Authority of Nature*, Chicago: University of Chicago Press, pp. 109–13.

Davidson, J. (2009), *Breeding: A Partial History of the Eighteenth Century*, New York: Columbia University Press.

De Jaegher, H. (2009), 'Social understanding through direct perception? Yes, by interacting', *Consciousness and Cognition* 18.2: 535–42.

De Jaegher, H. and E. Di Paolo (2007), 'Participatory sense-making: An enactive approach to social cognition', *Phenomenology and the Cognitive Sciences* 6.4: 485–507.

Dehaene, S. (1997), *The Number Sense*, Oxford: Oxford University Press.

Dennett, D. (1988), 'Quining qualia', in A. and E. Bisiach Marcel (eds), *Consciousness in Modern Science*, Oxford: Oxford University Press, pp. 42–75.

Dennett, D. (1991), *Consciousness Explained*, Boston: Little, Brown and Company.

Dennett, D. (1992), 'The self as a center of narrative gravity', in F. Kessel, P. Cole and D. Johnson (eds), *Self and Consciousness: Multiple Perspectives*, Hillsdale, NJ: Erlbaum, pp. 103–15.

Dennett, D. (2008), *Kinds of Minds: Toward an Understanding of Consciousness*, New York: Basic.

Dennett, D. (2017), *From Bacteria to Bach and Back: The Evolution of Minds*, London: Allen Lane.

Descartes, R. [1641, 1657] (1971), *Discourse on Method and the Meditations*, trans. F. E. Sutcliffe, Harmondsworth: Penguin Books Ltd.

Descartes, R. [1637] (1993), *Optics*, in *The Philosophical Writings of Descartes, Vol. 1*, ed. J. Cottingham, R. Stoothoff and D. Murdoch, Cambridge: Cambridge University Press, pp. 167–75.

Descartes, R. [1637] (2013), *Discourse de la méthode*, Milton Keynes: JiaHu Books.

Dewhurst, K. and N. Reeves (1978), *Friedrich Schiller: Medicine, Psychology, Literature*, Oxford: Sandford.

Di Paolo, E. (2005), 'Autopoiesis, adaptivity, teleology, agency', *Phenomenology and the Cognitive Sciences* 4.4: 429–52.

Di Paolo, E. (2009), 'Extended life', *Topoi* 28: 9–21.

Diderot, D. [1749] (1916), 'Letter on the blind for the use of those who see', in *Diderot's Early Philosophical Works*, trans. M. Jourdain, Chicago: Open Court, pp. 68–141.

Donald, M. (2001), *A Mind So Rare: The Evolution of Human Consciousness*, New York: Norton.

Drayson, Z. (2009), 'Embodied cognitive science and its implications for psychopathology', *Philosophy, Psychiatry and Psychology* 16.4: 329–40.

Dreyfus, H. (1979), *What Computers Can't Do: The Limits of Artificial Intelligence*, 2nd edn, New York: Harper & Row.

Dreyfus, H. and J. Haugeland (1978), 'Husserl and Heidegger: Philosophy's Last Stand', in M. Murray (ed.), *Heidegger and Modern Philosophy*, New Haven: Yale University Press, pp. 222–38.

Duffy, J. J. (1970), 'Problems in publishing Coleridge: James Marsh's first American edition of *Aids to Reflection*', *New England Quarterly* 43.2: 193–208.

Eisenstein, E. (1980), *The Printing Press as an Agent of Change*, Cambridge: Cambridge University Press.

Elam, H. R. and F. Ferguson (2005), *The Wordsworthian Enlightenment: Romantic Poetry and the Ecology of Reading*, Baltimore: Johns Hopkins University Press.

Ellis, R. D. (2005), *Curious Emotion: Roots of Consciousness in Motivated Action*, Philadelphia: John Benjamins Publishing.

Emerson, R. W. [1836] (2003), *Nature and Selected Essays*, ed. L. Ziff, New York: Penguin Books.

Fara, P. (2012), *Erasmus Darwin: Sex, Science, and Serendipity*, Oxford: Oxford University Press.

Ferrand, N. (2002), *Livre et lecture dans le roman français du XVIIIe siècle*, Paris: Presses universitaires de France.

Fielding, H. [1748] (1974), *The History of Tom Jones*, ed. F. Bowers and M. Battestin, 2 vols, Oxford: Clarendon Press.

Fielding, S. and J. Collier [1754] (2018), *The Cry: A New Dramatic Fable*, ed. C. Woodward, Eighteenth-Century Novels by Women series, Lexington: University Press of Kentucky.

Finucci, V. and K. Brownlee (2001), *Generation and Degeneration: Tropes of Reproduction in Literature and History from Antiquity through Early Modern Europe*, Durham, NC: Duke University Press.

Flower, L. S. and J. R. Hayes (1981), 'The pregnant pause: An enquiry into the nature of planning', *Research in the Teaching of English* 15: 229–43.

Fodor, J. and Z. W. Pylyshyn (1997), 'Connectionism and cognitive architecture: A critical analysis', in J. Haugeland (ed.), *Mind Design II*, Cambridge, MA: MIT Press, pp. 309–50.

Follett, D. (2015), 'The tension between immanence and dualism', in S. Laniel-Musitelli and T. Constantinesco (eds), *Romanticism and Philosophy: Thinking with Literature*, New York: Routledge, pp. 209–21.

Ford, J. (2005), *Coleridge on Dreaming: Romanticism, Dreams and the Medical Imagination*, Cambridge: Cambridge University Press.

Foucault, M. (1961), *Folie et déraison: histoire de la folie à l'âge classique*, Paris: Plon.

Fox, C. (ed.) (1987), *Psychology and Literature in the Eighteenth Century*, New York: AMS Press.

Fox, C. (1988), *Locke and the Scriblerians: Identity and Consciousness in Early Eighteenth-Century Britain*, Berkeley: University of California Press.

Fox, C., R. Porter and R. Wokler (1995), *Inventing Human Science: Eighteenth-Century Domains*, Berkeley: University of California Press.

Fracastroro, G. (1555), 'De sympathia', *Opera*, Venice.

Frankfurt, H. (1998), *Necessity, Autonomy, and Love*, Cambridge: Cambridge University Press.

Fraser, F. (1986), *Beloved Emma: The Life of Emma, Lady Hamilton*, London: Macmillan.

Fry, H. P. (1990), *Physics, Classics, and the Bible: Elements of the Secular and the Sacred in Barthold Heinrich Brockes' Irdisches Vergnügen in Gott, 1721*, New York: Peter Lang.

Fuchs, T. (2005), 'Corporealized and disembodied minds: A phenomenological view of the body in melancholia and schizophrenia', *Philosophy, Psychiatry and Psychology* 12.2: 95–107.

Fuller, S. (1989), *The Cognitive Turn: Sociological and Psychological Perspectives on Science*, Dordrecht: Kluwer Academic.

Funnell, P. (1982), 'The symbolical language of antiquity', in M. Clarke and N. Penny (eds), *The Arrogant Connoisseur: Richard Payne Knight, 1751–1824*, Manchester: Manchester University Press, pp. 56–64.

Gallagher, S. (2004), 'Neurocognitive models of schizophrenia: A neurophenomenological critique', *Psychopathology* 37: 8–19.

Gallagher, S. (2005), *How the Body Shapes the Mind*, Oxford: Oxford University Press.

Gallagher, S. (2008), 'Direct perception in the intersubjective context', *Consciousness and Cognition* 17.2: 535–43.

Gallagher, S. (2013), 'The socially extended mind', in M. Merritt, S. Vargar and M. Stapleton (eds), *Socializing the Extended Mind*, special edition of *Cognitive Systems Research* 25–6: 4–12.

Gallagher, S. (2017), *Enactivist Interventions: Rethinking the Mind*, Oxford: Oxford University Press.

Gallese, V. and G. Lakoff (2005), 'The brain's concepts: The role of the sensory-motor system in conceptual knowledge', *Cognitive Neuropsychology* 22.3–4: 455–79.

Gaukroger, S. (2010), *The Collapse of Mechanism and the Rise of Sensibility: Science and the Shaping of Modernity, 1680–1760*, Oxford: Oxford University Press.

Geyer-Kordesch, J. (1990), 'Georg Ernst Stahl's radical Pietist medicine and its influence on the German Enlightenment', in A. Cunningham and R. French (eds), *The Medical Enlightenment of the Eighteenth Century*, Cambridge: Cambridge University Press, pp. 67–87.

Gibbs, R. (1994), *The Poetics of Mind: Figurative Thought, Language, and Understanding*, Cambridge: Cambridge University Press.

Gibson, J. J. (1977), 'The theory of affordances', in R. Shaw and J. Bransford (eds), *Perceiving, Acting, and Knowing: Toward an Ecological Psychology*, Hillsdale, NJ: Erlbaum, pp. 67–82.

Gibson, J. J. [1979] (1986), *The Ecological Approach to Visual Perception*, Hillsdale, NJ: Erlbaum.

Gisler-Huwiler, M. (2004), 'From Naples to London: The fate of the first Hamilton collection', in S. Schütze and M. Gisler-Huwiler (eds), *The Collection of Antiquities from the Cabinet of Sir William Hamilton*, Cologne: Taschen, pp. 34–9.

Glacken, C. J. (1967), *Traces on the Rhodian Shore: Nature and Culture in Western Thought from Ancient Times to the End of the Eighteenth Century*, Berkeley: University of California Press.

Goldin-Meadow, S. (2005), *Hearing Gesture: How Our Hands Help Us Think*, Boston, MA: Harvard University Press.

Goldin-Meadow, S. and S. Wagner (2005), 'How our hands help us learn', *Trends in Cognitive Sciences* 9.5: 234–41.

Goodman, K. (2005), *Georgic Modernity and British Romanticism: Poetry and the Mediation of History*, Cambridge: Cambridge University Press.

Gottschall, J. and D. S. Wilson (eds) (2005), *The Literary Animal: Evolution and the Nature of Narrative*, Evanston: Northwestern University Press.

Gould, S. J. (1996), 'Evolution by walking', in *Dinosaur in a Haystack: Reflections in Natural History*, London: Jonathan Cape, pp. 248–59.

Grafton, A. (2003), *The Footnote: A Curious History*, Cambridge, MA: Harvard University Press.

Greenblatt, S. (1980), *Renaissance Self-Fashioning: From More to Shakespeare*, Chicago: University of Chicago Press.

Gregory, R. (1993), *Mind in Science*, New York: Penguin.

Hagstrum, J. H. (1987), 'Towards a profile of the word conscious in eighteenth-century literature', in C. Fox (ed.), *Psychology and Literature in the Eighteenth Century*, New York: AMS Press, pp. 23–50.

Halmi, N. (2001), 'Mind as microcosm', *European Romantic Review* 12.1: 43–52.

Halsband, R. (1973), *Lord Hervey: Eighteenth-Century Courtier*, Oxford: Oxford University Press.

Hamilton, P. (1983), *Coleridge's Poetics*, Stanford: Stanford University Press.

Hamilton, P. (2007), *Coleridge and German Philosophy: The Poet in the Land of Logic*, London: Continuum Press.

Haney, D. P. (2001), *The Challenge of Coleridge: Ethics and Interpretation in Romanticism and Modern Philosophy*, University Park: Pennsylvania State University Press.

Haraway, D. J. (1991), 'A manifesto for cyborgs: Science, technology and socialist feminism in the 1980s', in D. J. Haraway (ed.), *Simians, Cyborgs and Women: The Reinvention of Nature*, New York: Routledge, pp. 149–81.

Harloe, K. (2013), *Winckelmann and the Invention of Antiquity: History and Aesthetics in the Age of Altertumswissenschaft*, Oxford: Oxford University Press.

Harré, R. (2002), *Cognitive Science: A Philosophical Introduction*, London: Sage Publications.

Harrison, P. (2005), 'Physico-theology and the mixed sciences: The role of theology in early modern natural philosophy', in P. R. Anstey and J. A. Schuster (eds), *The Science of Nature in the Seventeenth Century: Patterns of Change in Early Modern Natural Philosophy*, Dordrecht: Springer, pp. 165–83.

Hartley, D. (1749), *Observations on Man, his Frame, his Duty, and his Expectations*, 2 vols, London: S. Richardson.

Hartley, D. [1749] (1971), *Observations on Man, his Frame, his Duty, and his Expectations*, 2 vols, New York: Garland.

Harvey, S. (2013), *Transatlantic Transcendentalism: Coleridge, Emerson, and Nature*, Edinburgh: Edinburgh University Press.

Haskell, F. (1987), 'The Baron d'Hancarville: An adventurer and art historian in eighteenth-century Europe', *Past and Present in Art and Taste: Selected Essays*, New Haven: Yale University Press, pp. 30–46.

Haskell, Y. (2003), *Loyola's Bees: Ideology and Industry in Jesuit Didactic Poetry*, Oxford: Oxford University Press.

Haskell, Y. (2019), 'Performing the passions: Pierre Brumoy's *De motibus animi* between didactic and dramatic poetry', in Y. Haskell and R. Garrod (eds),

Changing Hearts: Performing Jesuit Emotions between Europe, Asia and the Americas, Leiden and Boston: Brill, pp. 43–62.

Haugeland, J. (1998), 'Mind embodied and embedded', in *Having Thought: Essays in the Metaphysics of Mind*, Cambridge, MA: Harvard University Press, pp. 207–37.

Haven, R. (1959), 'Coleridge, Hartley, and the mystics', *Journal of the History of Ideas* 20.4: 477–94.

Hawley, J. (1990), 'Laurence Sterne and the circle of sciences: A study of *Tristram Shandy* and its relation to encyclopedias', PhD thesis, University of Oxford.

Hay, D. (2000), 'Master and servant in England: Using the law in the eighteenth and nineteenth centuries', in W. Steinmetz (ed.), *Private Law and Social Inequality in the Industrial Age*, Oxford: Oxford University Press, pp. 227–64.

Hayles, N. K. (1999), *How We Became Posthuman: Virtual Bodies in Cybernetics, Literature, and Informatics*, Chicago: University of Chicago Press.

Hayles, N. K. (2014), 'Cognition everywhere: The rise of the cognitive nonconscious and the costs of consciousness', *New Literary History* 45.2: 199–220.

Haywood, E. [1735] (2001), *The Dramatic Historiographer*, in *The Dramatic Historiographer and The Parrot*, ed. C. Blouch, A. Pettit and R. Sayers Hanson, from *Selected Works of Eliza Haywood*, set II, vol. 1, gen. ed. A. Pettit, 6 vols, London: Pickering and Chatto.

Hazlitt, W. (1854), *The Miscellaneous Works of William Hazlitt*, 2 vols, Philadelphia: Henry Carey Baird, <https://catalog.hathitrust.org/Record/008618315> (last accessed 31 January 2019).

Hedley, D. (2000), *Coleridge, Philosophy and Religion: Aids to Reflection and the Mirror of the Spirit*, Cambridge: Cambridge University Press.

Herder, J. G. (1989), *Italienische Reise: Briefe und Tagebuchaufzeichnungen 1788–1789*, ed. A. Meier and H. Hollmer, Munich: Beck.

Herder, J. G. (2002), *Sculpture: Some Observations on Shape and Form from Pygmalion's Creative Dream*, trans. J. Gaiger, Chicago: University of Chicago Press.

Herder, J. G. (2006), *Fourth Critical Grove*, in *Herder: Selected Writings on Aesthetics*, trans. G. Moore, Princeton: Princeton University Press, pp. 177–290.

Heringman, N. (2013), *Sciences of Antiquity: Romantic Antiquarianism, Natural History, and Knowledge Work*, Oxford: Oxford University Press.

Herman, D. (ed.) (2011), *The Emergence of Mind: Representations of Consciousness in Narrative Discourse in English*, Lincoln: University of Nebraska Press.

Hess, J. (2012), 'Coleridge's fly-catchers: Adapting commonplace-book form', *Journal of the History of Ideas* 73.3: 463–83.

Higginson, R. (2011), *A History of the Study of South Italian Black- and Red-Figure Pottery*, Oxford: Archaeopress.

Hill, J. (1754), *On the Management and Education of Children, a Series of Letters Written to a Neice; by the Honourable Juliana-Susannah Seymour* [sic], London: printed for R. Baldwin.

Hilton, N. (1983), *Literal Imagination: Blake's Vision of Words*, Berkeley: University of California Press.

Hobbes, T. (1655), *Elementorum philosophiae sectio prima de corpore*, London.

Hohwy, J. (2013), *The Predictive Mind*, Oxford: Oxford University Press.

Holland, N. (1988), *The Brain of Robert Frost: A Cognitive Approach to Literature*, London and New York: Routledge.

Holmström, K. G. (1967), *Monodrama, Attitudes, Tableaux Vivants: Studies on Some Trends of Theatrical Fashion 1770–1815*, Stockholm: Almqvist and Wiksell.

Hooper-Greenhill, E. (1992), *Museums and the Shaping of Knowledge*, London: Routledge.

Hope, J. (2010), *Shakespeare and Language: Reason, Eloquence and Artifice in the Renaissance*, London: Arden.

Huebner, B. (2014), *Macrocognition: A Theory of Distributed Minds and Collective Intentionality*, Oxford: Oxford University Press.

Hume, D. [1777] (1975), *An Enquiry Concerning Human Understanding*, ed. P. Nidditch, Oxford: Clarendon Press.

Hume, D. [1748] (2001), *An Enquiry Concerning Human* Understanding, vol. XXXVII, part 3, The Harvard Classics, New York: P. F. Collier & Son, <www.bartleby.com/37/3/> (last accessed 31 January 2019).

Hume, D. [1738] (2012), *A Treatise of Human Nature*, <https://www.gutenberg.org/files/4705/4705-h/4705-h.htm> (last accessed 31 January 2019).

Hurley, S. (1998), *Consciousness in Action*, Cambridge, MA: Harvard University Press.

Hurley, S. (2010), 'The varieties of externalism', in R. Menary (ed.), *The Extended Mind*, Cambridge, MA: MIT Press, pp. 101–53.

Hurley, S. and A. Noë (2003), 'Neural plasticity and consciousness', *Biology and Philosophy* 18: 131–68.

Hurst, S. (2003), *The Diaries of Sarah Hurst, 1759–1762: Life and Love in 18th Century Horsham*, transcribed by B. Hurst, ed. S. C. Djabri, Horsham: Horsham Museum Society.

Hutchins, E. (1995), *Cognition in the Wild*, Cambridge, MA: MIT Press.

Hutto, D. (2008), *Folk Psychological Narratives: The Sociocultural Basis of Understanding Reasons*, Cambridge, MA: MIT Press.

Hutto, D. and E. Myin (2012), *Radicalizing Enactivism: Basic Minds without Content*, Cambridge, MA: MIT Press.

Ione, A. (2016), *Art and the Brain: Plasticity, Embodiment, and the Unclosed Circle*, Leiden and Boston: Brill.

Iseli, M. (2015), *Thomas De Quincey and the Cognitive Unconscious*, Basingstoke: Palgrave.

Iser, W. (1988), *Tristram Shandy*, Cambridge: Cambridge University Press.

Israel, J. I. (2010), *A Revolution of the Mind: Radical Enlightenment and the Intellectual Origins of Modern Democracy*, Princeton: Princeton University Press.

Jackendoff, R. (1987), *Consciousness and the Computational Mind*, Cambridge, MA: MIT Press.

Jackson, H. J. (2001), *Marginalia: Readers Writing in Books*, New Haven and London: Yale University Press.

Jackson, H. J. and J. R. de J. Jackson (eds) (1995), *The Collected Works of Samuel Taylor*

Coleridge: Shorter Works and Fragments, 2 vols, Princeton: Princeton University Press.

Jackson, N. (2003), 'Critical conditions: Coleridge, "common sense", and the literature of self-experiment', *English Literary History* 70.1: 117–49.

Jackson, N. (2008), *Science and Sensation in Romantic Poetry*, Cambridge: Cambridge University Press.

Jacyna, L. S. (1983), 'Immanence or transcendence: Theories of life and organization in Britain, 1790–1835', *Isis* 74.3: 310–29.

Jager, C. (2011), 'Can we talk about consciousness again? (Emergence, natural piety, Wordsworth)', in T. Kelley (ed.), *Romantic Frictions*, Romantic Circles Praxis Series, <http://www.rc.umd.edu/praxis/frictions/HTML/praxis.2011.jager.html> (last accessed 1 February 2019).

Jajdelska, E. (2007), *Silent Reading and the Birth of the Narrator*, Toronto: University of Toronto Press.

Jajdelska, E. (2016), *Speech, Print and Decorum in Britain, 1600–1750: Studies in Communication and Social Rank*, Abingdon: Routledge.

Jeannerod, M. (1994), 'The representing brain: Neural correlates of motor intention and imagery', *Behavioural and Brain Sciences* 17.2: 187–245.

Jeannerod, M. (2001), 'Neural simulation of action: A unifying mechanism for motor cognition', *NeuroImage* 14: 103–9.

Jenkins, I. (1996), '"Contemporary minds": William Hamilton's affair with antiquity', in I. Jenkins and K. Sloan (eds), *Vases and Volcanoes: Sir William Hamilton and his Collection*, London: British Museum, pp. 40–64.

Jenkins, I. and K. Sloan (eds) (1996), *Vases and Volcanoes: Sir William Hamilton and his Collection*, London: British Museum.

Jesseph, D. (1997), *Berkeley's Philosophy of Mathematics*, Chicago: University of Chicago Press.

Johnson, M. (1987), *The Body in the Mind: The Bodily Basis of Meaning, Imagination and Reason*, Chicago: University of Chicago Press.

Kant, I. (1900–), *Kants gesammelte Schriften*, Königlich Preußische Akademie der Wissenschaften, 29 vols, Berlin: De Gruyter.

Kant, I. [1790] (1973), *Critique of Judgment*, trans. J. C. Meredith, Oxford: Clarendon Press.

Kant, I. [1784] (1985a), 'An answer to the question, what is enlightenment?', in *Kant's Political Writings*, ed. H. Reiss, trans. H. B. Nisbet, Cambridge: Cambridge University Press, pp. 54–60.

Kant, I. [1783] (1985b), *Prolegomena to any future metaphysics that will be able to come forward as science*, in *Kant's Philosophy of Material Nature*, trans. J. Ellington, Indianapolis: Hackett Publishing Co.

Kant, I. [1768] (1992a), 'Concerning the ultimate ground of the differentiation of directions in space', in *Immanuel Kant: Theoretical Philosophy, 1755–1770*, trans. D. Wolford, Cambridge: Cambridge University Press, pp. 361–72.

Kant, I. [1770] (1992b), *Inaugural Dissertation*, in *Kant's Latin Writings*, trans. L. W. Beck, New York: Peter Lang Publishing, pp. 119–60.

Kant, I. (1996a), *Critique of Pure Reason*, trans. W. S. Pluhar, Indianapolis: Hackett Publishing.

Kant, I. [1786] (1996b), 'What does it mean to orient oneself in thinking?', in *Immanuel Kant: Religion and Rational Theology*, trans. A. Wood, Cambridge: Cambridge University Press, pp. 1–18.

Kant, M. (2015), 'What do we mean when we speak about the body politic?', unpublished conference paper delivered at 'Embodied Cognition at the Goethezeit', Cambridge.

Keach, W. (2010), 'Romanticism and language', in S. Curran (ed.), *The Cambridge Companion to British Romanticism*, Cambridge: Cambridge University Press, pp. 103–26.

Keats, J. (1934), *John Keats's Anatomical and Physiological Notebook: Printed from the Holograph in the Keats Museum Hampstead*, ed. M. Buxton Forman, Oxford: Oxford University Press.

Keats, J. (1958), *The Letters of John Keats: 1814–1821*, ed. H. E. Rollins, 2 vols, Cambridge, MA: Harvard University Press.

Keats, J. (2009), *Keats's Poetry and Prose*, ed. J. N. Cox, New York: Norton.

Kemp, R. (2012), *Embodied Acting: What Neuroscience Tells Us about Performance*, London: Routledge.

King, J. (2012), 'Coleridge's *Aids to Reflection*, print culture, and mediated spiritual community', *European Romantic Review* 23.1: 43–62.

King, K. (2017), 'Frances Brooke, editor, and the making of the *Old Maid* (1755–6)', in J. Batchelor and M. Powell (eds), *Edinburgh Companion to Women and Print Media, 1690s to 1820s*, Edinburgh: Edinburgh University Press, pp. 606–31.

Kirk, R. (2005), *Zombies and Consciousness*, Oxford: Clarendon Press.

Kirsh, D. (1995), 'The intelligent use of space', *Artificial Intelligence* 73: 31–68.

Knights, B. (2010), *The Idea of the Clerisy in the Nineteenth Century*, Cambridge: Cambridge University Press.

Koehler, M. (2012), *Poetry of Attention in the Eighteenth Century*, New York: Palgrave Macmillan.

Kramnick, J. (2010), *Actions and Objects from Hobbes to Richardson*, Stanford: Stanford University Press.

Kripke, S. (1972), *Naming and Necessity*, Oxford: Blackwell.

Krueger, J. and T. Szanto (2016), 'Extended emotions', *Philosophy Compass* 11.12: 863–78.

Kukkonen, K. (2014), 'Bayesian narrative: Probability, plot and the shape of the fictional world', *Anglia* 132.4: 720–38.

Kukkonen, K. (2017), *A Prehistory of Cognitive Poetics: Neoclassicism and the Novel*, Oxford: Oxford University Press.

La Fontaine (1991), *Oeuvres complètes*, Paris: Gallimard.

La Mettrie, J. O. d. and A. Thomson (1996), *Machine Man and Other Writings*, Cambridge: Cambridge University Press.

La Mettrie, J. O. d. and A. Vartanian (1960), *L'homme machine: A Study in the Origins of an Idea*, Princeton: Princeton University Press.

Lacan, J. (1981), *The Language of the Self*, trans. A. Wilden, Baltimore: Johns Hopkins University Press.

Lada-Richards, I. (2003), 'Mobile statuary: Refractions of pantomime dancing from Callistratus to Emma Hamilton and Andrew Ducrow', *International Journal of the Classical Tradition* 10.1: 3–37.

Lakoff, G. (1987), *Women, Fire and Dangerous Things: What Categories Reveal about the Mind*, Chicago: University of Chicago Press.

Lakoff, G. (2003), 'How the body shapes thought: Thinking with an all-too-human brain', in A. J. Sanford and P. N. Johnson-Laird (eds), *The Nature and Limits of Human Understanding: The 2001 Gifford Lectures at the University of Glasgow*, London: T&T Clark, pp. 49–74.

Lakoff, G. and M. Johnson (1980), *Metaphors We Live By*, Chicago: University of Chicago Press.

Landa, L. A. (1963), 'The Shandean homunculus: The background of Sterne's "Little Gentleman"', in C. Camden (ed.), *Restoration and Eighteenth-Century Literature*, Chicago: University of Chicago Press, pp. 49–68.

Lanham, R. (1973), *Tristram Shandy: The Games of Pleasure*, Berkeley: University of California Press.

Leavis, F. R. (1962), *Two Cultures? The Significance of C. P. Snow*, London: Chatto & Windus.

Lemmings, D., H. Kerr and R. Phiddian (2016), *Passions, Sympathy and Print Culture: Public Opinion and Emotional Authenticity in Eighteenth-Century Britain*, Basingstoke: Palgrave Macmillan.

Lennox, C. (1753–4), *Shakespear Illustrated: or the Novels and Histories, On which the Plays of Shakespear are founded, collected and translated from the Original Authors, with Critical Remarks by the Author of the Female Quixote*, 3 vols, London.

Levere, T. (1971), *Affinity and Matter*, Oxford: Clarendon Press.

Levere, T. H. (2002), *Poetry Realized in Nature: Samuel Taylor Coleridge and Early Nineteenth-Century Science*, Cambridge: Cambridge University Press.

Liedtke, R. (1996), *Die Hermetik: Traditionelle Philosophie der Differenz*, Paderborn: Schöningh.

Lindop, G. (2004), 'Romantic poetry and the idea of the dream', *Keats-Shelley Review* 18: 20–37.

Littau, K. (2006), *Theories of Reading*, Cambridge: Polity Press.

Llinas, R. (2001), *I of the Vortex: From Neurons to Self*, Cambridge, MA: MIT Press.

Lloyd, H. M. (2013), *The Discourse of Sensibility: The Knowing Body in the Enlightenment*, New York: Springer.

Lochman, D. (2019), 'Pierced with passion: Brains, bodies and worlds in early modern texts', in M. Anderson and M. Wheeler (eds), *Distributed Cognition in Medieval and Renaissance Culture*, Edinburgh: Edinburgh University Press.

Locke, J. (1969), *An Essay Concerning Human Understanding*, vols 1–2, Freeport: Books for Libraries Press.

Locke, J. [1690, 1693, 3rd edn] (1975), *Essay Concerning Human Understanding*, ed. P. Nidditch, Oxford: Clarendon Press.

Logan, P. M. (1997), *Nerves and Narratives: A Cultural History of Hysteria in Nineteenth-Century British Prose*, Berkeley: University of California Press.

Londry, M. (2004), 'Our dear Miss Jenny Collier', *Times Literary Supplement*, 5 March 2004, pp. 13–14.

Lyons, C. (1997), 'The Neapolitan context of Hamilton's antiquities collection', *Journal of the History of Collections* 9.2: 229–39.

McCarthy, J. A., S. M. Hilger, H. I. Sullivan and N. Saul (2016), *The Early History of Embodied Cognition 1740–1920: The Lebenskraft-Debate and Radical Reality in German Science, Music, and Literature*, Leiden: Brill Rodopi.

McFarland, T. (1969), *Coleridge and the Pantheist Tradition*, Oxford: Clarendon Press.

Macintosh, F. (2013), 'From sculpture to vase-painting: Archaeological models for the actor', in G. Harrison and V. Liapis (eds), *Performance in Greek and Roman Theatre*, Leiden: Brill, pp. 517–33.

McKenzie, D. F. (1969), 'Printers of the mind: Some notes on bibliographical theories and printing-house practices', *Studies in Bibliography* 22: 1–75.

McKeon, R. (1942), 'Rhetoric in the middle ages', *Speculum* 17.1: 1–32.

McKitterick, D. (2003), *Print, Manuscript and the Search for Order 1450–1830*, Cambridge: Cambridge University Press.

McKusick, J. (1986), *Coleridge's Philosophy of Language*, New Haven: Yale University Press.

McLane, M. N. (2000), *Romanticism and the Human Sciences: Poetry, Population, and the Discourse of the Species*, Cambridge: Cambridge University Press.

Makdisi, S. (2015), *Reading William Blake*, Cambridge: Cambridge University Press.

Malabou, C. (2008), *What Should We Do with Our Brain?*, trans. S. Rand, New York: Fordham University Press.

Malachuk, D. S. (2000), 'Coleridge's republicanism and the aphorism in *Aids to Reflection*', *Studies in Romanticism* 39.3: 397–417.

Malafouris, L. (2004), *The Cognitive Basis of Material Engagement: Where Brain, Body and Culture Conflate*, Cambridge: McDonald Institute Monographs.

Malafouris, L. and C. Renfrew (2010), *Cognitive Life of Things: Recasting the Boundaries of the Mind*, Cambridge: McDonald Institute.

Malafouris, L. and C. Renfrew (2013), *How Things Shape the Mind: A Theory of Material Management*, Cambridge, MA: MIT Press.

Manley, K. A. (2012), 'Subscription and circulating libraries', in S. W. Brown and W. McDougall (eds), *The Edinburgh History of the Book in Scotland, Volume 2: Enlightenment and Expansion 1707–1800*, Edinburgh: Edinburgh University Press, pp. 337–71.

Maravati, A. and A. Iriki (2004), 'Tools for the body (schema)', *Trends in Cognitive Science* 8.2: 79–86.

Marsh, C. (2002), 'Sacred space in England, 1560–1640: The view from the pew', *Journal of Ecclesiastical History* 53.2: 286–311.

Marsh, R. (1959), 'The second part of Hartley's system', *Journal of the History of Ideas* 20.2: 264–73.

Maturana, H. R. and F. J. Varela (1980), *Autopoiesis and Cognition: The Realization of the Living*, Dordrecht: D. Reidel.

Mayne, Z. (1728), *Two Dissertations Concerning Sense, and the Imagination. With an Essay on Consciousness*, London: printed for J. Tonson.

Mazzeo, T. J. (2013), *Plagiarism and Literary Property in the Romantic Period*, University Park: Pennsylvania State University Press.

Mee, J. (2011), *Conversable Worlds: Literature, Contention and Community 1762–1830*, Oxford: Oxford University Press.

Menary, R. (2007), *Cognitive Integration: Mind and Cognition Unbounded*, Basingstoke: Palgrave Macmillan.

Menary, R. (ed.) (2010), *The Extended Mind*, Cambridge, MA: MIT Press.

Mensch, J. (2004), 'Kant on Truth', *Idealistic Studies* 34.2: 163–72.

Mensch, J. (2006), 'Kant and the problem of idealism: On the significance of the Göttingen Review', *The Southern Journal of Philosophy* 44.2: 297–317.

Mensch, J. (2013), *Kant's Organicism: Epigenesis and the Development of Critical Philosophy*, Chicago: University of Chicago Press.

Merlin, D. (2001), *A Mind So Rare: The Evolution of Human Consciousness*, New York: Norton.

Metzinger, T. (2004), *Being No One: The Self Model Theory of Subjectivity*, Cambridge, MA: MIT Press.

Miall, D. S. (1993), '"I see it feelingly": Coleridge's debt to Hartley', in T. Fulford and M. Paley (eds), *Coleridge's Visionary Languages: Essays in Honour of J. B. Beer*, Rochester, NY: Brewer, pp. 151–63.

Mill, J. S. (1969), *Essays on Ethics, Religion, and Society*, ed. J. M. Robson, Toronto: University of Toronto Press.

Milnes, T. (2010), *The Truth about Romanticism: Pragmatism and Idealism in Keats, Shelley, Coleridge*, Cambridge: Cambridge University Press.

Miner, P. (2002), 'Blake's London: Times and spaces', *Studies in Romanticism* 41.2: 279–316.

Mitchell, R. (2013), *Experimental Life: Vitalism in Romantic Science and Literature*, Baltimore: Johns Hopkins University Press.

Monro, A. (1783), *Observations on the Structure and Functions of the Nervous System*, Edinburgh: William Creech.

Montini, D. (2014), 'Language and letters in Samuel Richardson's correspondence', *Journal of Early Modern Studies* 3: 173–98.

Moore, G. (2006), *Herder: Selected Writings on Aesthetics*, Princeton: Princeton University Press.

Moravia, S. (1978), 'From homme machine to homme sensible: Changing eighteenth-century models of man's image', *Journal of the History of Ideas* 39: 45–60.

Moretti, F. (2000), 'Conjectures on world literature', *New Left Review* 1: 54–68.

Moretti, F. (2013), *Distant Reading*, London: Verso.

Morton, R. (1720), *Phthisiologia: Or, A Treatise of Consumptions*, London: W. Innys.

Most, G. (2002), 'Preface', in G. Most (ed.), *Disciplining Classics: Altertumswissenschaft als Beruf*, Göttingen: Vandenhoeck & Ruprecht.

Mullan, J. (1990), *Sentiment and Sociability: The Language of Feeling in the Eighteenth Century*, Oxford: Clarendon Press.

Muri, A. (2006), *The Enlightenment Cyborg: A History of Communications and Control in the Human Machine, 1660–1830*, Toronto: University of Toronto Press.

Murley, S. (1998), 'The use of marginalia in Coleridge's *Aids to Reflection*: Collaboration as supplementation', *European Romantic Review* 9.2: 243–52.

Natarajan, U. (1998), 'One undivided spirit: Hazlitt, Coleridge, and the unity of imagination', *Studies in Romanticism* 37.2: 235–58.

Nellhaus, T. (2006), 'Performance strategies, image schemas, and communication frameworks', in B. McConachie and F. E. Hart (eds), *Performance and Cognition: Theatre Studies and the Cognitive Turn*, London: Taylor & Francis, pp. 76–94.

Noë, A. (2004), *Action in Perception*, Cambridge, MA: MIT Press.

Noë, A. (2009), *Out of Our Heads: Why You Are Not Your Brain, and Other Lessons from the Biology of Consciousness*, New York: Hill & Wang.

Noë, A. (2015), *Strange Tools: Art and Human Nature*, New York: Hill & Wang.

Nolta, D. (1997), 'The body of the collector and the collected body in William Hamilton's Naples', *Eighteenth-Century Studies* 31.1: 108–14.

Norton, R. E. (1991), *Herder's Aesthetics and the European Enlightenment*, Ithaca: Cornell University Press.

Nussbaum, F. (2010), *Rival Queens: Actresses, Performance, and the Eighteenth-Century British Theatre*, Pennsylvania: Philadelphia University Press.

Nussbaum, M. C. (2010), *Not for Profit: Why Democracy Needs the Humanities*, Princeton: Princeton University Press.

Nusselder, A. (2009), *Interface Fantasy: A Lacanian Cyborg Ontology*, Cambridge, MA: MIT Press.

Nuttall, A. D. (1974), *A Common Sky: Philosophy and the Literary Imagination*, Berkeley: University of California Press.

Nuzzo, A. (2008), *Ideal Embodiment: Kant's Theory of Sensibility*, Bloomington: Indiana University Press.

Nye, E. (2011), *Mime, Music and Drama on the Eighteenth-Century Stage: The ballet d'action*, Cambridge: Cambridge University Press.

O'Regan, J. K. and A. Noë (2001), 'A sensorimotor account of vision and visual consciousness', *Behavioral and Brain Sciences* 24: 939–1031.

Odling-Smee, J., K. Laland and M. Feldman (2003), *Niche Construction: The Neglected Process in Evolution*, Princeton: Princeton University Press.

Ortolano, G. (2005), 'F. R. Leavis, science, and the abiding crisis of modern civilisation', *History of Science* 43: 161–85.

Outram, D. (1995), *The Enlightenment*, Cambridge: Cambridge University Press.

Pagden, A. (2013), *The Enlightenment: And Why It Still Matters*, Oxford: Oxford University Press.

Pashler, H. E. (1998), *Attention*, Hove: Psychology Press.

Paster, G. K., K. Rowe and M. Floyd-Wilson (eds) (2004), *Reading the Early Modern*

Passions: Chapters in the Cultural History of Emotion, Philadelphia: University of Pennsylvania Press.

Patey, D. L. (1997), 'The institution of criticism in the eighteenth century', in H. B. Nisbet and C. Rawson (eds), *The Cambridge History of Literary Criticism*, Cambridge: Cambridge University Press, vol. 4, pp. 3–31.

Pearce, S. (1992), *Museums, Objects and Collections: A Cultural Study*, Leicester: Leicester University Press.

Pepys, S. (1971–83), *The Diary of Samuel Pepys*, ed. R. C. Latham and W. Matthews, 11 vols, London.

Perry, S. (1999), *Coleridge and the Uses of Division*, Oxford: Clarendon Press.

Petronius (1996), *The Satyricon*, trans. P. G. Walsh, Oxford: Clarendon Press.

Petsalis-Diomidis, A. (2014), 'Ancient Greek vases and modern British bodies', unpublished paper, APGRD seminar series, University of Oxford.

Phillips, N. M. (ed.) (2016a), *Distraction: Problems of Attention in Eighteenth-Century Literature*, Baltimore: Johns Hopkins University Press.

Phillips, N. M. (2016b), 'Scattered Attention: Distraction and the rhythm of cognitive overload', in N. M. Phillips (ed.), *Distraction: Problems of Attention in Eighteenth-Century Literature*, Baltimore: Johns Hopkins University Press, pp. 97–131.

Phillipson, T. (2017), 'Calculators: Latest gadget to obsolete relic', History of Distributed Cognition Project, <http://www.hdc.ed.ac.uk/lectures/calculators-latest-gadget-obsolete-relic> (last accessed 1 February 2019).

Pickering, M. J. and S. Garrod (2013), 'An integrated theory of language production and comprehension', *Behavioral and Brain Sciences* 36: 329–92.

Pinch, A. (1996), *Strange Fits of Passion: Epistemologies of Emotion, Hume to Austen*, Stanford: Stanford University Press.

Pocock, J. G. A. (1976), 'The classical theory of deference', *The American Historical Review* 81.3: 516–23.

Poe, E. A. (1836), 'Recollections of Coleridge', *Southern Literary Messenger* 2 (June 1836): 451–3.

Porée, C. (1726), *L'homme instruit par le spectacle, ou le théâtre changé en école de vertu*, Paris.

Porée, C. (1736), *De libris qui vulgo dicuntur romanenses oratio*, Paris.

Porée, C. (2000), *De theatro/Discours sur les spectacles*, ed. E. Flamarion, trans. P. Brumoy, Paris: Champion.

Price, C. J. (2012), 'A review and synthesis of the first 20 years of PET and fMRI studies of heard speech, spoken language and reading', *NeuroImage* 62: 816–47.

Prickett, S. (1979), 'Coleridge and the idea of the clerisy', in W. B. Crawford (ed.), *Reading Coleridge: Approaches and Applications*, Ithaca: Cornell University Press, pp. 252–73.

Priestley, J. (1778), *Disquisitions Relating to Matter and Spirit*, London: British Library.

Priestley, J. [1777] (2005), *Disquisitions Relating to Matter and Spirit*, Whitefish, MT: Kessinger Publishing.

Putnam, H. (1975), 'The meaning of "meaning"', in K. Gunderson (ed.), *Language, Mind, and Knowledge*, Minneapolis: University of Minnesota Press, pp. 131–93.

Puttenham, G. (1589), *The Arte of English Poesie*, London.

Quesnel, P. (1755), *The Spiritual Quixote*, London.

Quinlan, S. (2013), 'Shocked sensibility: The nerves, the will, and altered states in Sade's *L'Histoire de Juliette*', *Eighteenth-Century Fiction* 25: 533–56.

Radway, J. A. (1984), *Reading the Romance: Women, Patriarchy, and Popular Literature*, Chapel Hill: University of North Carolina Press.

Ramachandran, V. S. (2006), 'Mirror neurons and the brain in the vat', *Edge: The Third Culture* 176, <http://edge.org/3rd_culture/ramachandran06/ramachandran06_index.html> (last accessed 1 February 2019).

Ramachandran, V. S. and D. R. Ramachandran (1996), 'Synaesthesia in phantom limbs induced with mirrors', *Proceedings: Biological Sciences* 263: 377–86.

Rauser, A. (2015), 'Living statues and neoclassical dress in late eighteenth-century Naples', *Art History* 38.3: 462–87.

Raven, J. (1988), 'New reading histories, print culture and the identification of change: The case of eighteenth-century England', *Social History* 23.3: 268–87.

Reeves, C. (2010), *A Cultural History of the Human Body in the Age of the Enlightenment*, Oxford and New York: Berg.

Reid, C. (2005), 'Speaking candidly: Rhetoric, politics and the meanings of candour in the later eighteenth century', *British Journal for Eighteenth-Century Studies* 28: 67–82.

Revonsuo, A. (2000), 'Prospects for a scientific research program on consciousness', in T. Metzinger (ed.), *Neural Correlates of Consciousness*, Cambridge, MA: MIT Press, pp. 57–76.

Richards, R. J. (2002), *The Romantic Conception of Life*, Chicago: University of Chicago Press.

Richardson, A. (2001), *British Romanticism and the Science of Mind*, Cambridge: Cambridge University Press.

Richardson, A. (2010), *The Neural Sublime*, Baltimore: Johns Hopkins University Press.

Richardson, A. and E. Spolsky (2004), *The Work of Fiction: Cognition, Culture, and Complexity*, Aldershot: Ashgate.

Richardson, R. C. (1982), 'The "Scandal" of Cartesian interactionism', *Mind* 91.361: 20–37.

Richardson, S. [1741] (2012), *Pamela in her Exalted Condition*, ed. A. Rivero, vol. 3 of *The Works and Correspondence of Samuel Richardson*, Cambridge: Cambridge University Press.

Richter, K. (2002), 'Teleskop und Mikroskop in Brockes' *Irdischem Vergnügen in Gott*', in P. A. Alt, A. Kosenina and W. Riedel (eds), *Prägnanter Moment. Studien zur deutschen Literatur der Aufklärung und Klassik: Festschrift für Hans-Jürgen Schings*, Würzburg: Königshausen und Neumann, pp. 3–18.

Riskin, J. (2002), *Science in the Age of Sensibility: The Sentimental Empiricists of the French Enlightenment*, Chicago: University of Chicago Press.

Riskin, J. (2015), *The Restless Clock: A History of the Centuries-Long Argument over What Makes Living Things Tick*, Chicago: University of Chicago Press.

Rivers, I. and D. Wykes (eds) (2011), *Dissenting Praise: Religious Dissent and the Hymn in England and Wales*, Oxford: Oxford University Press.

Rizzolatti, G. and C. Sinigaglia (2008), *Mirrors in the Brain: How our Minds Share Actions and Emotions*, trans. F. Anderson, Oxford: Oxford University Press.

Roach, J. (1993), *The Player's Passion: Studies in the Science of Acting*, Ann Arbor: University of Michigan Press.

Roberston, L. A. (2011), 'Soulful sensorium: The body in early British romantic brain science', *La Questione Romantica* 3.1: 17–28.

Robinson, B. (1907), *The Abdominal and Pelvic Brain: With Automatic Visceral Ganglia*, Chicago: Frank S. Betz.

Roby, C. (2018), 'Physical sciences: Ptolemy's extended mind', in M. Anderson, D. Cairns and M. Sprevak (eds), *Distributed Cognition in Classical Antiquity*, Edinburgh: Edinburgh University Press, pp. 37–56.

Roche, D. (2006), 'Encyclopedias and the diffusion of knowledge', in M. Goldie and R. Wokler (eds), *The Cambridge History of Eighteenth-Century Political Thought*, Cambridge: Cambridge University Press, pp. 172–94.

Roger, J. and K. R. Benson (1997), *The Life Sciences in Eighteenth-Century French Thought*, Stanford: Stanford University Press.

Rosenberg, J. (1997), 'Connectionism and cognition', in J. Haugeland (ed.), *Mind Design II: Philosophy, Psychology, Artificial Intelligence*, Cambridge, MA: MIT Press, pp. 293–308.

Ross, D. (2007), *Distributed Cognition and the Will: Individual Volition and Social Context*, Cambridge, MA: MIT Press.

Ross, T. (1996), 'The emergence of "literature": Making and reading the English canon in the eighteenth century', *ELH* 63: 397–422.

Rousseau, G. S. (1968), 'Science and the discovery of the imagination in Enlightened England', *Eighteenth-Century Studies* 3.1: 108–35.

Rousseau, G. S. (1972), *Organic Form: The Life of an Idea*, London: Routledge & Kegan Paul.

Rousseau, G. S. (1975), 'Nerves, spirits and fibres: Toward the origins of sensibility', in R. F. Brissenden (ed.), *Studies in the Eighteenth Century*, Canberra: Australian National University Press, pp. 137–57.

Rousseau, G. S. (1989), 'Discourses of the nerve', in F. Amrine (ed.), *Literature and Science as Modes of Expression*, Dordrecht: Kluwer Academic, pp. 29–60.

Rousseau, G. S. (1990), *The Languages of Psyche: Mind and Body in Enlightenment Thought – The Clark Library Lectures, 1985–1986*, Berkeley: University of California Press.

Rousseau, G. S. (1991), *Enlightenment Borders: Pre- and Post-Modern Discourses: Medical, Scientific*, Manchester: Manchester University Press.

Rousseau, G. S. (1993), 'The perpetual crises of modernism and the traditions of Enlightenment vitalism: With a note on Mikhail Bakhtin', in F. Burwick and P. Douglass (eds), *The Crisis of Modernism: Bergson and the Vitalist Controversy*, Cambridge: Cambridge University Press, pp. 15–97.

Rousseau, G. S. (2004), *Nervous Acts: Essays on Literature, Culture and Sensibility*, Basingstoke: Palgrave Macmillan.

Rousseau, G. S. (2007a), 'Brainomania', *British Journal for Eighteenth-Century Studies* 30.2: 161–92.

Rousseau, G. S. (2007b), 'Temperament and the long shadow of nerves in the eighteenth century', in H. Whitaker, C. U. M. Smith and S. Finger (eds), *Brain, Mind and Medicine*, New York: Springer, pp. 353–70.

Rowlands, M. (1999), *The Body in Mind*, Cambridge: Cambridge University Press.

Rowlands, M. (2010), *The New Science of the Mind: From Extended Mind to Embodied Phenomenology*, Cambridge, MA: MIT Press.

Rupert, R. (2009), *Cognitive Systems and the Extended Mind*, Oxford: Oxford University Press.

Rupert, R. (2011), 'Empirical arguments for group minds: A critical appraisal', *Philosophy Compass* 6.9: 630–9.

Rupert, R. (2013), 'Memory, natural kinds, and cognitive extension', *Review of Philosophy and Psychology* 4.1: 25–47.

Rupert, R. (2014), 'Against group cognitive states', in S. Chant, F. Hindriks and G. Preyer (eds), *From Individual to Collective Intentionality: New Essays*, Oxford: Oxford University Press, pp. 97–111.

Russell, G. (2007), *Women, Sociability and Theatre in Georgian London*, Cambridge: Cambridge University Press.

Sacks, O. (1995), *An Anthropologist on Mars*, New York: Vintage Press.

Sahai, S. (2011), 'Reading dance, performing research: Meaning, interpretation, context, and recontextualisation in dance performance and research', in U. Sarkar Munsi and S. Burridge (eds), *Traversing Tradition: Celebrating Dance in India*, New Delhi: Routledge, pp. 104–23.

Santamaria-Garcia, H., M. Burgaleta and N. Sebastian-Galles (2015), 'Neuroanatomical markers of social hierarchy recognition in humans: A combined ERP/MRI study', *Journal of Neuroscience* 35.30: 10843–50.

Sassen, B. (ed.) (2000), *Kant's Early Critics: The Empiricist Critique of Theoretical Philosophy*, Cambridge: Cambridge University Press.

Scheler, M. (1973), *The Nature of Sympathy*, Hamden, CT: Archon Books.

Schnapp, A. (1992), 'La pratique de la collection et ses conséquences sur l'histoire de l'Antiquité. Le chevalier d'Hancarville', in A. F. Laurens and K. Pomian (eds), *L'Anticomanié: la collection d'antiquités aux 18e et 19e siècles*, Paris: École des Hautes Études, pp. 209–18.

Schnapp, A. (2013), 'The antiquarian culture of eighteenth-century Naples as a laboratory of new ideas', in C. Mattusch (ed.), *Rediscovering the Ancient World on the Bay of Naples, 1710–1890*, New Haven: Yale University Press, pp. 209–18.

Schofield, R. (ed.) (1978), 'Joseph Priestley on sensation and perception', in P. K. Machamer and R. G. Turnbull (eds), *Studies in Perception: Interrelations in the History of Philosophy and Science*, Columbus: Ohio State University Press, pp. 336–54.

Schrödinger, E. (1944), *What Is Life? The Physical Aspect of the Living Cell*, Cambridge: Cambridge University Press.

Schultz, J. [1784] (1995), *Exposition of Kant's Critique of Pure Reason*, trans. J. Morrison, Ottawa: University of Ottawa Press.

Schütze, S. (2004), 'Collection of Etruscan, Greek, and Roman antiquities from the cabinet of the Hon. W. Hamilton', in S. Schütze and M. Gisler-Huwiler (eds), *The Collection of Antiquities from the Cabinet of Sir William Hamilton*, Cologne: Taschen, pp. 6–33.

Schütze, S. and M. Gisler-Huwiler (eds) (2004), *The Collection of Antiquities from the Cabinet of Sir William Hamilton*, Cologne: Taschen.

Sgard, J. and G. Sheridan (1992), 'Préface', in G. H. Bougeant, *Voyage merveilleux du Prince Fan-Férédin dans la Romancie*, Saint-Étienne: Publications de l'Université de Saint-Étienne, pp. 7–31.

Sha, R. C. (2013), 'Romantic physiology and the work of Romantic imagination: Hypothesis and speculation in science and Coleridge', *European Romantic Review* 24.4: 403–19.

Shaffer, E. (1980), *'Kubla Khan' and the Fall of Jerusalem: The Mythological School in Biblical Criticism and Secular Literature, 1770–1880*, Cambridge: Cambridge University Press.

Shakespeare, W. [1604–5] (2006), *Hamlet*, ed. A. Thompson and N. Taylor, The Arden Shakespeare, London: Arden.

Shanahan, M. (2010), *Embodiment and the Inner Life: Cognition and Consciousness in the Space of Possible Minds*, Oxford: Oxford University Press.

Shanton, K. and A. Goldman (2010), 'Simulation theory', Hoboken: John Wiley & Sons, <http://fas-philosophy.rutgers.edu/goldman/Simulation%20Theory.pdf> (last accessed 1 February 2019).

Sheehan, J. and D. Wahrman (2015), *Invisible Hands: Self-Organization and the Eighteenth Century*, Chicago: University of Chicago Press.

Sheets-Johnstone, M. (2011), *The Primacy of Movement*, 2nd edn, Amsterdam: John Benjamins.

Shelley, P. B. [wr. 1821/pub. 1840] (2001), 'A defence of poetry', *English Essays: Sidney to Macaulay*, vol. XXVII, The Harvard Classics, New York: P. F. Collier & Son, <http://www.bartleby.com/27/23.html> (last accessed 1 February 2019).

Shelley, P. B. (2010), *Percy Bysshe Shelley: A Longman Cultural Edition*, ed. S. Behrendt, New York: Pearson.

Simpson, M. C. T. (2012), 'Institutional libraries', in S. W. Brown and W. McDougall (eds), *The Edinburgh History of the Book in Scotland, Volume 2: Enlightenment and Expansion 1707–1800*, Edinburgh: Edinburgh University Press, pp. 323–30.

Sinding, M. (2012), '"A sermon in the midst of a smutty tale": Blending in genres of speech, writing, and literature', in I. Jaén and J. J. Simon (eds), *Cognitive Literary Studies: Current Themes and New Directions*, Austin: University of Texas Press, pp. 145–61.

Siskin, C. and W. Warner (2010), 'This is Enlightenment: An invitation in the form of an argument', in C. Siskin and W. Warner (eds), *This Is Enlightenment*, Chicago: University of Chicago Press, pp. 1–33.

Slaby, J. (2014), 'Emotions and the extended mind', in C. von Scheve and M. Salmela (eds), *Collective Emotions: Perspectives from Psychology, Philosophy, and Sociology*, Oxford: Oxford University Press, pp. 32–46.

Slaney, H. (2016), 'Perceiving in depth: Landscape, sculpture, ruin', in S. Butler (ed.), *Deep Classics: Rethinking Classical Reception*, London: Bloomsbury, pp. 87–105.

Slaney, H. (2017), 'In the body of the beholder: Herder's aesthetics and classical sculpture', in A. Purves (ed.), *Touch and the Ancient Senses*, London: Routledge, pp. 105–20.

Small, H. (2013), *The Value of the Humanities*, Oxford: Oxford University Press.

Smith, A. [1759] (1976), *Theory of Moral Sentiments*, Oxford: Oxford University Press.

Smith, A. [1762] (1978), *Lectures on Jurisprudence*, ed. R. L. Meek, D. D. Raphael and P. G. Stein, Oxford: Oxford University Press.

Smith, C. U. M. (1999), 'Coleridge's "Theory of Life"', *Journal of the History of Biology* 32.1: 31–50.

Snow, C. P. [1959] (1993), *The Two Cultures*, ed. S. Collini, Cambridge: Cambridge University Press.

Solomon, R. (2004), 'Emotions, thoughts, and feelings', in R. Solomon (ed.), *Thinking About Feeling*, Oxford: Oxford University Press, pp. 76–90.

Sparkes, B. (1996), *The Red and the Black: Studies in Greek Pottery*, London: Routledge.

Spolsky, E. (1993), *Gaps in Nature: Literary Interpretation and the Modular Mind*, Albany: State University of New York Press.

Sprevak, M. (2009), 'Extended cognition and functionalism', *The Journal of Philosophy* 106.9: 503–27.

Sprevak, M. (2011), 'Neural sufficiency, reductionism, and cognitive neuropsychiatry', *Philosophy, Psychiatry and Psychology* 18.4: 339–44.

Spufford, M. (1981), *Small Books and Pleasant Histories*, Cambridge: Cambridge University Press.

Starr, G. (2013), *Feeling Beauty: The Neuroscience of Aesthetic Experience*, Cambridge, MA: MIT Press.

Stein, E. [1917] (1989), *On the Problem of Empathy*, Washington, DC: ICS Publications.

Stephanson, R. and D. N. Wagner (2015), *The Secrets of Generation: Reproduction in the Long Eighteenth Century*, Toronto: University of Toronto Press.

Sterelny, K. (2003), *Thought in a Hostile World: The Evolution of Human Cognition*, Malden: Blackwell.

Sterelny, K. (2010), 'Minds: Extended or scaffolded?', *Phenomenology and the Cognitive Sciences* 9: 465–81.

Sterelny, K. (2014), *The Evolved Apprentice: How Evolution Made Humans Unique*, Cambridge, MA: MIT Press.

Sterne, L. (1930), *A Facsimile Reproduction of a Unique Catalogue of Laurence Sterne's Library*, London: J. Tregaskis.

Sterne, L. (1978–84), *The Life and Opinions of Tristram Shandy, Gentleman, The Florida Edition of the Works of Laurence Sterne*, 3 vols, Gainesville: University Press of Florida.

Sterne, L. (2009), *The Letters, The Florida Edition of the Works of Laurence Sterne*, 2 vols, Gainesville: University Press of Florida.

Stewart, P. (1973), *Le Masque et la parole: le langage de l'amour au XVIIIe siècle*, Paris: Corti.

Stillinger, J. (1991), *Multiple Authorship and the Myth of Solitary Genius*, Oxford: Oxford University Press.

Sutcliffe, F. E. (1971), 'Introduction', in R. Descartes, *Discourse on Method and the Meditations*, Harmondsworth: Penguin Books, pp. 7–23.

Sutton, J. (1998), *Philosophy and Memory Traces: Descartes to Connectionism*, Cambridge: Cambridge University Press.

Sutton, J. (2006), 'Distributed cognition: Domains and dimensions', *Pragmatics and Cognition* 14.2: 235–47.

Sutton, J. (2010), 'Exograms and interdisciplinarity: History, the extended mind, and the civilizing process', in R. Menary (ed.), *The Extended Mind*, Cambridge, MA: MIT Press, pp. 189–225.

Swearingen, J. (1977), *Reflexivity in Tristram Shandy: An Essay in Phenomenological Criticism*, New Haven: Yale University Press.

Tallis, R. (2011), *Aping Mankind: Neuromania, Darwinitis and the Misrepresentation of Humanity*, Durham: Acumen.

Taylor, C. (1989), *Sources of the Self*, Cambridge: Cambridge University Press.

Taylor, D. (2003), *The Archive and the Repertoire: Performing Cultural Memory in the Americas*, Durham, NC: Duke University Press.

Terrall, M. (1996), 'Salon, academy, and boudoir: Generation and desire in Maupertuis's science of life', *Isis* 87.2: 217–29.

Thomasius, C. [1699] (2004), *Versuch vom Wesen des Geistes oder Grund-Lehren so wohl zur natürlichen Wissenschaft als der Sitten-Lehre*, ed. K. Zenker, Hildesheim: Olms.

Thompson, E. (2005), 'Sensorimotor subjectivity and the enactive approach to experience', *Phenomenology and the Cognitive Sciences* 4: 407–27.

Thompson, E. (2007), *Mind in Life: Biology, Phenomenology, and the Sciences of Mind*, Cambridge, MA: Harvard University Press.

Thompson, E. (2011), 'Reply to commentaries', *Journal of Consciousness Studies* 18.5–6: 1–40.

Thompson, E. (2015), *Waking, Dreaming, Being*, New York: Columbia University Press.

Thompson, E. and M. Stapleton (2008), 'Making sense of sense-making: Reflections on enactive and extended mind theories' *Topoi* 28: 23–30.

Thomson, A. (1981), *Materialism and Society in the Mid-Eighteenth Century: La Mettrie's Discours preliminaire*, Geneva: Librairie Droz.

Tierney-Hynes, R. (2012), *Novel Minds: Philosophers and Romance Readers, 1680–1740*, Basingstoke: Palgrave.

Tollefsen, D. P. (2006), 'From extended mind to collective mind', *Cognitive Systems Research* 7.2: 140–50.

Touchette, L.-A. (2000), 'Sir William Hamilton's "pantomime mistress": Emma Hamilton and her attitudes', in C. Hornsby (ed.), *The Impact of Italy: The Grand Tour and Beyond*, London: British School at Rome, pp. 123–46.

Traugott, J. (1954), *Tristram Shandy's World: Sterne's Philosophical Rhetoric*, Berkeley: University of California Press.

Trendall, A. D. (1989), *Red Figure Vases of South Italy and Sicily: A Handbook*, London: Thames & Hudson.

Tribble, E. (2005), 'Distributing cognition in the Globe', *Shakespeare Quarterly* 56.2: 135–55.

Tribble, E. (2011), *Cognition in the Globe: Attention and Memory in Shakespeare's Theatre*, Basingstoke and New York: Palgrave Macmillan.

Tribble, E. and N. Keene (2011), *Cognitive Ecologies and the History of Remembering: Religion, Education and Memory in Early Modern England*, Basingstoke and New York: Palgrave Macmillan.

Tribble, E. B. and J. Sutton (2012), 'Minds in and out of time: Memory, embodied skill, anachronism, and performance', *Textual Practice* 26.4: 587–607.

Trompf, G., J. Gough and O. Eckhart (1988), 'Western folktales in changing Melanesia', *Folklore* 99.2: 204–20.

Tsur, R. (1992), *Towards a Theory of Cognitive Poetics*, Amsterdam: North-Holland.

Turbayne, C. (1955), 'Kant's refutation of dogmatic idealism', *The Philosophical Quarterly* 5: 225–43.

Turner, M. (1991), *Reading Minds: The Study of English in the Age of Cognitive Science*, Princeton: Princeton University Press.

Turner, M. (1996), *The Literary Mind: The Origins of Thought and Language*, Oxford: Oxford University Press.

Turner, T. (1984), *The Diary of Thomas Turner 1754–1765*, ed. D. Vaisey, Oxford: Oxford University Press.

Vallins, D. (2000), *Coleridge and the Psychology of Romanticism: Feeling and Thought*, Basingstoke: Macmillan.

Van Cleve, J. and R. E. Frederick (eds) (1991), *The Philosophy of Right and Left: Incongruent Counterparts and the Nature of Space*, Dordrecht: Springer Verlag.

Varela, F. J. (1991), 'Organism: A meshwork of selfless selves', in A. I. Tauber (ed.), *Organism and the Origins of Self*, Dordrecht: Kluwer Academic, pp. 79–107.

Varela, F. J. and J. P. Dupuy (1992), *Understanding Origins: Contemporary Views on the Origin of Life, Mind and Society*, Dordrecht: Kluwer Academic.

Varela, F. J., H. R. Maturana and R. Uribe (1981), 'Autopoiesis: The origin of living systems, its characterization and a model', *Cybernetics Forum* 10.2–3: 7–13.

Varela, F. J., E. Thompson and E. Rosch (1991), *The Embodied Mind: Cognitive Science and Human Experience*, Cambridge, MA: MIT Press.

Vermeule, B. (2010), *Why Do We Care about Literary Characters?*, Baltimore: Johns Hopkins University Press.

Vickers, N. (2004), *Coleridge and the Doctors: 1795–1806*, Oxford: Oxford University Press.

Vygotsky, L. [1930] (1978), *Mind and Society: The Development of Higher Mental Processes*, Cambridge, MA: Harvard University Press.

Vygotsky, L. [1934] (1986), *Thought and Language*, ed. A. Kozulin, trans. E. Hanfmann and G. Vakar, Cambridge, MA: MIT Press.

Wade, N. (2000), *The Emergence of Neuroscience in the 19th Century*, London: Routledge/Thoemmes Press.

Walls, L. D. (2008), 'Ralph Waldo Emerson and Coleridge's American legacy', in J. Vigus and J. Wright (eds), *Coleridge's Afterlives*, Basingstoke: Macmillan, pp. 112–27.

Walsh, M. (2009), 'Scholarly editing: Patristics, classical literature and Shakespeare', in M. Suarez and M. Turner (eds), *The Cambridge History of the Book in Britain 1695–1830*, vol. 5, Cambridge: Cambridge University Press, pp. 684–98.

Ward, D. (2012), 'Enjoying the spread: Conscious externalism reconsidered', *Mind* 121.483: 731–51.

Ward, D. (2014), 'Enactivism', History of Distributed Cognition Project, <http://www.hdc.ed.ac.uk/seminars/enactivism> (last accessed 1 February 2019).

Waugh, P. (1984), *Metafiction: The Theory and Practice of Self-Conscious Fiction*, London: Methuen.

Weir, T. H. (2012), *Monism: Science, Philosophy, Religion, and the History of a Worldview*, Basingstoke: Palgrave Macmillan.

Welle, F. (2009), *Der irdische Blick durch das Fernrohr. Literarische Wahrnehmungsexperimente vom 17. bis zum 20. Jahrhundert*, Würzburg: Königshausen und Neumann.

Wellek, R. [1955] (1981), *A History of Modern Criticism 1790–1950, Volume 2: The Romantic Age*, Cambridge: Cambridge University Press.

Wengelin, Å., M. Torrance, K. Holmqvist, S. Simpson, D. Galbraith, V. Johansson and R. Johansson (2009), 'Combined eyetracking and keystroke-logging methods for studying cognitive processes in text production', *Behavior Research Methods* 41.2: 337–51.

Wheeler, M. (2004), 'Is language the ultimate artefact?', *Language Sciences* 26.6: 693–715.

Wheeler, M. (2005), *Reconstructing the Cognitive World: The Next Step*, Cambridge, MA: MIT Press.

Wheeler, M. (2010a), 'In defence of extended functionalism', in R. Menary (ed.), *The Extended Mind*, Cambridge, MA: MIT Press, pp. 245–70.

Wheeler, M. (2010b), 'Mind, things and materiality', in L. Malafouris (ed.), *The Cognitive Life of Things*, Cambridge: McDonald Institute, pp. 29–37.

Wheeler, M. (2011), 'Mind in life or life in mind? Making sense of deep continuity', *Journal of Consciousness Studies* 18.5–6: 148–68.

Wheeler, M. (2015), 'Extended consciousness: An interim report', *Southern Journal of Philosophy* 53: 155–75.

Wheeler, M. and A. Clark (2008), 'Culture, embodiment and genes: Unravelling the triple helix', *Philosophical Transactions of the Royal Society B: Biological Sciences* 363.1509: 3563–75.

Wheeler, M. and E. Di Paolo (2011), 'Existentialism and cognitive science', in J. Reynolds, J. A. Woodward and F. Joseph (eds), *The Continuum Companion to Existentialism*, London: Continuum, pp. 241–59.

Whitaker, H., C. U. M. Smith and S. Finger (2007), *Brain, Mind and Medicine: Essays in Eighteenth-Century Neuroscience*, New York: Springer.

White, D. (2006), *Early Romanticism and Religious Dissent*, Cambridge: Cambridge University Press.

Whyman, S. (2009), *The Pen and the People: English Letter Writers 1660–1800*, Oxford: Oxford University Press.

Willey, B. (1946), *Coleridge on Imagination and Fancy*, Warton Lecture on English Poetry, Oxford: Oxford University Press.

Williams, A. (2016), *The Social Lives of Books*, New Haven: Yale University Press.

Wilson, E. (1999), *Emerson's Sublime Science*, Basingstoke: Palgrave Macmillan.

Wilson, R. A. (2005), 'Collective memory, group minds, and the extended mind thesis', *Cognitive Processing* 6.4: 227–36.

Winckelmann, J. J. (2006), *History of the Art of Antiquity*, trans. A. Potts, Los Angeles: Getty.

Winkler, K. (2005), 'Berkeley and the doctrine of signs', in K. Winkler (ed.), *The Cambridge Companion to Berkeley*, Cambridge: Cambridge University Press, pp. 125–65.

Winkler, K. (2008), 'Berkeley and Kant', in D. Garber and B. Longuenesse (eds), *Kant and the Early Moderns*, Princeton: Princeton University Press, pp. 141–71.

Wojciehowski, H. C. (2019), 'Metaphors they lived by: The language of early modern intersubjectivity', in M. Anderson and M. Wheeler (eds), *Distributed Cognition in Medieval and Renaissance Culture*, Edinburgh: Edinburgh University Press.

Wolfe, C. T. (2012), 'Forms of material embodiment', in M. S. Landers and B. Muñoz (eds), *Anatomy and the Organization of Knowledge*, London: Pickering & Chatto, pp. 129–44.

Wolfe, C. T. (2014), 'The brain is a book which reads itself: Cultured brains and reductive materialism from Diderot to J. J. C. Smart', in C. Danta and H. Groth (eds), *Mindful Aesthetics: Literature and the Science of the Mind*, London: Bloomsbury, pp. 73–90.

Wolfe, C. T. and O. Gal (eds) (2010a), *The Body as Object and Instrument of Knowledge: Embodied Empiricism in Early Modern Science*, Dordrecht: Springer.

Wolfe, C. T. and O. Gal (2010b), 'Introduction', in C. T. Wolfe and O. Gal (eds), *The Body as Object and Instrument of Knowledge: Embodied Empiricism in Early Modern Science*, Dordrecht: Springer, pp. 1–5.

Wordsworth, W. (1979), *The Prelude: 1799, 1805, 1850*, New York: Norton.

Wordsworth, W. (2001), 'The Preface to *Lyrical Ballads*, 1802', *Prefaces and Prologues*, vol. XXXIX, The Harvard Classics, New York: P. F. Collier & Son, <http://www.bartleby.com/39/36.html> (last accessed 1 February 2019).

Wordsworth, W. (and S. T. Coleridge) (1798), *Lyrical Ballads with a Few Other Poems*, retrieved from <https://www.gutenberg.org/files/9622/9622-h/9622-h.htm> (last accessed 4 March 2019).

Wright, J. P. and P. Potter (eds) (2000), *Psyche and Soma: Physicians and Metaphysicians on the Mind-Body Problem from Antiquity to Enlightenment*, Oxford: Oxford University Press.

Wright, L. (2010), *Samuel Taylor Coleridge and the Anglican Church*, Notre Dame: University of Notre Dame Press.

Yolton, J. W. (1983), *Thinking Matter: Materialism in Eighteenth-Century Britain*, Minneapolis: University of Minnesota Press.

Yousef, N. (2004), *Isolated Cases*, Ithaca: Cornell University Press.

Zahavi, D. (2014), *Self and Other: Exploring Subjectivity, Empathy, and Shame*, Oxford: Oxford University Press.

Zeleny, M. (1981), *Autopoiesis: A Theory of Living Organizations*, New York: North Holland.

Zimmermann, J. G. (1794), *Solitude Considered with Respect to its Influence upon the Mind and Heart*, London: Dilly.

Zuckert, R. (2009), 'Sculpture and touch: Herder's aesthetics of sculpture', *The Journal of Aesthetics and Art Criticism* 67.3: 285–99.

Zunshine, L. (2010), *Introduction to Cognitive Cultural Studies*, Baltimore: Johns Hopkins University Press.

Index

Note: Page numbers in *italics* indicate illustrations. Page numbers followed by 'n' indicate footnotes.